# The Washington Post

## Guide to Washington

*Revised Edition*

# The Washington Post

## Guide to Washington

Revised Edition

edited by
**Laura Longley Babb**
of the Washington Post Writers Group

**McGraw-Hill Book Company**
New York • St. Louis • San Francisco
Düsseldorf • Mexico • Toronto

Photo credits:
P.7: left, Charles Del Vecchio—*The Washington Post;* right, United Press International. P. 47: top, James K. W. Atherton—UPI; bottom, Linda Wheeler—*The Washington Post.* P. 94: Harry Naltchayan—*The Washington Post.* P. 95: Douglas Chevalier—*The Washington Post.* P. 119: left, Library of Congress; right, Charles Del Vecchio—*Washington Post.* P. 160: left, Frank Johnston—*The Washington Post;* right, Bob Burchette—*The Washington Post.* P. 212: top, Tom Allen—*The Washington Post;* bottom, Harry Naltchayan—*The Washington Post.* P. 326: top, Tony Hathaway; bottom, Matthew Lewis—*The Washington Post.*

Editor's note: If you go to an art gallery we recommend and you find only rubble from the wrecker's ball, if you patronize a restaurant we praise and find a hot dog stand, if you dial a number and it's been disconnected, please forgive us. But, you see, change is a constant in this town. We'll do everything we can to update future editions.

Book design by Jules Perlmutter
A Good Thing Inc.

3 4 5 6 7 8 9 MUMU   8 3 2 1

**Library of Congress Cataloging in Publication Data**

Washington Post Writers Group.
The Washington post guide to Washington.
Includes index.
1.  Washington, D.C.—Description—1951–    —
Guide-books.   I.  Babb, Laura Longley.    II.  Anderson, Claudia.    III.  Parks, Sabina.    IV.  Washington post.
V.  Title.    VI.  Title:  Guide to Washington.
F192.3.W34 1978    917.53′04′4    78-7668
ISBN 0-07-068429-4

# Contents

## The Power & The Glory

## The Ceremonial City

# Floor Plans and Maps

# Preface

*By Benjamin C. Bradlee*

Washington became the capital of the free world almost accidentally during World War II. And ever since, newspapering in this city has been as close as a journalist can get to the history that will last until the historians take over.

This is the revised edition of a book about Washington by Washington reporters, men and women who have walked the streets reporting the giant events and the little happenings that are life in this vitally important place. And because of this involvement, they know more than their peers and understand more about Washington than others. A sight for visitors' eyes is often a slice of history for reporters' eyes.

As a visitor to Washington, you will surely cross Pennsylvania Avenue from Lafayette Park to the broad sidewalk on the north side of the President's house. I can't take that short walk today without thinking of an early afternoon in November, 1950, when I burst off a trolley car (yes, trolley tracks split Pennsylvania Avenue in those days) and crossed the street on my hands and knees. It was seconds after the Puerto Rican Nationalists Grisello Torresola and Oscar Collazo had tried to shoot their way into Blair House and assassinate President Truman. The body of Torresola lay sprawled in the middle of the street, and Officer Leslie Coffelt lay dying a hero's death near the steps of Blair House.

Your tour guide will tell you that the empty ornate shell that is now the Willard Hotel once housed Ulysses S. Grant (when he was President of the United States) and a pretty fair country newspaperman by the name of Samuel Clemens, better known by his by-line Mark Twain. Reporters remember it for that—and more. I remember it particularly for the day in June, 1949, when I

Benjamin C. Bradlee is executive editor of *The Washington Post* and author of *Conversations with Kennedy* (W. W. Norton).

crawled out on the ledge behind a low iron railing on the 14th floor to listen to two cops and a priest talk a bewildered young GI out of jumping to his death.

All reporters have similar memories, and all the reporters in this guide book work for a newspaper whose life and times have been fixtures on the Washington scene for 100 years, and whose impact on the Washington scene is unique. *The Post* has some 169 reporters, backed by 147 editors, 2,000-plus other employees, producing more than half a million copies daily and close to a million copies Sunday, on nine presses in a large building five blocks north of the White House.

This is the city they know and love.

# Introduction

*By Haynes Johnson*

When I was young I often felt I had been born too late. How wonderful it would have been to have lived in London, in the days of Boswell, Paris, in the time of the French Revolution, New York, in the Twenties. Washington, well, Washington was merely there, a half-remembered scene from a boyhood trip, a city sleeping in the summer sun, a place of wide and empty avenues offering glimpses of marble monuments surrounded by dark stands of trees and greensward. It seemed a sterile city, all stone and no soul. That was long before I came to know, and love, this special city along the Potomac.

I have heard it said that Washington is dull, that it lacks culture, that it is a fearsome city, that it is a one-industry town, that it is cliquish, expensive, tasteless, ill-governed, too hot, too cold, too humid, unlivable. All true, in part. Yet I know of no city that combines the ingredients that make Washington so exciting and charming a community.

Twenty years have passed since I first arrived in town, but that first morning remains indelible. I left the rooming house in which I was temporarily staying and walked east down G Street past the Corcoran Gallery, along the curving sidewalk by the old War and State Departments, around the White House grounds and the Ellipse and then down Pennsylvania Avenue to my newspaper office in sight of the Capitol looming ahead. It was a hot, muggy August day, Washington at its worst, but I knew with a rush of emotion that this was where I wanted to be. No matter how far away my newspaper assignments have carried me over the years since, I still experience that same sense of excitement upon returning to the capital. To me there is no more moving

Haynes Johnson, who has won a Pulitzer Prize for reporting, is a columnist for *The Washington Post* and the author of several books.

sight than you see flying in low over the Potomac at dusk: the city and its memorials bathed in a pale light below. I know it is illusory, I know the noble marble often masks ignoble deeds, I know of the constant clashes between ambition and principle, and I know that, for all its imperfections, no other place promises so much to so many.

None of the numerous guides to Washington, the nation's ceremonial center, captures Washington, the city, where we work and live. In these pages you will find both Washingtons. It is not a conventional guide we are offering. Nor is it a prose valentine to Washington the Magnificent, a latest version of a Chamber of Commerce bromide. Here you will find candor, humor, criticism, irreverence and, yes, practical advice about where to go, what to see, when to start, and how to sample the myriad sides of city life.

In reading these articles, from the contributors and staff of *The Washington Post,* a most individualistic newspaper, I was struck by two things. Few of the writers represented here are natives of Washington. They are, literally, from across the country. In this, they are typical Washingtonians. They are typical in another sense: no matter how different their backgrounds, or how critical they are, at times, of certain aspects of Washington, they all obviously love the city. For them, too, it is home, a treasured city, not merely a good professional place to work.

You can gauge their true feelings in the words of David Broder, the distinguished political commentator, as he describes one of his favorite scenes, the view from the outdoor balcony and terrace on the Capitol's west front which sweeps out across the city, past the monuments, museums, and memorials, and beyond "to the land that is America, stretching west, in your mind's eye, to the Pacific" . . . in the way in which Wolf Von Eckardt, the architecture critic, expresses his admiration for Pierre Charles L'Enfant's original plan for the city, a plan that still leaves experts "awed by its grandeur" . . . in the reaction of Christopher Dickey, a poet's son, as he stands before the three original charters of American freedom and justice—the Declaration of Independence, the Constitution, and the Bill of Rights—inside the massive and cold Exhibit Hall of the National Archives and wishes the designers of that place had not insisted on so stuffy and deadening a repository for such vibrant and living symbols . . . in the reverence of Paul Richard, the art critic, as he speaks about Washington's Louvre, the National Gallery of Art, "the sort of place paintings would aspire to if masterpieces went to heaven" ... in the prose of Henry Mitchell, a Southern student of Faulkner and one of the most sensitive writers ever to grace the Washington scene, as he sketches the natural life in which the capital glories and comments that "nowhere else in the world can you enjoy vultures, sea gulls and crows, none of them essentially urban fowl, so close to a Capital dome."

I fancy myself something of an amateur expert on Washington lore, but after reading my colleagues I find there are many things about this city I didn't know. I wasn't aware that the Smithsonian, vast as it is, largest museum in the world and all, contains so sprawling a collection of artifacts and memorabilia that 98 per cent of its items are not on public display; that Andrews Air Force Base, out in the rolling countryside of Maryland's Prince Georges County, is the busiest such base in the world and that three specially equipped jets stand ready around the clock, in all seasons, to get the nation's commander-in-chief instantly into the air in the event of a nuclear emergency; that Fort McNair, guarded by a heavy iron gateway in southwest Washington not far from the Capitol, is the nation's oldest active military post or that Lincoln's assassination conspirators were hanged there (a tennis court now covers the ground where the scaffold stood); that the site of the Marine Barracks, where so many have thrilled to the tattoo ceremonies of the Corps' drill and bugle corps, was personally picked by Thomas Jefferson after a carriage ride around the new capital city in 1801; that in northwest Washington, at Piney Branch Road and Quackenbos Street, remnants of an old fort at which a young Union lieutenant colonel named Oliver Wendell Holmes saw a tall civilian standing on the ramparts during a Confederate attack and shouted sharply, "Get down, you fool!"—and that Abraham Lincoln promptly got down; that L'Enfant, who designed a city for the people, planned Lafayette Park as the President's personal front yard, but that George Washington, so often thought of now as our first imperial President, an executive who wished to be called His Excellency, instead proposed that the ground be purchased as a public park for the people. It was, and remains one of the city's ornaments.

All these, and much more, form the narrative sketch of our portrait of Washington, capital and city.

Years ago, when I was closeted for nights and weekends in a Library of Congress study room doing research for a book about early life in Washington, I came across an expression by a long-forgotten Supreme Court justice. The capital of a nation, he said, although it may lie as ours does at the level of the sea, in a true sense must be a city that is set upon a hill and cannot be hidden. In the nature of things it draws to itself not only the eyes of its own people, but, if it is the capital of a great nation, the eyes of the world. Then he said:

"This capital of capitals should be no mean city. . . .whether we will it so or not it will become a symbol—a symbol of the great Republic whose visible throne is here. . . .It is wisdom, then, to see that the symbol shall be worthy of the love and veneration it expresses."

I don't know about veneration. We are critical and chary of excessive emotion. I do know about our love. If you're not careful you'll wind up the same way and, like all of us, want to call Washington home.

# The
# Power
# &
# The
# Glory

# I
# The White House

## The Presidency
### By Lou Cannon

Soon after Franklin Delano Roosevelt was named Assistant Secretary of the Navy in the Woodrow Wilson administration, he and his young wife Eleanor went calling on the distinguished historian Henry Adams in his residence overlooking Lafayette Square. Roosevelt was full of the accomplishments of the new administration, and he extolled them and Wilson to his host. Old Adams, the descendant of two Presidents, shook a finger in Roosevelt's patrician face and said, "Young man, I have lived in this house many years and seen the occupants of the White House across the square come and go, and nothing that you minor officials or the occupants of that house will do will affect the history of the world for very long."

Adams' view was not the usual one held of Presidents, especially by Presidents themselves and by the men and women who work for them. Some fifty years later, just after Richard Nixon was elected President for a second term, a reporter complained to a White House official about a presidential action he considered high-handed. The aide gave no defense of Nixon's conduct. Instead, he said, "That's up to the President. The President can do anything he wants."

The historian's conviction that Presidents are ultimately insignificant and the aide's belief in presidential omnipotence express the polarities of the strangest and most vital office in the world. Throughout its history, the American presidency has been the living embodiment of the revolutionary idea that government is the servant of the people rather than its master. And the man in

Lou Cannon is a national staff writer for *The Washington Post*.

the White House has been both celebrated as the champion of the people and reviled as a betrayer of the people's will.

Both the views of Adams and of the Nixon aide have something to recommend them. For while it sometimes seems as if a modern President, possessed of powers of life and death over the planet's civilization, can actually do "anything he wants," most Presidents instead confess to a sense of powerlessness in the face of events they can neither control nor comprehend. With all the cost in human life and material wealth extracted by the Indochina War, it is doubtful if the extraordinary exertions of Lyndon Johnson made a substantial difference in the outcome of the struggle for Vietnam. The most pervasive revelation of the Nixon White House tapes is the inability of either the President or his chief aides to gain control of events they had set in motion. Abraham Lincoln, writing to a friend in the spring of the climactic Civil War year of 1864, declared: "I claim not to have controlled events and confess plainly that events have controlled me. Now, at the end of three years' struggle the nation's condition is not what either party, or any man devised, or expected."

And yet the President is a very powerful man. Franklin Roosevelt, only a few years after he labored with great skill and much delay to persuade Congress to permit him to send a few destroyers to beleaguered Great Britain, with a stroke of his pen decreed that the Japanese-American population of the western United States should spend World War II in concentration camps. Harry Truman, who complained that he could not get the White House staff to prepare a decent old fashioned, with a similar stroke of a pen ended the shameful segregation of the United States armed forces that had persisted even during a war fought in the cause of freedom. With another concise decision Truman authorized the atomic bombing of Hiroshima and Nagasaki.

The sheer scope and magnitude of the presidency has fascinated the nation's citizens and outsiders alike since the time of Alexis de Tocqueville. No American has captured it so well as the British political scientist Harold J. Laski in his famous 1940 study, *The American Presidency:*

"No one can examine the character of the American presidency without being impressed by its many-sidedness," Laski wrote. "The range of the President's functions is enormous. He is ceremonial head of state. He is a vital source of legislative suggestion. He is the final source of all executive decision. He is the authoritative exponent of the nation's foreign policy. To combine all these with the continuous need to be at once the representative man of the nation and the leader of his political party is clearly a call upon the energies of a single man unsurpassed by the exigencies of any other political office in the world."

These conflicting duties sometimes get in the way of each other, as Presidents have learned to their sorrow. Taken together, they probably are impossible of fulfillment by any one man. Some Presidents fail as party leaders, others as the "vital source of legislative suggestion." A few have been incapable of decisive executive action. Most modern Presidents have been obsessed with foreign policy, seeing it as the stage upon which the historical drama critics of the future will rest their judgments. But preoccupation with foreign policy is not merely the province of modern Presidents. The Louisiana Purchase, the greatest single real estate transaction in history, was an act of foreign policy. So were the presidential decisions that led to the acquisition of California and to the Mexican-American war.

It also is foreign policy that has given the presidency its present character. "It was during World War II, in Roosevelt's third term, rather than in the early New Deal years, that the foundations of modern presidential government were laid," wrote historian James MacGregor Burns. "The courts sustained presidential curtailment of liberties, such as those of the Japanese-Americans. Congress was surly and prickly on minor issues, generally acquiescent on the big. Under the pressure of war, the presidential staff proliferated: the 'presidential press' had a wider role; the bureaucracy was refashioned for war."

The presidency, and the executive branch that the President heads, have changed under these pressures. Washington, the center of government, has changed with it. When the federal government moved to Washington from Philadelphia in 1800, the bureaucracy consisted of 130 employees, most of whom were clerks. The government had 7,000 employees by the end of the Civil War, 28,000 by 1901, 140,000 by 1940—and has over 350,000 today. Small wonder that modern Presidents often have despaired of being able either to control or to direct this vast, varied, and multi-skilled bureaucracy. John F. Kennedy once became so discouraged that he told an aide not to abandon a minor remodeling project in Lafayette Park. "Hell, this may be the only thing I'll ever get done," he said.

President Carter's official White House staff—down to 431—has almost 150 employees fewer than when Ford took office, not counting the 1,584 men and 24 women Secret Service agents, plus the 867 officers of the Secret Service Uniform Division, the uncounted numbers of military persons detailed to the White House mess, the medical staff, and various gardeners and chauffeurs. The size of the staff is ever-changing and the actual number somewhat meaningless, since all modern Presidents also employ "detailees," who appear on the payrolls of other federal departments. This practice probably reached its apogee—or its nadir, depending on how it is regarded—during the Johnson administration, when the 250 persons officially on the White House staff were outnumbered by 326 persons detailed from other agencies. President Nixon, expressing a public desire for "accuracy and candor" and a private concern for directing the entire bureaucracy from the White House, substantially reduced the practice of detailing personnel. But he also made himself less accessible than any previous President to Cabinet officials, Congress, and the press, and he appointed the greatest number of presidential assistants ever. Many of these aides rarely, if ever, saw the President, but some of them caused great, if temporary, havoc in attempting to put into the principal agencies men who bore the Nixon stamp of approval. In contrast, the Carter White House is noticeably more relaxed than any administration in recent memory, owing to the Georgia influence and Carter's expressed concern that he be a "people's President."

Despite the misgivings that arose in the wake of Watergate about faceless assistants acting in the President's name, the handpicked White House staff is here to stay. The complexity of the issues facing the President and the sheer size of the bureaucracy probably make it a necessity. But there is no way to draw a precise organization chart describing how this staff works; its functions and its uses depend almost entirely on the character and needs of the men in the White House. The executive branch, which presidential adviser Clark Clifford once compared to a chameleon that takes on the coloration of whoever is President, can best be considered as a series of concentric circles—with the President at the center, surrounded by successive circles representing the staff, the Executive Office of the President, and the several departments. The independent regulatory agencies, where the President's power is largely the power of appointment, occupy slightly overlapping circles of their own.

It would be next to impossible to describe a proper circle for the Cabinet, which according to early constitutional doctrine would rank next to the President himself. But Cabinets frequently have been of lesser importance than the President's personal advisers on the White House staff. Andrew Jackson, the seventh President of the United States, set the pattern by relying on a group of unofficial advisers who came to be known as the "Kitchen Cabinet." No Cabinet official in the Woodrow Wilson administration had as much influence as presidential adviser Colonel E. M. House. Franklin Roosevelt relied on Harry Hopkins, Dwight Eisenhower on Sherman Adams, Nixon on H. R. Haldeman. When the defeated Wendell Willkie visited the White House and expressed his distrust of Hopkins, Roosevelt replied:

"I can understand that you wonder why I need that half man around me. But some day you may well be sitting here where I am now as President of the United States. And when you are, you'll be looking through that door over there and knowing that practically everybody who walks through it wants something out of you. You'll learn what a lonely job this is, and you'll discover the need for somebody like Harry Hopkins who asks for nothing except to serve you."

Carter, like Roosevelt, knew the importance of personal style from the beginning. It is particularly important in the American presidency when that style seems to convey the best notions of the democratic ideal. The frontier democrat that lurks in most of us revels in the story of "the people" trampling precious White House furnishings at the Jackson inaugural. Few Americans know or care that Jackson also had plumbing installed in the White House, that he redecorated the residence in the French style, and that he insisted on the use of good china and fine wines. The Teddy Roosevelt of our childhood fancies charges endlessly up San Juan Hill, forever busting the trusts with a big stick while crying, "Bully." In our own time we all share with each other in some secret place that cares about our country the memory of particular Presidents. Our ears recall the Roosevelt fireside chat, our eyes remember the Eisenhower grin. All but the youngest voting generation of Americans still hear the Boston accents of Kennedy ringing hard above the snow on Inauguration Day.

President Kennedy and U.N. Ambassador Adlai Stevenson leave the White House by the seldom-photographed South Portico.

Harry S Truman is welcomed back to Washington after his smashing defeat of Thomas E. Dewey in 1948.

Even the youngest know about the Kennedy flame. And Carter brought the New South to Washington. From the prayers of Martin Luther King, Sr. at his inauguration, to the first family's walk to the White House, to Miss Lillian—our "First Mama"—Carter wore being a Washington outsider like a badge of honor.

We have also learned, some of us, that if style is not substance, it can at least be a clue to presidential character. Nothing betrayed the restlessness and insecurity of Richard Nixon more than his unwillingness to remain in the White House if he could spend the night somewhere else. Ford, by contrast, would travel immense distances in the middle of the night during his campaigning to return, even for a few hours, to the White House.

Beyond the question of presidential lifestyle lies the fundamental issue of presidential power—the central focus of the presidency ever since the founders, after much deliberation, chose to embody the powers of the executive branch in a single person, and then to limit and constrain him with the checks and balances of other branches. "Power is poison," Henry Adams observed more than half a century ago. Its effect on Presidents has always been tragic, chiefly as an almost insane excitement at first, and a worse reaction afterward; but also because no mind is so well balanced as to bear the strain of seizing unlimited power without habit or knowledge of it . . ."

However, it has also been argued that a President's powers can be too diffused, too restrained. Arthur Schlesinger, Jr., in his introduction to *The Imperial Presidency*, cautions for a middle ground. "The answer to the runaway presidency is not the messenger-boy presidency," he wrote.

How is this middle ground to be attained? Who will restrain runaway Presidents and embolden weak ones? The answer, ringing through two centuries of presidential experience, is the Constitution—but only if its purposes are solidly supported by the people. "The Constitution could not hold the people to ideals it was determined to betray," observed Schlesinger. Four years before he was elected President, Abraham Lincoln said that "our government rests in public opinion. Whoever can change public opinion, can change the government . . ."

Each President is both a molder of that public opinion and molded by it. "Lincoln was a sad man because he couldn't get it all at once," Roosevelt once said. "And nobody can." Laski, who thought less of the American presidential system than he did of the British parliamentary one, concluded that Roosevelt's performance showed decisively "what an immense impact the personality of a President can make when he is able to arouse and retain the conviction that something of real importance is afoot . . . His ideas, his policies, his purposes will shape the mental climate as will those of no other man in America." Roosevelt had been effective, Laski believed, because he had dramatized the big issues confronting America, the issues upon which men's lives and livelihoods depend. He had been—in company with such other "positive Presidents" as Jefferson, Jackson, Lincoln, Theodore Roosevelt, and Wilson—a forward-looking President rather than a backward-looking one. This idea has found an expression in our time in the words of John Kennedy: "Each President is the President not only of all who live, but in a very real sense, of all those who have yet to live."

It is this forward-looking presidency that Americans celebrate in looking backward at the performance of their Presidents across two centuries. It is this forward-looking presidency that still gives hope to Americans who have become much more disillusioned about their capacity to govern themselves than they used to be. "Your old men shall dream dreams, your young men shall see visions," President Kennedy said in quoting Scripture the night before his assassination. "Where there is no vision, the people perish."

# *Public House, Private Home*

### By Sarah Booth Conroy

The White House is the only residence of a head-of-state in the world regularly open free. In the United States, it has always been that way. But public access isn't as free and easy as it was before the turn of the century, when anyone who wanted to see the President just walked in, by gad, and went upstairs to his office above the East Room. In 1842, Charles Dickens, with an official presidential invitation in hand but no servant or anyone to greet him, strolled into an open White House as if it were a public train station. To his amazement, as he recalled in his *American Notes,* he found idle men lounging and standing by for no apparent purpose in the first-floor state rooms. Upstairs, to his disbelief, fifteen or twenty more determined men were unrelentingly spitting on a drawing room carpet while waiting to see the President.

Now the public and official visitor are restricted to certain parts of the house. Yet, the perpetual open house at **1600 Pennsylvania Avenue, N.W.,** attracts almost 2 million visitors a year—which says something about what the White House means to the nation's citizens.

But the public house is also a private home, and the two sometimes conflict. For more than one hundred years, the second floor housed both first-family quarters and working presidential offices. Seekers of the President's attention, applicants for offices, lobbyists, and indeed sight-seekers lounged about the second floor hall at a sad sacrifice of the family's privacy.

From the beginning it was a major project of Presidents' wives to move the presidential offices and aides of the house altogether. The most elaborate plans for separating public house from private home were those Mrs. Benjamin Harrison commissioned architect Fred D. Owen to do, which included an immense

Sarah Booth Conroy, the editor of *The Washington Post's* Living section, has covered the White House East Wing, among other assignments.

greenhouse to extend clear across the south façade. Presidents Grover Cleveland and William McKinley also had plans drawn.

But it was President Theodore Roosevelt who finally moved the presidential offices into what he considered a temporary building, the West Wing. His large family needed all the living space on the White House second floor that they could get. The "temporary" office wing that Roosevelt ordered constructed in 1902 was doubled in size in 1909, and enlarged again in 1927 and 1934.

The West Wing is the working section of the White House. It is not open to the casual tourist. It's all strictly business. And, more than the ceremonial center section of the White House, it moves with the times and the administration. President Nixon remodeled the West Wing in 1969, adding a driveway and portico on the north side, facing Pennsylvania Avenue, and the West Wing Reception Room for his callers.

Presidential callers or newspeople coming to the Press Secretary's briefings come in through the West Gate, presenting their credentials to a uniformed White House guard (who does not wear the comic-opera costume today that he did during a few of the Nixon days). The officer checks names from a list provided by the appointments office. Finding the name, he'll ask the caller the date and place of his birthday—it isn't that he cares about astrological signs, it's just a way of checking identification.

Official presidential callers now wait in the formal West Wing Reception Room, which until 1969 was the informal, leather-chaired Press Lobby where reporters lounged about waiting for a story. But Nixon floored over the White House swimming pool and moved the press quarters there, and made room for an Appointments Lobby for presidential callers. While waiting for an audience, a presidential caller is bound to notice the American landscape paintings, including Winslow Homer's "Maine Coast," and the official gifts presented to the President arranged in a breakfront bookcase, all in the Appointments Lobby.

Finally, the big moment comes, and the visitor is ushered into the Oval Office, which is used by President Carter for ceremonial purposes. The President often greets visitors in front of his desk, flanked by the President's flag on the left and the United States flag on the right. Lest the caller forget where he is, the presidential seal is molded into the ceiling's plaster medallion. There is a marble-manteled fireplace here, too, and Presidents have been known to sit with guests on chairs and settees around the fire.

The President often pins medals on honorees in the Rose Garden, when the flowers are in bloom, or holds an occasional press conference. The Rose Garden, extending beyond the French doors and portico of the Oval Office, is familiar as the President's reception area for famed and foreign callers.

If the West Wing is his, the East Wing is hers. The East Wing and its arcade to the house were added in 1902, rebuilt and enlarged in 1934 to tuck a bomb shelter underneath, and a tunnel to the Treasury—used, it is said, as a secret escape route for White House brides leaving on their honeymoon.

The First Lady's official visitors are shown into the dark-paneled appointments lounge with Whistler's "Nocturne" on the wall. Her staff has offices on a floor above. Visitors also wait in a less stiffly formal Garden Room overlooking the Jacqueline Kennedy Garden, as Mrs. Lyndon Johnson named it. Mrs. Richard Nixon called it (firmly) "the east garden." Counterpart to the West Wing Rose Garden, the garden is frequently used by the First Lady to greet guests.

If you should be invited to a social/official function of both the President and First Lady, you come in through one of two "their" entrances on the north and south, as opposed to "his" and "her" entrances on the west and east. The north entrance facing Lafayette Park is under the porte-cochère designed for Thomas Jefferson by Benjamin Latrobe (with some borrowings from James Hoban's original White House plans). This is the carriage entrance, favored for heads of state.

If you are anything less, but still august enough to come for a state party, the route is through the south entrance and the Diplomatic Reception Room. The south entrance is also the first-family entrance. The Diplomatic Reception Room was originally the basement and at one point the furnace room, with vaulted ceilings of the times. Today, it is embellished with "Scenic America," a wallpaper mural printed in 1834 by Jean Zuber et Cie in Alsace and installed by Jacqueline Kennedy during her renovation. Before its now elegant decoration, Franklin Delano Roosevelt used the Diplomatic Reception Room as a broadcast studio for his famous "fireside chats."

Guests arriving for a state dinner (a first-class invitation, or

# The White House

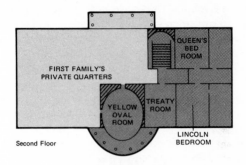

Second Floor

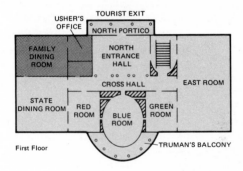

First Floor

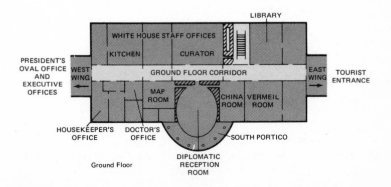

Ground Floor

for the entertainment after dinner (second class), first pass through the southwest gates, showing invitations as they go. Invitations to the White House are not transferable.

The south entrance walk is a fine place to stop and look out at the Jefferson Memorial and the White House south lawn—this is the landing spot, marked by tiny red squares, of the President's helicopter. Heads of state customarily arrive here by helicopter to a 21-gun salute. Once a highly unscheduled helicopter, violating the President's air rights, was forced down here and its pilot marched off to jail. The event spurred a new flurry of discussion of presidential security—as such events do.

---

### THE STATE ROOMS

To invited guest and tourist alike, the five state rooms of the White House are the most important—beginning with the East Room and extending through the Green, Blue, and Red Rooms in the center, and finally the State Dining Room on the house's west side. In the morning visiting tourists are ushered through these rooms, and in the evening visiting heads of state, dignitaries and even American officials are wined, dined, and wooed. It is in these rooms over the years that most of the decorating attention of presidential occupants has been lavished—and for good reason, for the hard wear that these rooms receive necessitates their frequent renovation.

To see the state rooms, tourists form long lines on Tuesday through Saturday from 10 to 12 on the east sidewalk, along by the rhododendrons kept at bay by the tall bayonetted fence with the recorded messages about the house recited from hidden speakers, keeping the waiting lines entertained.

It's wise to write your congressman and ask to get on the VIP tour at 8 A.M. But grander than that is the tour offered some afternoons for those who have indicated their desire to make a substantial donation to the White House's collection of furniture and decorative objects. The VIP tour includes some rooms not open to the general tour, such as the White House Library. And the prospective donor's tour also includes an amusing and informative discourse.

The most recent decorating upheaval of the state rooms came during the Nixon administration, under the supervision of

Curator Clement Conger and his adviser, architect Edward Vason Jones (who also worked on the Metropolitan Museum's American wing). Conger has said that his aim is to redo the White House as it should have been done in the first third of the nineteenth century—if the early occupants had all the taste and money that was needed.

Not everyone agrees with the Conger concept. But Conger has raised the necessary money—close to $2 million—hired the technical expertise, lectured on the results (with always a commercial asking for more donations), bid at auction, hunted in antique shops, people's houses, and museums, and in general run the renovating show. On one memorable occasion, Mrs. Nixon told a press group, "We want the antiques from people's attics." Conger interrupted forcefully to correct her, "not attic, drawing room." But the Conger charm, humor, and his offer of income tax deductibility for gifts to the nation have won more than 400 antiques plus the great sum of money.

The greatest decorating changes have been made in the three parlors in the central, south section of the house—the Green, Blue, and Red Rooms.

The Green Room may have been so called since James and Elizabeth Monroe in their restyling efforts used green silks to decorate the room. Following the Monroe lead, no doubt, Jacqueline Kennedy in 1962 restored the room with a wall covering of green moire silk. Pat Nixon used the same fabric in 1971 in her renovation.

The room originally served different purposes for the early Presidents. James Madison used it as a sitting room adjoining the East Room where his cabinet met. It was a Card Room for whist-playing guests during the Monroe administration. John Quincy Adams made it into a green drawing room, which it has remained.

Earlier, President Jefferson used this room as his intimate dining room. Instead of a rug, he had a green painted canvas floor cloth, which he rolled up after every meal.

The Green Room boasts early nineteeth century classical furniture in the style of English furniture designer Thomas Sheraton, as interpreted in the New York workroom by Duncan Phyfe. The Duncan Phyfe chairs are signed and dated 1810 on the stretchers. The Duncan Phyfe benches were made for Robert

Livingston, a New Yorker who helped draft the Declaration of Independence. His descendant, Edward Cox, married Tricia Nixon.

If the Green Room reflects James Monroe's taste, the Blue Room is dominated by it. Washington had appointed Monroe as Minister to France in 1744, where he developed a penchant for elegant French décor. The Monroes, as first occupants of the White House after the British burned it in 1814, ordered French Empire mahogany furniture by Pierre Antoine Bellange for the Blue Room. Bellange, against Monroe's instructions, insisted that the furniture be gilded because ordinary mahogany was "not suitable for even a gentleman's house."

In Monroe's days, lighted by a gilt-bronze chandelier shaped as an eagle holding 50 candles, the Blue Room served as the south entrance through French doors since Hoban's South Portico was not constructed until 1824. Standing in the middle of a tier of three oval rooms, the Blue Room was conceived by Hoban as the most elegant room in the house.

The Red Room, the third of the parlors, is American Empire, 1810–1830, and a much more cheerful room with its lipstick red suggested by the portrait of Dolley Madison, which hangs here. Only when Dolley Madison held court at her socially glittering Wednesday night gatherings, it became the "Yellow Drawing Room." The room now serves as a reception room as do the other two, but in earlier days it was also a family music room.

Records show that Monroe had ordered Empire furnishings for the Red Room, as well as for the Blue Room, and in 1962 during Jacqueline Kennedy's restoration the American Empire style was returned to the room.

First families usually gathered in the Red Room during the nineteenth century on Sunday evenings, but it was a Saturday night gathering of political importance that gave the Red Room fame. In this room, in 1877, Rutherford B. Hayes was clandestinely sworn into office at a Saturday soirée hosted by retiring President Grant. Neither Hayes nor opponent Tilden had won a majority vote from the Electoral College. An Electoral Commission appointed by Congress to determine the issue, since as a body it had been unable to do so, had decided for Hayes. Yet Tilden persisted in opposing the Commission's decision. So the secret swearing settled the affair and ensured the succession of the presidency—the only time in history when it was in doubt. The following Monday, the official inauguration services were performed at the Capitol.

Next door to the Red Room, the State Dining Room was once much smaller, and by the 1850s too small to seat guests that included a growing number of congressmen and diplomats of a nation expanding in size and power. So, in the 1902 renovaton of Theodore Roosevelt by the prestigious architectural firm of McKim, Mead & (Stanford) White, more space for the room was gained by sacrificing an adjacent grand staircase.

The fireplace mantel in the State Dining Room is a 1962 copy of a mantel with carved buffalo heads ordered by Theodore Roosevelt in 1902. Inscribed on the mantel by another Roosevelt, Franklin Delano, are the words of John Adams written on his second night as first White House occupant. The inscription reads, "I pray Heaven to Bestow The Best of Blessings on THIS HOUSE and All that shall hereafter Inhabit it. May none but Honest and Wise Men ever rule under this Roof."

It was in the State Dining Room at a 1962 dinner honoring Nobel Prize winners that President Kennedy described his guests as "the most extraordinary collection of talent, of human knowledge, that has ever been gathered together at the White House, with the possible exception of when Thomas Jefferson dined alone."

The Cross Hall, which leads from the State Dining Room across the north entrance of the White House past the three parlors and into the East Room, is often filled with small tables and chairs at large evening entertainments. But its principal function is to serve as a ceremonial marble hall to lead people into the East Room, the grandest of them all.

The East Room, the most ceremonial and historic of all White House rooms, was the last to be completed and furnished, 29 years after the house was occupied. Abigail Adams hung her wash in the drafty, unfinished East Room. Seven presidents have lain in state in this room, including Lincoln, who two weeks before his death foresaw his catafalque in the East Room in a dream, and John F. Kennedy, whose wife copied the black draping of the windows from pictures of the Lincoln mourning.

But Hoban's "Public Audience Room" has also seen happy

occasions, such as weddings, which included Alice Roosevelt Longworth's. She came to the next one, Lynda Bird Johnson Robb's.

Possessions in the White House come and go, as do the occupants. Each new family moving into the White House brings with it the knowledge that the lease is not easily renewable and can be canceled for high crimes and misdemeanors. Even though the lodgings are temporary, every new presidential family—in the spirit of "throwing the rascals out"—tends to throw out the way the previous residents lived in the house. Moving the furniture around, if not the walls, is, of course, a prerogative of everyone who lives in a furnished house, even one that is government issued.

Each first family can choose from a wealth of furniture left behind in storage by previous tenants. The private quarters on the second and third floors are usually redecorated to each new tenant's tastes. In earlier times, this was also true of the public state rooms. In Grover Cleveland's administration, the now stately gold-and-white and furniture-sparse East Room was adorned in the latest mode with large ferns, flowers, and ottomans. Theodore Roosevelt added a moosehead and other mounted-animal-head trophies to the State Dining Room. President Chester Arthur's choice of décors was Tiffany's art nouveau—to make room for it, he sold 24 wagonloads of household effects at public auction.

But Mrs. Kennedy's restoration in 1961, when many antiques were acquired, resulted in national legislation that established the historic interest of the White House furniture and prohibited any more public auctions. In 1964, President Johnson by Executive Order created a permanent position of curator for the White House and a Committee for the Preservation of the White House which must approve any proposed changes in the state rooms.

So now the public house, private home is also a national living museum. It is difficult to believe that Theodore Roosevelt's children once roller-skated in the East Room, or that President Harrison did his own grocery shopping, bringing it home in a basket, or that Jefferson had to pay for his own servants and for his own dinners, of which the wine bill was considerable.

Today, the house, certainly still not a palace by European standards, has 75 employees on the permanent staff, headed by

Chief Usher Rex Scouten, who does everything except usher. He runs the staff, calls the plumber, keeps the books and the peace. His job calls for almost superhuman abilities at pleasing an unlikely assortment of people, while keeping primary loyalties to the house and the history it represents.

That's a job that Presidents also have as they occupy the house that is more public than private. For as President Franklin Delano Roosevelt once told the nation in one of his fireside chats, "I never forget that I live in a house owned by all the American people and that I have been given their trust."

**The White House, 1600 Pennsylvania Avenue, N.W., 456-1414.** Visitor entrance at East Gate, East Executive Avenue. Public tours Tuesday–Saturday 10 A.M.–noon; closed Thanksgiving and Christmas. During the summer tickets will be available at 8 A.M. for the day of the tour; tours will begin 10 A.M.

# *The Presidents' Other Homes*
## By Mel Elfin

During the eight months when Gerald R. Ford was Vice President of the United States, he used to fend off embarrassing questions about his aspirations for the White House by telling and retelling the same story: "Every time I leave my office late at night and get into my car for that long drive home to Alexandria, I look over at 1600 Pennsylvania Avenue and think to myself: Jerry, if you lived here, you'd be home by now." In August, 1974, "Jerry"

Mel Elfin is Washington bureau chief of *Newsweek*.

Ford stopped commuting to work and moved into what another White House aspirant, Hubert Humphrey, once jokingly referred to as "the nation's foremost public housing project." On the day the Fords' moving van pulled up to 1600 Pennsylvania Avenue, their red-brick rambler at **514 Crown View Drive in Alexandria, Virginia,** was added to the Washington area's most exclusive real estate list—the houses and apartments where the nation's Presidents lived before and after taking the oath as chief executive.

Time, and the wrecker's ball, of course, have taken their toll of many former presidential residences. Of those which remain standing, only five are open to the public:

• George Washington's 500-acre estate at **Mount Vernon, in Virginia** (which almost was turned into a resort hotel in the nineteenth century by its non-sentimental owners).

• **The Octagon at 1799 New York Avenue, N.W.,** headquarters of the American Institute of Architects Foundation—once the temporary home of James and Dolley Madison, who fled the White House in 1814 after it was burned (*See* Chapter V, "Monuments and Memorials") by British invaders.

• The elegant federal-period offices of the Arts Club of Washington at **2017 I Street, N.W.,** where James and Elizabeth Monroe lived from his inauguration in March, 1817, until the refurbished White House was made habitable again in December of that year.

• **Decatur House at 748 Jackson Place, N.W.,** home of Martin Van Buren when he was Secretary of State from 1829 to 1831, and where, according to legend, he had an attic window cut into the side of the red-brick building so he could secretly signal President Andrew Jackson across Lafayette Square in the White House. (*See* Chapter V, "Monuments and Memorials.")

• The gracious, 23-room, Georgian-style house at **2340 S Street, N.W.,** to which Woodrow and Edith Galt Wilson drove from the Capitol immediately after watching Warren Harding being sworn in as his successor and where the 27th President lived until he died in 1924. (*See* Chapter V, "Monuments and Memorials.")

Most of the other homes associated with the Presidents are closed to the casual visitor—or are in places like Plains, Georgia—because they are privately or institutionally occupied or else because they are devoted to nonpublic uses by the federal government. These include such venerable Washington landmarks as:

• **Woodley,** the Georgian manor house at **3000 Cathedral Avenue, N.W.,** built by a nephew of Francis Scott Key in 1836, and which, in pre-airconditioning days, served as a nineteenth century summer White House for Presidents Van Buren, John Tyler, James Buchanan, and Grover Cleveland (and where both George Patton and Henry L. Stimson lived in the twentieth century). The estate now functions as the home of a private school.

• The U.S. Soldiers' and Airmen's Home at **Rock Creek Church Road and Upshur Street, N.W.,** a neo-gothic cottage which also served as the summer White House in the administrations of Buchanan, Abraham Lincoln, Rutherford Hayes, Ulysses Grant, and Chester Arthur.

• **Blair House, at 1651-53 Pennsylvania Avenue, N.W.,** across from the White House, where Andrew Johnson lived between his inauguration as Vice President in March, 1865, and Lincoln's assassination five weeks later. Harry, Bess, and Margaret Truman lived there, too, from 1948 until 1951, when the White House was undergoing its most extensive reconstruction since the post-burning rehabilitation of the Madison and Monroe era.

But it is among Washington's non-landmark and lesser known presidential residences that the best insights can be gained into the tastes and lifestyles of the nation's chief executives, particularly those who served and lived here in the twentieth century.

The Washington residential neighborhood richest in such presidential homes centers around the Woodrow Wilson House on S Street. Besides Wilson, three other chief executives lived in the area within a brief span of years a half century ago. Herbert and Lou Hoover lived just a few steps east of the Wilson house, at **2300 S Street, N.W.,** from 1921 until 1929. They entertained there lavishly and frequently amid black and gold Oriental-style trappings. The three-story, painted-brick house is now occupied by the Chancery of Burma. Shortly before Hoover moved into the neighborhood, his future successor in the White House, Franklin Roosevelt, moved out. FDR lived in a 17-room, $6^1/_2$-bath house at **2131 R Street, N.W.,** now the residence of the

Ambassador of Mali. Roosevelt, who came to Washington in 1913 as a young and ambitious Assistant Secretary of the Navy, initially lived in a house at **1733 N Street, N.W.,** which was torn down in 1963 to make way for a new apartment building. But in 1917, needing more room for Eleanor and their five growing children, the Roosevelts moved up to the R Street house.

After FDR lost the race for Vice President in the 1920 election year the Roosevelts left Washington. The same election brought moving vans to another house in the same neighborhood—the one at **2314 Wyoming Avenue, N.W.,** that belonged to Warren and "Duchess" Harding. The Hardings had lived in the small, heavily planted three-story Georgian house with its brick-arched driveway since 1915 and were still there when he was elected President five years later. Following Harding's death in California in 1923, the formidable "Duchess" auctioned off almost all of the family's furniture and moved back to Ohio.

When the widow Harding held her "presidential garage sale," another former chief executive was living just one block away. From 1922 until his death in 1930, William Howard Taft, by then Chief Justice of the United States, lived in a large, white-pillared house at **2215 Wyoming Avenue, N.W.** With nine bedrooms, several fireplaces, and a dining room that could seat 16 comfortably, the house was large enough to accommodate the corpulent Chief Justice, who weighed more than 300 pounds. The red-brick house has been owned by both the Egyptian and Syrian governments, but it is, nevertheless, one of the few former presidential residences marked by an appropriate historical plaque.

There's no such appropriate plaque at **Connecticut Avenue and Woodley Road, N.W.,** at the sprawling **Sheraton Park** complex, which has provided lodgings for three Presidents. Taft lived there for a brief time until he bought the Wyoming Avenue house; Brigadier General Dwight David Eisenhower spent the winter of 1942 there before going to England to take command of United States troops in the European theater (after the war from 1945 until 1948, Ike lived at **Fort Myer,** near **Arlington Cemetery, in "Quarters One,"** traditionally assigned to the Army Chief of Staff); and Lyndon Baines Johnson occupied a hotel apartment there for a few months in 1961 when he was Vice President.

Of all recent Presidents, LBJ, who spent 35 years in Washington, seems to have had more homes than any other chief executive—at least nine, besides the White House. Two can be found near the Sheraton, just north of the National Zoo: on the **east side of Connecticut Avenue** is the huge **Kennedy-Warren** apartment building where Johnson lived in 1940, shortly before moving across the street to an apartment in the **Woodley Park Towers at 2737 Devonshire Place, N.W.**

The Washington residence where LBJ lived the longest, from 1943 until 1961, is a three-story, white brick, gray-shuttered pseudocolonial house at **4921 Thirtieth Place, N.W.,** in the suburb-like Forest Hills section of the District, two long blocks east of Connecticut Avenue.

From there LBJ, Lady Bird, and their two daughters moved into what is perhaps the most sumptuous of recent Presidents' homes in Washington—**The Elms.** In 1961 Perle Mesta sold to the recently sworn-in Vice President her mansion at **4040 Fifty-Second Street, N.W.** The house, set back from the hilly street about 100 feet, is so secluded by foliage that only the turreted roof is visible from the driveway. The house is now owned by the Republic of Algeria.

At the other end of the scale, perhaps the most modest of all the surviving presidential residences in Washington is the two-bedroom apartment at **4701 Connecticut Avenue, N.W.,** where Harry Truman lived from 1941 until 1945. Here a bit of history is commemorated in the building lobby by a large autographed portrait of the former President and by a gold plaque noting that he lived there as a senator from Missouri, as Vice President, and, for a few days, as President. After FDR's sudden death on April 12, 1945, Bess Truman had to rush down to the White House to witness her husband's swearing-in before she'd had time to prepare supper for Harry and Margaret. Consequently, Harry Truman's first meal as President of the United States was a sandwich prepared by a neighbor at 4701 Connecticut. When the neighbor asked the new chief executive what it was going to be like living next door to the President, Mr. Truman replied, "Well, it'll cause you plenty of trouble, so as soon as we can we'll move out." A week later the Trumans moved temporarily into Blair House, and a week after that into the White House.

Georgetown, which was the citadel of "Camelot" during John Fitzgerald Kennedy's 1,000 days in the White House, was also JFK's home for most of his 14 years in Washington as a congressman and senator. During his first term in the House of

Representatives, from 1947 until 1949, Kennedy, then a bachelor, lived in a typically small, narrow Georgetown rowhouse at **1528 Thirty-First Street, N.W.** In 1949, as social obligations became more demanding for the rising young congressman, JFK moved to a larger, four-story red-brick corner house at **1400 Thirty-Fourth Street, N.W.,** where his sister Eunice served as his hostess. Four years later, Senator Kennedy moved with his new bride, Jacqueline Bouvier, into a two-story white-brick house at **3271 P Street, N.W.** In 1954, the Kennedys, who hoped to have a large family, shifted to **Hickory Hill,** an estate with sprawling green lawns located on **Chain Bridge Road just off Route 123** in suburban **McLean, Virginia.** But after Jackie lost their first child by miscarriage in 1956, they returned to Georgetown, to a federal-style townhouse at **3307 N Street, N.W.,** where they lived until they left for the White House on January 20, 1961.

Gerald Ford was once a Georgetowner, too. From 1949 until 1951 when he was a freshman member of the House, Mr. Ford lived in the large apartment house overlooking Rock Creek Park at **2500 Q Street, N.W.** Then, he and Betty and their infant son, Michael Gerald, moved to the Virginia suburbs. From June, 1951, until March, 1955, the Fords lived in a secluded rowhouse at **1521 Mount Eagle Place,** in a section of Alexandria called **Parkfairfax.** During his very early days at Parkfairfax, Ford could have walked out his front door, through a patch of woods, to a similar rowhouse at **3538 Gunston Road,** then occupied by another rising young Republican congressman, Richard Milhous Nixon.

Richard and Pat Nixon left the suburbs and moved into the District of Columbia in July, 1951, shortly after he became a member of the Senate. Their first home in D.C. was a corner white-brick house with bay windows out past American University at **4801 Tilden Street, N.W.** Six years later Nixon, by then Vice President and earning $35,000 a year, upgraded his lifestyle by buying a sumptuous, 21-room stone Tudor-style house at **4308 Forest Lane,** in the wealthy Wesley Heights section of northwest Washington.

By contrast, Calvin Coolidge lived in far more modest surroundings when he was Vice President. From 1921 until 1923, Coolidge and his wife Grace occupied an $8-a-day suite in the **Willard Hotel** at **Fourteenth and F Streets, N.W.,** now closed but once the social center of Washington where Taft, Wilson, and Harding also lodged on occasion.

Although it would not occur until the end of the Ford administration, many Washingtonians have long felt that the Vice President should have an official residence, and in 1923 the widow of Senator John B. Henderson of Missouri offered to deed her red-stone, castle-like mansion at 2200 Sixteenth Street, N.W., as a home for the Vice President. However, Mrs. Warren Harding, who did not like either of the Coolidges, would have none of it. "Do you think I'm going to have those Coolidges living in a house like that?" she stormed. "A hotel apartment is plenty good enough for them." And so the Vice President stayed at the Willard—until fate forced "Duchess" Harding to move out of the White House to make way for "those Coolidges."

Shortly after the 1977 inauguration, Vice President and Mrs. Walter Mondale moved into the official vice-presidential residence. On the grounds of the Naval Observatory at **Massachusetts Avenue and Thirty-fourth Street, N.W.,** the house was acquired during the Ford administration. The residence is not yet open to the public but plans call for having tours at some later date.

# II
# Congress and the Capitol

## Congress
### By David S. Broder

The Capitol policeman—a member of the special force hired by the members of Congress for their own protection—is familiar with the routine by now. The anxious tourist rushes up and wants to know what part of the building the President's office is in. Patiently, the policeman explains: the President and his staff work at the White House, at the other end of Pennsylvania Avenue. The Senate and House of Representatives are the only official bodies housed in the Capitol building. "Oh," says the tourist, "I thought this was where the government was."

It is more than accidental that the **Capitol,** which is between **Constitution and Independence Avenues at First Street,** is firmly lodged in the public's mind as the symbol of government. Members of Congress complain constantly, and often with good reason, that the power has moved elsewhere. Across the street is the Supreme Court, which sometimes crosses the line between interpreting or applying the law and writing its own policies into law. Downtown, there are the White House and the hundreds of executive agencies whose directives and regulations may determine more of the impact of government on our everyday lives than the broad statutes written by Congress.

All that may be true, but Congress and the Capitol still symbolize the essence and the spirit of our Republic. "Here, sir, the people govern," said Alexander Hamilton, and it is in the Capitol, where the people's representatives gather, that the workings of the democracy are most real.

They should also be most visible here, but the visitor to the Capitol often leaves with a sense of puzzlement and frustra-

David S. Broder is a Pulitzer Prize-winning political commentator, an associate editor of *The Washington Post*, and author of *The Party's Over* (Harper & Row).

tion—and not just because he or she has been told that the President doesn't work here. Ushered through endless corridors of statuary on the official tour, the citizen-spectator is seated for a few minutes in the public gallery of the House or Senate and treated to the doubtful entertainment of some unidentifiable person orating to a nearly empty set of chairs. If this is where "the people govern," the manner in which their sovereignty is exercised by their elected representatives seems mysterious indeed. Many a visitor, I am afraid, leaves the Capitol puzzled about where the representatives and the senators are, what they are doing, what kinds of decisions they make and how they make them.

The reason for that puzzlement is that Congress is a complex institution, whose members must do several jobs in a single day—and frequently seem more frantic than fulfilled at the end of their labors. The House and the Senate are parts of a single whole—the Congress—but they operate independently on most matters, and there's a good deal of rivalry between them. To become law, a bill must be passed in the same form by both the House and Senate. Reaching that agreement is never easy. Each of the 435 Representatives (each representing a district with about 500,000 residents) and the 100 senators (two from each state, regardless of population) has his or her own ideas. Finding a majority to support any measure is a matter of patient negotiation and sometimes tough debate.

That job of legislation may be the most important of a congressman's many tasks, but it is certainly not the most time-consuming: most members of Congress spend a good deal less than half their working day on the House or Senate floor. Each member of Congress is also a representative of his state or district, whose assignment it is to look out for its interests everywhere in the web of government that is Washington, and this takes many more hours than legislation does. He or she is also a member of several congressional committees and subcommittees, which not only draft laws in their specialized areas but maintain a degree of supervision over related executive agencies and their actions. In addition, the member is also a host to visitors from his district; a trouble-shooter for constituents who have problems with the government; a source of information for journalists covering Congress; an object of lobbying by spokesmen for every conceivable interest group; and, of course, a political party member and a politician hoping to win another term (two years in the House and six years in the Senate) at the next election.

The Congress is the reflection of its members, and they, in turn, reflect the great diversity of regions, communities, races, and viewpoints in this continental republic—a richness of variety that gives spice to Congress as it does to the country. The way to think about what is taking place in the Capitol is to imagine what you would confront if you were one of 535 people, chosen from your 200 million fellow-citizens, set down in Washington, D.C., and told you must help decide how much the government should spend and what its laws should be—while simultaneously keeping an eye on what it is already doing, and helping anyone from home who needs help in any area where government ought to be of assistance.

That is what is happening in Congress every day, and if the Capitol leaves the visitor puzzled, it is because there is so much going on—not so little—that it's hard to separate out and comprehend.

There is, however, a way to get a real insight into Congress on a short visit, particularly if you are fortunate enough to be in Washington while the House and Senate are in session. (The most active days in the Capitol are generally Tuesday, Wednesday, and Thursday. Congress tries to schedule its summer and holiday recesses well in advance, so a letter to your congressman will usually enable him or her to advise you whether Congress will be in session when you plan to arrive.)

With a bit of luck, you can get a very good idea of the role of Congress and the work of congressmen within 24 hours. Any member of the House or Senate will be happy to give you a pass to the public galleries in both chambers, enabling you to visit them at your own convenience, without being part of a tour. Unless you have reason for some other choice, my suggestion would be to go to the office of the representative from your district. Senators are big-shots who get plenty of visitors; your representative likes to know that his constituents know and care about him, and you're almost guaranteed a warm welcome in his office.

You will not find his office in the Capitol. While it hasn't grown quite as fast as the rest of government, Congress has spread out from the Capitol to three main office buildings for House members and two for senators. The House office buildings are just to the south of the Capitol; the Senate office buildings, just to the north. A phone call in advance (call 224-3121 and ask for your representative by name) will tell you the exact building and room number you want.

Personally, I think late afternoon is the best time to drop in on your congressman. After 3 P.M. or so, the office begins to relax a bit. The big morning rush of visitors has passed; the most urgent crises have been handled; the mistakes have been corrected—or covered up. As a journalist, I've found that walking the corridors of one of the congressional office buildings in late afternoon, you can turn in at almost any door and find members and their assistants having coffee, signing letters, planning the next day's schedule—and ready to talk.

It's a good time for you as a constituent to learn about the first and most important of the worlds of your representative—that of his or her office. This is the center of each member's Washington operation, where his own assistants work, where he maintains contact with his district via phone and letter, and where he holds most of his meetings with those who are seeking his help or support.

Whether or not your representative is there (and if he is, he'll almost surely want to greet you), plan to spend a half-hour or so in the office. (Congressional offices are short of space, but they'll never throw a constituent out in the hall.) After you've introduced yourself, tell the assistant who has greeted you that you'd like to understand more about how your congressman does his job. Ask about the size of the staff and the duties of the various aides. Ask them to show you the equipment they use for answering correspondence. Ask if the congressman has other office space around the Capitol as well—many do have "annexes" or secondary offices—and ask what kind of work is done there.

I think you'll be impressed with how hard most congressional offices work to keep up with the requests for assistance and information from the constituents. But you'll also learn that not all those "personal" letters you get from your congressman are typed by hand, let alone seen by him. And you'll discover how much staff and equipment is available to the representative for making himself well and favorably known at home. You have every right to be inquisitive, for you, as a taxpayer, are paying for every bit of it.

Then ask your host or hostess to tell you about what's been

going on that day. How did the congressman spend his time? Did any big problems come up in the district which required his help? Did he put out any announcements for the press or radio or television today? What meetings did he have? What other visitors came by—a White House lobbyist, an environmental group? What did they want? If your host or hostess is at all candid, you ought to have a much better idea of the daily demands on your representative when you've finished this discussion. And if you have an opinion you want to express on some issue, or a problem you want some help with yourself, the aide should certainly invite you to speak your piece.

If straight answers aren't forthcoming, by the way, that's a pretty good tip-off that your representative isn't running the kind of congressional office you deserve.

There's one more thing you can do effectively during this late-afternoon visit: plan your next day's activities at the Capitol. Ask your contact in the office what of interest is going on the next day in the House and Senate. Start with the schedule of committee meetings. Mornings, usually, are given over to committee meetings, where most of the detailed work of Congress actually gets done. The schedule of each day's committee meetings is announced the previous afternoon, and is published each morning in *The Washington Post*. Thanks to recent reforms, most congressional committee meetings are open to the public, but occasionally, when secret matters are involved, they are closed, and that fact is noted in the published schedule.

Your best bet, in most instances, is to go to the meeting of the committee on which your own representative serves. More than anything else you can possibly do, watching him in action on his own committee will give you a good clue to his competence, his influence, and the degree of respect he commands from his colleagues. Besides, if you tell him you will be there, he'll have to be on the job.

Your congressman or his assistant should be able to brief you on the subject matter of the hearing and give you a copy of the bill they'll be discussing or a summary of the previous testimony they've heard. Once again, if your request gets no sensible response, you'd better start wondering about your representation. It may be that your congressman is going to be testifying before some committee other than his own on a matter of interest to him or the district. By all means, ask if you can accompany him to that committee and then go with him to his own committee when he goes there.

If, by chance, his committee is not meeting, or if it's a closed meeting, or if the subject matter is so deadly dull you can't bear the thought of hearing it, there are some other options. You can ask the representative's assistant to find out what other hearings the next morning sound interesting. A complete run-down is available from the press gallery, or your host can get suggestions from other members' offices, or from the senators from your state. It may turn out that the Secretary of State is going to be testifying on the foreign aid bill and you'd like to see what he really looks like; or that some big investigation you've been following is going to have a "mystery witness." Your representative's office should be able to tip you off about this kind of treat the previous afternoon, tell you the time and the room number and, perhaps, even help you get a seat in the hearing room.

There are as many different kinds of committee meetings as there are functions for Congress, and you can learn something from any one of them about the work of Congress. Most meetings are devoted to receiving testimony on a pending piece of legislation. By listening to the parade of witnesses, you can get some idea of the variety of pressures that come to bear on even the simplest legislative decision. And you can tell, from the members' questioning, how they try to balance those pressures, determine the equities, and build a record that supports the policy decision they hope to see the committee make.

A second type of committee meeting is the "mark-up session," where the drafting of the legislation and the voting on its provisions actually takes place, after all the testimony has been received. This is the heart of the legislative process, where all the political pressures collide with the substantive policy questions. It is at this stage that most of what finally will be in the bill is decided. If you find yourself in a committee "mark-up session," you will have a civics lesson that cannot be topped.

A third type of committee meeting is an "oversight" or investigative session, where the members are examining the operations of a government agency or probing some area of public life that may require future legislation. These investigative sessions can be quite dramatic, but even if the subject matter lacks the suspense of a grade-A thriller, there's something you can learn from such a meeting. That is the enormous difficulty of maintaining effective control over the operations of the bureaucracy by the elected representatives of the people.

With any luck at all, your morning in the committee rooms of Congress ought to give you an understanding of some or all of the legislative, investigative, and political phases of Congress' work—as well as a better "feel" for your own representative's contribution (if any) to the process.

By the time you have visited your congressman's office and spent a morning in committee, you'll be ready to move on to the more obvious elements of Congress at work: the full floor sessions of the House and Senate. Normally, each chamber starts its work at noon, but the starting time may vary from day to day, so you may want to check with your congressman or in *The Post*'s listing of the day's congressional schedule.

Most people are disappointed by floor debate. The House, with its large membership, limits the time any member may speak. Often, what you hear sitting in the visitors' gallery is more of a fragment of an argument than an understandable exposition of the issue. Still, you ought to look in, even briefly, on the House in session, just to get a sense of the flavor of the body and the styles of its members.

Roll-call votes in the House used to be fun to watch, because the names were called alphabetically, and you could literally hear, in the welter of accents, the voices of America's people. But now the House has a modern electronic voting system, with a fancy lighted scoreboard, and the romance has all departed.

The Senate maintains more of the tradition of debate and it still has real roll-call votes, so it is there that one can best get the sense of floor action. But don't expect too much. If you wander in on an afternoon when no votes are scheduled, you may find only a handful of senators on the floor—one or two engaged in desultory debate, the others visibly bored at listening. There are certain speeches that are made for the record—to establish the senator's views on the issue for his own constituents. Senators do not expect their colleagues to waste their time listening to such speeches.

Once again, a bit of advance planning usually can make your visit to the Senate much more interesting. The Senate these days operates with a good deal of schedule planning. By calling your senator's office the afternoon before your visit (or having your representative's assistant make the call for you while visiting that office), you can find out if there are any recorded votes scheduled for the next day and, if so, what time they are likely to come up. Plan to be in the Senate gallery an hour of so before the scheduled time for the vote.

The last hour of debate is usually reserved for the chief supporters and opponents of the bill or amendment that is coming to a vote. That's when you're likely to hear the best exchanges. And when the bells sound for the roll-call vote, you'll see the senators streaming onto the floor to answer when their names are called. That's the time for celebrity-gawking, to see what those familiar television visages really look like in the flesh. I just hope you're not too disappointed.

After the Senate vote, if you move quickly to the elevator that takes you to the basement, you're likely to bump into (literally) some of those same Senators, headed for the little subway trains that shuttle to and from their office buildings. You can hop a ride with them, if you like, or stroll the corridors of the Capitol with the confident sensation that you now have a much better understanding of the work that's done in this place. The guides are very good about pointing out the historical spots, and there is a great sense of history in the Capitol. (*See* the following article, "The Capitol Building.") From the caucus room in the Old Senate Office Building, where dozens of famous investigations have been held and many a senator has announced his candidacy for the White House, to the House Judiciary Committee hearing room, where in 1974 the people's representatives sat in judgment of the President, the power of the legislative branch of government is manifest on Capitol Hill.

There have been great changes in our country and its government since the first Congress met in Philadelphia. But, considering the differences between our America and theirs, the continuity of the system is even more impressive.

The Founding Fathers created a tripartite government, with independent and competing executive, judicial, and legislative branches. But they assumed and desired that the legislative branch—the Congress—would be at the center and the heart of that government, and, in some senses, dominate it. That is why they gave Congress the power to levy taxes and determine how they shall be spent, to declare war and ratify treaties, to regulate commerce, to confirm the chief appointees of the executive branch and all federal judges, to make the laws, and, if necessary, to try and remove from office all civil officers, including the President, who violate their oaths of office.

On your visit to Congress, you will undoubtedly see the most familiar view of the Capitol, the East Front, where every fourth January the inaugural stand is built on which the President and the Vice President take their oaths of office. There is an important symbolism in the President's coming to the home of the legislative branch to solemnize his oath, just as there is in his annual appearance before Congress to report on the State of the Union. Powerful as he has become in our government, he needs to be reminded that he does not make the laws by which we are governed; only the Congress may do that.

But, personally, I am not enamored of the imperial East Front on which the President takes his oath; nor do I much care for the vast parking lot that the East Front plaza has become. I would hope that when you have finished watching Congress at work, you might wander down the lovely interior staircase onto the outdoor balcony and terrace that provide the West Front of the Capitol. From its height, you can look out over the city of Washington, past the Justice and Labor and Commerce departments, the museums that line the Mall, past the White House and the State Department, the monuments to Washington and Jefferson and Lincoln, and out along the course of the Potomac to the land that is America, stretching west, in your mind's eye, to the Pacific.

You will understand, then, why the Capitol was placed on this hilltop, and why the Congress was given it as a home. And I hope you will feel, with Hamilton, that here, sir, the people still do govern.

# The Capitol Building

## By Sarah Booth Conroy

On nights when the Congress works late, a lantern burns high in the Capitol dome, like a signal bonfire, to show that the people's representatives are at work, running the country. Every nation has a symbol of authority, an emblem of government, but few seats of power rise so visibly and majestically as does the people's palace we call the Capitol.

In the District of Columbia, it is hard to forget the Capitol, whether you can actually see it or not. Its dome floats always in the mind's eye. In Washington, Capitol Hill is simply called "the Hill." It sounds irreverent, but it is not—the sobriquet merely confirms the Capitol's power. Distances are measured from it. Major streets radiate from it. City parties and previews fluctuate with its calendar. In an annual spring ritual, civil servants trek up to "the Hill" to report: what did they do with last year's money, and why do they need next year's. And, when a President is to be inaugurated, he goes up to the Hill.

What used to be called Jenkins' Hill was certainly, as Pierre L'Enfant said, an obvious "pedestal waiting for a monument." It is not known what the Powhatan Indians, who once camped there, thought of it.

Your taxi will come up the hill and stop before the East Front of the Capitol. Try, if you can, to forget that the grand plaza is now a dumping ground for automobiles, and imagine it as it is on Inauguration Day—flags flying, bunting waving, and the bands playing "Hail to the Chief" as the President makes his vows on the great central portico stage.

If your legs are strong and your heart is sound, there is a much more impressive way to arrive at the Capitol—by climbing up the long stairs on the West Front, up the terrace designed by Frederick Law Olmsted in 1874–1875. Until they were added, it was said that the Capitol looked as though it were teetering on the hill's edge.

Sarah Booth Conroy is an editor of *The Washington Post's* Style section.

Standing at the top at the West Front, looking back at the city, is a good time to imagine that fine fall day, September 18, 1793, when President George Washington climbed the hill to lay the cornerstone of this edifice. The best description of that day is Daniel Webster's, who later said of Washington:

"He heads a short procession over naked fields, he crosses yonder stream on a fallen tree, he ascends to the top of this eminence where original oaks of the forest stood as thick around as if the spot had been devoted to Druidical worship, and here he performed the appointed duty of the day."

While you're there, look closely at the West Front because it is the original sandstone façade. George Washington, who lived down the Potomac at his estate, Mount Vernon, had a vested interest—some might say a conflict of interest: he recommended the sandstone from his quarries at Aquia Creek. This Virginia sandstone, with its tendency to decompose, has been a constant worry to the Architect of the Capitol ever since, leading the successive holders of that office to recommend all sorts of fanciful schemes to replace the original sandstone with marble. If the Architect of the Capitol had his druthers, the West Front would be extended and be made of marble. But protest by the American Institute of Architects and other history buffs, including United States congressmen, has halted for the time being that further tampering with the historic building. Yet George Stewart, a former Architect of the Capitol, had his way on the East Front. He extended the east façade $32^1/_2$ feet; this extension was completed in 1961, in time for John F. Kennedy's inauguration. The new front is built of Georgia marble.

Before you go into the Capitol (you may wish to enter from the East Front), take a minute to get your bearings and hear a bit more history. The original design was by Dr. William Thornton, a gifted amateur student of architecture, who entered the competition for the plan three months late. Nevertheless, he was chosen to receive the prize, $500 and a city lot, over the other 16 entrants, after George Washington recommended the design: "The grandeur, the simplicity and the beauty will . . . I doubt not, give it a preference in your eyes as it has in mine."

Washington's eyes were never to see the reality of the grand design. He died in December, 1799. Almost a year passed before the Capitol was occupied, and then only because President John Adams insisted.

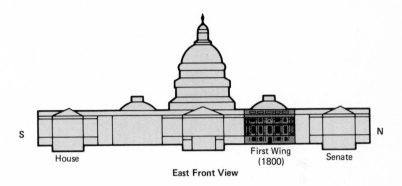

S     N

House     First Wing (1800)     Senate

**East Front View**

The first part of the Capitol was finished in 1800. It was a square, two-story section now just to the north of the center, domed section. This small building held the 32-member Senate, the 106-delegate House, the Library of Congress, the Supreme Court (in 1801), and the District of Columbia Circuit Court. The crowding caused a congressional-judicial musical-chairs—temporary moves that lasted until the Supreme Court moved out in 1935 into its own architecturally noteworthy building.

The first joint session of Congress was held in that first, square, two-story section on November 22, 1800. The Senate and House came down from Philadelphia to attend and then stay on. President Adams congratulated the congressmen on their permanent home.

The south, or House, wing was finished around 1807, under the direction of Benjamin Henry Latrobe, who in 1803 was ap-

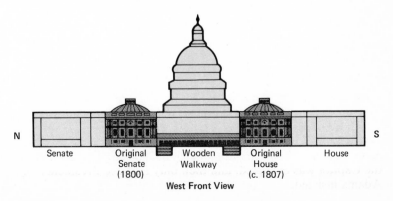

N     S

Senate     Original Senate (1800)     Wooden Walkway     Original House (c. 1807)     House

**West Front View**

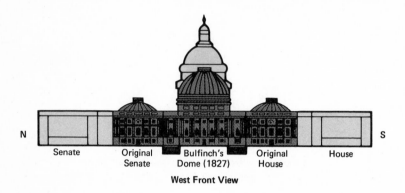

N                      S

Senate      Original      Bulfinch's      Original      House
            Senate     Dome (1827)    House

**West Front View**

pointed Architect in Charge of the Capitol by Jefferson. Then, Latrobe turned his efforts to repairing the north, or Senate, wing, where the plaster was prematurely dropping on the hallowed heads of the forefathers. Latrobe stayed on at the Capitol until 1811. The Capitol now consisted of two separate structures, a north and a south wing, which were connected by a wooden walkway. The Capitol was still domeless.

Then, in 1814, Admiral Cockburn of the British Navy held a kangaroo court in what is now called the "Old Supreme Court chamber" and handed down a decision to burn the Capitol, which they did on August 24th. But a gale of a rainstorm came up and subdued the flames, and saved the Capitol from total destruction. Latrobe, calling the Capitol "a magnificent ruin," returned to Washington in 1815 to rebuild it. He stayed until 1817. After the war, private citizens publicly subscribed money to build the "Brick Capitol" where the Supreme Court is now (First and East Capitol Streets, N.E.). From 1815 to 1819, it was Congress' home until the Capitol was repaired. Amid serious talk of moving the capital city (the House defeated such a proposal by a bare 9 votes), the Brick Capitol served to keep Congress in Washington and local businessmen happy.

Finally, 1827, the Capitol's central section between the wings was completed under Charles Bulfinch, Latrobe's successor. It was crowned with a wooden, copper-sheathed dome. Bulfinch's dome was low, in harmony with Thornton's and Latrobe's design.

Congress, never satisfied unless it was forever building ever more stately mansions, authorized still more extensions at either end of the Capitol in 1851. Then, too, they had cause. Congress was under some pressure to house representatives from the new states which were then emerging from the new lands of the 1803 Louisiana Purchase. The House extension was completed in 1857, the Senate in 1859, under the direction of Thomas Ustick Walter. Naturally, Walter had to add a dome bigger than Bulfinch's to make the aspect ratio work.

Walter's dome, finished in 1863, took 9 million pounds of iron that could have been used against the Rebels. Abraham Lincoln knew—before Carl Jung—that people survive by symbols, and he ordered the dome completed. The iron was needed more for "a symbol that our nation will go on." The dome proved as durable as the Union. Its ingenious construction with inner and outer shells allows it to expand and contract with the weather —and it does, about four inches.

If you stand on the East Front's plaza, the "Statue of Freedom" atop the dome is 287 feet, $5^1/_2$ inches from the ground underneath your feet. Freedom, who is a woman, was designed by sculptor Thomas Crawford, cast in bronze, ironically by slave labor at a Bladensburg Road, N.E., foundry, and mounted in 1863. She was originally called "Armed Liberty" and wore a Liberty Cap, the sort worn in Rome by freed slaves. But Jefferson Davis, soon to be president of the Confederacy, protested—and Crawford gave her instead an eagle helmet (and platinum lightning rods).

Before you, underneath her feet, the Capitol stretches from north to south more than 751 feet long and from east to west, 350 feet wide. The 540 rooms occupy $16^1/_2$ acres of floor space. There are four grand staircases, and many more strange and secret ones. There are even some tiny staircases being used as secretaries' offices. And underneath it all is the subway linking the Capitol with the Senate and House office buildings. When there is a roll call, elevators are reserved for members of Congress.

As you climb the grand steps from the East Plaza, through the East Portico, leading into the Rotunda are the huge bronze "Columbus" doors, sculpted by Randolph Rogers in 1858. The door panels memorialize the discoverer of America with scenes of his deeds as he prepared for his adventure.

The Rotunda, which circles under the dome, is the Capitol's grandest room and Constantino Brumidi's masterpiece. The Rotunda is 180 feet high and 96 feet across. Constantino Brumidi was an Italian-born artist of Greek descent who came to the United States in 1852 as a political refugee. Grateful for his freedom here, he spent 25 years painting the Capitol's interior, and many months stretched on his back atop a 180-foot scaffold.

Gracing the top of the dome, like a canopy, is a 4,664-foot true fresco, pigment onto wet plaster, by Brumidi, "Apotheosis [Glorification] of Washington." In five groupings it depicts early incidents in the nation's history, allegorically, of course. Graceful gods and goddesses intermingle with George Washington, Ben Franklin, and the growth of the nation. Brumidi's sweeping figures are 12 to 15 feet tall so they will look life-sized from the ground. Brumidi finished the painting in 1865. He was 60.

The Rotunda frieze, also in fresco—according to legend, done with a mixture of cream and cottage cheese and milk—was begun in 1877 by Brumidi (then 72). It illustrates American history in an 8-foot high, 300-foot circumference. Brumidi had painted about a third of it when, in 1879, while painting Penn signing a treaty with the Indians, he slipped from the scaffold. He caught himself and held on by one hand, hanging 58 feet above the floor, until he was rescued. He died a few months later.

His helper and student, Filippo Costaggini, painted eight more panels from Brumidi's drawings. But a 30-foot gap lasted from 1888 until 1953, when Allyn Cox finished the frieze.

Eight large historical paintings hang in the Rotunda. Four are by John Trumbull, who served for a time on Washington's Revolutionary War staff. There are some interesting contradictions in Trumbull's painting of the signers of the Declaration of Independence—he shows 47 instead of the actual 56 signers, and five of Trumbull's 47 were not signatories. In another of the Rotunda paintings, "The Baptism of Pocahontas," by John G. Chapman, one of the Indians is shown with six toes, which allegedly he actually had.

The Rotunda's Lincoln marble sculpture is by Vinnie Ream, a 17-year-old Virginia girl who wanted to do a statue of Lincoln. On her behalf, Congressman James Rollins of Missouri took up the matter with Lincoln, who scarcely heard the request until he was told she was young and poor. Assuming his country drawl, Lincoln said, "Well, that's nothing agin' her." During the last five months of his life, Vinnie Ream was allowed to sketch Lincoln while he worked.

Most people come to the Capitol with the stated intention of seeing their senator and representative in action. Well, the likelihood is you will not find them in the House or the Senate, but rather tucked away in some hidden committee room, if not in their offices, or home campaigning. Stop by their offices anyway, in the appropriate buildings—the two Senate office buildings are just north of the Capitol, the three House buildings (the Rayburn is especially ugly) are south—and pick up your pass to the galleries. The legislative chambers themselves are in dreary 1949 style, the year they were remodeled.

The House Chamber is, of course, the largest, 139 feet by 93, and one of the largest legislative halls in the world. In both chambers, the Republicans sit to the left of the Speaker and the Vice President and the Democrats to the right—one might say in reverse of their political views.

But while passing through the halls of the Senate wing, do take a moment to admire the Minton tiles from Liverpool, England, paving the way between the Senate Chamber and the Rotunda. Recently, the Smithsonian Institution, which also has some Minton tiles in their old Arts and Industries building, and the Capitol Architect made a joint order to the original factory's successors for replacement tiles. But most have lasted well over the 100 years.

In the Senate wing, on the ground floor, be sure to notice the decorative murals by Constantino Brumidi, in the "Brumidi Corridor." The House members, in more plebeian taste, had voted long ago their preference for "plain brown democratic walls." But jealousy overcame them finally, in 1972, and they hired Allyn Cox, then 76, to paint some murals on the walls and hall ceilings outside the House restaurant.

The three Capitol rooms you should definitely see are the most historic and the most interesting—Statuary Hall, and old Senate and Supreme Court chambers. All three are newly restored—the Capitol's first restorations, and a Bicentennial commemoration.

Statuary Hall, south of the Rotunda, was the House of Representatives chamber until 1857. The room was highly praised by Jefferson, who declared that only Latrobe could have designed it. But the acoustics have always been strange. John Quincy Adams was the first to realize and take advantage of the fact that at a certain spot, you could hear everything being whispered across the

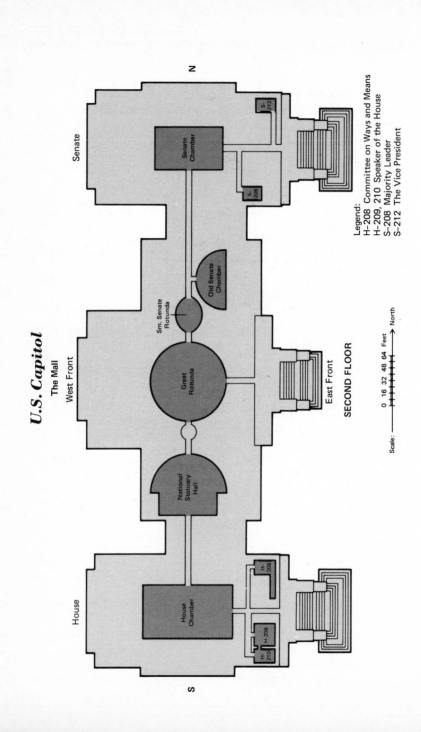

# U.S. Capitol

## The Mall

West Front

Senate

Senate Chamber

S-212

S-209

Old Senate Chamber

Sm. Senate Rotunda

Great Rotunda

National Statuary Hall

House Chamber

H-206

H-209

H-210

House

N

S

East Front

SECOND FLOOR

Scale: 0 16 32 48 64 Feet ⟶ North

Legend:
H-208  Committee on Ways and Means
H-209, 210  Speaker of the House
S-208  Majority Leader
S-212  The Vice President

room. What he heard may have served him well, because he later became our sixth President. Oddly enough, in 1848, he died of a stroke at that same spot, at 81. But only after serving eight more terms in the House, having returned there after his presidency. A plaque on the floor marks the spot where Adams was stricken. Statuary Hall is restored to its 1857 appearance, complete with its red draperies—which congressmen hoped, futilely, would improve the acoustics (and no doubt prevent the eavesdropping).

The Old Senate Chamber, north of the Rotunda, was used by the Supreme Court for 75 years, until it occupied its own building in 1935. It was here, in the Old Senate Chamber, that President John Adams (Quincy's father, if you remember your history) addressed the first joint session of Congress on November 22, 1800. On March 4, 1801, Thomas Jefferson was inaugurated here. Originally, the Old Senate Chamber was a single room, two stories high; Latrobe, while repairing the north wing, divided the room into two separate stories. In 1810, the Senate moved into the top story and the Supreme Court into the lower. The rooms were to be redone again after the 1814 Capitol fire. After that British destruction, Latrobe wrote that "great efforts were made to destroy the Court room, which was built with uncommon solidarity, by collecting into it, and setting fire to, the furniture of the adjacent rooms. By this means, the columns were cracked exceedingly; but it still stood, and the vault was uninjured."

Then, on January 4, 1859, in another musical-chambers turn, the Senate moved out into its new wing, and the Supreme Court moved up in 1860, leaving the old Supreme Court chamber below as a law library, and eventually as a dusty store room. But in May, 1975, the old Supreme Court chamber had been restored to its 1860 glory, at a cost of about $478,000, and opened to the public.

The chamber is considered one of Latrobe's masterpieces, if not his finest interior. You can approach it through the small Senate Rotunda, and admire the tobacco leaves and blossoms on the top-level columns, and the corn-cob capitals on the lower-level columns. Latrobe always said he had received more praise for those bits of Americanism than for all else he had designed. The Supreme Court justices, however, had no such high opinion of the room, finding it so dim, dank, and dingy that they preferred to meet at the tavern across First Street.

Today, the Supreme Court Chamber is chiefly notable for its

remarkable ceiling, described variously as an umbrella or half a pumpkin shell. The beams culminated in three splendid arches. The Chief Justice sat in the middle of the center arch where the dome in the ceiling made sort of a halo over his head. The vault fell when first constructed, killing the builder. Latrobe redesigned it and it has stood well since although some years later, braces were added after a bomb went off here.

For all the trials in designing and building such a "palace for the people," for all its pretensions and faults, the Captiol is what it is: a monument in stone to a land and its people—a monument as diverse and as constant as the people and the system it symbolizes there on the Hill.

**The Capitol Building, between Constitution and Independence Avenues at First Street, 224-3121.** East Front entrance at East Capitol Street. Open daily, 9:00–4:30, except Thanksgiving, Christmas, and New Year's. Tours leave every 10 minutes from 9:00–3:45, in the Rotunda. The Capitol Rotunda and Statuary Hall are open in the summer until 10 P.M. The House and Senate Wings are also open when either of those legislative bodies is in night session.

# III
# The Supreme Court

## By James E. Clayton

Perhaps no building in Washington so well represents its occupant as does the one on Captiol Hill housing the Supreme
Court. This magnificent "marble palace" exudes power and
majesty. Yet, it is quiet and simple. There are no trappings of
power—no bustle, no aides scurrying about, no sense of urgency,
no visible sign that much happens here. The long corridors are
often deserted and the high ceilings are reminiscent of those in memorials to things long gone. The decorations on its exterior and
on its walls are historical and extend back not just through the life
of the United States but through the history of the civilized world.
A sense that this is a unique place and that what goes on here is
different from what goes on elsewhere is easy to gain from a visit
to this building. That is appropriate, because there is no other
court on earth like the Supreme Court of the United States and
there is no other part of government anywhere whose power rests
so heavily on so simple a thing as an idea.

It is that idea—the deeply held belief that rules called law
provide the best way to settle disputes without violence—that
permeates everything that exists and happens here. The massive
bronze scenes cast into the main entrance doors trace part of the
history of that law beginning with the trial scene from the shield
of Achilles as described in *The Iliad*. The sculptured marble
panels around the top of the courtroom depict the great lawgivers
of history—from Menes, Hammurabi, Moses, and Solomon to
Charlemagne, King John, Blackstone, and Marshall. The effort to
carry out that idea of law marks the arguments the justices hear.

James E. Clayton, an award-winning Supreme Court reporter, is now a member of
the editorial page staff of *The Washington Post*.

Their opinions are generally accepted as providing the best fulfillment of the idea that we are capable of expressing.

So accustomed have we become to the Supreme Court's existence that it is easy to forget its unique position. No other major nation has granted so much power to its judges and then accepted their exercise of it so fully. This Court's decisions, since it first sat in New York City in 1790, have shaped American government and society as much as the actions of Congress and the Presidents. Early in our nation's history, the Court fostered the development of a strong national government, and without its active encouragement the government in Washington might well have withered, as did the original national government under the Articles of Confederation.

Later, one of the Court's decisions (in the case of Dred Scott) nudged the country to the brink of the Civil War. More recently, the Court changed American society by ordering an end to racial segregation in all phases of public life, forced an equitable redistribution of political power within the states by compelling the one man–one vote reapportionment of their legislative seats, and helped bring about the first resignation of a President by directing him to yield up certain tape recordings he wanted to keep secret.

This is power, in its truest sense, for it rests not on money (the Court has only that to spend which Congress provides) or troops (the Court must rely on the President to see that its orders are obeyed) or politics (the Court has no constituents to whom it turns), but on that idea called law and on the prestige that the Court's members have nurtured carefully for almost two hundred years.

"We are very quiet there," Justice Oliver Wendell Holmes once wrote, describing the Court, "but it is the quiet of a storm center." The issues that come to the Court for resolution are among the most divisive the nation faces. How do you square the commands of the Constitution against compelling self-incrimination and against unreasonable arrests and searches with the need of the public for protection from criminals? How do you determine whether prayer in the public schools violates the First Amendment guarantee of free exercise of religion and its bar against the establishment of a state religion? What do the vague words of a Constitution—"due process of law," "equal protection of laws," and the regulation of "commerce"—mean today,

Demonstrations have been a Washington feature; this is the Martin Luther King, Jr., 1963 March on Washington.

The Supreme Court mourns Chief Justice Warren, July 11, 1974.

almost two centuries after they were written? The Court's answers to these, and dozens of other questions, have kept it almost
constantly in that "storm center," but respect for that idea called
law and for those who interpret it here have kept the Court safe
from the storm itself. Perhaps the words chiseled in marble over
the main entrance to the Court building—Equal Justice Under
Law—express better than anything else what the nation is all
about.

If you are fortunate enough to hear the Court in action, the
vitality of this idea will become clear. In the hall where the justices meet to hear arguments, nothing counts but the quest for
what the law is or ought to be. On four days a week, two weeks a
month, October through April, the justices sit from 10 A.M. to 3
P.M. with an hour off for lunch. They hear fifteen or so cases each
week and they have no time to squander. A lawyer usually has 30
minutes, occasionally an hour, and rarely more than that in which
to present the critical facts and the crucial arguments on which
his case turns. That case must be important—otherwise it would
not be heard in this Court—and no lawyer ever feels he has been
allowed sufficient time. His presentation will be interrupted,
sometimes completely disrupted, by questions from the nine justices in as full and as frank a discussion of complex issues as you
will ever hear. Time is precious on both sides of the bench, and
the justices do not tolerate well the occasional lawyer who cannot
cope with their questions, nor do they tolerate flowery or bom-
bastic speeches. Their interest is in getting to the heart of the
issue as quickly as possible, and they let little interfere with that.
If you hear a case that is well argued (the schedule is printed daily
in *The Washington Post* when the Court is sitting), you should
be able to follow most of the discussion. If you hear the entire
presentation of a case and you cannot understand what is involved, chances are the case was poorly argued. Even the most
complex issues are stripped down to simple terms in this Court if
the lawyers do their job properly.

On three Mondays a month, more or less, the justices begin
their session by announcing their opinions and orders. Sometimes, they have little to report. At other times—particularly in
May and June, when they may sit on other days of the week solely to announce decisions—there will be many items on the
docket. Each year now, the Court is asked to review more than

4,000 civil and criminal cases that have originated in the state and federal courts. Since they can handle only 100 to 150 a year, they pick the most significant, seeking cases that involve major principles. Only rarely does the Court hear a case solely because the justices believe an injustice was committed by the lower courts. This is a court of law, not a court to correct wrongs.

The announcement of opinions is always a fascinating event. The justice who wrote the opinion usually takes time to state the facts of the case and to explain why the Court has decided it the way it has. Other members of the Court then may announce their concurrences in that opinion or their dissents from it. This procedure, almost unique in American courts, is sometimes criticized as a waste of time. But the justices seem to enjoy it, and those who hear the announcements gain an understanding of the case, and of how the justices feel about it, that the written word cannot convey. Occasionally, tempers flair as these opinions are announced. One day, after Justice Felix Frankfurter had concluded an opinion, Chief Justice Earl Warren hunched forward to say angrily that he would have had a dissent if the written opinion really contained what Mr. Frankfurter had just said it contained. In his oral announcement of a decision on another day, Justice Frankfurter referred to the Constitution's first amendments as the "so-called Bill of Rights." When he had finished, Justice Hugo Black mustered all the vast scorn at his command and started his dissent with these words: "This case involves the Bill of Rights, not the so-called Bill of Rights." On still another day, the second Justice John Marshall Harlan, who was a master at summarizing the most complex case in a few words, told the spectators he would read his dissent from a decision he bitterly opposed because he feared his emotions would lead him into extravagant criticism if he spoke extemporaneously.

The justices, then, are not men devoid of emotion, although most of them usually give that impression from the bench. All of them develop strong views of what kind of government our Constitution was meant to establish, and their differences are openly and frankly displayed. But none of them casts votes lightly and most justices cannot be influenced by anything other than their own, personal convictions. Taking note several years ago of a series of articles attributing the justices' votes to their early education or to political views they espoused before coming to the bench, Justice Black remarked, somewhat wistfully, "I wish that just once, someone would write that I voted like I did because I thought it was right."

Most of the work of the Court, of course, takes place in parts of the building that you cannot see. There is, on the back side of the building, a conference room where the justices meet regularly. Only the nine members of the Court attend these meetings, and no one else really knows what happens inside them. Each justice has a small suite of offices, usually terribly crowded with books, and a staff consisting in most cases of only two law clerks, a secretary and a messenger. This means, quite simply, that each justice does his own work. Each must vote on every one of the 4,000 or so cases—either to hear it or reject it; there are no committees. The task is formidable and, on at least one occasion, has been more than a member of the Court could physically and mentally stand. One justice, still on the Court, commented soon after his arrival that he had surveyed what he had to do and worked out a schedule giving himself barely enough time in which to do it, only to discover he had forgotten to leave time for writing opinions. Since each justice will write 20 or more opinions a year, that is a major part of the job. If you drive past the Court late at night and notice lights burning in one of the windows on the main floor, a justice or his clerks may still be there, trying to get a typescript ready for the private printing shop in the building's basement.

It is not difficult to see the Court, but you need to be lucky to spend much time listening to it. The courtroom holds fewer than 200 spectators, so the delay in gaining access is sometimes long, and when many are seeking entrance, your allotted time may be quite brief. When major cases are argued, like the school desegregation cases of the 1950s, the prayers-in-the-schools cases of the 1960s, or the Nixon tape case of 1974, the waiting line may extend out of the Court building and down the long flight of stairs on the Capitol side.

Even if you are not fortunate enough to see the justices on the bench, there is much to be gained from a visit to the Court. Free guided tours are conducted about every 30 minutes from 9:30 A.M. until 4 P.M. on days the Court is not sitting, and at 3:30 and 4 on days when it is. The tours will take you through all the building's public areas, but you are also generally free to roam those areas as you choose. The most noted features of the building are the two elliptical spiral staircases that connect five stories.

They are not so free-standing as they look—each marble step was built into the wall of the stairwell. Elsewhere in the building, there are busts of all the Chief Justices, paintings of some other members of the Court, and various symbolic pieces of sculpture.

You may wish to have lunch in the Court's cafeteria, which is located on the ground floor and is open to the public except during brief, peak periods when the Court's staff gets priority. It is one of the best in town—and there is always a chance to see a justice eating there.

The Court building, designed by architect Cass Gilbert, was begun in 1932 and completed in 1935 at a cost of slightly less than $10 million. Of that amount, 30 per cent was spent for marble of various kinds, most of it from Vermont and Georgia. Prior to the construction of the building, the Court had met for years in a room in the basement of the Capitol, which has recently been refurbished. (*See* Chapter II, "The Capitol Building.") When the new building was completed, one member of the Court, Justice Louis Brandeis, refused to use the suite of offices assigned to him. He thought the building too massive and not conducive to the spirit of humility he believed those who sit on the Court, and govern by the power of reason, should have. But the majesty of the building is brought down to human scale in the courtroom where the justices sit and where anyone can come to hear them discuss with lawyers, and sometimes with each other, the way in which those rules called law should be applied in preserving the republic in a constantly changing world.

The **Supreme Court** is directly east of the Capitol, at **1 First Street, N.E.** The main entrance is on the west side of the building facing the Capitol.

For additional current information on the term, weekly schedule, tours and lectures, and parking (or lack of it) nearby, call 252-3000.

# IV
# The Cults and Communities

## *A Typical Community*
### By Art Buchwald

Sometime ago I watched Barbra Streisand on a TV special from the Kennedy Center where she sang at a benefit for the Special Olympics for the Mentally Retarded.

She received a tremendous ovation after one of her songs, and she said she was surprised because she thought people in Washington were "stuffy."

It occurred to me that Miss Streisand was speaking for many Americans who somehow think that those of us who live in the nation's capital are different from other people in the country.

Well, it's not true. We're just simple folk with the same dreams and aspirations as everyone else. In the morning we insert our legs in our pants, one at a time, just as men and women do in Topeka and Peoria. And after a breakfast quite similar to ones eaten all over America, we go to our offices where we do our simple work.

The work is no different than that done in Hartford, Connecticut, or Atlanta, Georgia. Some of us will pass laws; others will filibuster, and still others will follow Amy Carter to school. One man in a small office might give a squadron of jets to an Arab country, and another man in a small office will send missiles to Israel.

We could give a billion dollars to the space program, or cut $500 million to education. We'll tap telephones if we have to and add to files of suspected subversives.

Art Buchwald writes a syndicated humor column that appears in *The Washington Post* and is also the author of several books.

Some people might be assigned to following Russian diplomats all over town, and others could be in charge of selling them wheat.

We might work on ways of giving the American people a tax cut or figure out methods of bailing large corporations out of debt.

Some of us will lunch with lobbyists, while a few will eat with their secretaries and take the afternoon off.

People should stop thinking just because we live in Washington we're different.

We indict Attorneys General and White House aides, pardon previous Presidents, defend multimillion-dollar antitrust suits, and try to get government agencies off our clients' backs.

We cut food stamp aid, raise Social Security rates, and declare budget deficits. Some of us lie to grand juries, and others lie to Senate committees. We make speeches for TV audiences and hand out press releases telling how wonderful we are.

Some of us work for the media and, no matter what we say, we're always right.

We're a typical community. After work we may go over and have a few drinks with the ambassador of Iran or play a game of tennis with the Secretary of the Treasury. On some nights we might go to have dinner with the Carters, and on other evenings we'll have the Mondales in for bridge and a light buffet.

If the weather is good we could have a cookout at the Tidal Basin or wander down to the local tavern and have a few beers with Zbigniew Brzezinski. If there is a good movie in town and Barbra Streisand is singing beforehand, we might even go to that. Otherwise we'll stay at home and read the *Congressional Record*.

It's sad that although we live in Washington people think we're something special. We're just average Joes, a little better educated, more informed, rarely in error and confident that nobody knows better than we do what's good for the country. How could Barbra Streisand think we're stuffy?

# Social-Political Washington

### By Sally Quinn

Everyone has his or her idea of what this city is all about, but there is one aphorism with which most will agree: Washington is a company town. It has one industry: government. What happens socially in Washington revolves around the administration, Congress, the courts, and those who report and comment on them.

Social prominence in Washington has little to do with traditional social credentials or wealth. It has to do with power. If you have power, you are in. If you haven't, you are out. If you have power, you don't need to try to make it. You already have.

Because everything of significance socially is political, a party is not a party in this town. It is a working occasion where the only concession to the hour is that people change their clothes and take a drink.

If you are invited to a high-powered party in Washington, you will find several things happen naturally that would never happen in another town. First, the guest list will be carefully balanced to include at least: one senator, one congressman, one ambassador, one member of the administration (the closer to the President the better), one political columnist, one reporter, one editor, one TV correspondent, and one good gossip who will spread the word the next morning about what a success the party was and who was there.

You will find that no Washington party ever fails to have a discussion of politics and of those in power. Then, later, in order to discuss and work out various political strategies, there is a dividing up of interested parties, i.e., a politician with a journalist, an ambassador with an administration official, a columnist with an ambassador—always with a gossip looking on, listening

Sally Quinn is a writer for *The Washington Post* Style section and the author of *We're Going to Make You a Star* (Simon & Schuster) about her experiences as a TV anchorperson.

in. You can judge who is in power—or who is not—by who attracts the party reporter. Dressed to blend in, the reporter can usually be identified by the notebook almost always in hand.

For visitors to Washington the social life looks pretty dead. It's nothing like New York, Chicago, or Los Angeles. There are no fashionable nightclubs and hardly any very elegant restaurants where people go to dine at night. There is a reason why the town seems lifeless by 8 P.M., and why it seems especially so on weekends: Washington's power elite socialize publicly at lunch and privately at dinner—and they do it so energetically during the week that on the weekend people rarely go out to eat or even entertain.

During the day, the place to be seen is, without question, the Sans Souci, often referred to as "The Sans" (pronounced as in "sands") only by those who can get a table at a moment's notice or who can speak fluent French. It is there that the pols and the press hang out to see and be seen, to conduct business, put out stories, get stories, and trade gossip. There are other restaurants in Washington, fairly good ones too, but this is the one where a visitor, at lunch—if he or she can get a reservation—will get a capsulized version of what happens at night in the inner sanctum of social-political Washington. The evening private social scene is made up of these same people, minus the social climbers (generally recognizable by their asking for a phone at their table to make calls as opposed to those who are brought a phone to receive them).

The parties after dark always used to be very formal, but social-political Washington is relaxing these days. Where once you would have found butlers behind every chair, finger bowls, place cards, and seating charts, today you will as often find a cabinet minister sitting on the floor with a plate on his lap, chatting, while a senator or congressman is dispatched to the kitchen for another bottle of wine.

Perhaps it is inflation that has caused a deformalizing of lifestyles. Or just an honest recognition, belated maybe, that most of those in power in Washington haven't the money or the time (or, for that matter, the social background) to entertain in the grand manner. They have eliminated the affectations, and they've quit trying to impress others by entertaining in a way in which they don't normally live.

What many visitors to Washington forget is that this is a transient town, the only town in America where the word *nouveau* is laudatory. Most people come and go, get elected, then defeated, appointed, then resign, or get fired. Every six years there is a senatorial election, every four years a presidential election, and every two years the entire House must face re-election. This creates a constant changeover in Washington; additionally, there's always an influx of new faces in the diplomatic corps, in the military, among those who come and go with the elected or appointed.

To name names of who's in power and who's not would be to immediately condemn this piece to obsolescence before it reaches print, for the reasons mentioned above. Everything that's important in Washington is ephemeral—the power, the personalities, the plans, the programs, the prestige.

There seem to be only three institutions which still have stability: the Supreme Court, old social Washington, and the press.

The Court is hardly where the action is socially. And social Washington sits back in ivy-covered houses in Georgetown and Chevy Chase, going to private clubs, exclusive little dancing groups, observing the whole power circus as it parades by, occasionally taking a quick turn in it, then stepping back out to watch from a careful distance.

But old social Washington could be considered useful in the way it provides perspective. For this is the group that provides the gossips, the tongue-waggers, the ones who project a sense of who and what people really are, who provide a setting for the minuet. They have always been there. They always will be.

Journalists, it appears, reached their peak of power during Watergate, when a President was forced to resign largely because of the efforts of the press. Because of that, the tone of the power structure changed quite a bit, and today you'll find politicians asking reporters for their autographs, and Presidents and Vice Presidents accommodating those who they realize will be there long after they have gone.

All this may change. In fact, it probably will. For Washington is a city where the balance of power shifts every day, where it can happen, has happened, that the ranking guest seated on the hostess's right will lose an election, be fired, or recalled, in the middle of the meal—and another, suddenly more high-ranking, will take his place.

It is that element of precariousness, of transiency, of fluctuation, that draws people to Washington, captivates them, and never truly lets them go.

# International Washington

### By Judith Martin

Everybody knows what diplomatic life is like in a great capital. Titled people in white tie or diamond tiaras gather nightly in gilt-and-Aubusson drawing rooms to sip champagne, nibble caviar, and utter tiny witticisms in which half the words are italicized. Once or twice a year, an approximation of that scene actually takes place in Washington. There are no tiaras, diamond or otherwise, and the caviar is either scarce or lumpfish or both, but a White House reception or State Department dinner for the diplomatic corps tries to live up to that Old World ideal. Usually, it is about the only white-tie party in the whole of Washington for the entire year, and the smell of mothballs could kill you.

Ordinary diplomatic life, though, goes on in Washington relentlessly, every day and every night, and if the hundreds of people who participate do not sip and nibble and utter, they are at least out there drinking and eating and gossiping in the name of peaceful international relations. It is a difficult trade, with long hours and peculiar working conditions, little glamour and less glory. A diplomat does the routine work of taking in information

Judith Martin is a reporter and columnist for *The Washington Post* Style section and the author of *The Name on the White House Floor* (Coward, McCann & Geoghegan).

and putting out an image, and when something exciting comes along, such as a world crisis, it is handled by his bosses on a summit or over a hot line.

There are those, therefore, who say that diplomacy is obsolete. Gone are the days when ambassadors made their own world-shaking or world-calming decisions during the days or months it took to send home for instructions. It is hard enough for a modern diplomat to get through the mountains of information he finds in the local newspapers and magazines—where is he going to get time to dig around for more on his own? You can hardly have multiple personal contact in a diplomatic corps so huge that if everyone made the old required formal visits to heads of missions, there would be no time for anything else. Still—who knows what clashings of nations are now being avoided by the skillful swervings of officials, and what changes are being made in the course of history by secrets indiscreetly dropped into diplomatic ears?

In any case, 133 countries are represented in Washington, and more than 2100 diplomats work for them. That is not even counting the 25 missions accredited to the Organization of American States, which forms another Washington-based diplomatic corps, although the staffs often overlap. In fact, a small country may have the same ambassador accredited to the United States, the Organization of American States, and the United Nations in New York, thereby saving on salaries, although running up a large bill on the airline shuttle.

Signs of diplomatic life can be seen all over Washington, although rarely in the form of exotic dress, which is more likely to denote an ethnically inclined student, foreign or American. Modern diplomatic uniform is a gray suit (double-breasted for Eastern Europeans) or a black dress. But everybody in Washington notices DPL-tagged cars, especially when they are illegally parked; or, when street parking spaces are few, legally parked in those all-too-many "Diplomatic Cars Only" areas; or when they have effectively stopped rush-hour traffic while 300 diplomats try to drive into one ambassadorial driveway for a 6:30 to 8:30 party. Other common sights are: uniformed Secret Service officers clustered in front of certain embassies that occasionally attract bombers; leafleteers or marchers demonstrating in front of innocent office buildings that happen to be 500 feet away from an embassy (as near as one can legally go to picket a particular embassy); and diplomats explaining to store clerks that they do not have to pay sales tax.

Whatever friction these events create among the natives—and they do—it is somewhat tempered by the memories of Washingtonians who have lived abroad with privileged status. Washington has a sort of "returned foreign service" that includes returned diplomats, Navy wives who learned flower arranging in Japan and form clubs here, and high school kids—who get easy French or Spanish credits on the basis of what they learned from the maids abroad.

Some of the biggest and wildest controversies in Washington have centered on the location of foreign chanceries—the offices of diplomatic missions where the day-to-day work is done. An embassy, technically used only as the ambassador's private residence, may be located anywhere an ordinary house can be. But in recent years the location of chanceries (or office space) has been limited to certain areas zoned for such use.

The **Soviet Embassy** office situation includes all three of the typical solutions to diplomatic space problems: an old mansion, too expensive to be kept up by private citizens; a new glass-and-steel building complex at **Wisconsin Avenue and Tunlaw Road, N.W.;** and overflow space all over town. The Russians' mansion at **1125 Sixteenth Street, N.W.,** near the White House is known to old Washingtonians as "the Pullman mansion" because it was built by the sleeping-car family. Its luxurious interior (including a jewel-box elevator that was the first such machine in Washington), plastered over with poster-sized portraits of Lenin and other heroes, is considered one of the great ironies of Washington.

Then there is the **People's Republic of China,** which solved its space problem by simply purchasing an entire hotel, the **Windsor Park, 2300 Connecticut Avenue, N.W.**

The **British, Brazilians, and Iranians** have expanded their old-mansion embassies with neighboring modern buildings near **Whitehaven Street** on **Massachusett Avenue, N.W.,** which is often called Embassy Row. Once **Sixteenth Street,** less fashionable now, had its day, and **Italy** (which has plans for a new place), **Spain, Mexico, Ghana, and Poland** are among the embassies inhabiting huge residences there. Other handsome old embassies are those of the **Belgians,** who occupy a miniature chateau at **2300 Foxhall Road, N.W.,** and of the **Taiwan Chinese,** who are in

**Twin Oaks, 3225 Woodley Road, N.W.**, the estate that once belonged to Alexander Graham Bell. Some modern embassies—such as the **Danish (3200 Whitehaven Street, N.W.)**, the **German (4645 Reservoir Road, N.W.)**—are considered examples of splendid design. The **Kuwaiti Embassy, 2940 Tilden Street, N.W.**, is considered splendid in another way, complete with the pillowed salon that immediately became known around town as the Seduction Room.

There are large embassies with huge staffs, many of whom are popularly suspected of being spies, and embassies of one, two, or three people, who are also suspected of being spies. Some represent countries with volumes of daily traffic with the United States in trade, culture, science, and matters of mutual political interest; and there are others whose only function is the vain hope of drumming up tourist business.

Some governments represented in Washington have not existed for decades. Diplomats from Estonia, Latvia, and Lithuania—appointed before those countries were incorporated into the U.S.S.R.—scrupulously follow all the steps of diplomatic life. Their ranks, however, are steadily depleted, since there is no home government to name new diplomats as the old ones die.

The headquarters of the **Organization of American States** is the **Pan American Union, Seventeenth Street and Constitution Avenue, N.W.**, where concerts and art shows are also organized to represent the member countries. What the tree-filled courtyard has in drama for a party setting was considered by some to be offset by the liability of its resident live birds' occasionally molting into people's drinks. The first thing the new O.A.S. Secretary General did when he came into office was to send them packing—to the Zoo.

There are ambassadors who spend personal family fortunes entertaining, and third secretaries who live in dingy apartments suffering from loneliness and culture shock—and there are also third secretaries who are enjoying a fling abroad before returning to their aristocratic lives at home, and awkward ambassadors who have not yet mastered the language.

At some state functions, it is considered expedient to have the whole diplomatic corps rolled into one, and that one is the Dean of the Diplomatic Corps, the ambassador who has been in Washington for the longest consecutive time. The Nicaraguan Ambassador, Guillermo Sevilla-Sacasa, obviously enjoys this duty, greeting every successive American President as "my very good friend," and displaying all the medals he has collected in glass cases in his living room. On those white-tie occasions when he manages to wear them all, one side of his jacket hangs a good four inches below the unadorned side.

United States headquarters for diplomatic activities is, of course, the **Department of State, 2200 C Street, N.W.,** the eighth floor of which has been painstakingly fitted out with American antiques and paintings, after much pleading with American collectors. It is on that floor, with its panoramic-view terrace, that most American entertaining of diplomats is done, although the President's Guest House (the Blair-Lee House) across the street from the White House has also been used by American officials when no foreign potentate is in residence. These affairs are run by the State Department's Office of Protocol, which is capable of shuffling the names of everybody in the world, including our own democracy, and coming out with them in strict order of rank. In the early '60s, Protocol came out of its cookie-arranging function for a while to join in the civil rights movement, with the argument that discrimination against black diplomats adversely affected American foreign policy. The next step of the argument—that it was bad policy for black diplomats to observe discrimination against black Americans—seemed to carry weight even with people who had no objections to discrimination against our own citizens when they thought no one else was looking.

For many reasons, embassies tend to act or be treated as cliques. The most chic ones are the grand old European powers, although a newcomer with style can make it for a while. One year, the Moroccans abandoned the common small-country practice of serving imitation French food in imitation French surroundings and went native, with pillow-filled tents, exotic dancing girls from downtown Washington, and couscous *sans* forks. They immediately skyrocketed socially, taking a lot of the Arab world up with them—but the aftermath of the Seven-Day War with Israel wiped that out until the recent peace initiatives.

There are touches of the native culture in some Asian, African, and Latin American embassies, but for the most part they are what might be called Basic Diplomatic. It is a curious cultural phenomenon that diplomats tend to resemble one another more than they do their countrymen. Possibly it is because they all eat the same food. The similarity of the cuisine in all the embassies

# Embassy Row

(A selected listing for architectural or historic interest.)

1. U.S.S.R. Embassy, 1125 16th Street
2. Canadian Chancery, 1746 Massachusetts Avenue
3. Ghana, 2460 16th Street
4. Inter-American Defense Board, 2600 16th Street
5. Lithuania, 2622 16th Street
6. Poland, 2640 16th Street
7. Italy, 2700 16th Street
8. Spain, 2801 16th Street
9. Mexico, 2829 16th Street
10. Israel, 1621 22nd Street
11. Luxembourg, 2200 Massachusetts Avenue
12. Turkey, 1606 23rd Street
13. Vietnam (closed), 2251 R Street
14. Ireland (Ambassador's Residence), 2244 S Street
15. Egypt (Ambassador's Residence), 2301 Massachusetts Avenue
16. Venezuela, 2445 Massachusetts Avenue
17. Japan, 2516 Massachusetts Avenue
18. France (Ambassador's Residence), 2221 Kalorama Road
19. People's Republic of China, 2300 Connecticut Avenue
20. Islamic Center (Mosque), 2551 Massachusetts Avenue
21. Denmark, 3200 Whitehaven Street
22. Brazil, 3000 Massachusetts Avenue
23. Iran, 3005 Massachusetts Avenue
24. Great Britain, 3100 Massachusetts Avenue
25. U.S. Vice President's House
26. Taiwan China (Ambassador's Residence), 3225 Woodley Road
27. Site of new USSR complex, Wisconsin Avenue near Tunlaw Road

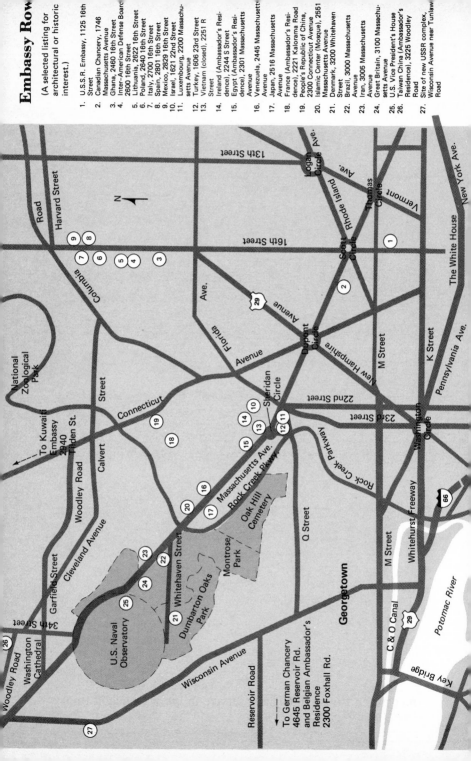

has a lot to do with the size of the catering firms that reach into every gilt corner of foreign Washington with the same standard menus. An embassy that saves money by making its diplomats' wives cook will often have the most interesting meals.

African embassies and other so-called Third World representatives are courted by American blacks, as the Israeli Embassy is by American Jews. Most isolated are the Eastern European embassies, whose staffs stick close together, either because of nervousness on their part or nervousness on the part of Americans who know about security checks made on natives who entertain such foreigners. On their national holidays, the Eastern Europeans send one another identical oversized red-and-white flower arrangements.

It is understood that once a year each embassy will entertain the rest of the diplomatic community, or at least as much of it as it is on political speaking terms with; that is on its National Day. Embassies are also expected to entertain on their military holidays; when their heads of state are in town; every fall when their finance ministers come for World Bank and International Monetary Fund conferences; and to say goodbye to high-ranking staff members who are being transferred to different posts. If possible, diplomats also give parties for American ambassadors and other top-ranking officials going to their countries. Lunch and dinner parties are considered part of the average working day. Some even give parties just for fun, but not many.

Most embassies complain about the meagerness of their entertainment allowances, and as inflation has been spreading around the globe, the complaints have been getting louder. One may hear, for instance, that the cream served with the strawberries at Queen Elizabeth's birthday party, which is the British Embassy National Day party, is flown in from Devonshire. What the logistics of such a stunt would do to the dairy product is not what horrifies British diplomats, but rather what the expense would do to their yearly budget. (As a matter of fact, the cream comes from local cows.)

The British Embassy is also the subject of a popular cocktail-circuit story illustrating how things have improved in what is modestly known locally as the "Capital of the Free World": some time ago, but not all that long ago, London revoked the ruling that recognized British diplomats' service in the Washington tropics as a "hardship."

# The Defense Establishment

## By Michael Getler

On August 11, 1941—four months before Japanese planes attacked Pearl Harbor—construction workers broke ground for a huge five-sided office building on a swampy wasteland of mud flats and automobile junkyards on the Potomac River's west bank. By fall, the cornerstone of what would be called the Pentagon was set in place by the U.S. Army Corps of Engineers.

No ceremony marked the occasion. Perhaps, as some theorized, the Army did not want to draw attention to a structure that had already started controversy in Washington. Even then, some congressmen argued that the vast new "concrete cobweb"—meant to house the scattered headquarters of the old War Department and the U.S. Army Command in one place—was too big, too expensive, and unnecessary. In January, 1943, the building was completed. Since then "Pentagon" has become a global buzzword, an instantaneously recognizable part of international language.

The Pentagon is many things to many people, but mostly it symbolizes the nerve center and command post of the massive American military arsenal spawned by World War II and the nuclear era. To be sure, a shrinking in the defense establishment's size followed each of the big build-ups for World War II, Korea, and Vietnam. But in sheer military power and influence none of those contractions ever quite brought back the prewar size, and the importance of the Pentagon has grown steadily over the past quarter century. Now, the Department of Defense is, in simple fact, the nation's (if not the world's) biggest spender and largest employer. It budgeted almost $100 billion in fiscal 1977, using 4 to 5 million people to do it: 2.1 million men and women in uniform, another 1 million civilian employees, and yet another 1 to 2 million people working in defense plants scattered throughout the

Michael Getler, a *Washington Post* foreign correspondent based in Bonn, has served on the national staff specializing in defense affairs.

United States. Despite increased domestic government spending in recent years, the military still accounts for more than 30 per cent of the so-called "controllable" portion of the total federal budget.

Put another way, the Pentagon is the world's largest corporation housed in the world's largest office building ($249.5 billion in assets; real estate worth $44.3 billion; the five-sided structure on the Potomac has three times as much space as New York's Empire State Building). Its size is not only real, but legendary, sparking stories of the Western Union boy who went in to deliver a message, got lost, and next emerged 25 years later as a full colonel. It has never lost its ability to generate controversy. The building itself was the forerunner of those modern "cost overrun" problems that have plagued large-scale military projects for decades. The Army, pressured by the White House to make the price look reasonable, first estimated the cost of the building at $31 million. It wound up costing $83 million.

For years, unlike the military ministries of virtually all other countries, the Pentagon was open to the general public, its financial supporters. On May 19, 1972, during sporadic turmoil around the nation, a bomb went off in a fourth-floor washroom; since then, the Pentagon has been closed to visitors unless they are on business or know someone who works there.

What goes on inside and how well the men and women of the Pentagon do their jobs in one way or another affects the politics and taxes of every American—and the security of most of the world.

In a third floor office, the civilian Secretary of Defense runs America's military establishment from behind a desk once used by General "Black Jack" Pershing, the commander of America's forces in World War I. On the second floor is the national military command center, or "War Room," where, as battle plans unfold in a crisis, theater-size screens reveal the positions and readiness of U.S. and potential enemy forces. Nearby, the Washington-Moscow "hotline" (a teletype, not a "Dr. Strangelove" telephone) directly links the American President with Soviet leaders in the Kremlin. On the fourth floor, a group of Navy admirals dressed in business suits might be developing new tactics for the Sixth Fleet in the Mediterranean, in case a new Middle East war brings about a U.S.-Soviet confrontation—while on the second floor, an official might be telephoning the Defense Supply Agency to complain about a price hike in the 3 million sets of underwear the military needs next year.

Most of the offices are off limits to persons without security clearance. But for the ordinary visitor a walk through even part of the 17$\frac{1}{2}$ miles of corridors conveys both a sense of vastness, perhaps symbolic of what goes on in the Pentagon, and a sense of contrast. Along the central corridor, a large collection of paintings by American combat artists depicts the turmoil, courage, pathos and exhaustion of war. The walls of this corridor are a reminder that the American fighting man has done his job well. At another corridor's end is the new Hall of Heroes, dedicated to Medal of Honor winners, another reminder of individual valor on the battlefields. There are no visible reminders, however, of the My Lai massacre and the long agony of Vietnam that sent tremors through this building and the entire military establishment. Nor are there visible signs of the well-known bureaucratic foul-ups that occasionally produce fabulously expensive weapons that do not work; or of the huge C-5A jet transport or the F-111 attack plane, or the Navy's F-14 fighter, all of which, when finally made operable, cost so much that far fewer were bought than originally planned. Perhaps C. W. Borklund summed up the Pentagon's contrasts best. "It is," he wrote, "a complex, curious contradiction of waste and efficiency, brilliance and stupidity, patriotism and pork-barrel politics, courageous vision and reactionary caution."

Though the Pentagon is the real and symbolic center of the defense establishment, the pervasiveness of defense-related jobs, facilities, and activities in the D.C. area is much greater than most visitors, or even Washingtonians, realize. For if the "business" of Washington is government, then the single largest item of business done by the government is "defense."

---

### OUTSIDE THE PENTAGON

Scattered throughout the District of Columbia and the surrounding counties in Virginia and Maryland are some 59,757 armed-forces men and women with an estimated 200,000-plus dependents. Another 81,742 civilians work here for the Department of Defense. More than $2 billion in military and civilian defense salaries flow into the area economy each year. On top of all this, another 60,000 or so military retirees are believed to live around Washington, plus thousands more civilian defense retirees.

The brass is here in force—460 generals and admirals. Washington is a headquarters area rather than the home of huge operating bases like Norfolk and San Diego; consequently, the officer-to-enlisted-man ratio in Washington is much higher than one finds in most "military" towns. Since there are really no big bases, and many upper-echelon officers, most of the brass live off base—thus Washington provides many American officers with much more exposure to civilian life than they might encounter on duty elsewhere in the world.

The Pentagon keeps in close touch with Congress. On Capitol Hill, where "defense" accounts for more testimony and hearings, year in and year out, than any other single topic, legislative liaison offices are maintained by each armed service—not only to inform, but to be informed. More than one hundred senators and representatives hold reserve or National Guard commissions, as well.

The military's links with industry are perhaps more extensive than its ties with the government. As President Eisenhower said farewell to the nation over radio and television on January 17, 1961, he called attention to the dangers he saw waiting for America, among them the rise of the "military-industrial complex." Aside from Fairchild Industries in nearby Germantown, Maryland, there are few defense plants near Washington, but about 100 American defense companies make sure they have corporate offices here. Many maintain large staffs for lobbying on Capitol Hill and keeping watch on the Pentagon.

Keeping watch is the business, too, of information-gathering arms of the defense establishment. Before the summer of 1973, people driving to Washington via the George Washington Parkway or the Dolley Madison Highway (Route 123) might never have known that the headquarters of the nation's foreign intelligence operation—the **Central Intelligence Agency**—was just behind the trees in **Langley, Virginia.** In the winter, when the leaves have fallen, the vast, gray, sweeping lines of the building are just visible from the road. For years, the only sign nearby announced the "Fairbank Highway Research Station." In the spirit of more "open" government in 1973, however, the Nixon administration ordered big road signs pointing the way to the CIA.

During the first months of the Carter administration a dramatic step occurred that included a televised tour preceding the now public tours of the facility(351-1100). It's still safe to say that your neighbors or relatives going to work there will not tell you what they or the other 12,000 employees do when they get inside.

An even more super-secret organization, the **National Security Agency,** is headquartered at **Fort Meade, Maryland.** Several thousand people there and scattered all around the world work on such arcane tasks as code-breaking and analysis of intelligence information gathered from radar scanners, airplanes, ships, submarines, and satellites that intercept communications. If you travel north from Washington along the Baltimore-Washington Parkway near the Route 23 exit, you can just glimpse part of the nine-story concrete building that marks the National Security Agency complex.

Whereas NSA remains quite inaccessible to the public, at least one of Washington's military installations is almost invisible. At **Fort Ritchie, Maryland,** an entire command post is underground. If Washington were under atomic attack the President might be taken there—but he would go to Fort Ritchie only if the White House helicopters could not get him to Andrews Air Force Base. Three specially equipped four-engine jets are there, standing ready to get the Commander-in-Chief into the air as fast as possible in a nuclear emergency. Even in the midst of peace and detente, Andrews is the busiest Air Force base in the world, serving Washington's and the world's hierarchy, and the largest employer in Prince George's County, Maryland. Tuesday through Thursday at 10 A.M. tours lasting 45 minutes can be arranged for groups of ten or more, three weeks in advance, through the Office of Information (981-4511) at **Andrews AFB, Menoher Drive near Arnold Avenue, Camp Springs, Maryland.**

---

### MILITARY HISTORY

A visitor to **Fort Lesley J. McNair, Fourth and P Streets, S.W., 545-6700,** walks through a heavy iron gateway onto the oldest (1790) active military post in America. Today, the fort is the home of the National War College, the most prestigious of the military schools for senior officers and a virtual "must" for promotion to the top ranks.

More than a century ago there was a prison at Fort McNair.

On July 7, 1865, four prisoners, including the woman Mary E. Surratt, were hanged for conspiracy in the assassination of President Lincoln. The body of John Wilkes Booth lay secretly buried nearby until 1867. Now, the site of the scaffold is a tennis court. The prison remains have been remodeled into more comfortable living quarters for junior officers and their families.

Across the Potomac, what was once the Civil War home of Confederate General Robert E. Lee is now the U.S. Army's **Fort Myer (Arlington Boulevard and Pershing Drive, Arlington, Virginia, 545-6700).** It is now the home of the Third U.S. Infantry, the nation's pre-eminent ceremonial unit. It is the Army's oldest active infantry outfit, and guards the Tomb of the Unknown Soldier.

The **Marine Corps Barracks at eighth and I Streets, S.E., 545-6700,** is the service's oldest post (1801). President Thomas Jefferson, after a carriage ride around the swampy new capital city, personally picked the site because it was so close to the Navy Yard and within marching distance of the Capitol in case protection was needed. The Marines' famed ceremonial guard company, the drill team, band, and bugle corps, all combine to put on a band concert and spectacular parade within the barracks' grounds each Friday evening at 8:20 from mid-May to mid-September.

The nearby **Navy Yard (Eighth and M Streets, S.E., 545-6700)** does not build ships any more. The site, which was purchased by President John Adams in 1799, does still house the Navy Memorial Museum, and this, along with the Truxtun-Decatur Naval Museum near the White House, provides some of the nation's best displays of American nautical history. Because it is tucked away inside the Navy Yard, the **Navy Memorial Museum** (accessible via the Ninth and M Streets sentry station) is frequently overlooked by visitors and Washingtonians alike. Yet, in one of the longest buildings in the world, one can find biscuits baked on *Old Ironsides* in 1854, a Japanese Kamikaze plane, a hand-cranked submarine from America's Civil War, even a bottle of grog salvaged from the fleet of John Paul Jones. (*See* Chapter XV, "Of Special Interest to Children.")

The **Truxtun-Decatur Museum** is in a portion of the home of the former naval hero, Stephen Decatur, at **1610 H Street, N.W., 783-2573.** Inside are small, high-quality exhibits of ship models, naval photos, guns, and flags.

Elsewhere, youngsters can climb over old cannons and picnickers can lunch under the trees of two old forts. A tiny one-block park at **Piney Branch Road and Quackenbos Street, N.W.,** marks the site of **Fort Stevens.** In 1864, Lieutenant Colonel Oliver Wendell Holmes had to shout at a tall civilian on the ramparts, "Get down, you fool!" President Lincoln had been watching the Confederates advance on the city, not noticing the bullets tearing overhead. To the south of the city, opposite Mount Vernon on the Maryland side of the Potomac, sits **Fort Washington Park, Potomac River and Fort Washington Road, off Indian Head Highway, 292-2112.** Intended to protect the river route to the capital, the fort unfortunately was not finished in time to stave off the 1814 British attack. Its steep ramparts, walls, and moat, though, are well-preserved examples of that era's most modern coastal defenses.

---

## MODERN TIMES

It is a long way, in development, from cannons to the weaponry of the 1970s. The military technology that burgeoned after World War II produced the age of atomic weapons and ocean-spanning missiles. On the one hand, this technology is responsible for two of the world's best-known medical facilities—the Army's **Walter Reed Center, 6825 Sixteenth Street, N.W. (545-6700),** and the **Naval Medical Center, Wisconsin Avenue near Jones Bridge Road, Bethesda, Maryland (545-6700)**—while on the other, scientists at the **Naval Ordnance Lab, White Oak, Maryland (545-6700),** develop missiles that carry TV cameras in their nose-cones to help them find their target.

For 25 years, the people who worked at the Army's **Fort Detrick** in Maryland wore a kind of "black hat" image among their neighbors. It was at Detrick, in dozens of different laboratories, that scientists and technicians worked on the dark science of biological weapons—the tools of germ warfare. In 1969, President Nixon renounced the use of such weapons for offensive purposes. Some work on defensive techniques continues, but 98 per cent of the labs at Fort Detrick have now been converted to cancer research under the Department of Health, Education and Welfare.

The transition at Fort Detrick may be a symbol of things to come. At the Atomic Energy Commission and the National

Aeronautics and Space Administration headquarters, in Washington, the awesome technologies first developed for atomic bombs, nuclear warheads, and intercontinental ballistic missiles have been adapted to the peaceful goals of supplying electricity to American homes and industry and the exploration of outer space. In the summer of 1974, an old World War II Navy torpedo factory along the waterfront in Alexandria, Virginia, was even converted into a vast working area for artists.

Some "swords" have been turned into "plowshares," and torpedoes into paintbrushes, but the world still seems a long way from the time when the "Pentagon" will cease to be a household word; when Americans need not worry what happens in the Pentagon's counterparts around the world, and "all peoples will come to live," as President Eisenhower prayed they would, "in a peace guaranteed by the binding force of mutual respect and love."

# *Invisible Washington: The CIA and the Intelligence Community*

## By Laurence Stern

It soars over the Virginia treetops near McLean, its neo-colossal mass surrounded by teams of blue-uniformed General Service Administration guards, miles of 12-foot chain-link fence, and acres of lawn. And until recently the headquarters of the Central Intelligence Agency of the United States had no tour buses or

Laurence Stern is assistant managing editor/national of *The Washington Post.*

visitors' centers, no shooting galleries, no exhibit halls. The only public space in the building, the Rendezvous Room, was, until the tours, a sort of decontamination chamber separating the world outside, with its dense and toxic leakage of security violations, from the hushed and controlled space within. It is still the room where congressmen, journalists, consultants or visitors from other agencies pick up and return their identification badges and CIA escorts. *All those who enter these portals,* the building seems to say, *had damned well better be on official business.*

It is no wonder that those who work in CIA headquarters regard themselves as set apart. The architecture reinforces the institutional discipline. Agency persons tend to huddle together, in their own skeet-shooting clubs and softball leagues, or at the more exalted social levels, at dinner parties in McLean or Georgetown where many tend to drink too much.

Now it purports to be different. The tours. The television cameras. Can this alter an environment that has an architecture that sets itself apart? Probably not. The difference is that the inhabitants of the CIA headquarters are undergoing a kind of institutional culture shock. They have been invaded. It's safe to say that they don't like it much either.

The building is the main trunk of an extended family that includes operatives and analysts, secretaries and alumni. CIA personnel are tucked away in other government agencies such as the Library of Congress, Treasury and Post Office Departments, in business "proprietaries" (wholly owned by CIA) or under genuinely private corporate cover, such as an oil company or a PR firm. Alumni of the intelligence service are scattered everywhere: they grace the pages of the social register, the senior partnership lists of important law firms, editorial page mastheads, and signed columns of major daily newspapers. One career operative for the CIA served, after retirement, as a senior political adviser to Eugene McCarthy in 1968. E. Howard Hunt and James McCord of Watergate fame worked in the Nixon re-election campaign in 1972. CIA graduates are people of differing politics, careers, and personal style; but many have in common the special bond of affinity for their alma mater.

At a bar in McLean, old operatives gather to exchange gossip and talk about retirement plans, to recall adventure. The discipline of lifelong secrecy makes their camaraderie of a different sort than you would find in American Legion halls. One retired veteran of countless covert escapades in Europe, Africa, and Indochina holds up his left hand with two missing fingers and quietly asks an acquaintance at the bar, who is also missing his full complement of digits: "Where'd you get yours?"

One fall day in the mid-1960s a black limousine pulled up punctually at 12:30 P.M. to the curb of my newspaper office where the then Deputy Managing Editor and I were waiting to be taken to Langley for a VIP tour and lunch with the Director. Neither of us had ever visited the building before. It is a pleasant drive of some twenty minutes along the Potomac, past the spires of Georgetown University and past the ranch-style contemporary houses along the Washington Palisades.

We emerged at Langley in an underground garage where we were greeted by the public affairs officer for the agency, a perpetually worried-looking man with an ID badge hanging from a chain around his neck. Visitors' badges were issued to us. Pleasantries and introductions were exchanged. We were whisked upstairs past rows of high, narrow doors bearing no names or titles to the Office of the Director, a career Navy man who had won his celebrity spurs by building a new generation nuclear submarine. His tenure as Director of Central Intelligence was brief and controversial. He had been a man of the sea who had a penchant on *terra firma* for implanting his foot in his mouth. He could not cope with the world of Byzantine bureaucratic nuance and maneuver and the closely knit old-boy network which governed the CIA since its inception.

During drinks in the Director's suite, we were surrounded by senior staff aides, deputy directors, and special assistants, all tall, competent-looking men in their late forties and fifties with strong handshakes. The Director was addicted to the mangling of big words ("mino-skewly" for minuscule, "denegredate" for denigrate), which produced tiny winces, like faint electric sparks, around the room. The old man lectured us on the efforts by enemies of the CIA ("the com-symps in this country and abroad") to destroy the image of the agency. "They-are-trying-to-denegredate-this-agency-and-weaken-our-national-defenses," he complained, spitting out the words in evenly spaced military formation.

I wondered whether he would confront me with the fact that I had just written an anonymous piece on the CIA for *Esquire,* which was about to hit the newsstands the following Monday and

might well have fit into his rubric of "com-symp disinformation."
My fears were groundless.

At lunch there were printed place cards. My boss, the Deputy Managing Editor, had been placed at the wrong end of the table, in the thick of the deputy directors. I was positioned on the Director's right, a flaw of intelligence and official etiquette he compounded by patting me on the shoulder twice and speaking noisily of "we who sit above the salt and know the loneliness of command." (As we left the building the public affairs man ran after us to murmur embarrassed apologies about the seating arrangement.)

Despite the inanities of the luncheon chit-chat, the Director's intellectual striptease before the embarrassed underlings, there was in the CIA dining room overlooking the Langley woods a pulse of power that haunts only a few other official spaces in Washington—the power to overthrow political leaders or annihilate their governments. It is a sense of power that makes hookers of gifted men, who spend entire careers scrambling and scheming to sit in such offices and preside over such tables.

In most of the important agencies and departments of the government, the struggle for position is visible to anyone sufficiently curious to learn the players and study the program. Inside The Company it is a more complicated exercise of Kremlinology. There were, at least in the old days, no public confrontations over policy or internal status. Leaks were few. A carefully selected press clientele of bureau chiefs and managing editors was given access—but only for deep background guidance. Heads rolled quietly and no questions were asked.

The late Stewart Alsop wrote in his book *The Center* of an important social dichotomy in the CIA separating "The Bold Easterners"—the WASP, Ivy League elite gathered by Allen Dulles—from the "Prudent Professionals", who had climbed the ladder up through the working levels without the benefit of pedigree and contacts. The era of the Bold Easterners is now bygone, its passing personified by the departure and eventual conviction of Richard M. Helms and the painful withdrawal of Theodore Sorensen's nomination by Jimmy Carter to the final approval of Admiral Stansfield Turner as director of the agency.

Under the old-boy network of Allen Dulles, John McCone, and Richard Helms, the CIA carried out the most controversial excesses of foreign intervention and domestic snooping, beyond even the flexible limits of the agency's charter, allegedly at the direction of—certainly with the concurrence of—Presidents Eisenhower, Kennedy, Johnson, and Nixon. It took an outsider, James G. Schlesinger, and the explosive impetus of the Watergate scandal, to blow the whistle on the agency's illegal spying within the United States. It then fell to William E. Colby, the Prudent Professional who won accession to the directorship to disclose the excesses of his former bosses in repeated appearances before congressional committees and executive tribunals. It was Colby's name that was being hissed in the prominent living rooms of Washington to which he is not invited and where Helms was coveted as a dinner partner.

The big white building behind the chain-link fence at Langley will continue in a state of siege for some time. Hundreds of agents are being shown to the gate. The support of the corporate, political, and social elites that were influential in shaping American foreign policy abroad, determining national security priorities in Washington, and governing the social pecking order in Georgetown and Cleveland Park is less than enthusiastic. Now the agency's constituencies and supporters are shaken and divided by the way in which the top-heavy agency is being trimmed. Both sides charge a kind of intra-agency blackmail, but one thing is certain and that is that the bitterness that followed the revelations of illegal conduct and the then almost surgical removal of the agents will be debated on both sides of the Potomac—and by operatives around the globe—for many years to come.

# Money and the Bureaucracy
## By William H. Jones

If one accepts the notion that 90 per cent of politics has to do with money and that Washington has to do with politics, the idea that Washington has plenty to do with money makes plenty of sense. In the capital, money is not only made—literally—at the Treasury's Bureau of Engraving and Printing. It is also controlled by the Federal Reserve Board, managed by the Office of Management and Budget, appropriated by Congress, funneled around the federal bureaucracy, channeled out to the American people, and taken back by the IRS.

Washington may not always have had its fingers dipped up to the palm in the nation's economic pie. But there is no getting around the fact that the federal city and its rulers have been preoccupied with money ever since the capital was created.

Even more fundamental than the federal power to decide how money will be used is the creation of money—and Washington owns that franchise, too. Not only are all American dollars printed in the capital city but also government officials here decide periodically how much new money will be put into circulation—acts of judgment that remain secret in the Federal Reserve Board for 45 days at a time but that are central to the business cycles of growth, inflation, and recession in this and every other country. Official Washington then influences the way these dollars are spent, either directly through government spending, controls, and policies favoring specific investment; or indirectly through an array of regulatory and judicial restraints—perhaps most important, through its ability to collect revenues through taxation (at rates that can be changed to reflect new policies).

The growth of Washington as the economic capital of America has not been overlooked by the institutions that control

William H. Jones is an assistant editor in the financial news section of *The Washington Post*.

jobs and distribute wealth—labor unions and corporations. Organized labor is represented here not only by individual headquarters for principal unions, but also collectively by the AFL-CIO (only a block away from the White House). Nearly every major corporation has Washington offices and a retinue of Washington lobbyists. They, like the unions, are represented collectively too: the trade associations are legion, looking out for everything from aerospace to zoos. Big business organizations, such as the U.S. Chamber of Commerce and National Association of Manufacturers, rival Ralph Nader's associates and the Consumer Federation of America for attention. The whole city, in fact, is a battleground for a uniquely American government that responds, more often than not, to well-executed pressure and influence from one or many segments of the population.

One consequence of all this is an absorbing economic drama, but there is little of the drama out in the open for a visitor to watch. In the **Commerce Department lobby (Fourteenth Street and Constitution Avenue, N.W., 377-2000),** there is a "clock" measuring the U.S. population, and other business displays. A small exhibit at the **Treasury Department on East Executive Drive opposite the White House (566-2000)** is open to the public; and thousands flock yearly to the **Bureau of Engraving and Printing, Fourteenth and C Streets, S.W. (566-2000),** where from well-guarded ramps they wistfully watch paper money and stamps roll off the presses.

The most far-reaching decisions, monetarily, are often those of the **Federal Reserve Board (Twentieth Street and Constitution Avenue, N.W., 452-3000),** the nation's central bank since 1914. Here, under a cloak of secrecy unrivaled in the American government's superstructure (with the possible exception of the CIA), seven persons appointed by the President, each for a 14-year term, are charged with maintaining the monetary integrity and health of the country and its largest banks. In concert with a staff of economists and money experts, plus the leaders of 12 regional Federal Reserve Banks, America's central bankers decide if and when to expand or reduce the growth of new money and credit. The independence of the Federal Reserve in thus massaging the economy was dictated by Congress, intending to free the monetary system from potential political influence by the executive branch. In reality, the Federal Reserve consults regularly with the administration in power, so even though its actions do not require presidential endorsement, they generally do not come as a surprise at the White House.

The chairman of the Federal Reserve Board, who does not have to account to the Treasury or to Congress for the way his agency manipulates the economy, is a powerful money man— more powerful than the Secretary of the Treasury, and way more powerful than the printer at the Bureau of Engraving. Nevertheless, the printer puts on a better show for the Washington visitor; generally tourists are not welcome in the Federal Reserve's headquarters on Constitution Avenue. No tours or exhibits here, and the guards let you inside only on official business—all of which adds mystery and a bit of intrigue.

---

## THE SPENDING

Once dollar bills are created—either in an expansion of the money supply or simply to replace old bills—they are distributed throughout the banking system. Eventually, the dollar may be in an American citizen's pocket; just as likely, it may be channeled through one of the international financial establishments headquartered in Washington—the World Bank, International Monetary Fund, Export-Import Bank, Inter-American Development Bank—to build a road in Latin America, send arms or airplanes overseas.

The dollars may return to Washington in payment for overseas trade or in the form of industrial and individual tax collections by the Internal Revenue Service, a branch of the Treasury, and be spent again on a government project. If they do not return as trade payments or as taxes, still they will return eventually —an old dollar, faded, ragged, or torn, is sent to Washington for burning at the Bureau of Engraving and Printing. (The Bureau of the Mint is part of the Treasury but no coins are minted in Washington; the mints are in Philadelphia and Denver.)

Inside the historic Treasury Department, built 1838–1842 and symbolically blocking a direct line of sight that city planner Pierre L'Enfant designed for Pennsylvania Avenue between the Capitol and White House, officials carry out the policies of disbursing American money.

In theory, the power to design federal programs and appropriate funds resides on Capitol Hill. In practice, the Congress does not initiate many of the ways Washington spends its money, but rather responds to proposals of the White House, special interest groups, or the vast federal bureaucracy. The operations of that bureaucracy, as well as of regulatory agencies and commissions, are, of course, overseen by Congress. Public hearings on the activities of the bureaucrats can be the most interesting and/or entertaining events in Washington.

One in-depth aid to looking in on the operations of the agencies, bureaus, and commissions, as well as Congress, is being provided by a Ralph Nader storefront office at **Fifteenth and M Streets, N.W.,** called the **Public Citizen Visitors Center (659-9053).** The office provides a daily agenda of government goings-on that affect the consumer—who is, after all, helping fund the whole business of government.

Outside of government agencies, Washington offers little for a visitor to see that has to do with money—though it is possible to look on the city as a whole as an exhibit that has to do with money. The capital and its suburbs have become a major urban center—eighth largest in the U.S.—and a financial center of growing importance. The basic industry in Washington is a service industry—federal government—which alone employs, at recent count, some 351,000 people, or about one-fourth of the area's work force. Real estate and construction have grown to house the expanding government and its relatively affluent civil service. Tourism became a significant business in the years just before World War I; printing and mass communications spread rapidly with the growth of graphic arts, photography, and broadcasting. Technology and scientific research firms have been formed in Washington by the hundreds. Lawyers have seen their profession boom in this city under the weight of an adversary system where government and private interests stage confrontations. A warehouse and wholesale industry has circled the city, adjacent to the postwar Capital Beltway and serving the whole Middle Atlantic region; retailers from coast to coast climbed over each other to find room in booming suburban shopping centers, which now serve the richest per-capita marketplace in the nation, ringing up total annual sales volumes exceeded only in six much bigger cities.

At times, the commingling of commerce and government in the nation's capital has not been looked upon with favor. But George Washington had no doubts about it. The wealthy landowner and businessman who went from nearby Mt. Vernon to the presidency was the city's unofficial chamber of commerce from the start. He saw Washington as a great mercantile center and promoted the construction of a canal—recognizable today as the Chesapeake and Ohio—to the west, where he saw cities developing in future years that would need goods from the East Coast and overseas.

The drive to build canals was a factor in promoting strong central government, and General Washington was a strong factor in the site selected for the capital. When the first government buildings were under construction, Washington built two houses as speculative ventures north of the Capitol—mainly to encourage other similar developments. That investment contributed also to the start of a real estate industry that has been thriving ever since in the knowledge that America's government continues to grow.

When considering what Washington has become, it is worthwhile to remember how it began. It was a compromise agreement, involving money, that caused the capital city to be built on the banks of the Potomac River, far from the heavily populated states to the northeast. One evening in 1790, Secretary of the Treasury Alexander Hamilton and Secretary of State Thomas Jefferson were joined for dinner at Jefferson's New York residence by two Virginia congressmen. A North-South impasse over selection of the capital's site was settled when the Virginians agreed to support Hamilton's bill to have the federal government assume the various states' Revolutionary War debts, and when Hamilton in return agreed to gather northern support for what would be a southern city.

So, in the beginning, a decision over money created the capital on the Potomac. So it continues, as now, with money decisions still wielding the capital's power.

# The Fourth Estate

## By Richard Harwood

It is the spring of 1964. Lyndon Johnson is in the White House dreaming of a Great Society, the grave at Arlington is still fresh, and *Esquire* magazine has just published for the benefit of the American people a guide to that fascinating institution, the Washington Press Establishment.

The author, Karl Meyer, concluded that "it is . . . an impregnably self-confident Establishment, tolerant of wayward ideas because it is indifferent to them. It is supremely sure of its own virtues—indeed, one might unkindly say, it is smug. In this respect, it is unlike its consanguinal cousin, the Senate Establishment. . . . There has been a collapse of self-esteem in the past two years in the Senate, a melancholy tendency to soul-searching. This is abhorrent to the Press.

"The better comparison is with the Civil Service, with which the Press Establishment has symbiotic relations and which in signal qualities is very much like the Fourth Estate. Both are permanent institutions, and tend to regard with disdain the scuffle of elective politics; Administrations come and go, but Arthur Krock is there forever."

Today's visitor to Washington, therefore, should be able to take his *Esquire* guide in hand and visit the old established precincts of Washington journalism to watch the great men and women of the Fourth Estate making their rounds, bearding Presidents and senators and Cabinet officers, firing off the incisive question on "Meet the Press," rubbing shoulders with kings and kingmakers.

Unfortunately, however, it wouldn't work. For the Press Establishment of 1964 proved to be less permanent than the editors of *Esquire* assumed. Arthur Krock, its symbolic dean, is dead. So are a dozen others among the 50 men and women who comprised the "power elite" of that Establishment a dozen years ago. They

Richard Harwood is the deputy managing editor of *The Washington Post*. With Haynes Johnson, he is co-author of the pictorial biography *Lyndon* (Praeger).

included Drew Pearson, Walter Lippmann, Marguerite Higgins, Edwin Lahey, Doris Fleeson, David Lawrence, and Stewart Alsop. Still another dozen have entered into what one hopes are the felicitous years of retirement, among them Joseph Alsop, Kenneth Crawford, Walter Trohan, J. Russell Wiggins, Alfred Friendly, Benjamin McKelway, Newbold Noyes, Fletcher Knebel. Yet another group has fallen onto bad times, professionally, and would no longer make anyone's list of the Power Elite.

Death and disability also have taken their toll of some of the leading institutions of the 1964 Establishment. *Life* magazine is dead. *Look* magazine is dead. *The Reporter* magazine is dead. *The New York Herald Tribune* is dead. *The Washington Daily News* and *The Chicago Daily News* are dead.

So that is lesson Number One about the Washington Press Establishment: it is a mortal, constantly changing institution whose members, like the politicians with whom their lives are intertwined, are vulnerable to the turns of fate; their lights flame briefly, and then vanish in the void. A Dan Rather is at the White House one night and the next night someone else is there.

There has been a second and more profound change in the Press Establishment since 1964. It has suffered, as the government and the nation itself have suffered, a "collapse of self-esteem." On the face of it, such a statement makes little sense in the aftermath of Watergate and other journalistic triumphs of recent years—but the fact is that the Press Establishment, as such, had little or no part in those triumphs. It was not the celebrated columnists, nor the White House correspondents, nor the members of the hallowed Gridiron Club who did the reporting on the CIA or the My Lai massacre or the Pentagon papers, or who laid the groundwork for the fall of the Nixon administration. These journalistic coups were, in each case, the work of unheralded outsiders (Seymour Hersh, Woodward and Bernstein, Neil Sheehan), or the work of somewhat gamy members of the fraternity such as Jack Anderson and Leslie Whitten.

The result has been a deep psychological shock to the Establishment, a shock that has set off a binge of unprecedented soul-searching, rather like that which the government has gone through in trying to discover what went amiss in Vietnam. So the Establishment today is introspective, unsure and insecure. There is no certitude, no solid sense of place or function. That is why, when you watched the televised news conferences of recent years, you were met with scenes of shouting and disorder and general disarray. The poor fellows were going through hard times.

There are other symptoms of fundamental change in this institution which plays such a large role in the workings of the American system. In 1964, Karl Meyer correctly observed in the *Esquire* article that the National Press Club and the Gridiron Club were the "twin fortresses" of the Washington Press Establishment. Today they are not. The Press Club, located in an aging structure in central Washington, has become a plebeian watering hole, frequented by minor lobbyists and minor journalists. Some offices in the tall old building are deserted; many of the prestigious news organizations have moved elsewhere.

The Gridiron Club, limited to 50 male members throughout its history, recently succumbed, reluctantly, to the demand of women for admission. But all that aside, it is not the same. Presidents, as often as not, now ignore the Club's annual dinner, which was once the high point of the Washington social season. Other men and women of power have followed suit and the unthinkable has finally happened: membership invitations to the club are being declined. It simply does not count for much any more.

Finally, in charting the decline of the old Washington Press Establishment, one must take note of two other developments. Half of the people on *Esquire*'s list of the journalistic Power Elite in 1964 were columnists or radio-television commentators. As a class, these men and women are now in decline. They rose to prominence as the confidants of Presidents and other men and women of parts. They told us not only what the leaders of government were doing, but explained the workings of their minds, their grand strategies, their hopes and aspirations for the nation and the world. They gave us "critical analyses," forewarnings of things to come, "inside reports" on mood and style, such as William S. White's account of his bedside visit with Lyndon Johnson on the night of John Kennedy's assassination. Or the "definitive" story on the Cuban missile crisis by Charles Bartlett and Stewart Alsop.

That kind of thing is now more or less passé.

The new elite of the Washington Press Establishment fall into four principal categories. First are the investigative reporters who have developed or stumbled upon the great stories of the past decade. In each case these stories have assaulted the mystique, reputation, and credibility of major institutions of the American corporate and governmental Establishment—the White House and the presidency, the FBI, the CIA, the Pentagon, the oil industry, the huge multinational companies such as ITT. In nearly every case, the stories were done by "outsiders," meaning reporters who were not assigned to report on the doings of these great Establishment institutions. That accounts, in large measure, for the loss of self-esteem within the old Washington Press Establishment. Those reporters were shown to be gullible or lazy or jaded or insensitive or a combination of those negative qualities.

The second new cadre of elite is comprised of the profane and iconoclastic writers and essayists who have brought a new realism to the journalism of Washington. Their work may appear in *New York* magazine, *Esquire, Playboy,* or *Rolling Stone,* or in the news columns and Style section of *The Washington Post.* These "new realists" also write from an essentially anti-Establishment point of view. Unlike the investigators, they do not seek to show that men in the White House or Pentagon may be dishonest or criminal. Rather, they depict Establishment people in terms of the human fallibilities that afflict us all; they tell us that Presidents, like their butlers, put on their pants one leg at a time, commit social gaffes, stumble over their words, snarl at their wives and children. They make the point, in short, that the Emperor and his retinue may have no clothes.

The third category of elite in 1978 is made up of the ideologues of the editorial and op ed pages of the leading journals—columnists, cartoonists, illustrators, and editorialists. They, too, come on as basically anti-Establishment in their point of view. They give an intellectual and ideological coherence to the revelations of the investigators and to the commentaries of the "new realists." They can be both savage and sentimental, depending on whether the subject is the oppressor or the oppressed. The important thing is that they have a fairly consistent view of the system and how it works; it is neither a Marxist nor a Socialist view and, in fact, rarely offers substantive alternatives to the System. But it is consistently critical and dissatisfied with the status quo.

Finally, among the new elite are the managers and owners of the media who have discovered, encouraged, and given voice to the investigators, the new realists, and the ideologues. They are in no sense anti-Establishment themselves. They have had qualms about the rise of the new press elite. They have sometimes held them in check. But they have also sensed the inadequacies of the old Washington Press Establishment and have acceded to and, sometimes unconsciously, aided its demise. That is what "Agnewism" was all about—it lamented the death of a journalistic system in which a partnership of sorts existed between press and government, a partnership in which the government and its institutions were always dominant. The symbol of that dominance was the American war correspondent prior to Vietnam, who wore a military uniform and insignia of rank, and who submitted his stories routinely to the censor. The other symbol was the columnist or White House correspondent who could win a Pulitzer Prize for a mere interview with a President—Arthur Krock of *The New York Times,* for example. It was a system in which, as President Lyndon Johnson once said to the White House correspondents, "I can make big men of you."

The new Washington Press Establishment, Professor Paul Weaver has written, is creating an "adversary" system of journalism that threatens "the capacity of the press to help the American system realize its ideals.... For the press can make its contribution to the system only by maintaining close access [to the government]—a closer access ... than can ever be provided by law. The price of such access is some degree of co-operation and sympathy for government—*not* a slavish adulation, as is sometimes said, but a decent respect for authority, a willingness to see government and persons in government given the opportunity to do their job, and at least a slight sense of responsibility for and commitment to the goals inherent in those jobs. When these are not present, access diminishes. And when newsmen begin to assert they are positively the adversaries of government, access diminishes drastically, and with it not only the contribution journalism can make but also the openness and flexibility of government itself."

*Fortune* magazine has published a similar criticism: "In the long run, the greatest danger to the national press is probably posed, not by public unhappiness with its political position but by the intense feeling among executives, in business and government, about what they see as its systematic distrust of all established institutions."

These criticisms carry a superficial weight of authenticity.

But they miss the main point, the main point being that a New Establishment is arising in Washington and that the New Press Establishment is quite in tune with it; the bureaucracy has an adversary relationship with itself, as does Congress, so the new posture of the New Press Establishment is no impediment to access. One could easily argue, in fact, that there is more access now than in the past.

In any case, there *is* a new elite in Washington journalism. It is composed, on the whole, of younger, more educated, and more affluent men and women than in the past. The affluence needs emphasis because in material terms the New Press Establishment is very definitely upper class. The average American family earns about $13,000 a year. A 25-year-old reporter on *The Washington Post* earns a *minimum* of $25,000 a year if he can claim four years experience. The new elite of the Press Establishment, of course, earns far more. Incomes upwards of $50,000 a year are not uncommon when salaries are combined with lecture fees, book and magazine royalties, television appearances, and so on. James Reston earned $126,000 in 1974. An Art Buchwald or a Jack Anderson commands in excess of $200,000. The major television news personalities are in those brackets too.

The life styles of the Washington correspondents are consistent with their incomes. While the divorce rates are high, they tend to be family oriented, with homes in the upper-income districts of metropolitan Washington—Georgetown and the northwest neighborhoods of the District of Columbia, the suburbs of Maryland and Virginia. They vacation frequently in Europe and the Caribbean. They drive appropriate automobiles, are accustomed to $20 and $30 lunches, and the best hotels when traveling to the provinces, which is a frequent occupation. They are physically pampered—like the old Establishment—by the White House, Congress, and corporations.

They work long hours, have a fair quota of ambitious and liberated wives and lovers, and for all the glamour and excitement, often lead fearful and insecure lives as they contemplate the mortality and attrition of their colleagues and hear, always, in the background, the footsteps of younger, brighter competitors. They seem to age too fast, to become young fogies obsessed with their own careers and the materials of their craft. But they have had and continue to have an impact on their country that the Old Establishment could not have dreamed of.

## PRESS HEADQUARTERS AND HAUNTS

Below are some of the places around Washington where the new elite, and old elite, and regular "working" journalists—often accompanied by "sources"—work and hang out.

**Haunts:**

**Chez Camille, 1737 DeSales Street, N.W.**

**The Class Reunion, 1726 H Street, N.W.** (for drinkers)

**Duke Zeibert's, 1722 L Street, N.W.**

**Federal City Club, Sheraton Carlton Hotel, Sixteenth and K Streets, N.W.** (The Number One place for journalists.)

**Hawk and Dove, 329 Pennsylvania Avenue, S.E.**

**Kay's Sandwich Shoppe, 1733 G Street, N.W.**

**Madison Hotel, Fifteenth and M Streets, N.W.**—various restaurants, but particularly the buffet lounge ("Connie's Place") off the Montpelier Restaurant.

**Mr. Henry's, 601 Pennsylvania Avenue, S.E.**

**National Press Club, National Press Building, 529 Fourteenth Street, N.W.**

**The Palm, 1225 Nineteenth Street, N.W.**

**Paul Young's, 1120 Connecticut Avenue, N.W.**

**Le Provençal, 1234 Twentieth Street, N.W.**

**Sans Souci, 726 Seventeenth Street, N.W.** (This is *the* place to find Art Buchwald and other "name" columnists and TV personalities, but rarely the place to find a "working" journalist.)

In addition, local television and radio people can often be found in **Alfio's La Trattoria, 5100 Wisconsin Avenue, N.W.,** and **The Chase, 4400 Jenifer Street, N.W.,** both close to many of the broadcast houses.

**Headquarters:**

*The Washington Post,* **1150 Fifteenth Street, N.W.,** offers one-hour public tours Monday, Wednesday, and Friday, every hour on the hour from 10 A.M. to 4 P.M. Visitors must be at least age 12; maximum number per tour is 40. Call **233-7971** a week in advance for a reservation.

*The Washington Star,* **225 Virginia Avenue, S.E., 484-5000.**

Most of the major **news bureaus** have their offices in the central business district, many within walking distance of the White House.

The **broadcast stations** are clustered in northwest Washington.

# The
# Ceremonial
# City

# V

# Monuments and Memorials

## By Phyllis C. Richman

### WASHINGTON MONUMENT

**Fifteenth Street near Constitution Avenue, N.W.; 426-6839.** Open 9 to 5 in winter, 8 A.M. to midnight in summer. No admission charge.

The Washington Monument acts as a beacon of welcome to the city. It even winks at you at night. Whether you are flying into National Airport or driving into the city, the Washington Monument, it being the tallest building around—twice as tall as the Capitol—gives you your bearings. As a vertical shaft in an essentially horizontal city, visible from every part of town, it serves as a focal point for determining one's location.

Isolated on a grassy mound set in an open plain, the Washington Monument is, give or take a few hundred feet, the axis of a cross formed by the Capitol on the east, the Lincoln Memorial on the west, the White House on the north, and the Jefferson Memorial on the south. The site is L'Enfant's, with some adjustment for the foundation's sake. His exact axis selection for a memorial to Washington was too marshy.

This simple obelisk, the Washington Monument, was a center of controversy and a victim of money shortages during the time of its construction, which dragged on from 1848 to 1884. Some architects of the era called it the ugliest building in the world, claiming that when an architect is incompetent he resorts to obelisks.

The construction delays came not without their blessings. For, initially, the now-magnificent obelisk was not meant to be so simple. Surrounded at its base by a circular Greek temple in Rob-

Phyllis C. Richman is on the staff of *The Washington Post Magazine*.

ert Mills' original and winning design in 1836, the obelisk as first conceived looked like a huge firecracker rising out of an oversized, overdecorated birthday cake. Forty years later, in 1876, the monument still unconstructed, foundation problems and presumably changes in taste saved the day and caused abandonment of the encircling Greek temple.

Inside the monument's shaft, inscribed memorial blocks were donated by countries, cities, states (and even such special interests as temperance groups and fire companies). The inscriptions on the state stones, voicing opinions about the Union, trace the increasing tension between the North and South until, in 1854, vandals believed to be from the American Party, the "Know Nothings," stole and destroyed the stone donated by Pope Pius IX, which they objected to as a "Papist" gift. Still not content, in 1858 they seized office records and actually claimed possession of the monument. This further sabotage and the advent of the Civil War left the 156-foot stub unfinished until further funds were appropriated by Congress in 1876. As a result, the color of the marble abruptly changes to a slightly different tone, indicating the limits of the unfinished stub that for almost 30 years stood as a monument to dissension in the country.

When the Corps of Engineers took over construction in 1865, the stub was found to be tilting. A new base was laid in 1880 in the sandy clay under the old foundation, correcting that situation. Construction proceeded rapidly after that, and in 1884, during a winter storm, the aluminum tip of the monument was finally laid in place.

The 555-foot, $5^1/_8$-inch monument is now considered quite admirable by architects, though something of a mystery. For unknown reasons, hot spells cause condensation so great that it actually rains inside.

By merely standing tall and breathing—it really does expand and contract—the monument causes discomfort and violence in its surroundings. Birds dash themselves against its walls. Even the presidential helicopter has come pretty close in a high wind. By 1949, the obelisk had been the site of five suicides; to prevent further deaths, wire mesh was installed in the windows.

The monument has been restored to more joyful purposes recently. After years of being banned, kites fly again on the monument grounds, and an annual spring kite festival presents one of the most colorful pageants the city offers. On other spring days boomerang meets, Nordic Day and other assorted festivities stretch across its grounds. (*See* Chapter XVI, "Sports.")

For the city's children, the Washington Monument holds a fascination from the moment they identify it as representing "downtown." But the monument has an exposition air about it that fascinates all children, who seem represented more here than at other monuments, if only because they clamor to be lifted so they can see from the monument windows at the top, where they frequently monopolize the panoramic views.

And, an important rite of passage for children, as well as other tourists, has been walking up the 898 steps to the top. But the steps became too congested, so now the trip up can be made only by elevator, which takes 70 seconds, and the hardy can walk down and read the 189 memorial stones along the way.

### LINCOLN MEMORIAL

**Twenty-third Street off Constitution Avenue, N.W.,** at the entrance to Memorial Bridge; **426-6895.** Always open.

Although more tourists visit the Lincoln Memorial than the Washington Monument, it is a less obvious measure of the tourist level because there are no lines around its base waiting to enter. Rather, the circle on which it stands is a reasonably accurate traffic gauge, one that many Washington area residents pass on the way to and from work.

At night, the troubles of the city are often taken to Lincoln. It is traditional to mull over one's worries with the 19-foot-tall stone Lincoln—or with his visitors, as Richard Nixon once did in May, 1970, at 5:00 A.M., with sleeping student anti-war demonstrators who were camped out at Lincoln's feet. The diffused overhead lights, reflecting from the luminous, beeswax-saturated, marble-paneled ceiling, help to make it one of the most serene spots in Washington.

Originally, Henry Bacon's Greek temple modeled on the Parthenon was considered too elaborate a memorial for Honest Abe, and its site too absurd. Joseph G. Cannon, then Speaker of the House of Representatives, predicted that the memorial "would shake itself down with loneliness and ague" set in its inaccessible swamp, which then housed only snakes, bullfrogs, and mosquitoes. Today, however, even the most carping critics would agree that the solid Lincoln Memorial with its oblong Reflecting Pool stretching toward the Washington Monument forms not only a perfect complement to that soaring obelisk, but a stately balance to the west end of the Mall.

Far from lonely now, Daniel Chester French's massive seated statue of Lincoln, surrounded by one column for each of the 36 states at the time of his death, now receives a constant stream of company—from Chief Justice Earl Warren retiring from the Supreme Court on its steps, to opposing senatorial candidates both kicking off their campaigns at the same time. Whenever there were lynchings in the South, groups of black people showed up to pray before Lincoln. When President Kennedy was assassinated, the mood of the country was portrayed by cartoonist Herblock in the statue of Lincoln, weeping.

Since its completion in 1922 the memorial has been a mecca for the oppressed. It served as a concert site for Marian Anderson in 1939 when the Daughters of the American Revolution refused to let a black woman sing in their Constitution Hall. In August, 1963, 250,000 people gathered to hear Martin Luther King, Jr., in full view of Lincoln, deliver his "I have a dream" speech. In 1968, as many as 2,500 citizens of the Poor People's Campaign made a makeshift summer camp of tents, shacks, and mud beside the Reflecting Pool, and called it "Resurrection City." They came to campaign in the halls of Congress, to influence the passage of antipoverty legislation. On June 8, 1968, the Robert F. Kennedy funeral procession, after passing the Lincoln Memorial, stopped for a few moments at Resurrection City on its long journey to Arlington National Cemetery across the Potomac. It was night by this time, and everyone along the way held candles. Over the soft, flickering candlelights, mourning voices began to slowly sing "Mine eyes have seen the glory of the coming of the Lord . . ." After a few verses, the cortege moved on into the darkness. The "Battle Hymn of the Republic" was shared by Lincoln and Kennedy that night.

The most reproduced work of art in the world, the memorial has appeared on more than 80 billion pennies and more than a quarter of a trillion $5 bills. When the Chief Engraver of the U.S. Mint, Frank Gasparro, first etched the Lincoln Memorial on the penny in 1959, he did not even realize that there was a statue inside. When he finally visited the memorial in 1971, he was so moved by the statue that he redesigned the penny, moving aside the columns to show the statue.

From each side of the statue, best seen at night, a different mood of Lincoln is depicted. Strong and determined from the front, Lincoln seems to be frowning from the left and smiling from the right. Flanked by the Gettysburg Address and his Second Inaugural Address, Lincoln was until recently protected by stern rulings against visitors talking above a whisper or appearing without coats and ties. However, nothing protected him against the assaults of the vast communities of pigeons that have made the memorial their home. And nothing kept him from being shot at during World War II, by a guard on top of the Department of the Interior building who fell asleep against the firing pin of his rifle.

By the early 1960s, magazine articles deplored the casual mode of dress at the Lincoln Memorial—but they hadn't seen anything yet. The demonstrations in the late '60s introduced nude bathing to the Reflecting Pool. By 1974, Lincoln had hosted a champagne breakfast (at the Reflecting Pool, as liquor is not allowed inside national monuments) and a wedding—unexpectedly attended by 40 Russian visitors who thought it was a guided tour.

## JEFFERSON MEMORIAL

**On the Tidal Basin on the south end of Fifteenth Street, S.W.; 426-6822.** Always open.

If one thing bred contentment with the design of the Washington Monument and Lincoln Memorial, it was the proposal for the Jefferson Memorial. By the time anyone got around to planning a memorial to Jefferson (in 1934), the lone remaining southern site on the cross-like plan for the memorials was on the Tidal Basin, which was already ringed by the beloved 2,000 cherry trees Japan had given this country in 1912.

In the late 1930s, the proposed Jefferson Memorial became the center of bitter controversy—first over displacement of the cherry trees (some protesters chained themselves to the trees), then over presenting Jefferson as toga clad. Eventually, Jefferson was depicted 19 feet high in bronze, aloof in a fur-trimmed coat. The greatcoat copies the one given to him by the Polish ally of the Revolutionary War, General Thaddeus Kosciusko.

A surprise birthday breakfast of extraordinary elegance at dawn in the midst of the Washington Monument and Lincoln Memorial, 1974.

**National Capital Parks employee John R. Roberts applies a scrubbing brush to the face in the massive Lincoln Memorial, 1959.**

Despite the memorial's being modeled after Jefferson's own design for the rotunda at the University of Virginia, the John Russell Pope building lacks inspirational force, coming long after the heyday of Classic Revival architecture. Ringed by his famous words, and introduced by a frieze depicting the committee who drafted the Declaration of Independence, the Jefferson Memorial is considered by some too cold and weak to symbolize the man who is said to have been the last educated man to encompass all the learning of his time.

Except during the concerts four nights a week in summer, the Jefferson Memorial is visited primarily by people who happen on it at cherry blossom time or get lost looking for the bridge to Virginia. It is somewhat of an attraction for intellectuals and high school social studies classes. It is, according to the National Park Service guards, the cleanest of the major memorials.

---

### MOUNT VERNON

**17 miles south of Washington via the George Washington Parkway,** past National Airport and through the city of Alexandria; **780-2000.** Open daily, 9 to 5. Admission: $2.00 adults, $1.00 kids 6-11.

The Washington Monument, impressive focal point that it is, conjures up little of Washington, the man. For that, you must travel to Mount Vernon, a delightful jaunt taking you through wooded vistas of the Potomac via George Washington Parkway. Or you can go by boat (Wilson Boat Line, Sixth and Water Streets, S.W.), in poor imitation of John F. Kennedy's yacht procession which preceded his historic dinner party at Mount Vernon, in 1961, for Pakistani President Mohammed Ayub Khan.

In either case, if you travel on weekends or in the summer, the first impressive feature of Mount Vernon will be the crowds—sometimes waiting 45 minutes to get into the house. But even George Washington himself complained about the steady stream of visitors, declaring, "My house is like a well resorted tavern."

In some ways the estate is quite different than in George Washington's day—reduced to 500 acres from 8,000, for instance. Meticulous efforts have been made by the Mount Vernon

Ladies' Association to restore this Georgian plantation as closely as possible to the form in which Washington left it.

Americans considered it a pretty impressive place, but for Europeans it was not particularly magnificent, its façade being wood painted to appear as stone, its windows slightly askew. One visiting Englishman compared it to the house of a minor squire; it was either Queen Elizabeth or Prince Philip who called it a "cozy place."

The outbuildings give unusual insight into the life style of the period: the well-equipped kitchen, the smokehouse hung with hams and bacon, the slaves' quarters with clothing hanging and tables set, the coach house, the spinning house with the plantation's own spinning and weaving instruments. The formal, meticulously kept flower and vegetable gardens and the path below the stables to George Washington's tomb are worth the strolling time. Besides a small museum housing George Washington's artifacts, there is a fascinating archaeology exhibit showing how the house was restored. You can spend any leftover time sitting in the Windsor armchairs on the veranda, overlooking the river.

Near Mount Vernon are **Woodlawn Plantation** (3 miles south of Mount Vernon on Route 1; **780-3118**), which George Washington gave to his adopted daughter (*see* Chapter XV, "Of Special Interest to Children"), and the **Pope-Leighey House** (on the grounds of Woodlawn; **780-3264**), designed by Frank Lloyd Wright (*see* Chapter IX, "Architecture") and moved to that site by the National Trust for Historic Preservation, which maintains both houses. They are open from 9:30 to 4:30 daily, and charge an entrance fee.

---

### ARLINGTON NATIONAL CEMETERY

**Across Memorial Bridge, behind the Lincoln Memorial, in Virginia. Open 8 to 7 daily. The Custis-Lee Mansion, 557-3153, is open 9:30 to 6:30 daily. No admission charge.**

Carved out of land officially confiscated in 1864 from Robert E. Lee for failure to pay questionably imposed back taxes, Arlington National Cemetery is the burial site of military men from Presidents on down. With at least half a dozen funerals a day, there is barely enough space left to last until the year 2000. Thus, requirements on who would be permitted burial here were made more strict in 1967. Even so, visitors can often happen onto the pageantry and poignancy of a military funeral, or a wedding in the chapel on weekends.

Primarily, visitors come to the cemetery to **John F. Kennedy's grave** and to the **Tomb of the Unknown Soldier.** Completed in 1967, Kennedy's grave has, like the Lincoln Memorial, attracted people as a place to seek solace in troubled moments. Perhaps the eternal flame serves as a magnet. The site is unpretentious, though its setting is a spectacular panorama of the city's skyline. On a low wall are quotations from Kennedy's Inaugural Address, which serve as the monument to the man entombed in a simple marble terrace flanked by his two infant children; the **grave of Robert F. Kennedy** is nearby.

The Tomb of the Unknown Soldier is a legendary tribute. Sentinels from the Third U.S. Infantry, America's most distinguished honor guard, called the "Old Guard," protect the tomb in perhaps the most intricate ritual one might see in this country. A robotlike white-gloved inspection precedes the changing of the guard, an elaborate series of salutes, clicking heels, and rifle maneuvers which occurs every half hour during the day, less frequently at night. Guards march without moving from the waist up, their trousers taped to them so that no belt bulges their uniforms. Feet never leaving the mat, rifle always on the shoulder away from the tomb, the guard patrols 21 steps, stops for 21 seconds, and repeats.

Besides these two sites, the lovely rolling hills of Arlington National Cemetery are ornamented by the 49 chimes of the **Netherlands Carillon,** a gift of the people of the Netherlands commemorating American aid during World War II. The grounds are crowned by **Arlington House**—less officially known as Custis-Lee Mansion—and the **Robert E. Lee Memorial.** The stubby pillars in front of the mansion are more impressive from a distance than from close up, but then the view back toward the city makes up for the disappointment. It seems fitting that the **tomb of Pierre L'Enfant,** Washington's city planner, lies in front of Arlington House, etched with a plan of the city, and in view of the city's panorama. (*See* Chapter IX, "Architecture.")

The adopted son of George Washington, George Washington Parke Custis built Arlington House as the family seat; his son-in-law, Robert E. Lee, later called it "a house that anyone might see with half an eye," so prominent was its site. When Lee joined the Confederacy and his wife left the house, the army took it over and began burying their dead on its slopes. Years later, the Lees sued the government and received $150,000 for the house.

## U.S. MARINE CORPS WAR MEMORIAL

**Over Memorial Bridge, turn right, follow the signs.** Always open.

On Route 50 west, on the periphery of Arlington National Cemetery, stands the **Marine Corps War Memorial.** Commonly known as the **Iwo Jima statue,** this powerful sculpture of six servicemen raising the flag on Iwo Jima's Mount Suribachi is a bronze rendition of a Pulitzer Prize-winning photograph by Joe Rosenthal, taken toward the end of World War II. From it, a cloth flag flies 24 hours a day. Besides being a main attraction for visiting Marines, the statue sits on a spectacular spot of land which serves as a site for evening parades in the summer. Only three of the six men depicted in the statue survived the battle, one of the bloodiest the Marine Corps ever fought. In 1974, the statue was the rallying point for protesting Navajos who claimed that insufficient credit had been paid them for their part in the war, not the least of which was an unbreakable code which consisted of the Navajo language being spoken backwards.

On Tuesday evenings at 7:30, June through August, you can watch a ceremonial lowering of the flag performed by the Marine Drum and Bugle Corps and the Silent Drill Platoon.

## FORD'S THEATRE AND THE HOUSE WHERE LINCOLN DIED

**Ford's Theatre, 511 Tenth Street, N.W., 426-6924.** Open daily 9 to 5, except during matinees Thursdays and Sundays and during rehearsals. **The House Where Lincoln Died, across the street; 426-6830.** Open daily 9 to 5. No admission to either place, except to the Ford's theatrical performances.

Back in the District of Columbia, the most lively of the memorials commemorates a death: the assassination of Abraham Lincoln at Ford's Theatre on April 14, 1865. It took a hundred years before restoration revived this theater, the third floor of which collapsed in the meantime. It took more than one hundred years before it was again visited by a President, Gerald Ford, in April, 1975. The Secret Service took an entire week to prepare the theater for that presidential visit.

In the basement, a small museum traces Lincoln's early life, political career, and presidential life with artifacts. The assassination paraphernalia—John Wilkes Booth's derringer, the doctor's surgical equipment, the flag that draped Lincoln's casket —are there. Upstairs, the theater now houses live performances with family appeal. Patrons of the theater are compelled to absorb the environment of Lincoln's day, though cushions have been added to the authentically uncomfortable seats, and rest rooms have been installed, whereas formerly back alleys served the purpose.

Fewer visitors see Petersen House across the street, officially known as "The House Where Lincoln Died." It takes but a short visit to view the three simple rooms, a little rundown, and noisy from the street traffic. It appears a plain, sad place for such a great life to have ended, his feet hanging over the side of a bed that was too small. This is not the actual bed in which he died—the real one, also too small, is in the Chicago Historical Society museum.

---

## LAFAYETTE SQUARE

**Lafayette Square faces Pennsylvania Avenue on the south, H Street, N.W., on the north, between Jackson Place and Madison Place.** Summer walking tours of the park begin in July, each Friday and Saturday afternoon at 2 P.M.; assemble at Lafayette Park kiosk facing H Street.

**Decatur House, 748 Jackson Place, N.W., 638-1204.** Open daily, 10 to 2 weekdays; 12–4 weekends and holidays. Admission.

**St. John's Church, Sixteenth and H Streets, N.W., 347-8766.** Open 7 to 5 daily.

Lafayette Square Park, flower laden and grassy, witnesses city life from political demonstrations to chess tournaments. The square is part of the President's Square, which includes Lafayette Square on the north, the White House in the center, and the Ellipse on the south. So, while passing through the square you are apt to see television cameras and commentators using the White House as a backdrop to report on the day's activities of the chief resident in the mansion across Pennsylvania Avenue.

But since the White House was erected, across from the Pierce family's apple orchard, the square has become a historic district in its own right. L'Enfant planned Lafayette Square as the President's front yard, but in 1791 George Washington proposed that the site be purchased as a public park. Benjamin Latrobe designed **St. John's Church,** the second building, after the White House, to be erected on the square (in 1816). Since President Madison first selected it, pew 54 has been reserved for presidential worshippers.

The first private home on Lafayette Square, **Decatur House,** built in 1819, was also Benjamin Latrobe's design, and is now a National Trust house. (*See* Chapter I, "The Presidents' Other Homes," *and* Chapter IX, "Architecture.") It has been restored on the first floor as it was when Commodore Stephen Decatur lived in it (for one year only, before he was killed in a duel), and upstairs in the Victorian-style of a later owner, General Edward F. Beale. By day a museum, the house serves by night for receptions given by embassies, historical groups, for naval events and such. The back garden has been used as a puppet theater. Even the carriage house is now a naval museum. All these activities coincide with "adaptive use," a new trend in historic preservation, and one supported by the occupant and manager of Decatur House, The National Trust for Historic Preservation. The Trust's headquarters offices in Decatur House are part of its complex of three houses, at 740, 744, and 748 Jackson Place, N.W. (Check out the **National Trust Bookstore at 740 Jackson Place, N.W.**)

Across the square, in another version of adaptive use, the Federal Judiciary Center occupies the **Dolley Madison House,** on the southeast corner of **Madison Place and H Street.** The house, no longer open to the public, was the social center of the square in its 1840s heyday. All the power-seekers and the social elite lived there then, when Lafayette Square was called the "lobby of the White House." Widowed Dolley Madison lived there until she died in 1849.

A major, well-celebrated event in the square's history was the dedication in 1853 of the Jackson Monument, which stands in the center of the square. Maybe it was reminiscent of Jackson's clamorous inauguration when, to entice the mobbing crowds away from the White House, tubs of hard, liquid refreshments were sent to the square. It was later, after that statue's dedication, the Congress designated the park as Lafayette Square, which explains the puzzle of why Lafayette should stand in the southeast corner of the square and Jackson in its center.

## WOODROW WILSON HOUSE

**Wilson House, 2340 S Street, N.W., 387-4062.** Open daily 10 to 4. Admission. (*See* Chapter I, "The Presidents' Other Homes.")
Wilson House, a second National Trust house in the District of Columbia, is uptown, off Connecticut Avenue. The block surrounding the house has not needed the efforts of a preservation society, for it is still in its prime, housing embassies and the **Textile Museum, 2320 S Street, N.W., 667-0441.** Wilson House, built in 1915 and occupied by Mrs. Wilson until 1961, seems more contemporary than historic.
It is furnished not too differently from the old family homes in nearby city neighborhoods like Kalorama and Cleveland Park. Like Decatur House, it is frequently rented for receptions compatible with its historic nature. But the mark of President Wilson shows itself throughout.

## THE OCTAGON

**The Octagon, 1799 New York Avenue, N.W., 638-3105.** Open Tuesday-Saturday, 10 to 4; Sunday 1 to 4. Donation requested. (*See* Chapter I, "The Presidents' Other Homes," *and* Chapter IX, "Architecture.")
If you were an old house in need of restoration, you could hardly do better than to be owned by the American Institute of Architects Foundation. That has been the good luck of the Octagon, originally built in 1800 for the Tayloe family's winter entertaining. The house, designed by Dr. William Thornton, architect of the Capitol, is really six-sided, not eight. It served as temporary quarters for the French foreign minister during the War of 1812, and the French flag flying from its roof no doubt spared it.
And while the White House was recuperating from its battle injuries, President and Dolley Madison lived at the Octagon House for nine months. It was there, in the Treaty Room on the second floor, that President Madison officially ended the War of 1812 for the U.S. by signing the Treaty of Ghent, on February 17, 1815.

Visitors to the Octagon are met by guides who conduct tours that usually last 45 minutes.

Among least-known memorials in Washington is the **Franklin Delano Roosevelt Memorial.** A small marble stone set in an unkempt little triangle outside the National Archives **at Ninth Street, N.W., on Pennsylvania Avenue,** its modesty in accord with the wishes of FDR, it jolts belief when it catches the eye of the leisurely passerby. **Theodore Roosevelt** is immortalized, appropriately enough, by the **Potomac River island across from Kennedy Center** that bears his name, and by a statue, on the island, which almost attacks its sylvan surroundings. **Lyndon B. Johnson** is being remembered by a 45-ton rough-hewn granite mass on **George Washington Parkway between Memorial Bridge and Fourteenth Street Bridge,** amid a grove of pines.

# VI
# Churches and Statues

## By Christopher Dickey

Most of Washington's skyline is made of trees. From the Virginia side of the Potomac as one looks north and west toward the largest section of the city, the office buildings and houses are soon lost above the river's banks and only the spires of a huge cathedral dominate the horizon.

Downtown, in the bureaucracy and business district of the city, most of the trees have surrendered to concrete and asphalt pavement. So have many of the churches. As office buildings move in on them and their parishioners move away they close down; a congregation that lives in the suburbs wants its church there too. Only a few places of worship, with history on their side, have survived. And many of them only barely.

**Epiphany Episcopal Church, 1317 G Street, N.W.,** is surrounded by tawdry shops and parking lots. The nave cracked and almost fell in when construction of an office building next door undermined the foundation. That has since been repaired, and except for minor expansion and the surroundings, the graceful gothic structure looks much as it did a century ago when it catered exclusively to the upper echelons of Washington society.

The plot of land where the **Metropolitan African Methodist Episcopal Church** stands at **1518 M Street, N.W.,** was bought by the congregation in 1850. For more than 30 years free blacks and slaves worked to build the red Victorian gothic building that stands there now. They tore down their temporary quarters and cleaned the bricks to reuse them in the new church. Before the Civil War, when escaped slaves sought out the congregation, members would pass the hat to buy their freedom. Frederick Douglass—who was born a slave and became an abolitionist, author, orator, and ambassador—worshipped here.

Christopher Dickey is on *The Washington Post* Metropolitan staff.

The **Old Adas Israel Synagogue** has been restored, but no one worships there any more. Dedicated with President Ulysses S. Grant in attendance, for a while it served as a Greek Orthodox Church. Later the Church of God took over, and eventually it was used as a warehouse with a carry-out sandwich shop downstairs. Since it stood in the way of Metro subway construction, the synagogue-warehouse was almost torn down, but instead, finally, was moved to its present barren site at **Third and G Streets, N.W.,** its windows and façade, bricks and woodwork repaired and returned to their original condition. There is now a small museum where originally there were Hebrew classrooms.

There is another small collection of memorabilia in **Grace Reform Church at Fifteenth and O Streets, N.W.** It is devoted to Theodore Roosevelt, who laid the cornerstone and gave the dedication of the building. He attended services there with chronometric punctuality while he was Vice President and President, from 1901 to 1909. His family did not accompany him. They went instead to St. John's—about which more later.

It is common in Washington for a church to be identified by the Presidents who have frequented it. **St. Matthew's Cathedral,** for instance, has a great deal of Old World, Catholic appeal, from the massive Romanesque exterior at **1725 Rhode Island Avenue, N.W.,** to the vast interior with its ornate ceilings, burning candles, tourists, and panhandlers strolling through it at midday and children running in its aisles; but it is most often remembered as the church John Kennedy attended and the site of his funeral mass.

Herbert Hoover, a Quaker, worshipped at the **Friends Meeting of Washington, 2111 Florida Avenue, N.W.** Richard Nixon, who was reared as a Quaker, did not worship with the Society of Friends whose services consist, for the most part, of silent meditation. In fact, after thinly veiled remarks about Watergate cropped up in a service he attended down in Florida, Nixon decided to bring services to the White House, rather than venturing out for them on Sunday mornings.

It is **St. John's Episcopal Church, on Lafayette Square,** however, that calls itself "The Church of the Presidents." Those who were *regular* parishioners are neither so numerous nor so noteworthy as one might be led to believe. James Madison was the first and Franklin Roosevelt was the last to frequent pew 54. In between came James Monroe, Martin Van Buren, William Henry

Harrison, John Tyler, and Zachary Taylor. Chester Arthur was not a communicant, but his wife had been a singer in the church's choir when he met her. She died before he became President, but not long after he took office he installed a window to memorialize her in the south transept, positioned so that at night, when the light of the church shined through it, he could see it from his room at the White House. It was at St. John's that Gerald Ford worshipped alone before going on TV to pardon his predecessor.

John Hay and Henry Adams used to live across the street where a hotel named after them now stands. Hay was Secretary of State; Adams, one of the country's more prominent writers— just as his *Mont Saint Michel and Chartres* evoked the essence of medieval Europe, his novel *Democracy* and *The Education of Henry Adams* evoked the spirit of Washington in the middle and late nineteenth century. In that autobiography he does not mention the death of his wife. She died unexpectedly, perhaps unaccountably, and young. For her grave he commissioned, from his friend Augustus Saint-Gaudens, the single most moving and important piece of sculpture in the city. It stands in the midst of tall holly trees, in a setting designed by Stanford White, in Rock Creek Cemetery. (*See* p. 113.)

Also in the cemetery, **Saint Paul's Episcopal Church** of the Rock Creek Parish was burned in 1921, but was immediately rebuilt. It now stands, perhaps too immaculately restored, at **Webster and Third Streets, N.W., between New Hampshire Avenue and North Capitol Street,** which is, incidentally, far from Rock Creek Park. The original building was the first church in Washington, built in 1771 before the District of Columbia existed, before, in fact, the United States existed.

The surroundings are quiet as only long-used graveyards can be. This place is far from the center of the city. Breezes blow here. A huge old white oak, called "The Glebe Oak," has stood here since before the first outdoor services were held in 1715 or the first grave dug in 1719. Across the road is the **Old Soldiers Home,** originally built with the ransom money General Winfield Scott had extorted from Mexico City in 1848.

---

### BUFFALOES, LONGFELLOW, AND WAR AND PEACE

In the heart of the city there are no such intimate and peaceful memorials as at Oak Hill and Rock Creek. Instead, monumental statues preside over every public place—generals and politicians, labor leaders and foreign revolutionaries, nuns and priests, figures symbolical and abstract, buffaloes, lions, seagulls delicately suspended above a wave, tigers, and a prehistoric triceratops named Uncle Beazly (at the Museum of Natural History); there are even a few poets (**Longfellow on Connecticut Avenue at M Street, N.W., Dante** in Meridian Hill Park, **Sixteenth Street between Florida Avenue and Euclid Street, N.W.,** and the Ukrainian bard **Taras Shevchenko, P between Twenty-second and Twenty-third Streets, N.W.).**

One must marvel at some of the monuments that have been erected in this town, erected by interest groups that have finagled a piece of land and occasionally an appropriation by act of Congress to see their heroes and representatives immortalized in cold metal or stone. There is an elaborate monument to **Dr. Samuel Hahnemann, Scott Circle, N.W.;** he was the father of homeopathy, a branch of medical science roundly denounced by the American Medical Association. There is a waterless **"Temperance Fountain"** in front of a liquor store at **Pennsylvania Avenue and Seventh Street, N.W.** And there is a grotesque **Boy Scout Memorial on the Ellipse, Fifteenth between Constitution and E, N.W.** showing an intrepid young hiker backed up by scantily clad images of American Manhood and Womanhood. These are but a few.

Everywhere in the city there are men on horseback. Most of them go unnoticed by passing tourists and office workers. When they are noticed they are often unrecognized and if recognized, often unremembered. They are background. The green-streaked men in the parks are strangers.

Until the middle of the nineteenth century, however, they were not there at all; not in Washington and not in the country. Not since New Yorkers tore down their gilded lead effigy of George III at the beginning of the Revolution and melted him for bullets had there been a major equestrian statue in America.

In 1849 the Democratic Party thought it would be nice to erect a monument to a great Democratic President, **Andrew Jackson.** A committee chose Clark Mills, a self-taught sculptor who had never seen an equestrian statue, to create a suitable image of Old Hickory on horseback. After many difficulties, on January 8, 1853, the 38th anniversary of the Battle of New Orleans, Mills unveiled the statue in the **middle of Lafayette Park.**

According to James M. Goode's incredibly comprehensive and detailed book, *The Outdoor Sculpture of Washington, D.C.,* the cannon at the base of Jackson's monument are rare pieces he captured fighting the Spanish in Florida. They have names—El Aristo, El Apollo, Witiza, and El Egica—after Greek gods and Visigothic kings. They point, as it happens, in the direction of the Revolutionary heroes at the square's four corners: **Lafayette** himself commands the **southeast corner** near the tourist entrance of the White House; **Rochambeau, in the southwest,** commander of the royal French expeditionary force, seems to be directing his soldiers at the Old Executive Office Building; **Thaddeus Kosciusko,** the Polish officer who designed the impregnable fortress at West Point, is near the Veterans Administration, to the **northeast;** and **Von Steuben,** the Prussian who drilled Spartan discipline into American soldiers at Valley Forge and after, stands in his heavy cloak near Decatur House at the **northwest** corner of the park.

Some say Jackson is too small for his setting. Franklin Roosevelt wanted the statue exchanged for another Mills monument—the grim **George Washington** on a windswept horse at **Twenty-third and K Streets, N.W.** (Washington Circle). Everything from the rigidity of Major General Jackson's face to the excessive size of his sword has been criticized, but of course none of that matters. He still stands where he was originally placed and looks as he did when Henry James called him "the most prodigious of Presidential effigies . . . as archaic as a Ninevite king, prancing and rocking through the ages."

In line with Jackson and the White House is **Winfield Scott, straight up Sixteenth Street.** "Old Fuss and Feathers" he was called, and the portly figure sitting astride the lightweight mare—his favorite mount—looks every bit the part. (In a curious bit of nineteenth century sexism his descendants thought it unseemly that he should be riding a mare. All the sculptor, H. K. Brown, could do to rectify the situation was imbue the horse with male parts.)

Generals who turned to politics in the nineteenth century, especially after the Civil War, could always be fairly certain they'd be turned to bronze. This was true whether they were successful politicians or not, and in some cases regardless of the way their military careers fared. **Major Generals McClellan** and **Logan** were both "released" from command during the Civil War. The former ran against Lincoln as a peace candidate, the latter founded a veterans' organization and served three terms as a Senator. Now McClellan sits astride an uncomfortably collected horse at **Columbia Road and Connecticut Avenue, N.W.,** while Logan presides over the circle named for him at the intersection of **Vermont Avenue, Thirteenth and P Streets, N.W.**

Other, less politically inclined but more heroic and successful military men have been the subjects of rather more impressive statues. **General Philip Sheridan,** at **Massachusetts Avenue and Twenty-third Street, N.W.,** rallies his troops to fight at the battle of Winchester, his hat clenched in his hand, his horse bracing itself against the tension of the moment. **William Tecumseh Sherman** (the War Between the States brought in a bumper crop of Union bronzes—these are but a few) is mounted atop a veritable tower of stone in a small square at **Fifteenth Street and Alexander Hamilton Place, N.W.,** which faces the steps of the Treasury. Unfortunately, he presents his back and his horse's rump to most passers-by. In the summer, trees obscure Sherman's bare head and the best way to get a good look at him is from above, at the bar atop the Hotel Washington.

**Ulysses S. Grant,** commander of the Union's forces and President of the United States, had the most successful military career and the most scandalous political one of anybody memorialized in the city. His bronze monument is stupendous. It stands **at the foot of Capitol Hill on the Mall.** From the north there is a frozen cavalry charge, with Union soldiers dying, fighting, and pushing forward their flag, while from the south, horsedrawn artillery struggles its way toward the marble base of the main statue. Above it all sits Grant, unflappable, swordless, on his alert thoroughbred.

There is only one happy statue in the city. It is of a woman, the great educator **Mary McLeod Bethune,** in Lincoln Park, **between Eleventh and Thirteenth Streets on East Capitol, S.E.** Mrs. Bethune, who died in 1955, is shown raising two children up from ignorance, and the three of them seem to be having a pretty good time of it.

---

## MORE PLACES OF WORSHIP

The man who drew the first master plan for Washington, the redoubtable M. L'Enfant, had a notion that a national place of worship would be a valuable part of the new capital city. All

Americans could worship there if they pleased and, as in England's Westminster Abbey, the great men of each generation would be buried there to be remembered, memorialized, revered, and, in a pleasant sort of way, worshipped. It would be, as L'Enfant called it, a "national pantheon."

The chosen site, Eighth and F Streets, N.W., languished for several years until finally, at Andrew Jackson's request, a grand structure incorporating the classical beauties of an ancient Greek temple with the most up-to-date engineering advances was built on the spot. It would have been a suitable pantheon, but became, instead, the Patent Office. Across the city, near Georgetown, we do have, though, the National Cathedral.

The **National Cathedral** is a complex, with grounds that stretch all over Mount Saint Albans, the highest point in the city, at **Massachusetts and Wisconsin Avenues, N.W.** There are lovely gardens, two schools, an herb and spice shop, and several other buildings; and for its size and painstaking detail the still unfinished structure officially known as the Cathedral Church of Saint Peter and Saint Paul is the most impressive building in the city. Its design is gothic, modeled on, but not copying exactly, such European cathedrals as Notre Dame de Paris, Chartres, and Reims—places of worship that took centuries to build during the Middle Ages. By comparison, the National Cathedral is rocketing upward: its foundation stone was laid in 1907, and the towers of St. Peter and St. Paul should be completed in 1984. Embellishment will go on forever. No steel has been used in the construction, and no shortcuts have been taken that would in any way jeopardize the lifespan of the structure—expected to be at least 1,000 years. Everything is solid stone masonry.

Though it is nominally Episcopal, the Cathedral is genuinely a national place of worship, open to all denominations. It has not been unusual for Hebrew congregations to use its chapels while awaiting the construction of a synagogue.

The visitor's center is located on the crypt floor (downstairs) in the south transept. Nearby is a pleasant gift shop. Tours start at 10 A.M., Monday through Saturday, and last about 45 minutes. There is a short break for noonday services, and the final tour begins at 3:30. On Sunday there are tours at 12:15 P.M., 1:30, and 2:30. If for some reason these times are not convenient, the Cathedral publishes a superb guide to itself.

The Cathedral's pleasures are not limited to the eyes. Concerts, both religious and secular—including jazz, dance, and folk music—are often given there. Without any electronic amplification the sound of a bass fiddle, a flute, and a drum, playing in the crossing, can completely surround an audience with sound. So, as a matter of fact, can a little boy stamping his heels.

In 1914 the Catholic hierarchy approved the erection in Washington of a monumental national church—the **Crypt Church** was completed in 1927. The shallow, vaulted ceilings and the dim subterranean light of the place evoke an intimacy and a mood that is quite pleasant—one of the nicest aspects of the **Shrine of the Immaculate Conception, Fourth Street and Michigan Avenue, N.E.** (Crypt, incidentally, simply means underground. Bishop Thomas Shahan, who saw the Shrine through hierarchy approvals, is the only person buried here.) In the early 1930s the crypt area was extended south to include the Lourdes Chapel, a lobby known as Memorial Hall, and the Founders' Chapel. The architecture in these places is more reserved; the detail is less ostentatious and in several curious ways more interesting than in more prominent parts of the building.

Tours start every hour in Memorial Hall. Hundreds of names have been engraved on the walls in loving memory of all kinds of people. Chiseled in jet-black marble is a dedication to Babe Ruth. Elsewhere, etched in Italian travertine marble, is a memorial to the Bonanno family in Maryland, listing the names of several members, including an "Uncle Joe."

In 1932 work on the Shrine was discontinued for lack of funds. It didn't begin again until 1954, when an all-out drive was made to complete the structure. In 1957 the Knights of Columbus pledged a million dollars for a belltower, which was built alongside the Shrine and designed to be, in a strange Byzantine-Romanesque manner, intentionally reminiscent of the Washington Monument.

The Shrine was finally dedicated in 1959, but the decoration on the inside is still far from complete. Within the main body of the building there is the same kind of vastness apparent in the Washington National Cathedral. Some of the art (nearly all of which is factory mosaic, made of Venetian glass) is unfortunately bad, particularly the "Woman of the Apocalypse" in the West Apse. Some people object to the fierce expression of the enormous Christ surrounded by flaming tongues.

Whatever the structure's problems with design and conception, it is worth visiting for its color and its spectacle as much as its religious interest.

Nearby is the **Franciscan Monastery at Fourteenth and Quincy Streets, N.E.** Here, inside the Memorial Church, can be found a series of reconstructed shrines from the Holy Land, including the Altar of Calvary, the Stone of Anointing, the Grotto of Nazareth, and the Grotto of Bethlehem. Beneath the church is an abbreviated version of the Roman catacombs, and outside is "Gethsemane Valley."

No one who comes to this city along the Beltway from the north can miss seeing the dazzling white **Mormon Temple at 9900 Stoneybrook Drive in Kensington, Maryland.** It looms above the trees like a fairyland castle, the gigantic gilded angel Moroni— bearer of the revelatory "golden plates" to the church's founder, Joseph Smith—trumpeting his message from a spire that projects 30 feet higher than the Washington Monument. There is another, small Moroni atop the **Church of Jesus Christ of Latter-day Saints at 2810 Sixteenth Street, N.W.** The difference between the two places of worship is essential to Mormon beliefs. Only in a temple, for instance, may devout Mormons seal their own marriages (and the marriages of their ancestors) for all time, a central act of the faith. This is the only temple on the east coast of the United States, and there are 90,000 Mormons who may from time to time need to use it. No one, however, who is not devout may enter.

The **Islamic Mosque at 2551 Massachusetts Avenue, N.W.,** is not so exclusive. All it asks of you is that you remove your shoes and, if you are a woman, be decently attired.

The Mosque, and the Islamic cultural center it is part of, seem neither ostentatious, assertive, nor out of place, but exotic in the most attractive sense of the word. With its graceful minaret towering above and the designs on its walls delicately inter-mingling white and gold and turquoise, the Mosque is an under-stated building. Five times a day the recorded chant of a muezzin calls the faithful to prayer.

There seem to be endlessly various places to worship in Washington. It seemed to Henry Adams, who knew this city so intimately—with its countless monuments and myriad churches devoted in varying degrees to patriotism, society, politics, and God—that "the American layman had lost sight of ideals; the American priest had lost sight of faith." Adams came to that conclusion as he watched the mystified reaction of people who were brought to see the statue, so wrongly called "Grief," that he had placed above his wife's grave **(in Rock Creek Cemetery, Webster and Third Streets, N.W., between New Hampshire Avenue and North Capitol Street).** Everyone wanted to know its meaning. "Most took it for a portrait statue," Adams wrote. "The remnant were vacant-minded in the absence of a personal guide. . . . The only exceptions were the clergy. . . . One after another brought companions there, and apparently fascinated by their own reflection, broke out passionately against the expression they felt in the figure of despair, of atheism, of denial. Like others, the priest saw only what he brought. Like all great artists, Saint-Gaudens held up the mirror and no more."

Today the traffic noise from a nearby highway impinges on the enclosure of holly trees, the pebbled ground, and the curving marble bench Stanford White placed facing the statue Saint-Gaudens called **"The Peace of God."**

# VII
# The Smithsonian

By Kenneth Turan

Like the tolerant parents of some gargantuan adolescent, the people who run the Smithsonian Institution tend to be slightly apologetic about its size. No fair pointing at the more than 20 million annual callers who make it the largest single center for visitors in the United States, more than twice as popular as Disneyland, or at its 1978 operating budget of more than $115 million, or at its staff of more than 4,000, the largest of any museum in the world. For the Smithsonian is not one museum, its people say, it is a combination of many, collecting many different things. Just how many different things, most people have no idea.

Never mind all those hulking public buildings out on the Mall and all the determined hours spent trying to see everything that is shoehorned into them, trying to get it all down. It cannot be done. For the Smithsonian Institution's collection numbers roughly 78 million items and is growing by an estimated one million per year. It is so big no one has a precise idea of its size, so big that even its caretakers admit "nobody could ever comprehend what's here." So big, in fact, that about 98 per cent of it is not on public display.

No invidious plot is in operation here, just the simple fact that enough room does not exist to get it all out in the open. Curators manfully rotate exhibits, press for more space, make their private research collections as accessible to the public as humanly possible, but there still are oodles of articles behind those "Authorized Personnel Only" signs.

Since there is no one around now who knows exactly what the future will find interesting, there is a great reluctance on the

Kenneth Turan is a staff writer on *The Washington Post*'s Style section and a film critic.

Institution's part to give up anything it has. The feeling is, as one curator puts it, "Well, the Smithsonian Institution is here forevermore," and therefore has a concomitant obligation to collect for the ages. After all, says a Smithsonian official, "It behooves a museum to acquire. If we don't take care of the objects of the past, the future is not going to have them."

But let it be understood early on: the Smithsonian is not all *things*. A unique educational institution, the Smithsonian may be the most active living museum in the world. Many of its local activities revolve around the Smithsonian Associates program, and for a $18 resident or $12 national membership fee, an associate is pleasurably bombarded with an array of learning and discovery activities from a class in urban planning to hunting mushrooms or wildflowers. Or, with the Smithsonian, you can go on a foreign study tour in Spain and France to examine the Santander and Altamira paleolithic cave paintings.

Smithsonian Associates also receive the *Smithsonian* magazine, whose interests range from the true character of the hyena—predator or scavenger?—to the restoration of Canterbury's stained-glass leaded windows. One of the fastest growing magazines in the country, the *Smithsonian* since its première issue in April, 1970, has achieved, in a time of failing publications, an enviable circulation of nearly one and one half million.

The Smithsonian Institution sponsors one of Washington's summer highlights—the "Festival of American Folklife" on the Mall. There you can hear bluegrass music (not only the *nouveau* genre but also the genuine old mountain music), or watch a sheep-shearing, or take in a Ukrainian folk dance.

No less exciting is the **Anacostia Neighborhood Museum, 2405 Martin Luther King Jr. Avenue, S.E., 381-5656,** a Smithsonian arm which develops and holds exhibitions on topics of special interest to the black community.

In addition, the Smithsonian is involved in a staggering amount of scientific research. Not content with having backed more than 2,000 expeditions, the Institution runs an astrophysical laboratory in Cambridge, Massachusetts, a biological research center on the Chesapeake Bay, an oceanographic sorting center in Tunisia, and one of the world's leading tropical research institutes, based in Panama and Colombia.

There is also the Center for Short-Lived Phenomena, which

for $20 a year notifies presumably interested members of happenings like fireballs over Mexico, the disappearance of a Pacific island, even a rainstorm of red frogs over Minneapolis. Or, in the Washington, D.C., area, for 15 cents you can **Dial-A-Phenomenon, 737-8855,** and learn of oncoming space and earth phenomena—for instance, a "skylab" passage that will be visible locally on a particular date, and exactly when and where.

And, of course, one must not ignore the splendid Smithsonian art galleries—and we do not intend to. For a report on them and their highlights see Chapter VIII, "Art," as well as Chapter XII, "The Performing Arts," with details on the John F. Kennedy Center for the Performing Arts, which is also a part of the large Smithsonian family.

### Gifts

James Smithson, an illegitimate son of the Duke of Northumberland, put a quirky provision in his 1826 will: should his nephew die childless, the whole of his fortune—which turned out to be $541,379 and 63 cents—would go to a country he had never seen for the purpose of founding "at Washington, under the name of the Smithsonian Institution, an establishment for the increase and diffusion of knowledge among men." Smithson could not possibly have had all this in mind. No one could and no one did. "You couldn't look for a master plan," admits Robert Brooks, the Institution's No. 2 man. "There wasn't a plan a hundred years ago that would lead to what we see in the Smithsonian today."

For a while, it did not look as if there were going to be any Smithsonian at all. The money arrived, all right, in ten presumably very large boxes aboard the clipper *Mediator* in 1838, but Congress was not sure whether accepting the bequest of this quiet scientist, who apparently chafed under the social stigma of his birth, was the right thing to do. Accepting it, thundered the honorable Senator John C. Calhoun of South Carolina, "is beneath the dignity of the United States." Finally, in August of 1846, the bequest was okayed, and architect James Renwick began work on the red sandstone Romanesque "castle" that symbolizes the Smithsonian. Smithson himself was re-buried there in 1904, and the Institution's collection mania began there as well.

So now that it has just about everything, the Institution is convinced of its value. And no matter how seriously—and it is very seriously—the Smithsonian takes its role as the nation's repository for all time, the general public seems to take it more so. "You could tell the seasons by the letters we'd get," says Helga Weiss, the Smithsonian's registrar for 25 years and now retired. "People would clean out their attics during spring cleaning and we'd get a lot of strange offers." Among the unsuccessful proffers were a bathtub that had gone across the English Channel and a Jeep that went around the world.

Even in the face of the gift—soon returned—of an undershirt worn by a man whose wife warned that if he did not give it up she would give it to the Smithsonian, the Institution encourages unsolicited donations. Almost everything it has was a gift, including an elephant that weighed approximately 12 tons when alive and was announced by a seven-page letter from the hunter describing in great detail the three-year search-and-destroy mission that led to its demise.

Despite the tightness of space, the one thing the Smithsonian curators do not want to do is discourage people from still more and more giving. There is always room for something of quality, they emphasize, always room for one more whatever.

## WHAT YOU WILL SEE, WHAT YOU WON'T SEE

The greatest pleasure in seeing the Smithsonian is the opportunities it offers for pure serendipity, the making of delightful and unexpected discoveries completely by accident. It is impossible to see all the million square feet of exhibits on the 12 square blocks of the Mall occupied by the Smithsonian buildings and grounds; the best thing is just to wander in the buildings of your choice, letting chance guide and delight you. Or get in on a special museum exhibit or event; to find out what's happening, just **Dial-A-Museum** at **737-8811.**

Of course, some exhibits are of such interest that your friends back home would never forgive you for missing them. Lists of such "can't miss" items follow, plus glimpses of what the Institution has behind the scenes. But remember: serendipity, always serendipity.

**National Museum of History and Technology**—the modern shoebox on **Constitution Avenue, N.W., between Twelfth and**

**Fourteenth Streets,** open daily except Christmas, 10 to 5:30, during the summer until 9. **628-4422**

### Can't Miss:

• The Star-Spangled Banner—the original, by now tattered, 30-by-42-foot flag that Francis Scott Key was delighted to find flying above Fort McHenry in Baltimore on that famous 1814 dawn.

• The Foucault Pendulum—a copy of the original exhibited in Paris in 1851 by French physicist Leon Foucault to demonstrate the earth's rotation. The 240-pound brass ball swings back and forth, back and forth, on a 71.5-foot chain, periodically knocking over small markers to the delight of all concerned.

• George Washington's false teeth.

• Greenough's "George Washington"—a heroic 20-ton statue of the father of his country, seated naked to the waist in classic garb, all done up as the God Zeus. This 1840 work did not win sculptor Horatio Greenough a lot of friends. "Did anyone ever see Washington naked!" exclaimed Nathaniel Hawthorne. "It is inconceivable."

• Gowns of the First Ladies—everyone from Martha Washington on is represented by one swell evening dress.

• Genuine Country Store/Post Office—open in Headsville, West Virginia, from 1861 to 1914, and open once again in the museum's lobby. If you like this kind of thing, do not miss the completely equipped 1890s American pharmacy either.

• "We the People"—a truly awesome exhibit of 6,000 objects that was keyed to the Bicentennial celebration. Costing $500,000 and three years' planning, it consists of three vast sections: "Of the People," with the focus on our national symbols, such as the bald eagle; "By the People," telling the story of our rights and participation in government; and "For the People," about how the government affects every aspect of our daily lives.

• Also worth mentioning—the 75,000-item National Postage Stamp Collection, sitting quietly in 500 glass-covered frames.

### Behind the Scenes:

Political history—just for openers there are the original Teddy Bear made in 1903 for Theodore Roosevelt and the hound dog patented in 1912 to back the political career of Champ Clark. There are Thomas Jefferson's sleeping bag, Herbert Hoover's

Mrs. Richard Nixon examines her inaugural gown in the First Ladies Hall of the National Museum of History and Technology, 1970.

Alice Roosevelt Longworth: "That was the only picture at my wedding . . ." 1906.

fishing rod, a desk used by Abraham Lincoln, the hoods and shackles worn by his captured assassination conspirators, a vest made by former tailor Andrew Johnson, Everett Dirksen's eyeglasses, even a compass made from a nut which fell from a tree planted by George Washington.

Harpoons—there are more than 100, mostly assembled for London's 1883 International Fisheries Collection, and now hanging all in a row on a wall of the division's storeroom, waiting for Ahab, or at least Gregory Peck.

Musical instruments—when you have around 250 of them, keyboard instruments can be a problem, and the division of musical instruments, with the most comprehensive collection of American pianos anywhere, finally came up with the solution. The legs are taken off and the instruments are lifted onto cantilevered shelves with the aid of a special forklift truck. It's easy when you know how. The rest of the Smithsonian's 4,000 instruments are less of a problem, sitting quietly in long rows. Among the more interesting specimens are a sarrusophone (a double-reed saxophone type thing), the first Hammond organ, the piano on which Irving Berlin wrote "White Christmas," an 8-foot alpine horn, a weird percussion instrument called a jingling johnny, and a genuine cigarbox guitar.

Clothing—enough clothes to make Macy's envious, 16,000 items in fact, hang in special custom-made steel cabinets or sit flat in drawers lined with acid-free paper. Among the prizes therein are a dress worn to George Washington's inauguration, the earliest surviving Levis (*circa* 1870) and a whole collection of objects from the Copp Family of Stonington, Connecticut, who apparently never threw anything out.

**National Museum of Natural History**—the columned, domed affair on **Constitution Avenue, N.W., at Tenth Street.** Open daily except Christmas, 10 to 5:30, during the summer until 9. **628-4422.**

### Can't Miss:

• Fénykövi Elephant—shot in Africa in 1955 by a Hungarian engineer who donated it to the Smithsonian. This, the largest elephant ever recorded, is 13 feet, 2 inches high, and weighed 12 tons when alive. It took two years to mount; the result was worth every minute. Also notice the largest tiger ever taken in India, 11 feet, 1 inch long, weighing in at 857 pounds.

• Brontosaurus—a mounted skeleton of a *Diplodocus longus,* 12 feet high, 80 feet long, allegedly hampered by a brain the size of a pea when alive.

• Blue Whale—a 92-foot fiberglass model of the 135-ton beast hangs awesomely in midair.

• Oldest Known Fossil—the Fig Tree chert, hailing from South Africa, 3.1 billion years old if it's a day.

• The Hope Diamond—smuggled out of India in the seventeenth century, at 44.5 carats it is the largest blue diamond in the world. There's a curse on it, though, so don't look too hard. Also note the Star of India, at 330 carats one of the finest star sapphires around.

• Discovery Room—a touch, feel, smell and taste center for all ages, where you can compare your plants, animals and rocks with the museum's. There's also a 55-gallon salt water tank where you can come nose-to-nose with a sea urchin.

• Insect Zoo—an all-live exhibit with over 100 species of insects some of which you can handle. These include two-inch cockroaches that hiss, tarantulas, unicorn beetles and a six-inch Australian walking stick.

### Behind the Scenes:

Invertebrate zoology—one after another after another, the jars line up, filled with crabs, shrimps, lobsters, snails, mollusks, jellyfish and worms, 12 miles' worth of shelving, using up 2–3,000 gallons of alcohol a year without even trying. Highlighting the collection, aside from things like 130 years' accumulation of coral, are 400-million-year-old animals that look so much like plants they were originally classified that way, and the 13-foot Japanese king crab, once displayed under a P. T. Barnum-ish blockbuster sign reading "The Giant Crab of Japan."

Skeletons—even Kafka would have shuddered. Sitting in 3-foot-long drawers stacked 14 high and 63 long, in a narrow corridor, are 23,000 skeletal remains. Approximately two-thirds are skulls, which fit ten to a drawer, some of the older ones with prison-like numbers written on the forehead and little tags tied to each ear hole. Each specimen has its own six-digit number, and walking down the corridor one sees representatives from every part of the world from Malaysia to Bohemia to Mongolia, Afghanistan, and Nebraska.

Entymology—this section's storage space consists of more than 400,000 slides, 100,000 vials and 25,000 drawers, most of them full. The collection includes more than 6 million beetles, 3 million flies, 2 million wasps and bees and more just plain bugs than anyone except an entymologist would care to contemplate.

Minerals and gems—"The value here far exceeds the rest of the museum," says a curator. "You can't really assign a value, but for a rough estimate we say $20–$30 million. That's a lot of bucks." It is also a lot of jewels, with literally hundreds of diamonds, one of California's largest gold nuggets, and some of the best silver specimens in the country biding their time in the division's three big safes and a bigger vault.

Medical sciences—white teeth on a field of blue, teeth displayed as far as the eye can see, perhaps 100 sets of dentures, ivory hand carved ones, mother of pearl ones, Revolutionary War dentures made by the first great American dentist, Joseph LeMayeur. In fact, just about everything related to dentistry is here, and that includes drilling machines and even dentists' chairs, 50 of which are packed away out in the Silver Hill, Maryland, storage facility.

Besides teeth-oriented material, the collection includes a vast amount of pills and drugs, and as an additional treat, the Food and Drug Administration's collection of early twentieth century quack devices: stockings to help you lose weight, a helmet that sends curing electricity through your body, even a shower you step into to calm your nerves.

Vertebrates—"vertebrate" means having a backbone, and that means birds, fishes, reptiles, amphibians, and mammals, more than 3 million where the Smithsonian is concerned. Some are preserved in alcohol, some are skeletons, some are stuffed, with a diversity ranging from a preserved dugong, the marine mammal on which the legend of the mermaid is based, to the bones of Lexington, the sire of the famed racehorse Preakness.

**National Air and Space Museum**—in mid-1976, all air and space exhibits received a shiny new building all to themselves on **Independence Avenue at Seventh Street, S.W.,** right next to the trendy, doughnut-shaped Hirshhorn Museum and Sculpture Garden. In the past, much of the collection was housed in the Arts and Industries Building, that red brick Romanesque exhibition hall next door to the "Castle," as well as in an adjacent quonset hut. Because of renovation, the Arts and Industries building was closed as of August, 1975, and the Museum's collections were refurbished at the Silver Hill facility. Included are a theater for special films and exhibits covering 200,000 square feet. Open daily except Christmas, 10 to 5:30, during the summer until 9. **628-4422.**

### Can't Miss:
- The 1903 Kitty Hawk "Flyer."
- The "Spirit of St. Louis"—it took Charles Lindbergh all of 33 hours and 20 minutes to become an international celebrity by flying this plane nonstop from New York to Paris in 1927.
- Man on the Moon—a lunar rock brought back by the crew of Apollo 11, as well as the blackened command module "Columbia," which brought them all back home.
- "To Fly"—one-half hour film running every 45 minutes during the museum's open hours. Tour across the U.S. through flight-oriented eyes, on a screen five stories high, starting with a balloon ascension, through to flight in space.
- "Skylab" Orbital Workshop—visitors can walk through an actual space station to see how astronauts live.

### Behind the Scenes:
Discreetly tucked away in Suitland, Maryland, what is probably the world's largest collection of old airplanes sits amidst the splendors of suburbia, resting quietly in a series of 24 corrugated iron buildings at the Silver Hill facility, lonely but brave. There is the "Enola Gay," the plane that dropped the first atomic bomb over Hiroshima. There are gliders, aerobatic airplanes, a plane small enough to take off and land from dirigibles, fierce fighters like German Messerschmitts and Japanese Zeros, even a kamikaze plane called a baka bomb after the Japanese word for stupid. And there is also something called the "Old Miss," a Curtiss-Robin aircraft used in 1934 by the Key brothers, Al and Fred, to set a world endurance record by circling Meridian, Mississippi, for 653 hours and 34 minutes nonstop. "They were very big," says a man who knows, "in Mississippi."

Other major subdivisions of the Smithsonian Institution are discussed in detail as follows:

Chapter VIII, "Art": the Freer Gallery, the Hirshhorn Museum and Sculpture Garden, the National Collection of Fine Arts, the National Portrait Gallery, the National Gallery of Art, the Renwick Gallery.

Chapter XII, "The Performing Arts": the John F. Kennedy Center for the Performing Arts.

Chapter XIV, "Natural Life": the National Zoological Park.

Also, see Chapter XV, "Of Special Interest to Children," for detail on the Discovery Room in the Museum of Natural History, and the Explore Gallery in the National Collection of Fine Arts.

# VIII
## Art

### By Paul Richard

Washington is not really a citadel of all the arts or a capital of culture. It hasn't yet come up with the great American novel, movie, poem, university, or rock band. But Washington has more artists, art museums, commercial galleries, studios, openings, temporary shows, and international exhibitions than any other American city of comparable size. And its collections are a blessing; Rembrandts, Rodins, Ryders, Chinese bronzes, Victorian photographs, Persian carpets, presidential portraits—masterworks and minor works of old and modern art.

The city's museums, most of them at least, are free, hard to park near, generous to the public, and least crowded weekday mornings. They should be taken in small doses, lest the mind begin to wander, the feet give out, and the objects start to blur. Conservative by nature, they affect an air of antiquity—those that do not look like palaces or mansions look like Grecian temples—but most have not been here long. The National Collection of Fine Arts, the Phillips Collection, the Freer Gallery of Art, the National Portrait Gallery, the Renwick Gallery, Dumbarton Oaks, the Textile Museum, the Museum of African Art are all twentieth century institutions. The National Gallery of Art opened to the public only in 1941, and the Hirshhorn Museum and Sculpture Garden (its new East Building opening only in June, 1978), in 1974.

The Hirshhorn, a fortress-secure bunker on the Mall, reminds us that museum art is worth a lot of money. The government agrees: our tax codes are so written that with museum gifts come tax deductions for the giver. That is a fact fully appreciated by the surprisingly small number of American collec-

Paul Richard is art critic of *The Washington Post*.

tors—Andrew and Paul Mellon, Ailsa Mellon Bruce, Duncan Phillips, Charles Lang Freer, the Wideners and the Kresses, Chester Dale, Lessing J. Rosenwald, George Hewitt Myers, Mr. and Mrs. Robert Woods Bliss, Joseph H. Hirshhorn, and others— who, in recent years, chose most of the art displayed in Washington's museums, paid for it, enjoyed it, and then gave it away.

The capital's museums contain presents from the rich, presents to the American people. So don't miss the opportunity to open these treasure boxes and delight in their contents.

**The National Gallery of Art, on the Mall, Constitution Avenue at Sixth Street, N.W., 737-4215.** Summer hours are 10–9 Monday–Saturday, noon–9 Sunday; winter hours 10–5 Monday–Saturday, noon–9 Sunday. Among the highlights: Leonardo da Vinci's "Ginevra de' Benci," Raphael's "Alba Madonna," Fragonard's "A Young Girl Reading," Botticelli's "Adoration of the Magi," Monet's "Rouen Cathedral," Perugino's "Crucifixion," Picasso's "Femme Nue," Rembrandt's "Self Portrait," Renoir's "A Girl with a Watering Can," Titian's "Venus with a Mirror," Gilbert Stuart's "Portrait of George Washington."

Washington's Louvre, Washington's Prado, the National Gallery of Art is the sort of place paintings would aspire to if masterpieces went to heaven. The columns here are marble, a rosy hue hand-picked from a quarry in Tennessee; there are fountains in the garden courts; there is an atmosphere that is noble, monumental, deluxe. Though lesser artists, by the tens of thousands, have been rigorously excluded from these lofty precincts, admittance has been granted to the most sought-after masters of painting: Rembrandt, Vermeer, Ingres, Cézanne and Picasso, even Leonardo.

The display is chronological. If one approaches from the Mall, ascends the marble stairs, turns left at the fountain and heads for the Italians, one can survey, in sequence, the high points of art history; that, at least, is the intention.

The National Gallery of Art was built to introduce Americans to the aristocracy of European art. It is a monument to Western painting, and to the Mellons of Virginia. Andrew Mellon, who built it, was a "squillionaire" (the term is Bernard Berenson's), a Secretary of the Treasury, and Ambassador to the Court of St. James's. It was he who gave the Gallery its first 111 pictures, five of which came from Soviet politicians seeking money for a five-year plan. In 1931, they dipped into the Czar's collections at the Hermitage and sold Mellon a Van Eyck, a Botticelli, a Titian, a Raphael, and a Perugino for $3,247,695.

Though the Wideners and the Kresses, Lessing Rosenwald, Chester Dale, and other merchant-prince collectors soon followed his example, and though hundreds of Americans have since filled out its collections, the Gallery, in many ways, remains a Mellon Gallery. Ailsa Mellon Bruce, Andrew Mellon's daughter, gave the institution its finest Fragonard ("A Young Girl Reading"), its great Picasso cubist nude, America's only Leonardo da Vinci, and a hundred other precious pictures. Paul Mellon, Andrew's son, is the Gallery's present president and seems an exemplary trustee.

The National Gallery of Art has yet to be annoyed by the sort of public controversies that occasionally bedevil the Boston or the Metropolitan. It is superbly, confidently run. Its finest scholarly publications, the menus at its black-tie openings, and the flawless installations of its most ambitious exhibitions reflect standards of good taste commensurate with those of its collections.

Living artists are poorly represented at the National Gallery. Their works, at first, were banned entirely, but then the dwindling supply and great demand for important modern paintings—and the long life of Picasso—made the policy indefensible.

Andrew Mellon envisioned a collection of European masterpieces. Other visions, other attitudes toward art—some far more suggestive and inclusive—took concrete form in the collections of other Washington museums.

The most modern of the city's art museums is the Gallery's new East Building, opened in June, 1978. Designed by I.M. Pei, the two pink marble triangles make room for more exhibition galleries, a Center for Advanced Study in the Visual Arts (to open later) and an underground connecting link to the West Building that houses a pleasant café/buffet by a mesmerizing waterfall coming from street level.

**The Phillips Collection, 1612 Twenty-First Street, N.W., 387-0961.** Open 10–5 Tuesday–Saturday, 2–7 Sunday; closed Monday. Highlights: Eakins' "Portrait of Miss Van Buren,"

Renoir's "Luncheon of the Boating Party," Cézanne's "Jardin des Lauves," the room units of Paul Klee, Mark Rothko, Georges Braque, Pierre Bonnard, Georges Rouault.

A place of quiet harmonies, the Phillips Collection, which opened to the public in 1918, is truly the city's, and the nation's, first museum of modern art. A comfortable red-brick house in a comfortable old neighborhood, it is in itself a complex work of art, which Duncan Phillips composed of other people's pictures. There are pictures in the drawing room, pictures in the bedrooms, the stairways, and the halls. They brought Duncan Phillips joy.

Once, when a small child, he was taken to the circus where, to entertain the children, a clown tossed a boy-sized doll wheeling high into the air. The sight sent little Phillips into hysterics; he was rescued from his terror early the next morning by the colors of the flowers in the sunlight by his bed. The collection that he left us in his own home is a peaceful hymn to color.

Although Phillips bought a few old paintings (a Goya, an El Greco, and what might be a Giorgione), he believed in living artists (Bonnard, Klee, Augustus Vincent Tack, John Marin, Rothko) and he bought their works in depth. Phillips was a highly cultivated man, a connoisseur, a scholar, but his loyalty was always to the present.

That present was a time of revolution, of wars and manifestos, but the paintings he assembled never seem to squabble despite their differing conventions. They converse warmly with one another, hanging as they do in no chronological order, with no pretense at tracing the history of art. "Miss Van Buren," a sharply focused Eakins, might hang beside a moody Ryder or a messy Monticelli, just because, to Phillips' color-oriented eye, they looked right together. Even near the end of his life (he died in 1966), bedridden elsewhere, he would call the gallery to suggest small changes—perhaps that Marin or the Pollock should be moved from here to there—exploring with his mind's eye the fresh subtleties evoked by each new alignment. In their reliance on complex, interacting colors, Morris Louis and the other Washington color painters are, truly, Duncan Phillips' heirs.

**The Hirshhorn Museum and Sculpture Garden, on the Mall, Independence Avenue at Eighth Street, S.W., 628-4422.** Open 10–9 during the summer; to 5:30 every other day of the year. Collection highlights include Giacometti's "Dog," Rodin's "Burghers of Calais" and "Tribute to Balzac."

The most modern of the city's modern art museums is the Hirshhorn—on the Mall. That address, not to mention the building's architecture, has been a source of controversy. When the government announced that it was building a museum to house the art of a man considered, well, brasher than a Mellon or Mr. Phillips, some critics were offended. Hirshhorn's name, they argued, should not be linked with those of Washington and Lincoln on the sacred greensward of the Mall. Andrew Mellon, they contended, had behaved with greater modesty. But then, in the 1930s when the Mellon gift was first considered, Senator Robert La Follette asked what right had Mr. Mellon to call his personal collection of just 111 pictures a "National Gallery of Art"? The opening of the Hirshhorn stilled much of the grumbling.

Joseph H. Hirshhorn grew up in New York's slums, made a fortune first on the stock market, later from Canadian uranium mines, and spent much of it on art. He bought and bought and bought, half a dozen works today, a dozen more tomorrow. The collective result of his shopping sprees is impure, uneven, and wonderfully inclusive.

Though he sometimes hit the bull's-eye (look at his de Koonings or his David Smiths), he frequently missed. Still, his misses teach us, too. The installation is chronological with the oldest works in the basement, and the viewer who ascends can navigate many of the mainstreams of twentieth century art. But the Hirshhorn also hints at the dead ends and the byways.

The Hirshhorn is a museum of surprises: A Washington gallery, it has a New York air, and yet one finds here the influence of Paris and trends such as abstract expressionism. And it surprises in its sculpture. If the National Gallery and the Phillips concentrate on pictures, Joseph Hirshhorn, who says that as a child he never had a toy, never lost his yearning for things that he could touch. So he bought 2,000 sculptures, and it is said he shipped to Washington 500,000 pounds of art. More than worth their weight in gold.

**The Freer Gallery of Art, on the Mall, Twelfth Street and Jefferson Drive, S.W., 628-4422.** Open 10–9 in summer; to 5:30 otherwise. Although the Freer Gallery of Art, the third art museum on the Mall, opened to the public in 1923, there are many Washingtonians who don't know it's there. The Freer is almost never crowded, perhaps because it is a gallery of Oriental art. But Charles Lang Freer never expected his gift to the nation to attract the shuffling masses; in fact, the Freer Gallery, with its 40,000 volume library, is designed to serve the scholar, and much of its collection is not on display. No objects in the Freer are allowed to leave on loan, nor is the Freer allowed to borrow, lest its perfection somehow be polluted by works from other institutions. What you see here, then, is the exquisite collection of an aesthete who was determined to "promote high ideals of beauty" and certain that the taste of others was less exquisite than his own. He took great pains to see that nothing sullied his collections.

Charles Lang Freer did not inherit money. He left school after the seventh grade to work in a cement factory, but finally made enough building railroad cars to retire at 44. His later life was given to more rarefied pursuits: he collected Persian miniatures, Indian sculptures, American crystal, some works by James McNeill Whistler, including the astonishing Peacock Room; Japanese calligraphies, Chinese scrolls, screens, jades, porcelains and bronzes.

The emphasis is on the Oriental works, and here one can, if not fathom the Oriental mind, then perhaps gain some clues to its depths and directions. For instance, while most Westerners discriminate between the visual arts and the language, the artists of the Orient do not draw such distinctions. A Chinese character is, at once, a picture and a word. While Western poetry depends upon the music of rhyme and meter, Oriental poetry is directed at the eye as well as at the ear. Chairman Mao's calligraphies are reproduced in China because the inflections of his meaning can be seen as well as heard. Oriental painting, too, is a kind of literature. To the educated Chinese, each brush stroke sends a message. The Freer offers the Westerner the opportunity to find the meaning in these elegant messages.

**The National Collection of Fine Arts, Eighth and G Streets, N.W.,** and the **National Portrait Gallery, Eighth and F Streets, N.W.; 628-4422.** Both are open 10−9 in summer; otherwise to 5:30. The National Collection of Fine Arts is one of the oldest, and one of the newest, federal museums. Like the Hirshhorn's, its collections are surprisingly inclusive, though not exactly by design. It contains many of the formal portraits, seascapes, land-scapes, neo-classical statues, prints, and drawings that have been acquired in a most haphazard fashion by the Smithsonian Institution since 1846.

The Smithsonian, as everyone knows, collects everything —minerals, machines, bird skins, bicycles, bees—and art works, too. For years the works of art were stored in the most dusty corners of the Nation's Attic, until, in 1938, a bit of space was discovered in the Museum of Natural History behind the Fénykövi elephant. Although that space was clearly insufficient if not also inappropriate, and despite a national architectural competition in the 1930s (Eliel Saarinen, whose son Eero designed Dulles Airport, was granted first prize but his building was never built), a proper home for the Smithsonian's collection was not found until 1968.

What was found was the Old Patent Office Building, where President Lincoln had once waltzed, and Walt Whitman had once ministered to dying soldiers of the Civil War. Rescued from the wrecker's ball, it was extensively refurbished for the National Portrait Gallery and the National Collection of Fine Arts. Quite suddenly, or so it seemed, a remarkable profusion of art works by Americans began to pour out of the Nation's Attic—nineteenth century marble statues, Barbizon landscapes, American impressionists, conversation pieces, sentimental terracottas, paintings, prints, and drawings that most twentieth century Americans had never seen or thought about. While some of the frames bear famous names—Homer, Ryder, Stuart, West—many of the pictures are the work of painters long forgotten. American art in all its quirkiness, daring, innocence, and grandeur is the subject of the National Collection of Fine Arts, and its galleries are lessons in museum installation.

Far too many institutions tend to view the history of art as a linear progression, as if this work begat that one. At the National Collection one is not misled by such rigorous chronologies; instead, the nation's art is shown as a complex, shifting, open field in which all sorts of objects—WPA propaganda pieces, naked marble maidens, twentieth century abstractions—contribute to the whole. Nor are the walls the standard white; instead, their subtle colors complement the pictures. The National Collection, a superb museum, teaches everyone who sees it. It should not be missed.

The National Portrait Gallery, which occupies the southern half of the Old Patent Office Building, contains many busts and paintings, but it is more a gallery of people than a gallery of art. Faces are its subject, the faces of our Presidents, warriors, scientists, judges, authors, entertainers. Most of them pose stiffly in their dark and formal clothes. An elegant institution, elegantly installed, the National Portrait Gallery still seems a history museum with works that are not all beautiful: many of its subjects did more for the country than the professional portraitists they posed for did for the history of art.

**The Renwick Gallery, Pennsylvania Avenue and Seventeenth Street, N.W., 628-4422.** Summers 10–9; otherwise to 5:30.

Across Pennsylvania Avenue from the White House is a red-brick confection in the Second Empire style named today in honor of its architect, James Renwick. The inscription above the door reads "Dedicated to Art" and that is the Renwick's role as a division of the Smithsonian's National Collection of Fine Arts. But it hasn't always been so.

The building was commissioned in 1858 to house the art collection of William Wilson Corcoran, but soon after completion it went into the service of the Quartermaster Corps during the Civil War. After the war, it was restored to its original purpose—but briefly: Corcoran's growing collection outgrew the building and moved down Seventeenth Street to its present gallery. So the fanciful structure became the U.S. Court of Claims, and by 1958 it was scheduled for demolition, along with much of the Lafayette Square neighborhood. But some wise re-thinking during the Kennedy administration preserved the place, and in 1965 President Lyndon Johnson gave the building to the Smithsonian Institution.

Since the Renwick's opening as a gallery for the display of American design, crafts, and the decorative arts, it has held many shows, among them exhibitions of objects crafted of grass, of American Northwest Coast Indian art, of Shaker furniture, and of the industrial design of Raymond Loewy, complete with Avanti car in the front showroom.

**The Textile Museum, 2320 S Street, N.W., 667-0441.** Open 10–5 Tuesday–Saturday, closed Sunday and Monday. **The Museum of African Art, 316 A Street, N.E., 547-7424.** Open 11–5 Monday−Friday, noon−5 Saturday and Sunday. Both the Textile Museum and the Museum of African Art have self-explanatory names; both are small, specialized, private institutions; and both have occasionally lent items to one another, such as Eliot Elisofon photos from African Art enhancing an African textile exhibit.

The Textile Museum was founded in 1925 by George Hewitt Myers, a contemporary of Mellon, Phillips, and Freer who collected cloth and rugs. If you're interested in ancient Peruvian fabrics, old bits of Greco-Roman, Coptic, or Islamic cloth, flat-woven rugs, or Persian carpets, the museum will delight you. If you could care less about woofs and warps, better to concentrate your attentions elsewhere. The collection is large (8,500 textiles and some 800 rugs) and the museum does mount exhibits. Most of what it owns, however, is mainly available to scholars and not on display.

The Museum of African Art occupies the Capitol Hill houses where black editor and orator Frederick Douglass lived in the 1870s, and focuses on African origins.

Warren Robbins, who founded the museum in 1964, believes that traditional African art has much in common with the art of Klee, Picasso, Modigliani, and other European modernists, and he has organized a small exhibit to make that point. He has amassed a good collection of masks and gold pieces, fetishes and drums. Although some of these are awesome, many don't lend themselves to display in a museum, because traditional African carvings, unlike Western paintings or Oriental screens, were not made for exhibit. African masks and headdresses were made to be worn and danced with, moved about and used.

**Boutique Africa, 328 A Street, N.E.,** the museum's unique shop, carries sculptures, baskets, jewelry and textiles.

**The Dumbarton Oaks Byzantine and Pre-Columbian Collections, 1703 Thirty-Second Street, N.W., 232-3101.** Closed July 1 through Labor Day; open the rest of the year 2−5 P.M. Tuesday−Sunday, closed Monday and legal holidays.

There are three good reasons to visit Dumbarton Oaks in Georgetown: (1) the pre-Columbian collection of jade and gold and coiled serpents carved of stone that is housed in a small and oddly echoing jewel-box of a pavilion designed by Philip Johnson; (2) Washington's only fine collection of pre-Renaissance European art, most of it Byzantine, some of it Greek, some Roman; and (3) the gardens. Dumbarton Oaks, an early nineteenth century mansion with extensive grounds, was purchased by Mr. and Mrs. Robert Woods Bliss in 1920. They rebuilt the house, filled it with their art, entirely transformed the gardens, and then, in 1940, gave it all to the trustees of Harvard University.

It is now a research center for the study of Byzantine and medieval history and culture. Most afternoons the public is admitted to enjoy the art. (Many people, however, don't go inside, although that is probably understandable due to the diverting delights of the reflecting pools, lawns and winding paths, the forsythia, magnolias, roses, Japanese cherries and chrysanthemums.) Since Dumbarton Oaks obeys the academic year, it closes its galleries and gardens for much of the summer—a situation that has infuriated more than a few visitors.

**The Corcoran Gallery of Art, Seventeenth Street and New York Avenue, N.W., 628-9484.** Open 11–5 Tuesday–Sunday, closed Monday. Admission, Thursday to Sunday, adults $1.50, students 75 cents. Tuesday and Wednesday are free. Talk to local artists, dealers, or collectors, and the Washington museum you'll hear mentioned most often is the Corcoran. Thousands of local artists have studied at its art school, and hundreds have been given shows in its gracious, skylit halls.

A venerable institution, it was founded in 1859 by William Wilson Corcoran, a mid-Victorian mini-Mellon, but his taste does not pervade the museum that bears his name, nor do his times. The Corcoran offers an American art survey, plus some top-notch European pictures, but its permanent collections seem somehow less important than its endless sequence of temporary shows. Therein lies the Corcoran's greatest virtue, for even if the Hirshhorn and the Phillips are viewed as museums of modern art, their collections have been frozen: at the Corcoran, modern art stays modern and alive.

There are over 100 commercial galleries listed in the city's Yellow Pages and, as their changing shows imply, there are thousands of artists, painters, sculptors, printmakers, photographers, and cartoonists working in Washington. (For the latest shows, check the Weekend section of *The Post*.) While the nation's capital has long had first-rate objects, today it is also producing first-rate artists and collectors. And although fine American writers—Faulkner in Mississippi, Mark Twain in Missouri, and others—may have thrived in isolation, painters learn from paintings, and from one another, and from the standards set by great collections.

It is no accident that some cities, more than others, have been visited by art's muse. Slighting Sparta, Genoa, and Marseilles, she spent some time in Athens, Florence, Paris, and Manhattan, at least in part because the art scenes of those cities had achieved a certain density, a necessary, critical mass of interest, artifacts, and artisans. It is not yet reflected in the formal halls of the federal museums; but in the studios and the workshops, in the art schools and the salesrooms, one can feel that energy gathering in Washington.

# IX
# Architecture

### By Wolf Von Eckardt

Thomas Jefferson suggested that the new capital, like Philadel-phia, be built on a gridiron plan. L'Enfant objected. "The regular assemblage of houses laid out in squares and forming streets that are parallel and uniform," he wrote President Washington on April 4, 1791, is "tiresome and insipid [and] wanting a sense of the real grand and truly beautiful." L'Enfant wanted "a dimen-sion proportioned to the greatness which . . . the Capital of a pow-erful Empire ought to manifest."

If the capital manifests that greatness, and conveys a sense of the real grand, its architecture is not, for the most part, truly beautiful. Washington has few aesthetically outstanding build-ings. L'Enfant's dimensions, in fact, intimidate architects. In the early years of the Republic, the capital's architecture seemed small, humble, lost, and discouraged by the magnificent distances of unpaved streets and unlikely avenues leading through swamps. No one so much as thought of building a Place de la Concorde or a Trafalgar Square. In 1860, cows were grazing on the Mall and were only kept out of the President's garden by a whitewashed fence. It was not until 1870 that Pennsylvania Avenue got a gut-ter.

The basic outlines and pattern of L'Enfant's plan found their way into the cityscape. But as time passed many aspects were al-tered, ignored, and, finally, almost forgotten—not to be redis-covered until 1900 at a convention of the American Institute of Architects. From then on, architects were suddenly awed by its grandeur. Even the best of them, self-confident in New York or Chicago, are self-conscious in Washington, tongue-tied with stage

Wolf Von Eckardt, a member of *The Washington Post* editorial page staff, writes a weekly column of architecture criticism for the Style section.

fright. Some architects compensate for their anxieties with bravado. The inarticulate mass mediocrity of federal offices along Independence Avenue or the monstrous new Labor Department at the confluence of Pennsylvania and Constitution Avenues are examples of this method of coping. Since Washington's building-height limit and Fine Arts Commission inhibit architectural stunts, they show off like bullies. Edward Durell Stone hogs the city's loveliest site with his Brobdingnagian **John F. Kennedy Center for the Performing Arts.** Gordon Bunshaft built a Führer-Bunker on the Mall to house the **Hirshhorn Museum and Sculpture Garden.** The most brutally arrogant of the capital's new buildings, no doubt, is the **J. Edgar Hoover Building on Pennsylvania Avenue at Ninth Street, N.W.**

## PERIODS

Like art and fashion, architecture, of course, expresses the spirit of its period. Some periods seem more inspired than others. The first building to be constructed under the L'Enfant plan, the "President's Palace"—it was not officially called the **White House** until Teddy Roosevelt moved in—is a graceful neo-Palladian country house inspired by Jeffersonian civility. At that time civilization meant gentle manners and a quest for beauty, harmony, and knowledge. (Civilized men, however, condoned slavery.) Now civilization seems to mean perpetual progress—plumbing and pollution, megabombs and megastructures, Xerox and no-knock, pocket computers and psychological complexes. That, I'm afraid, is what the Hirshhorn and Hoover buildings express.

But then, the White House had no bathrooms in its first 78 years, and there was an awful fuss when Harry Truman added that balcony. The Hirshhorn is a marvel of engineered convenience and Bunshaft's Bunker has the biggest balcony in town. You just can't get out on it. *Verboten.* It interferes with the air conditioning.

When James Hoban, an Irishman practicing architecture in Charleston, South Carolina, won the $500 prize for the best design of the "President's House" in 1792, another architect, Benjamin Latrobe, called it "Hoban's pile—a litter of pigs worthy of the great sow it surrounds, and of the wild Irish boar, the father of her." Tastes change. Some future critic, no doubt, will like

Bunshaft's pile and the rest of the ill-mannered litter of modern monstrosities as much as I like Hoban's pile.

In any event, L'Enfant's plan absorbs it all—the changing styles and piles, the joys and follies, the deeds of hacks and land speculators and even highway builders. That says a lot for good planning, Appropriately enough, the best way to get a sense of the result is from **L'Enfant's grave**—his second one—on the crest of Arlington National Cemetery, a few steps south of the Custis-Lee Mansion. (*See* Chapter V, "Monuments and Memorials.")

Major Pierre Charles L'Enfant, born in France, trained as an artist, architect, and engineer, and volunteered in the American Revolutionary Army. His first grave was in Green Hill, Maryland, and what drove him to it was his dismissal less than a year after George Washington commissioned him to plan the capital. The General had had his portrait drawn by L'Enfant, during the Valley Forge winter of 1777–1778, and was impressed with his talents. Washington obviously liked L'Enfant's ideas for the new city, and he was reluctant to let him go, but the impetuous Frenchman left him no choice. L'Enfant continually refused to submit to the authority of the city commissioners. He simply demolished a house that was built where he did not want it. He procrastinated about getting maps printed that were needed to sell lots.

One hundred and seventeen years later, city commissioners stood solemnly around L'Enfant's exhumed remains, lying in state in a flag-draped casket in the Capitol Rotunda. President and Mrs. William Howard Taft, Vice President James Sherman, the French ambassador, senators, and representatives, paid their respects; so did thousands of people who most likely had hardly heard of L'Enfant. They all joined the grand funeral procession to Arlington Cemetery, where the French major was given full military honors. His city plan is carved on his tombstone.

As you can see across the river below, L'Enfant made nature part of his design. He fitted the city into a low plateau, rimmed by hills and the Potomac and Anacosti rivers. In the center of the plateau is Jenkins' Hill, which L'Enfant saw as "a pedestal waiting for a monument."

The monument is the **Capitol,** which dominates the entire composition and is the center and focus of Washington's geometry. L'Enfant envisioned a great water cascade tumbling down Jenkins' Hill and a grand avenue, a sort of Champs Elysées, lined with embassies, leading up to it. A mile and a quarter down that grand avenue, on the northern end of a cross axis, he located the capital's second most important building, the White House.

The city's geometry is a street grid on which diagonal avenues are superimposed. The Capitol marks the intersection of the grid's central north-south and east-west streets, and is also the focal point of the radiating avenues. The central streets are called North, South, and East Capitol Streets; what might have been West Capitol Street (L'Enfant's Champs Elysées) was turned into a greensward and is now the Mall.

The view from L'Enfant's tomb, or from the nearby overlook that is part of President John F. Kennedy's gravesite, will impress you with the simple, symbolic order of the federal city. Because of the tree-lined, radiating avenues, everything relates to the Capitol. Its domed majesty is enhanced by the green carpet rolling down to the river, with that incredible obelisk, the Washington Monument, as a dramatic centerpiece. The rim of green hills, accented by the Washington Cathedral and by the National Shrine of the Immaculate Conception, frames what is surely one of the world's finest urban compositions.

In one of those fits of megalomania that occasionally seize Washington planners, some Capitol architect proposed some years ago to continue the Mall on East Capitol and line it with government offices. The idea failed to enchant the residents of Capitol Hill, who are struggling, and with some success, to rehabilitate their neighborhood. The area has much of the charm, but less of the snob appeal, of Georgetown.

The Mall and the Capitol Streets divide the city into its northwest, southwest, northeast, and southeast quadrants. Each of them has its own alphabetical and numerical streets, each starting at the Capitol with its own A and First Streets. It is the simplest system ever invented to confuse innocent strangers, and if you don't remember your N.W. or N.E., you, your cab driver, and your mail are irretrievably lost.

The avenues are named after the States of the Union and L'Enfant conceived them as "lines of direct communications" between the city's most important buildings, providing what he called "a reciprocity of sight." This is a Renaissance idea, invented when artists proudly discovered perspective and architects hastened to build perspective lines into Renaissance cities. The idea was perfected by aristocratic French hunters, who found that by cutting straight clearings into the forests, they could spot game running from one wood to another. If these vistas intersected at acute angles, the hunter, standing at the intersection, could scan several pathways simultaneously. These *rond points,* as the French called them, became an important feature of baroque city planning. L'Enfant dotted the Washington cityscape with *rond points* circles and squares.

Every so often, some idiot comes along and claims that L'Enfant, Washington, and Jefferson planned all this so that, come the revolution, the establishment can shoot rebellious workers marching down the avenue, much as French noblemen shot game. The same has been said about the avenues Baron Haussmann planned under Napoleon III some 60 years later in Paris. There is no evidence to support his militaristic view in either case. No machine-gun emplacements have ever been seen at a *rond point,* although during the anti-Vietnam demonstrations President Nixon ordered the White House surrounded by a wall of bumper-to-bumper buses.

The Major's plan is not without flaws. The distance between the White House and the Capitol seems much too great, for instance, which may be why the intended reciprocal relationship is often lost. The small triangular parcels resulting from the combination of radial avenues and the street grid are awkward and often defeat the best efforts of architects and landscape architects.

L'Enfant never got around to suggesting what to do with the Potomac riverfront. He must have assumed that docks and harbor bustle would develop spontaneously, as they already had in Georgetown. But railroads replaced shipping, an aimless industrial mess took over, and before the planners did any serious planning, what should have been a lively park was turned into a visual battleground between the wormy Watergate complex and the corny Kennedy Center.

Oddly, L'Enfant forgot the **Supreme Court,** and maybe more oddly, neither Washington nor Jefferson and not even John Marshall reminded him. The court's logical location would have been opposite the White House, where the Jefferson Memorial now stands. The three branches of government would form a symbolic triangle. But this obvious idea seems never to have occurred to anyone. L'Enfant only once mentioned a specific site for what he called the "Judiciary Court," and that was in the context of such other buildings as "the national bank," "the grand church," "the play house," and the "market and exchange." L'Enfant's site for this Judiciary Court was to be on the present site of Judiciary Square, now bounded by Fourth and Fifth and D and E Streets, N.W.

But the Supreme Court was tucked away inside the Capitol instead. Early in this century, when Daniel Burnham and the McMillan Commission resurrected and reinterpreted the L'Enfant plan, they enlarged the monumental area around the Mall with landfill and created the Tidal Basin opposite the White House. But they placed the Jefferson Memorial behind it, rather than the Supreme Court. When the Court finally got a building of its own, in 1935, it was placed in the Capitol's backyard, next to the Library of Congress. The gleaming white solemnity of Cass Gilbert's Roman temple, however, makes up for the unimpressive address.

It has taken just about two centuries for the grand plan to take on the reality of a city. Washington is still not quite completed. It never will be if it stays alive. Like other organisms, a living city keeps changing and renewing itself. If Washington changes in a relatively orderly fashion, like a well-tended garden rather than a diseased jungle, we owe this not only to the genius of L'Enfant's basic structure but also to Jefferson's wisdom, "Boss" Alexander Robey Shepherd's ambition, and Daniel Burnham's "magic to stir men's blood."

Burnham's magic still sufficiently bewitches modern architects to keep them from disrupting the sort of planned order they have disrupted elsewhere. Periodically, a few businessmen and real estate speculators clamor for taller buildings. But not even the highway engineers have succeeded as yet in wrecking the traditional pattern, although they keep trying.

## JEFFERSONIAN CLASSIC

Jefferson, Shepherd, Burnham, and the moderns, who represent major phases in the development of the city, might also serve to categorize its architecture. Jeffersonian Classicism, Shepherdian Romanticism, Burnham Baroque, and Modern Mediocrity are no more arbitrary as categories of Washington's building styles than those you find in learned architectural history books. Architecture defies easy classification to begin with—no one can agree on the nomenclature. Therefore all I shall attempt is to point out some outstanding buildings that seem to me to sound the spirit of their time with sufficient distinction to contribute to the visual symphony of the city.

Because of Jefferson, the buildings are low and the symphony low-key. In notes on a discussion with President Washington about the new capital, dated November 29, 1790, Jefferson opposed setbacks of buildings from the street (they produce "a disgusting monotony") and favored a height limitation. "In Paris," he wrote, "it is forbidden to build a house beyond a given height, & it is admitted to be a good restriction, it keeps the houses low & convenient, & the streets light and airy, fires are much more managable where houses are low. This however is an object of Legislation."

The legislation was passed 120 years later. It was prompted not by Jefferson but by a dandy architect-developer named Thomas Franklin Schneider, known about town as "the young Napoleon." He built large numbers of flamboyant and very salable rowhouses in different parts of the city. One of the first to make use of high-rise steel-frame construction for a residence, he built the elegant **Cairo Hotel (1615 Q Street, N.W.)** in 1894, and appropriately decorated it with neo-Moorish ornamentation. It is 160 feet high.

This height shocked the neighbors and eventually led to the Act of 1910 in which Congress ordained that no building in the District of Columbia shall be higher than 20 feet plus the width of the street or avenue on which it stands. As always happens, the lawyers got into the act and complicated things no end. But basically, the "good restriction" prevails. Washington is a horizontal city and the **Capitol,** if not the town's tallest structure—that's still the Washington Monument—remains the capital's most dominant building.

The Capitol began with republican simplicity. The Greek and Roman classic style seemed as rational to Jefferson and the others as the decimal system they adopted for the new nation's currency. It offered the sense of proportion, the symmetry, and gracious refinements that their age of enlightenment brought to speech, manners, and dress. The design for the Capitol was obtained by a publicly announced design competition, still the best way to obtain the best possible design for a public building. The Capitol competition was won by William Thornton, a doctor, and, like Jefferson, an amateur in many of the arts. In those days, being an amateur (the word derives from *amare,* to love) was not deprecatingly taken to mean lacking in skill. It connoted, rather, an interest in, and often a talent for, a variety of pursuits.

The simple elegance of Dr. Thornton's design, executed in sandstone, still survives in the central portion of the Capitol's west front. The last two architects of the Capitol (George J. Stewart, 1959–1970, and George M. White, who succeeded him), supported by vandalistically inclined members of Congress, have proposed to bury Thornton's handsome sandstone façade behind a glossy marble expansion that would also destroy the magnificent terrace Frederick Law Olmsted designed in the 1870s. The architects argued successively that the Thornton façade is about to crumble, that more office space is needed, and that more tourists must be accommodated with cafeterias and public toilets. Experts have refuted all these arguments. What keeps saving us from the congressional edifice complex is not reason but lack of money, due to war, inflation, and recession. When we had a brief respite from all three under the presidency of Dwight D. Eisenhower, the Capitol architect promptly used the opportunity to puff out the East Front of the Capitol by $32^1/_2$ feet. To those who remember the dramatic old sandstone façade, all that gleaming white marble has a shallow gaudiness.

In 1803, Benjamin H. Latrobe, who was trained in England and Germany, took over Capitol construction. His work, interrupted by British arson in 1814, followed Thornton's design. Yet a somewhat richer, more ornate romanticism crept in, subtly reflecting the change in the nation's mood—the growth of American nationalism. Latrobe decorated the columns of the House and Senate chambers with American tobacco leaves and corn cobs, rather than Dorian and Corinthian motifs. No such corn, no conscious effort to create a specific American style of architecture was attempted again, except, perhaps, by Frank Lloyd Wright. Although it became increasingly romantic, federal architecture remained essentially Jeffersonian classic until nationalism, reinforced by steel, greased with oil, financed by ever-bigger banks, speeded by railroads, and tested in the torment of Civil War, arrived at unprecedented industrial power.

Symbolizing this power in painted cast-iron, Thomas Crawford's Statue of Freedom was placed atop the Capitol dome in

December, 1863. The dome itself is based on the dome of St. Peter's in Rome and was designed by Thomas Ustick Walter, who succeeded Charles Bulfinch as Capitol architect.

Most buildings that survived the ante-bellum period are around the White House. The oldest of them is Dr. Thornton's residence, the **Octagon House (1799 New York Avenue, N.W.),** skillfully designed in 1800 to turn one of L'Enfant's awkward corners. The house has historic interest because President Madison occupied it after the British had burned the White House. It has recently been restored by the American Institute of Architects, whose massive concrete-and-glass headquarters building gives the gentle house a crushing embrace.

Almost as old, equally simple and gentle are the **Blair-Lee House (1651 Pennsylvania Avenue, N.W.),** the guest house for visiting heads of state; the **Decatur House (northwest corner of Lafayette Square)** designed by Latrobe in 1818; and **St. John's (Sixteenth and H Streets, N.W.),** the church of Presidents, also designed by Latrobe, who was its first organist.

The old houses around Lafayette Square were about to be bulldozed in 1961. Their death warrant was already signed and working drawings for neo-neo-classic office buildings were already completed, when President John F. Kennedy, newly elected and nudged by his wife, asked architect John Carl Warnecke to propose a better solution. Warnecke saved the houses by placing the needed office buildings *behind* them. Simple. As the American Institute of Architects' *Guide to the Architecture of Washington* (McGraw-Hill, $7.95, and highly recommended) put it, the tall new structures—the New Executive Office Building and the U.S. Court of Claims—are still more dominant than one might have wished, but "the scale and fabric of Lafayette Square were not only saved but enhanced."

Of Washington's large government department buildings, the oldest—the **Treasury (1500 Pennsylvania Avenue, N.W.)**—is also one of the finest, with a handsome colonnade marching down a whole block of Fifteenth Street. The trouble is that it is in the wrong place. It obliterates L'Enfant's vista and hinders direct communication from Capitol to White House. The culprit is Andrew Jackson. He got impatient after Congress had bickered about the site for two years, stomped out of the White House, pounded his cane on the ground, and said, "Build it here."

Now the inaugural parade must make a ludicrous turn up Fifteenth to find Pennsylvania Avenue again and pass the White House reviewing stand. For a decade, an august commission appointed by President Kennedy to raise the status of Pennsylvania Avenue, headed by architect Nathaniel Owing, labored to correct Jackson's mistake. The solution Owing's group proposed was not to tear down the Treasury, which would have been sacrilege, but to tear down the Washington and Willard hotels, the National Theatre, the National Press Club, and a great many buildings in between, which would have been insane. Nor would that have straightened the quadrennial parade route. No one wanted Owing's "National Square" and the proposal finally collapsed under its own fatuity. A different Pennsylvania Avenue Development Corporation is now proposing nothing much more than to spruce up the place a bit, which is what should have been done all along.

Construction of the **Old Patent Office (Seventh and G Streets, N.W.)** was started in 1836, shortly before the Treasury. Robert Mills, the Treasury architect, who had worked as a draftsman for both Jefferson and Latrobe, also helped design the Patent Office. The porticos are purported to be exact reproductions of those of the Parthenon. But you can admire this only on the north façade. On the south, highway engineers sheared off the Periclean flight of steps in 1936 to Widen F Street for more automobile traffic. In 1969, the Patent Office was converted to house both the National Portrait Gallery and National Collection of Fine Arts.

In 1836, Robert Mills also designed what, in my view, turned out to be one of the most inspiring structures in all Christendom—the **Washington Monument, on the Mall.** At 555 feet and $5^1/_8$ inches it is also the tallest masonry structure ever built. Because of soil conditions, it was built some 100 yards southwest of the center of L'Enfant's geometric cross-axis, and every so often some geologist gets a big fit and a small headline predicting that the grand obelisk is tilting or sinking. All kinds of absurd political controversies and financial difficulties haunted and halted construction of this monument for decades—you can still see evidence of this in the change in color in the stone. Mills' idea of a circular neo-Greek peristyle temple, topped with statues of heroically snorting horses and such, fell by the wayside, but no one seems to miss it. I, for one, could also do without the circle of flags tickling the base of this great shaft.

The last notable building in the city's first half century is no longer classic but wholly romantic—the **Smithsonian "Castle"** on the Mall. Like the Treasury, it should not be where it is, encroaching on the grand vista, at **Jefferson Drive between Ninth and Twelfth Streets, N.W.** But it encroaches with such endearing charm that even the most severe pedants are inclined to forgive its trespassing.

The "castle," designed by James Renwick in 1849, is the first building of the Smithsonian Institution. It houses its administration as well as a family of owls that Dr. Ripley, the secretary of the Smithsonian, settled in the big tower some years ago. The fairy-tale gothic structure, with its turrets, towers, rosettes, pointed arches and ivy, seems made for owls.

But in case congressmen should have failed to fancy the gothic structure, Renwick had a Romanesque model of the same building prepared. A decade later he designed the city's first art gallery for William Wilson Corcoran now known as the **Renwick Gallery (Seventeenth Street and Pennsylvania Avenue, N.W.)** in French renaissance style. (After the Civil War, Corcoran built the present, bigger **Corcoran Gallery of Art** at **Seventeenth and New York Avenue, N.W.**) To architects like Renwick, style was somewhat like clothing. What mattered to them was the body and soul of their buildings. The Renwick, which served for many years as Court of Claims, was saved from demolition by President Johnson in the late 1960s and is now beautifully restored.

---

### SHEPHERD'S ROMANTIC ERA

In Washington, the Civil War was followed by what many called the "uncivil war," a period of corruption in the White House and in Congress and of municipal squabbles in the city. There was talk of moving the capital to the Mississippi Valley. Congress stilled it by appropriating millions for the State, War and Navy Building. Alexander Robey Shepherd stilled it by modernizing the city.

"Boss" Shepherd, who headed the Board of Public Works from 1871 to 1874, was possessed by the same dictatorial abandon as Baron Haussmann in Paris before him and Robert Moses in New York after him. His distinction was that Haussmann and Moses took decades to transform their cities, while Boss Shepherd did it in three years. He laid miles upon miles of sewers and water mains, graded and paved even more miles of streets, built sidewalks, erected streetlights, planted 16,000 trees, and bankrupted the city. The streets and sewers started an unprecedented building boom, and the trees not only shaded, but also hid, the buildings. That deficit has long been forgotten.

The **State, War and Navy Building (Pennsylvania Avenue and Seventeenth Street, N.W.)** turned out to be glorious. It was designed in 1871 by A. B. Mullett in the French Second Empire style, with granite columns piled upon columns. In its day it was the largest office building in the world. It was also denounced as being "without question the ugliest if not smuggest mass of masonry in Washington." Serious architects suggested that the building be wrapped in a neo-classic façade to match the Treasury on the other side of the White House.

The building, now called the Old Executive Office Building, houses White House staff, the Council of Economic Advisers, the National Security Council, and other agencies. Security keeps out sunshine and tourists. The gilded sumptuousness of the Indian Treaty Room, the cast-iron showboat exuberance of the State, Army, and Navy libraries, and all the other trappings, exemplify the gauche and gaudy grandeur of the gaslit era of Ulysses S. Grant.

Most architecture historians still, somewhat contemptuously, call this era "late Victorian," although the grouchy old Queen would hardly have been amused by all this boisterous American grandiloquence. Earlier in this century, "modernists" had nearly convinced us that it was all terrible. But now just about everyone has come to love the old buildings of that era—and young people in particular fight for their preservation.

The **Old Pension Building (Fifth and G Streets, N.W.),** a nicely proportioned red brick palazzo, does not seem grandiloquent until you enter—and gasp. Here is Washington's most dazzling interior space. The building, it turns out, is much like a barn—an excuse for one big astonishing hall. It was a favorite place for inaugural balls. Now it is temporarily used by the District Courts.

For all its granite massiveness, the **Old Post Office (Twelfth Street and Pennsylvania Avenue, N.W.)** has been destined to die for most of its life. It was designed in 1899 by W. Edbrooke in the Romanesque chateau style that H. H. Richardson had created a little earlier. In the 1920s, the builders of the Federal Triangle ordained its demolition for yet another segment of their planned bureaucratic labyrinth. The now constructed nine-block **Federal Triangle, bounded by Pennsylvania Avenue on the north and Constitution Avenue on the south, extends from the Commerce Department at its base, at Fifteenth Street, to the Federal Trade Commission at its apex, at Sixth Street.** The skyward thrusting Old Post Office Building stood near the center of this planned low-level triangular complex of red-tiled government buildings, and in fact finally prevented completion of a grand plaza between the Internal Revenue and Post Office Department buildings.

In the 1960s, President Kennedy's Pennsylvania Avenue Commission began the moment of truth for the Old Post Office Building. It proposed to kill the building, saving only the tower for a trophy, like the ear of a *toro*. Present hopes are to preserve the *toro* in toto. The lower stories and the enclosed court are to be converted into a tourist center with shops, restaurants, entertainment, and displays. The upper floors are to serve as offices for the National Foundation on the Arts and similar organizations.

The Shepherd period gave Washington more than romantic big buildings. It gave shape to the city. Between the Capitol and the White House, stores, theaters, banks, restaurants, and hotels began to form themselves into a "downtown." Most of these buildings were richer in imagery and uninhibited eclecticism than the usual "Victorian" architecture. Far too many of them have been paved over into parking lots or mutilated by "modernistic" façades. Among my favorite survivors are the **Franklin School,** built in 1868 by Adolph Cluss **(Thirteenth and K Streets, N.W.)** and the recently remodeled **National Savings and Trust Company (Fifteenth Street and New York Avenue, N.W.),** designed in 1880 by James Windrim, whose whimsical little turret seems to thumb its nose at the Treasury across the street.

The old downtown, or Central Business District, as the planners call it, was never worthy of a great capital. But Washington's downtown residential neighborhoods were once as pleasant as the well-to-do residential areas west of Sixteenth Street are now.

Boss Shepherd's paved streets and sewers and the growing federal bureaucracy attracted a number of men who had made their fortune out West and invested it in congressional seats and/or Washington real estate. They developed rowhouses by the block, most of them of charming and varied design, adorned with turrets and gables and all manner of iron and plaster ornaments ordered from builder's catalogs. As Shepherd's trees had grown to meet at their crown, many streets were like the naves of green cathedrals. They were free of unseemly traffic as coal, ice, and groceries were delivered from the alleys.

Elegant mansions clustered around **Logan Circle (Thirteenth Street and Vermont Avenue, N.W.)** whence they marched westward to Dupont Circle and beyond, as well as north, up Sixteenth Street. The sturdiest of them have survived as embassies. The oldest of them were saved by neglect: the Logan Circle area became so delinquent so fast that even the bulldozers would not enter. There are now efforts to restore it. Much of Shepherdian Washington, in fact, could still be rehabilitated, though its civilized style of living is probably irretrievable.

The poor, to be sure, lived in unspeakable "alley dwellings," sordid shacks without plumbing, which unscrupulous landlords put up in the alleys. Many were in the shadow of the Capitol, which gave a picture of America more often seen in the Communist press abroad than the capitalist papers at home. The alley dwellings were finally cleared in the 1950s by a process called "urban renewal," which succeeded admirably in pushing the slums from one end of town to another.

Life in Washington most likely reached its civilized apogee in Boss Shepherd's time. One got around most comfortably on a network of clanking streetcars, which took people to work as well as out into the country, as far as Chevy Chase and even Kensington, now considered practically in town. There was a farmers' market offering fresh produce in every district. Butchers, bakers, and milkmen delivered, and fresh fish could (and still can) be had down at the Maine Avenue waterfront. There were numerous theaters and other diversions. High ceilings and big fans in houses and offices got people through Washington's sticky summers. Malaria declined as the swamps were drained.

### BURNHAM BAROQUE

Only the Mall left much to be desired when, in 1900, Daniel Burnham and many of the nation's architects met to celebrate the capital's centennial. Architects of that era studied at the École des Beaux Arts in Paris, which advanced a somewhat pompous style of ornate classicism. The Burnham group had applied this lesson elsewhere in a picturesque temple city of white plaster, mirrored in a grand lagoon, which housed the Chicago Columbian Exposition of 1893.

This World's Fair stage set inspired the "City Beautiful" movement and its civic centers all across America. In Washington, in 1901, it inspired even more: a Senate "park commission," headed by Senator James McMillan of Michigan, which produced a grand plan and, eventually, the capital's picture postcard image.

L'Enfant had been fired before he could even think of translating his plan into three dimensions. The missing dimension was added by the McMillan group, led by Burnham, landscape architect Frederick Law Olmsted, Jr. (the son of the designer of New York's Central Park), architect Charles Follen McKim, and sculptor Augustus Saint-Gaudens. Theirs was a complete work of art on an urban scale. A large model of their ambitious scheme is still in the attic of the Fine Arts Commission, which contines to supervise the execution of the plan.

The Mall was a mess when the McMillan Commission finally went to work in 1910. It was a boggy meadow crisscrossed by muddy trails that led to a scattering of buildings, a bit of landscaping around the Smithsonian and the White House, a smoke-belching railway station at the foot of the Capitol, and malarial swamps along the river shore. Nothing less than an era of national optimism—a time of unbounded faith in progress, the blessings of wealth and education, and the righteousness of America's cause; the time of Teddy Roosevelt, John D. Rockefeller, John Dewey, and Woodrow Wilson—could have transformed this mess into an impressive cityscape. The auspicious beginning sustained the work through two World Wars and a Great Depression. Now, with luck, we shall soon see another row of trees and more cafes, carousels, and bicycle trails on the Mall, and the courts, or something, will stop an outrageous proposal to dig an eight-lane freeway trench under the Lincoln Memorial.

The architecture Washington owes to the stern maîtres of the École des Beaux Arts is well mannered. Though often pompous and always boastfully monumental, it still relates to people and human proportions and sensibilities, in contrast to late twentieth century buildings, which are designed to the length of steel beams and the capabilities of giant cranes.

The first Beaux Arts building in Washington is also, I think, the best of that school. No other building in Washington turns the corner so elegantly as the **Willard Hotel.** The corner is that of **Pennsylvania Avenue and Fourteenth Street, N.W.** The Pennsylvania Avenue Commission wanted to tear it down, a proposal that more than anything else led to the demolition of the Commission. Designed in 1901 by Henry Hardenbergh, who also designed the Plaza Hotel in New York City, the Willard was followed in 1902 by the former **Central Library (Eighth and K Streets, N.W.)** and in 1908 by the **District Building (at Pennsylvania Avenue and Fourteenth Street, N.W.).**

Daniel H. Burnham and his friends had been in Europe to seek inspiration for the McMillan plan at Versailles, Fontainebleau, Hampton Court, Schönbrunn, and other royal palaces. In London, Burnham met with Alexander J. Cassatt, the president of the Pennsylvania Railroad, and talked Cassatt into (a) removing his railroad station from the Mall and (b) letting him build a new railroad terminal close to the Capitol. The resulting **Union Station, Massachusetts and Delaware Avenues, N.E.,** is a noble and very Roman building also housing the National Visitor's Center. A new railroad terminal and garages are being constructed behind it.

The flexibility of the Beaux Arts style is demonstrated by the **Pan American Union (Seventeenth Street and Constitution Avenue, N.W.),** designed by Paul Cret in 1910. It blends North and South American motifs into a charming building whose interior patio is exceptionally delightful.

There are few, if any, such delights in the rest of the massive Beaux Arts buildings that make up Washington's monumental core. Considering that they were built over a period of more than half a century, they vary relatively little. The **National Archives (Eighth Street and Constitution Avenue, N.W.),** designed in 1935 by John Russell Pope, with a smaller site and different purpose than most, is one of the few with a distinctive configuration. **The Museum of History and Technology (Constitution Avenue at Fourth Street, N.W.),** built in 1960, was scraped of all classic columns, pediments, and trimmings, and it looks embarrassed in its nudity. On the other hand, the **Sam Rayburn House Office Building (Independence Avenue and First Street, N.W.),** built in 1965, is overdressed in oversized columns, pediments, cornucopias, and other marble ostentations, which would be only ludicrous if they were not so revoltingly gauche. The best of the lot, no doubt, is J. R. Pope's **National Gallery,** designed in 1942 **(Constitution Ave-**

nue at Sixth Street, N.W.). It not only serves its purpose well, but also has in its halls and rotundas the elegance the others are lacking.

The National Gallery has a second building that provides an essay in concise architectural geometry, of which its designer, I. M. Pei, is a master. The **Air and Space Museum,** across the Mall **(Independence Avenue at Seventh Street, S.W.),** shows less aesthetic promise. The difficulty may be that, for all of L'Enfant's monumental dimensions, the Mall is not the place for an airplane hangar.

## MODERN TIMES

Which brings us to modern architecture. It came late to Washington. The climate here is not receptive to innovation—the government hates to depart from traditional ways, and when it comes to private tastes and aspirations, this is a small town. The speculative office buildings along K Street, west of Connecticut Avenue, must be among the ugliest buildings ever.

The best modern architecture in town is found in the southwest urban-renewal area. The apartments and townhouses by Washington architects Keyes, Lethbridge & Condon, and Chloethiel Smith, are among the most handsome in the country. Harry Weese's **Arena Stage (Sixth and M Streets, S.W.)** is a jewel in concrete. But the new waterfront with its seafood restaurants is a disaster area, which replaced a smelly and lovely fish market and marina. (A few fishstands are left more or less by accident.)

Another planning disaster is **L'Enfant Plaza, along the Tenth Street Mall, between Independence Avenue and the Maine Avenue waterfront,** also a product of the urban renewal mania of the 1960s. Conceived by I. M. Pei, in 1965, with its buildings designed by Araldo Cossutta and Vlastimil Koubek, the Plaza is a ceremonial stage set without actors. The reason there is and can be no action is that the Forrestal Building, a sorry mediocrity, spans that Tenth Street Mall (which leads nowhere), effectively cutting off L'Enfant Plaza from the rest of the city. To make matters worse, the Plaza's shops have been buried. Only a hotel gives this necropolis an occasional flicker of life.

One of Washington's few handsome office buildings in the modern style is behind L'Enfant Plaza: the **Department of Housing and Urban Development (451 Seventh Street, S.W.),** designed in 1968 by Marcel Breuer. The rest, particularly the most recent crop—the new **FBI Building, Pennsylvania Avenue between Ninth and Tenth Streets, N.W.,** the **Labor Department Building, Constitution Avenue and Second Street, N.W.,** and the **U.S. Tax Court, Second and D Streets, N.W.** (at the edge of a freeway canyon)—express architecturally what Senator William Fulbright called the "arrogance of power" that has characterized American government in the past few decades.

One of the best modern buildings is the **Martin Luther King Jr. Memorial Library (901 G Street, N.W.)** designed in 1972 by Mies van der Rohe. This major work by the internationally important architect would not have happened without the efforts of William Walton, a painter and friend of President Kennedy, who persuaded the city commissioners that just one really outstanding government building could not possibly do any harm. Another handsome new building is I. M. Pei's **East Building of the National Gallery (Pennsylvania Avenue and Third Street, N.W.)** with its knife-sharp angles jutting out with clean elegance.

Frank Lloyd Wright designed two interesting private houses in this area: the **Pope-Leighey House,** which was moved to **Woodlawn Plantation near Mount Vernon** to save it from the highway bulldozers; **his son's house** at **7927 Deepwell Drive** in suburban **Bethesda, Maryland.** Walter Gropius' firm designed businessman **John Hechinger's house on Chain Bridge Road.** A gem among moderns is Philip Johnson's **Pre-Columbian Museum, Dumbarton Oaks, 1703 Thirty-second Street, N.W.,** designed in 1963. A tiny pavilion of marble, teak, and bronzed glass, it is as exquisite as the ancient treasures it displays.)

To see and experience what may well be the most livable historic urban environment in the country, take a stroll through Georgetown. (*See* Chapter XX, "Walking Tours: Georgetown.") Contrary to legend, the houses are predominantly Victorian rather than Colonial or Federal. The most intriguing place architecturally in Georgetown may be **Canal Square (1054 Thirty-first Street, N.W.)** where architect Arthur Cotton Moore in 1972 incorporated an old canalside warehouse into a lively commercial center. One of the most attractive Georgetown houses is at **1350 Twenty-seventh Street, N.W.,** and was designed by Hugh Newell Jacobsen. It shows that there is no need to compromise to fit a modern house into a historic setting.

To see that today's builders and architects can also create a livable environment, if only they try, drive out to **Reston, Virginia,** a new community planned in 1963 by Whittlesey and Conklin.

To see and experience a building whose lean, functional beauty is unmatched in the Washington area, visit the **Dulles International Airport terminal,** designed in 1962 by Eero Saarinen. It shows that the architecture of our time can be as good as any. I think L'Enfant and Jefferson would approve of it.

# X

# Archives and Libraries

## By Christopher Dickey

The world is on file in Washington, available, open to the public, in *hundreds* of libraries. Read the intimate letters of George Washington or listen to the gut-music of Huddie "Leadbelly" Ledbetter singing in his penitentiary cell. See the Civil War in 3-D, discover your ancestors in an old census, or watch ancient movies until you forget the meaning of daylight. Historical, cultural, geographical horizons open up. Here is Goering's scrapbook, or the finer points of gardening, unlimited knowledge.

The weight of the information is on government and economics. There is a great deal you can learn here about defense analysis and, at one time, how to make an atom bomb. But there is also a library for astrologers and one for railroad men. Architects and the Scottish Rite Supreme Council, the Daughters of the American Revolution and the National Zoo, the Red Cross and the Textile Museum, all have collections of reference material and all make them available to the public one way or another. The embassies, the lobbies, and the universities have quantities of books. The District of Columbia has a sizable public library system, as does every county in the greater Washington area. And there are three ultimate information warehouses: the Library of Congress, where you can find out something about virtually anything; the National Archives, where the Declaration of Independence, the Constitution, and the Bill of Rights are on display, and the best of the bureaucracy's red tape is in storage, available to scholars; and the Folger Shakespeare Library, which lets tourists glimpse and scholars explore the whole of the Renaissance.

Few of these libraries or "media centers" will let visitors take books or other materials out of the building. But many of the

Christopher Dickey is a member of *The Washington Post* Metropolitan staff.

buildings are wonderful in themselves, and in this perpetually unfinished city full of jackhammers, torn streets, and hot air, the reading rooms are oases of quiet, cool, and thought.

---

## THE LIBRARY OF CONGRESS

*" . . . of making books there is no end."*

ECCLESIASTES 12:12

**First Street between East Capitol and Independence Avenue, S.E.; 426-5000.** Open Monday–Friday 8:30 A.M.–9:30 P.M., Saturday 8:30–5.

In 1814 the British marched into Washington to teach America a lesson. They burned the White House and the Capitol and incinerated, among other things, the congressional library. It also happens that in 1814 Thomas Jefferson, leading the life of a retired President and patriarch at Monticello, had pretty well run out of money. He offered to sell Congress a better library than it had had before—his own.

There had always been some question in Congress whether an official library was worth having. A good many Americans thought of books, especially for congressmen, as a frivolous squandering of the taxpayer's money. Weren't congressmen supposed to be well informed *before* they took office? The reasoning ran something like that. Up until the conflagration of 1814, only 3,000 books had been collected in the Capitol, their content limited basically to law, history, and quotable literature. Jefferson was offering nearly 6,500 volumes collected over a lifetime of humanistic study: history and law, but also philosophy, science, "works of the imagination," and a few books with a decidedly atheistical bent. Some representatives thought this a bit much. But Jefferson argued that "there is, in fact, no subject to which a Member of Congress may not have occasion to refer." And, not quite so simply as that, and only by a narrow margin, Congress approved the purchase.

Under a succession of librarians the collection grew and gradually opened up to non-members of Congress. In 1863, President Lincoln appointed Ainsworth Rand Spofford as Librarian; Spofford had a goal, a national library, and he knew how to get it. By 1870 the Copyright Office had been assigned to the Library of

Congress, and with it came a deluge of material to be copyrighted. Soon Spofford literally had more books that he knew what to do with, and the collections were beginning to squeeze congressmen out of the Capitol. The library no longer had to struggle for an identity, but it had to battle for space. It was time for new quarters.

### The Buildings

When the outside of the congressional library was finished in 1897, the dome was covered with gold and there were those in the city who thought it rivaled the white iron Capitol for prominence on the Hill. The collections, and the structure, too, had been built by strong-willed, self-assured men who were fiercely proud of what they had done and what they planned to do. The building was the epitome of culture, as they saw it. The style was Italian renaissance, 400 years after the Medici. The craftsmen were all American. The structure was vast, and they thought it would house the world's accumulated knowledge for a century to come. The whole building gleamed with that sense of pride and possibility that would later let us think we could make the world safe for democracy. It is elaborate and innocent, like Disneyland or a good, old movie about the future.

By the 1930s space had run out and a new building was going up behind the old. Now, a third vast structure scheduled to open in 1980 (the James Madison Memorial Building) is rising across Independence Avenue.

But walk toward the old building from the Capitol, and try to take in the whole thing. The dome no longer glitters. The gold faded during the Depression and was removed. It might have been restored, but the building had grown a little dingy, too, and it was thought a newly gilded dome would clash. Now the copper, in its place, has turned green. But there is still an exciting and amusing opulence about the bulding, and inside, a fine extravagance about the vastness of its collections.

Look at the wildly decorated lampposts, and, near the street, the violent and powerful Neptune fountain with its nude women astride thrashing horse-fish. Walk up the steps above the fountain and stone faces peer from all over the front of the building. Multiracial keystones sullenly watch the driveway, classically robed women languish above the arches, the busts of literary greats stare down from the "bull's-eye" windows as cherubs irreverently dance and lounge around them. Up at the top of the façade, straining Atlantes support granite children watched over by a granite eagle.

Between the grim-faced Atlantes there are balconies. At the one on the left, above the bust of Emerson, there might sometimes be a living face. The Poetry Consultant has his office there, and since the 1950s Randall Jarrell, Robert Frost, James Dickey, and Stanley Kunitz, among others, have looked over Washington from that window.

The best way for visitors to enter the building is through the revolving doors on the ground floor. To the left is the information desk, where tours start every hour on the hour, Monday through Friday, from 9 to 4 (more or less precisely depending on which of the guides is giving them). To the right of the entrance is a place for hats and coats and a set of free lockers where briefcases, purses, shopping bags and the like can be stowed away to save the trouble of having them searched later. You may have to wait a little for the tour, but do take the tour. Each one is an original experience, there is no set script, and only the guides can get you into the library's heart and soul—the stacks.

Behind the desk on the ground floor there is a lobby where, from April to about Labor Day, pictures taken by the White House News Photographers are on display. They cover a great deal more than just the antics of the President. As fine journalism, art, and a summation of the past year, these photographs are as good as the best of *Life* used to be.

An elevator at the rear of the lobby rises to the visitor's gallery high above the eight-sided expanse of the Main Reading Room. From here you can gaze down at the readers far below, perching or pacing among the concentric rings of dark old desks. At the center of everything is the issue desk and away on the other side a massive array of card catalogues stretches out of sight into the next three rooms. The catalogues hint at the quantity of things kept here. The collections are incomprehensibly enormous and multiplying all the time, inexorably approaching 100 million pieces. Thousands of books and other items come in every day, several every minute, from hundreds of countries in 460 different languages, a whole litany of numbers. Much of the library's bureaucracy is wholly involved with winnowing through this avalanche for what is worth keeping. Some goes to the stacks, some to microfilm, some is traded for more useful material, and some is given away. Not everything, by any means, is kept. But there is enough.

The Library of Congress has Jefferson's original draft of the Declaration of Independence, covered with corrections, deletions, and additions as well as an occasional emendation scribbled by John Adams or Benjamin Franklin. Lincoln's draft of the Gettysburg Address is at the library too, written on a piece of Executive Mansion stationery, not the back of an envelope. Both these documents used to be displayed among other memorabilia in the exhibits on the second floor, but now, in the interests of preserving the paper, they are stashed away in climate-controlled vaults opened only to the most insistent scholars. Unfortunately, only copies are available for the public's eyes.

Grandiose stairways sweep down to the floor of the Great Hall. Nearby, rococo corridors branch off north and south, to administrative offices and the Congressional Research Service. The CRS is the official *raison d'être* of the library. Every year it answers hundreds of thousands of requests for information from senators and representatives, proving conclusively that Jefferson was right, there is "no subject to which a Member of Congress may not have occasion to refer."

Around the periphery of this huge lobby are a number of small exhibits, and under the vaulted mosaic ceilings near the doors of the Reading Room are two attractions really worth seeing: a couple of Bibles made in Mainz, Germany, 40 years before Columbus discovered America. They are in Latin, unintelligible to most, but no one would doubt they bear the word of God. One was handlettered by a single scribe. It took him fifteen months of continuous work to get from Genesis to the Apocalypse, but the calligraphy is so perfect and precise it seems a marvel he did it so quickly. The scribe may not have known it, but the modern world of mass production was on the verge of overtaking him: the other volume, produced at the same time, is one of the first books ever printed with moveable type, and one of the finest, a Gutenberg Bible. There are only two others like it in the world.

Five hundred years after these volumes were created they remain in better condition than books printed fifty years ago. They were done on vellum, which is goatskin, and which lasts. Modern paper, especially from the beginning of this century, is self-destroying. The basic problem with it is blind progress. New

The Library of Congress' first dinner party in history, in 1973. The reading room of the Library of Congress; students in large numbers bone up during their year-end holidays, 1961.

techniques developed in the middle of the 1800s allowed paper to be manufactured in previously unimagined quantities, enabling a much wider dissemination of reading materials and giving frustrated writers a chance to play wastepaper basketball. But the new techniques also created an acid residue in the paper which, over a period of years, turns it brown and brittle and finally into dust. New, more durable, papers are being developed and old manuscripts can often be "de-acidified" and laminated between protective sheets of acetate and tissue. But with bound volumes such steps are not possible, and as a result it has been estimated that at least 97 per cent of the books printed between 1900 and 1939 will be usable for less than fifty years. So much for the immortality of the printed word.

For people with the time and interest, the library's facilities are nearly limitless; even the most casual visitor could spend a day in each major division of the Library of Congress and feel fascinated and unfulfilled, because the more you find the more there is you seem to need to find. What begins as casual interest soon becomes an obsessive search. Before you know it, you have begun to take on the mentality of a detective, and what you are doing is the work of a scholar.

## THE NATIONAL ARCHIVES

Exhibit Hall entrance on **Constitution Avenue at Eighth Street, N.W.; 523-3099; recorded message of events—523-3000.** Open Monday–Saturday 9–6, Sunday 1–6. In the summer months open every day until 10.

The National Archives Building is like a mausoleum, half shrine and half safe-deposit box. Up the vast gray steps from Constitution Avenue and behind the portico of towering Corinthian columns is the biggest pair of bronze doors in the world. They slide shut like an enormous vault when the building closes. Inside, enshrined in the Exhibit Hall, are the three original charters of American freedom and justice: the Declaration of Independence, the Constitution, and the Bill of Rights.

A great show is made of keeping them safe. Behind the bronze doors and the brass gates and the armed guards, the pieces of parchment are sealed in inert helium, more brass, glass, dim yellow light, and black and white marble; in effect, embalmed, so paper and ink will not deteriorate any more than they already have. To one side of the Exhibit Hall is a working model of the gargantuan machine that lowers the documents into a sealed vault every night and raises them again in the morning, thus keeping the parchment and the ink on it safe from just about everything but A-bombs.

The building as a whole is a bland, blatant attempt to generate awe through design and decoration. The statues around the exterior are heavy and muscular in elephantine, inhuman ways; dull allegory is rampant—the past is an old man with a closed book, the future is a woman with an open book; facing Pennsylvania Avenue there are stone "Guardians of the Portal" dressed in Roman armor beside the business entrance; there are even cow skulls carved above some of the windows. On the inside of the rotunda are murals of stuffy looking founding fathers receiving the Declaration and the Constitution with such gravity they might be attending the death of a nation instead of its birth.

There is one nice little touch, though, right in front of the documents' shrine: a little step made of scroll-worked marble for children to stand on one by one and behold the documents and try to understand.

The Constitution has five pages, but only the two bearing the preamble and the signatures are on display. Beside them is the Bill of Rights. The words are faded, but still endure and can be read. But the Declaration of Independence, which stands vertically, hermetically sealed, above them (with little bronze doors all its own), is so faded and so far from the viewer that only a few words and letters are discernible even to those who know the first paragraphs by heart. People ask why the Declaration has faded so much over the years. There is no single explanation. It has been stored everywhere from a cloth bag in an empty house to a bombproof vault at Fort Knox. It has gotten wet, it has been in the sun, it has taken a beating, not because people did not care about it, but because they did. They wanted to see it, and until twentieth century technology came to its aid, there was no way to display the parchment and save it at the same time. Though some of the measures are extreme and silly (it was moved from the Library of Congress to the Archives in an armored tank), and there is little to look at any more, people find comfort knowing that the original Declaration still exists. Faded or not, it remains a symbol of liberty and equality in America.

On the sides of the Constitution and Declaration there are long, curving display cases where less famous papers representing "The Formation of the Union" are on exhibit: some of the journals of the Continental Congress, Washington's letter reporting the victory at Yorktown, the Treaty of Paris, which ended the Revolution, even Washington's own printed copy of the Constitution with notes he scribbled in the margins. If you can ignore the quasi-religiousness of your surroundings, you can sense through these documents something of what the people in 1776 felt—the exhilaration, but also the indecision and insecurity—before they were old heroes, before they were demigods, even before they were "founding fathers."

### Expeditions, Statistics, and A Great Deal More

The other half of the building, the "business half," is entered from Pennsylvania Avenue. Here, after signing in with a security guard, it is possible with minimal credentials to wade through considerable red tape and acquiring of ID cards, and eventually to delve into census records before 1900, explore the military records of your forebears, and generally (aside from the quantities of information restricted by law) peruse the ultimate results of all the paper-shuffling for which the bureaucracy is famous.

But there is more. The government has sponsored a great many expeditions and enterprises with the intent of recording what is going on in America and the world. The resulting reports are on file here, along with millions of photographs, and finally, movies. There is a "Hollywood on the Potomac," an assortment of movie-making government agencies intent on documentation, instruction, and persuasion. They produce films about toothbrushing, transportation, nerve gas, and the American Revolution. These, and other movies, wind up in the Archives.

In addition to the material officially produced in the U.S., the Archives have a sizable assortment of items officially confiscated by the American Armed Services during World War II. As elsewhere in the city, Nazi memorabilia abound, including the collections of the official Nazi photographer and his assistant, Eva Braun, who was noted for her rather intimate knowledge of the Führer. Her pictures suggest that old Adolf could look as innocuous and silly as anybody else. And then there is a quota of atrocity snapshots. The audio-visual department is not particularly free with its materials, but a casual visitor can see compilation films produced from the Archives' collections and shown, free to the public, several times a year.

---

### IF YOUR INTERESTS ARE SPECIAL

**Martin Luther King Jr. Memorial Library, 901 G Street, N.W., 727-1111.** This is the main branch of the District of Columbia Public Libraries. The building, designed by Mies van der Rohe, stands near the National Portrait Gallery and the National Collection of Fine Arts. Parking facilities are available underneath. Its collections and facilities are extensive, but if there is something you wish to find that is not there, you can refer to their copy of *Library and Reference Facilities in the Area of the District of Columbia,* ninth edition, and instantly be in touch with all the specialized information centers in the city. Of the nearly 500 that exist, these are a few of the more accessible and unusual:

• To find out more about the city—the **Columbia Historical Society Library, 1307 New Hampshire Avenue, N.W., 785-2068,** a quirky and seemingly disorganized collection of wonderfully detailed information about the history of the capital.

• To find out about your personal history—in addition to the relevant sections of the Library of Congress and the National Archives, there are valuable genealogy collections at the **National Society of the Daughters of the American Revolution Library** ($1 a day fee), **1776 D Street, N.W., 628-4980;** the **National Genealogical Society Library, 1921 Sunderland Place, N.W.** (near Dupont Circle), **785-2123;** and the **Society of the Cincinnati,** in marvelous old Anderson House at **2118 Massachusetts Avenue, N.W., 785-2040.**

• To find out about life, liberty and the pursuit of happiness—the **B'nai B'rith Women Four Freedoms Library, 1640 Rhode Island Avenue, N.W., 857-6600,** offers 7,000 volumes about the evolution of freedom and liberation movements, utopias, cooperatives, labor movements, socialism, Marxism and communism.

• To find out about Africa and its impact on America—Howard University's **Mooreland-Spingarn Research Center, Sixth and College Streets, N.W., 636-7239,** offers world-renowned facilities for the study of black culture and heritage; the **Frederick**

**Douglass Museum of African Art Library, 318 A Street, N.E., 547-7424,** is built around some 100,000 pieces of photography by Eliot Elisofon.

• To find out about native Americans—the **National Anthropological Archives** in the **Smithsonian Museum of Natural History, Room 60A, Tenth Street and Constitution Avenue, N.W., 628-4422,** offers the largest single collection in the country, including 50,000 photographs, relating to American Indians and the anthropologists who have studied them.

• To find out about farms and farmers—the biggest agricultural library in the world, including the not-to-be-missed **Poultry Hall of Fame,** is the **National Agricultural Library** out in **Beltsville, Maryland, at the corner of Route 1 and Route 495, 436-8221.**

• To find out about further travels—try the **National Geographic Society Library, Sixteenth and M Streets, N.W., 857-7000,** with its extensive information about every remote corner of the world. Even a casual visitor may browse the bound volumes of the society's magazine dating back, of course, to the very first issue.

• To visit Shakespeare's time—**The Folger Shakespeare Library, 201 East Capitol Street, S.E.; 546-4800.** Exhibit hall open Monday–Saturday 10–4:30, closed Sunday.

You step into the room and back four centuries to the great hall of a Tudor mansion with elaborately carved dark oak paneling, tile floors, and high, vaulted ceilings. Above one entrance is an out-of-place American eagle, but above the other is the Coat of Arms of Queen Elizabeth I. In the specially carved cases are all sorts of books by Elizabethan authors, copies of books about the Bard, music his plays were set to, knives used by famous Hamlets in nightly murders.

Beyond the gallery is a reproduction of a playhouse from Shakespeare's time (though not specifically The Globe.) In those days the theaters had a roofless yard; at the Folger this area is covered by a canopy bearing an impudent unicorn, but the feel is there for the place and times. What is more, though the theater was originally intended strictly as an exhibit, since 1970 it has housed a resident group of actors who put on some of the more innovative new drama to be seen around Washington, as well as performances of the old masterpieces.

During the winter months tours can be arranged, or can be

taken without prior notice at 1 and 2 P.M. In the summer, however, no tours are given.

After only a few minutes of browsing through the gallery and the theater at the Folger, whether guided or on your own, you begin to realize fully what an enormous and pervasive influence just one writer and his works have had on the culture, and in fact the entire civilization of the Western World.

# The
# Serendipity
# City

# XI
# Dining in Washington

## *Restaurants*

### By Phyllis C. Richman

Don't look for a Washington cuisine. Although the city is just a short drive from the Chesapeake Bay, this is not a seafood town, and its being below the Mason-Dixon line is rarely reflected in its restaurants. What Washington does reflect in its food is the presence of the Federal Government and embassies. Thus, Washington has an abundance of expense account restaurants and cuisines of every nationality from Afghanistanian (Bamiyan and Khyber Pass) to Serbian (Serbian Crown, 4529 Wisconsin Ave., N.W.). There are nearly seventy French restaurants at all price levels, some of them among the country's best, and Italian restaurants from pizza carryouts to the kind of elegant Italian cooking that made French cuisine what it is today. The 18th Street and Columbia Road neighborhood is locally famous for its Latin American restaurants, notably El Caribe and El Dorado at moderate prices, Omega and Churrerria Madrid for inexpensive meals. And Asian restaurants, from Vietnamese to Japanese, are increasing daily.

There is one local culinary tradition, however, that every tourist here between late spring and early fall should try. That is crab season, which Washingtonians, shirtsleeves rolled up and tablecloths replaced with brown wrapping paper, celebrate by hammering and picking at crabs steamed with red pepper. The ritual can be observed at The Dancing Crab, or at numerous crab houses in the Maryland suburbs.

Nor is there a whim of day or night that cannot be satisfied. A glass of wine at midnight? La Grenier Au Vin on the second floor of La Chaumiere. Sunday morning dim sum? Anywhere in

Chinatown, from 7th to 9th Streets between H and I Streets. Late-night cafés are found on Capitol Hill and in Georgetown, and at Kramerbooks you can buy a book as well as a beer and a sandwich at nearly any hour. You can eat in a penthouse overlooking the monuments, or on a downtown sidewalk. You can buy a picnic from a restaurant and eat on a lawn.

Here is but a small sample, for the Washington area now has about five thousand restaurants, with a few more opening every week and just as many closing.

Before you travel far for a particular restaurant, check its hours. Many in-town restaurants are closed for Saturday lunch and Sunday. Georgetown restaurants tend to choose Monday as their closing day.

Despite Washington having so many restaurants, the good ones (and even some of the bad ones) are often crowded. Make reservations if you can; at L'Auberge Chez Francois, make them two weeks in advance for dinner.

Most important, you should remember that this transient city is reflected in its restaurants; the one thing a Washington diner expects is change. Chefs move from restaurant to restaurant. Sometimes a whole new restaurant moves in under the old name, and sometimes an old restaurant takes on a new name. These reviews are up-to-date as of press time, April 1978. Beyond that, nobody can tell. Even as we went to press, several new promising restaurants were opening, too new to review. But look into The Bread Oven (19th and N Streets, N.W.) for a Continental breakfast, light lunch or dinner. Claude Bouchet, one of the city's best-known French chefs, was opening a new restaurant under his own name at 1329 Connecticut Ave., N.W. El Caribe just opened a Georgetown branch at 3288 M Street, N.W. And very tiny, very beautiful, very sophisticated is 209 $^1/_2$, a fixed-price continental restaurant at 209 $^1/_2$ Pennsylvania Ave., S.E.

Almost anything you want to eat you can find in Washington. And if there is no Scandinavian restaurant or Klondike cafe, you can be sure that if you wait long enough, one will come along.

**Alexander's III,**

**1500 Wilson Boulevard, Arlington. (527-0100).** Expensive.

In Washington you can eat French food in basements, on porches, in the middle of a sidewalk. Now, with Alexander's III having hired a French chef and moving the menu more towards Gaul, you can eat French food high above the city, lit by the lights of Georgetown, the glow of the Lincoln Memorial, and the shooting stars of jets swinging a course from lower right to straight over your head. The view has always been the thing at Alexander's III. Now, if you pick your way carefully, the food can match it. First, ask for a window table. Then, ask for the lobster bisque—no match for what you can find downtown, but nevertheless pleasant (or pate —you may need to add salt or pepper, but it is agreeably fresh and homey). Then beg the kitchen to do you a truite a la nage with beurre blanc. The sweet, gently cooked fish is strewn with onions and flower-carved carrot slices, napped in a soft, delicate, white butter sauce. It is a quietly glorious dish. Beyond that you chance a fairly good, highly garlicked rack of lamb slightly overdone, accompanied by a decent ratatouille, or a beef Wellington soggy of crust and bland, properly cooked but indifferent of ingredient quality. Overcooked shad roe, overhandled tart crust. Alexander's III has plenty of pitfalls, but if you stick to something simple (the prime rib looked impressive) or order what seems to be a chef's whim, you may find food as spectactular as the scenery.

**Ali Baba,**

**655 Pennsylvania Avenue, S.E. (543-5570).** Inexpensive.

If there were any justice in the world, Ali Baba would be left for the exclusive use of its Capitol Hill neighbors. It has, after all, only a handful of indoor seats, being a converted Little Tavern, its chrome storage shelves and bar stools intact. In nice weather, the rear garden expands its capacity and its appeal. But at its best it is a bare-bones eatery with well-meaning but halting service and some surprisingly good food. The lamb kebab is tangy, tender, nothing short of delicious, teamed with bright yellow rice heavily cumin-scented and studded with raisins. The portion is small, but you can fill up on tabbula, a very lemony cracked wheat and mint salad, a cubed melange of tomatoes, cucumbers, radishes, chick peas and scallions, the Ali Baba Special Salad, and a good version of the eggplant and sesame purée, baba ghanouj. Don't be talked into the lamb liver kebab or the spinach pie. It is a small menu with a long list of desserts, French and Middle Eastern pastries made by a neighbor. Impressive quality, those pastries, with the reine de saba, the flaky nut-layered bastila and the date-filled cookies outstanding. Tea at Ali Baba involves a choice of a half dozen, properly brewed in a rotund pot, or try a luxurious yogurt and fruit drink that could be concocted, were the season right, from fresh peaches or berries. Even the lemonade is the real thing.

### Angie's Italian Gardens,
**2317 Calvert Street, N.W. (234-4550). Inexpensive.**

The show worth seeing is weekday lunch, when the Omelet King rolls his kitsch-covered, butane fueled cart to your table and asks if you want yours wet or dry. Order it wet, and make it a Western. It comes with fries, salad, coffee, and a basket of great, greasy garlic bread reeking oregano and parmesan.

### Apana,
**3066 M Street, N.W. (965-3040). Expensive.**

Just as Chinese restaurants have grown opulent, Indian restaurants are on their way to being elegant places to dine. The first such Indian restaurant is Apana, a very handsome dining room set with brown tablecloths and candles, with balloon wine glasses—which serve well for beer —and with lovely Indian primitive paintings on the brown and rust walls. Plants and intricately patterned fabrics on the banquettes add even more lushness. The service and the food live up to the setting. Waiters are professional and readily guide you through the menu. And the food is beautifully garnished with enormous onion rings, tomatoes and greenery. As soon as you are seated, warm crisp pappadums appear. Of the seven fritters and kebabs which are offered as appetizers, lightly battered and fried shrimp bhujia are exceptional. Also good are the large, triangular, meat- and vegetable-stuffed samosas, bland until dipped in the wonderful, dark brown, tart and peppery tamarind sauce. Curries here are not powerfully hot unless you request them or fuel them with chutney. But they are distinctive, revealing layers of flavors and interesting contrasts such as tender beef with crisp nuts. And the puri here are nearly as light and puffy as helium balloons. Prices are, of course, higher than at plainer Indian restaurants. But the menu includes such delicacies as trout stuffed with lobster.

### Apple Tree,
**1220 19th Street, N.W. (223-3780). Moderate.**

A kind of decorator's version of a cave, the Apple Tree is strung with tiny white lights and furnished with more porch swings and sofas (with lap trays) than tables. What people eat at the Apple Tree comes from Eve's Garden, a salad bar as fanciful as the seating arrangement. It includes a couple of soups which inexplicably tasted mushy, and a long stretch of greens and raw things like broccoli and cauliflower, plus brownish bean sprouts and paler croutons. What knocks you out, though, is the fruit on the salad bar: melon, sliced oranges and apples, and other things in season. Dressings are the usual, except for one that tastes like caramel sundae sauce, and the breads are chewily robust. Besides the salad bar, there are some unusual but indifferent tidbits like apple fritters and teriyaki steak, mushrooms, burgers, omelets, crêpes, quiches and more serious platters. None of it would divert you from your conversation, and a lot of the nutrition consumed at the Apple Tree is liquid, from the vitamin C in the mimosa to the calcium in the banana tree.

### Arabian Nights,
**2915 Connecticut Avenue, N.W. (232-6684).** Moderate.

There are people who wish the Arabian Nights would not be discovered. As it is, it serves some of the best Middle Eastern food in town, at low prices, with no difficulty getting a table and no necessity to rush. The menu is similar to other Middle Eastern restaurants—hummous, baba ghanouj, kebabs, stuffed vegetables and such, with a few curries. But since it is Arabic, the food is spicier, more peppery than at other Middle Eastern restaurants. Although the place has been recently redecorated, it is still rather simple, with a tiled entry and wallpaper in an Arabic

sort of motif, relieved by travel posters and red curtains. The effect is simple, clean, and vaguely attractive. The service is similar; it does the job, but you don't much notice it. On the other hand, you will remember the food. Baba ghanouj is peppery and tantalizing. The yogurt tastes fresh. And the parsley, onion, cracked wheat and lemon salad known as tabbula, is irresistible. With the appetizers, warm, quartered loaves of flat bread, called pita, are served. Among main dishes, the shish kebab is tender and spicy, faintly peppered and strongly charcoal-flavored. Similar is the broiled chicken, fragrant from cinnamon as well as other spices. Curries are also delectable, not too hot, and slightly sweet from cinnamon. Or try a combination plate, showing off the rich stuffed cabbage, the charcoal-grilled kifta, and such. Even the rice is special, being very buttery and served with a pitcher of cinnamon-scented sauce. Salad and pastries don't live up to the rest of the meal, although the cigar-shaped pastry named burma is more successful than the rest. End the meal, of course, with Turkish coffee.

### Au Pied de Cochon,
**1335 Wisconsin Avenue, N.W. (333-5440).** Moderate.

Pick your way carefully through the menu of this French café, and you can eat well on little money. The daily specials deserve examination first, for there may be a fresh fish filet or a hearty stuffed veal. Make a lunch or light supper of the appetizers: unctuous, subtle rillettes or a glorious cold pig's foot, its creamy-looking remoulade sauce tart and biting, crunchy with parsley. Worth wading through the pockets of fat. On the dim side, the soups seem matters of convenience, and the restaurant is not above destroying a rich, winey coq au vin with overcooking. Dark wood and ceiling fans, the long bar and tiny marble tables lend a special character which even neglectful service and soggy pastries don't dispel. For a casual meal or a sandwich with a carafe of wine, Au Pied de Cochon is pleasant, if not necessarily inexpensive. And their heady ratatouille, which accompanies most main dishes, eclipses other deficiencies of the cafe.

## L'Auberge Chez François,

**332 Springvale Road, Great Falls, (759-3800). Expensive.**

Other inns could learn a lesson from François' move to the country. The restaurant is even more popular than when it was in the city; in fact, reservations must usually be made two weeks in advance. The anticipation at L'Auberge Chez François begins as you walk up to the door of this stuccoed and beamed replica of a French provincial inn. The kitchen window is open to the front and its excitement is transmitted to the diner. On a pleasant evening you can have drinks in the garden. Inside, a table of tarts and cakes at the entrance tempts you to finish all your dinner. As crowded as Chez François gets, its service is prompt and efficient, far from grand, but it accomplishes the job comfortably. And the dinners, which have a fixed price range from the familiar steak with peppercorns (perfectly cooked, flamed at the table, in a limpid brown sauce flavored rather than overwhelmed with pepper) to the unusual salmon soufflé Paul Haeberlin (a moist filet of salmon topped with a thin puff of a soufflé, in a pool of rich cream sauce). In summer there will be soft-shell crabs, in winter heavy Alsatian stews. I have heard complaints about the food and I have found the veal scallops pounded within an inch of their life. But the smooth, flaky-crusted quiche and the intense shrimp bisque are raised above clichés, the tarts and napoleons are crisp and delicate enough so you can remember why such indulgences were invented and the ivory-tinted Alsatian liqueur mousse is a cloud of perfume. Besides carefully picking a wine list, with several good buys and strong temptations, Chez François goes to the trouble of serving excellent breads, buttery vegetables recently acquainted with the garden, interesting potatoes and salads of quality. Copper serving dishes suit the decor, which is a simple matter of primitive murals and pottery, copper utensils hung against the stucco, and—the cleverest touch of all—windows left open to the country air in good weather.

### Le Bagatelle,
**2000 K Street, N.W. (872-8677).** Very expensive.

Most French restaurants in town look imposing or non-descript; Le Bagatelle, however, could be called pretty. Divided into small rooms by trellises and partitions with windows, the dining rooms hint of a very elegant garden. It certainly looks the setting for a pampered life. Nobody knows how to pamper better than the staff at Le Bagatelle, but it helps if you are a celebrity. Even if you are treated as part of the furniture, though, you can hardly help enjoying the food. They do particularly well with fish, as exemplified by the bass with red wine sauce; despite a few stray bones, it has been precisely cooked and perfectly fresh, napped with a sauce dark and glossy, yet light on the tongue, and decorated with a lovely fluted mushroom. They pay more attention than most to the vegetables which accompany their meals. While the wine list is expensive, it offers some excellent choices at the low end, and the expertise to guide you towards them. And Le Bagatelle presents an exquisite choice of desserts which are made in the house rather than bought from a bakery. The pastries are fine, the berries get a ladle of velvety sabayan, and one might be lucky enough to encounter a delicate frozen bombe drizzled with their own chocolate sauce.

### Bamiyan,
**3320 M Street, N.W. (338-1896). Khyber Pass, 2309 Calvert Street, N.W. (234-4362).** Moderate.

For all its worldliness, Georgetown has not supported many foreign restaurants. French and Italian, yes. Touches of Spanish. Indian. And hamburgers enough to support a large ranch. So the area was ripe for something new, and got it in Bamiyan, of all things, an Afghanistan restaurant, which then branched out to upper Connecticut Avenue as the Khyber Pass. The food is spicier than Greek, milder than Indian, intriguingly combining mint and yogurt and tomato with lots of black pepper and garlic. You can order something as familiar as shish kebab, marinated and charcoal-broiled. Or you can venture into homemade noodles stuffed with meat and scallions, topped with mint and yogurt. You could have the noodles steamed, fried, or in a soup. Try all three. Try everything. The bread is homemade, the rice is temptingly buttery. And for dessert you can linger over cardamom tea and nibble at a large, papery, fried pastry dusted with pistachios and sugar. All this in a subtly Oriental setting with tablecloths and fresh flowers and costumed waiters rushing to do your bidding.

**La Bergerie,**
**220 N. Lee Street, Alexandria.**
**(683-1007).** Expensive.

If awards were given for the restaurant that made the greatest strides in a single year, La Bergerie would be a strong contender. It always was a comfortable place to dine, with its soft curved banquettes and large, well-spaced tables. And it always was a restaurant that treated its guests with particular consideration. But in the last year, the menu has been revised to include many Basque dishes, and now has some of the most interesting possibilities in town, and the cooking seems to have livened to produce some of the best-executed dishes in town. La Parillade des Pecheurs, for instance, is an aromatic display of rockfish, scallops, shrimps, clams and mussels in a heady wash of tomato sauce with parsley and garlic, each item being tender and zesty, not even needing the punch of the pale coral spiced mayonnaise that accompanies it. Pilgrimages are made to Le Bergerie solely for confit de canard, the duck richly seasoned in a powerful brown sauce, with sauteed potatoes and mushrooms. While chicken with oysters is less forthright, it is cooked to a lovely moistness, and the oysters and shreds of mushroom add a pleasant note to the cream sauce. La Bergerie does well with soups, particularly garbure and fish soup, but its scallop terrine was watery and oversalted. Two interesting cheeses, particularly

the chiberta, are worth tasting. But dessert is a specialty here, from Izarra souffle or souffleed crepes to very fine pastries. While the almond-stuffed galette Basque is difficult to resist, remember that La Bergerie is nearly alone in restaurants where one dares to risk ordering a Napoleon and expect it to be light and crisp. Like a growing number of restaurants, La Bergerie offers fixed-price menus as well as a la carte, and they are very good meals for the money.

**The Big Cheese,**
**3139 M Street, N.W. (338-3314).**
Moderate.

Besides being one of the prettiest contemporary rooms around, the Big Cheese has one of the most unusual menus, emphasizing cheese dishes from around the world, but also including meat dishes. The menu changes monthly, generally including a crêpe dish, a Mexican dish, a noodle dish, a quiche, and so forth. Meals tend to be fresh, light, pretty, skillfully cooked. Salads are notable. While the cheese fritters are their all-time popular dishes, the Big Cheese lately has been presenting some excellent chicken and lamb dishes. But the standout has been their pastry tray, with crisp, flaky fruit tarts, tiny tortes with real butter cream, and éclairs never left to grow soggy. It is such satisfying food served in such a charming setting that people put up with waiting in line, paying only in cash, risking indifferent or rushed service at the Big Cheese. There is no place else like it in Washington.

### Cantina d'Italia,
**1214-A 18th Street, N.W. (659-1830).** Very expensive.

Elegant new Italian restaurants line K Street, overflow to L Street, spread to the suburbs. But the first of the northern Italian restaurants, Cantina d'Italia, continues to hold its own. It may not be as beautiful as its younger rivals, being a basement warren hung with plastic grape vines and studded with plaster statues, but its food is as exciting as any of them. The menu is just short of garish, and nearly everything is called a specialty. But then, the dishes usually taste like specialties. The food is not only fresh, but includes the best of the season—rugola in the salad or fresh basil in the pesto. Striped bass might be served hot with lemon and mushrooms or cold with a thick, homemade Piemontese mayonnaise. Sometimes the pasta has been known to miss, with the sauce too thin or the noodles lukewarm; but usually the homemade noodles steam in their thick parmesan-cream-butter coating or an unctuous lobster and tomato purée with cream. The gnocchi are light and buttery, the veal beautifully cooked. And they serve kidneys several ways, or duck with olives and mushrooms in a wine-cream sauce. The choices are intriguing

and ever-changing. Ingredients and their preparation are of high caliber. And nobody in town makes better cannole. The wine list is appropriately and exclusively Italian. As for the service—well, try not to hit a crowded time, or dine with somebody you want to get to know well.

### Chalet de la Paix,
**4506 Lee Highway, Arlington. (522-6777).** Expensive.

If it is not a special evening when you set out for Chalet de la Paix, it will become so. A homey cove of candles and flowers against a background of barn siding (almost the symbol of a Virginia French restaurant). Chalet de la Paix specializes in Southern hospitality (another trademark of the genre) and very good food, the best of which shows up in the main courses. Appetizers—pates, quenelles, the usual French array—are creditable but nothing more. But in game season the meal can reach a crescendo of tender marinated game in sauce potent but delicately balanced. In any season, the veal Normande is beautifully browned yet juicy, pale and subtle, layered with tart apples and masked in a subtly perfumed calvados sauce thick with cream rather than with starch. Desserts, like the starters, are creditable rather than exciting. One does not go to Calet de la Paix for its side dishes (soggy overcooked spinach) or its extensive menu (a dozen main dishes). Its wine list is reasonably priced and selective but not noteworthy. But one leaves Chalet de la Paix feeling well fed and well treated.

## La Chaumière,
### 2813 M Street, N.W. (338-1784). Moderate.

Pessimists that we are, we usually expect restaurants to get worse in time. La Chaumière, amazingly, has gotten better. Now more a restaurant than a café, it seems to be depending less on the microwave oven, which it had never mastered. Gone is the delicatessen counter, in its place more tables. Remaining is the large fireplace, the focal point of the room. The daily lunch specials are worth scheduling your week around, especially Wednesday's couscous, the raisin-studded grains surrounded by a sampler of fragrant cabbage, carrots, turnips, zucchini, beef and chicken, accompanied by a zesty cumin-flavored red sauce. Now the pleasures (fine pâté, nicely cooked artichokes) outweigh the disappointments (occasional overcooking and undercooking, undrained salads), particularly when the experience is oiled by a bottle from the individualistic, reasonably priced wine list. More and more, La Chaumière is a good choice for an unpretentious, casual meal. And upstairs, Le Grenier au Vin serves a few dishes chosen to go with the stunning choice of wines—at least a dozen of them sold by the glass as well as by the bottle. The wines are so well priced that you could set up an impromptu personal wine tasting and spend the evening educating your palate.

## Chez Camille,
### 1737 De Sales Street, N.W. (393-3330). Expensive.

Just as some wines don't travel well, some restaurants suffer from a change of location. And while long-time patrons still frequent Chez Camille, the old location is sorely missed. It is not just the Franco-Chinese nightclub look of the new quarters, or the threadbare carpet, or the flimsy hangers taped together so they will be strong enough to hold your coat. It is the food—the second-rate veal scallop which is further insulted by being overcooked. It is the vichyssoise, which tastes as if the leeks had been forgotten. The lively lunchtime crowd attests that you can still get a very good meal, and that new seasons still bring new surprises to the menu. Camille's ebullience still dominates. Cold dishes are apt to be good at lunch; try a pâté platter or the lovely assortment of salads and charcuterie which makes up the hors d'oeuvres variés. A stuffed veal roast or stuffed carp can be the find of the year. And, since the wine list offers many half-bottles, a light spring meal seated by the open windows looking out to Connecticut Avenue can be delightful. But the restaurant's personality wears thin after too many disappointments.

### Churreria Madrid,
**2505 Champlain Street, N.W. (483-4441).** Inexpensive.

Newcomers will always feel they discovered this tiny luncheonette-carryout, though there is regular traffic between this kitchen and the Spanish Embassy. With less than a dozen tables and prices bordering on charity, the Churreria Madrid is so unexpected that one wonders why there are no lines out front. The menu is limited to sandwiches, soups—all homemade—and a few platters and daily specials such as chicken stewed with olives and pigeon peas or meaty stuffed peppers, all served with mountains of rice. Small empanadas, flaky and piquant, or an omelet layered with potatoes—known as a tortilla—make good light lunches. Milanesa, a thinly sliced beef, marinated and then breaded and fried, is tasty even on its greasy days. Overall, the food is homestyle and hearty, reaching its height with its raison d'être, the teardrop-shaped doughnuts known as churros. Whatever else you try, save room for freshly made sugared churros, and more churros.

### Clyde's,
**3236 M Street, N.W. (333-9180).** Moderate.

More of a Georgetown spot, a place to go, than a restaurant, Clyde's nevertheless offers a wide choice of foods from foot-long hot dogs to prime ribs, omelets to fried chicken. Don't press your luck with the kitchen. The hamburgers are charcoal-broiled and juicy, the sandwiches are enormous, and their fried potatoes are justly renowned. They do some good soups, and the omelets in the omelet room are generally deftly made. But, despite being served with some fine fresh vegetables such as broccoli with a respectable hollandaise, the veal francaise is a waste of money, being as expensive as at some of the finest restaurants but nowhere near their quality. Keep in mind that this is a pub, and order pub food. The atrium and the omelet room are lovely places to eat, and the service is well meaning, though it gets lost in the crush of things on a crowded evening. Clyde's is at its best at breakfast or brunch, when everything served is light, fresh, pretty and unhurried.

### Company Inkwell,
**4109 Wilson Boulevard, Arlington. (525-4243).** Expensive.

A first visit to the Company Inkwell requires a leap of faith to overcome the slightly hokey horse-collar-and-barn-siding decor and the rote introduction by the waiter in black tie. The tall white tapers with flowers at their base are elegant, but their red velvet ribbons tie them into the hokeyness. But the food is serious, highly professional. Besides the standard menu—Dover

sole, quenelles, crabmeat en che-
mise, veal scallops, flamed steaks
and rack of lamb—some more
fanciful dishes are among the
daily specials. Sauces at the
Company Inkwell manage to be
light and rich, the best example
being a shallot cream on barely
poached oysters, or very fragrant
beurre blanc on the salmon. The
chef seasons with a strong hand,
which works well with the quenelles and steak au poivre, less
well with the tarragon-flavored
lamb and too-sweet veal with
grapes. Ingredients—top quality
lamb, well-aged beef, ivory veal,
good cognac for flaming—are excellent, and the tableside preparations show competence as
well as flourish. Attention, attention—it shows in the service, in
the salads, in the preparation, in
the wine list (which has better
prices at the low end, some
overpricing at the high end), in
the greeting on the phone and at
the door. Lest the finale be a let-
down, finish with fruit or a grand
marnier parfait, and don't
blunder into any dessert so elaborate as pastry. Where the Company Inkwell is good it is very,
very good, and these days the talent shows most clearly in the
sauces, as it has always shown in
the service.

## The Dancing Crab,

**4611 Wisconsin Avenue, N.W.
(244-1882).** Moderate.

In a handmade, down-home
rustic setting you can celebrate
the fact that the Chesapeake Bay
is only down the road a piece.
Hammer at peppery steamed
crabs on tablecloths of brown
paper. Feast on all-you-can-eat
specials of raw oysters and
clams, spiced shrimp and
steamed clams. Or eat nicely
fried filets of rockfish. But pass
up anything more ambitious,
such as stuffed shrimp. And don't
expect much from the french
fries or desserts. It is a shirt-
sleeves-beer-and-crab place.

## Dominique,

**1900 Pennsylvania Avenue, N.W.
(452-1126).** Very expensive.

When the applause goes
around to restaurants that have
made strides in the last year,
Dominique's will be among the
deserving. The menu has expanded to reflect what is seasonally fresh, a late-supper menu has
been added, desserts have been
much improved, and the food in
general is better than ever. Dominique's has always had certain
major assets, among them spacious quarters, romantic niches,
and a charming as well as remark-
ably competent hostess. The atmosphere has always been lively,
in part due to the elaborate hodge-
podge of stained glass and oriental carpets and knicknacks and
fabrics and polished wood. It is a
restaurant that seems to generate a lot of energy. And now it gen-
erates some very good food, particularly robust dishes. This winter the venison was impeccable,
rare and gamey, in a smooth, rich,
highly herbed sauce. The accom-

panying chestnut purée was subtle, buttery and exceedingly delicious. Several lobster dishes were served in casseroles, among them an excellent lobster with whiskey sauce, airy and creamy, though rather heavy on the whiskey, the lobster meat juicy and sweet. As an appetizer, shrimps in garlic butter with chunks of tomato are piquant and irresistible. Dominique's attends well to salads and vegetables, offers baked brie as a cheese course, then tempts with souffles and excellent cookie-crusted tarts and a cheesecake which is less remarkable for itself than for its highly perfumed Grand Marnier sauce. As for the wine list, it is expensive but well chosen, and if you ask from the second, smaller list, you will find some good buys. Perhaps the strongest asset of all, however, is that Dominique's stays open late in this city where there are many late-night cafés, but few late-night, full service restaurants outside of Chinatown.

**Duke Zeibert's,**
1722 L Street, N.W. (296-5030).
Expensive.

It is not just the food—the sturdy stuff that men are made of—that draws a devoted crowd to Duke Zeibert's; it is the scene. As noisy as Times Square and big-city brusque, Duke's makes you feel like a jock even in a three-piece suit. First, there are the powerful pickles that wake up your palate, and the crusty onion rolls and yeasty pumper-

nickel that start your digestive juices at full speed. Even the salads are hearty, with real turkey and lots of bacon that you know is bacon, and tuna and —such a refinement!—hard-cooked eggs with double yolks. If you order herring at Duke's, it's old-country-style and family-size. The ham steak is cut thick enough to really bite into. And the boiled chicken in a pot could cure anything you walk in with. Desserts are made to knock you off your seat; every one is twice as tall as you would expect and three times as rich. The cheesecake packs about a pound in each bite, groaning under a solid two inches of strawberries. Hefty food, hefty prices.

**L'Enfant Gourmet,**
470 L'Enfant Plaza, S.W.
(554-1345). Inexpensive.

Yes, there are grassy stretches at L'Enfant Plaza. And there are very good carryout foods to enjoy on them. L'Enfant Gourmet carries an amazing collection of snacks and appetizers like cumin-scented empanadas, wrapped in plastic and kept hot. There is also a wide selection of lunch meats and pâté for sandwiches, made into conglomerations called Eiffel Tower and Cannibal and Lafayette and the like. My particular favorite is an eclectic mixture named the Concorde, French bread bursting with rare roast beef, corned beef and bacon, a bit of lettuce, tomato and mayonnaise. A knockout.

### L'Escargot,

**3309 Connecticut Avenue, N.W. (966-7510).** Moderate.

If it weren't right smack on Connecticut Avenue, L'Escargot would be called a little, out-of-the-way French restaurant. It has an unpretentious air that makes you feel you have just discovered an unpolished gem. And usually it performs that way. The wine list is notable for its low prices as well as for its individuality. The menu emphasizes simple preparations of fish, stews, and hearty peasant dishes like sausage with potatoes, and cassoulet, at prices considerably below those in downtown French restaurants. Though sometimes the dishes are plain, bordering on dull, they know how to properly cook—and buy—fresh fish, and they serve a fine green salad with main courses. And if you are lucky enough to come across a homemade rum cake slathered with whipped cream, save room. With such a down-to-earth menu and prices, they are allowed a few mistakes, and they give you good, rough-textured, homestyle bread to fill in any crevices.

### Evans Farm Inn,

**1696 Chain Bridge Road, McLean. (356-8000)** Moderate.

It is not really old, it is not really in the country, but one does not really notice such things at the Evans Farm Inn. The forty acres are green and rolling, with machinery and statuary set among the flower gradens and fruit trees, goats and sheep and ducks roaming through the yards. The stone house is floored in flagstone, the walls punctuated with huge fireplaces and farm implements. It may not be authentic, but it works. Unlike other suburban inns the staff here is spirited and efficient, and a salad bar passes the time between courses. Since the salad bar is the best part of the meal, you might want to return to it often for tart homemade applesauce, sweet-sour marinated cucumbers and date butter in addition to the usual tossed salad, cottage cheese, cranberry relish and three-bean salad. The list of main courses is short, from smoked chicken to ham, duck, steak and roast beef, with a few daily specials; but hardly anything is not overcooked. The duck is crisp but stringy, the smoked chicken only faintly smoke-seasoned and dull. Smithfield ham, being authentic, is the happiest choice. Alongside comes spoonbread the texture of oatmeal and some vegetables that were recognizably fresh. Desserts tend to be too sweet, but the apple crisp nevertheless worthy of the farm setting. A mixed bag, but a pleasant place to take the family on a Sunday afternoon.

### Gandy Dancer,

**200 E Street, N.E. (546-3377).** Moderate.

Feast with your eyes at Gandy Dancer, the two levels a

smorgasbord of macramé and supergraphics on brick walls, a tribute to modern design. The food, too, is designed with flair, the salads in wide glass bowls, the platters and sandwiches garnished in depth. Nothing tastes quite as good as it looks, but it looks good enough to allow some leeway. Whatever there is, there is a lot of it—a lot of salad, a lot of omelet, a lot of soup, and a lot of service. The Baron de Barante omelet bursts with lobster, drips with two cheeses, and wafts the fragrances of mushrooms and port wine.

### Le Gaulois,
**2133 Pennsylvania Avenue, N.W. (466-3232). Moderate.**

The left bank, so to speak, of Foggy Bottom is settled squarely at Le Gaulois. Day by day the kitchen turns out very good bourgeois French cooking at modest prices, from homemade sausages to fish in white wine sauce. It has also cornered the local market for cuisine minceur with its small selection of diet dishes. Its only problem is that it is too well loved, so you may have to line up behind the faithful fans.

### Geppetto,
**2917 M Street, N.W. (333-2602). Inexpensive to Moderate.**

Geppetto is a small café with some of the best pizza in town. The thick crust is freshly made, and the sauce is light and spicy, with great pools of oozing cheese. The rest of the menu has some interesting hot sandwiches and a few daily specials worth exploring, plus a noteworthy creamy ricotta pie for dessert.

### Geranio,
**724 King Street, Alexandria. (548-0088). Moderate.**

If you stopped off at a trattoria of some repute in the Italian countryside, you would expect food the likes of which they serve at Geranio: tantalizing soups, homemade pastas with zesty sauces or stuffed with fragrant, light meat pastes. The cannelloni and lasagne would be light, the chicken breast lightly sautéed and mated with unctuous eggplant and peppers, the squid and lamb dishes heady with garlic. There is a good cook in this kitchen, using fresh vegetables and cream and cheeses and butter and oil and bushels of garlic. Also, in the dining rooms—two of the tiniest public rooms you will ever see, whitewashed and set with pink tablecloths, fresh flowers, and paintings of more flowers—the staff is as zesty and fresh as the food, having fun at their jobs and keeping a careful watch that the patrons, too, are having fun.

### Golden Palace,
**726 7th Street, N.W. (738-1225). Moderate.**

At the Golden Palace, if you go during the daytime, you will be handed a small golden lunch menu listing about two dozen dishes. Ask for the little pink dim sum menu instead, even though it is written entirely in Chinese—that will make you look knowledgable. You can hardly go wrong by pointing to any of them, but I particularly recommend No. 10, a gossamer version of egg roll, and the har gow (No. 8) and shu mai (No. 12), both steamed stuffed noodles. Among the heavier, fried dim sum are beautifully prepared taro root balls (No. 16) and glutinous fried triangles (No. 15). And for adventure, try the pancake-shaped, fried, sticky rice filled with various meats (No. 2) and, if you wish, topped with a fried egg (No. 1). To drink, chrysanthemum tea for your health.

### Golden Temple of Conscious Cookery,

**1521 Connecticut Avenue, N.W. (234-6134).** Moderate.

Vegetarian food has polished its image, thanks to the Golden Temple. No longer does vegetarian imply heavy, bland or boring. The Golden Temple serves vegetarian food from cuisines as diverse as Indian and Chinese, along with some downhome American tastes. They present the food attractively, and serve it with serenity that belies the crowds waiting for a table. Some of the food is highly peppered, so you might want to ask about that. Salads are excellent because the ingredients are very fresh, and their dressings are delicious. They elevate the most humble dishes, like baked potato slathered with sour cream and sautéed mushrooms, ringed by a salad. Their breads and desserts are similarly agreeable. And the setting, blond wood and white walls, with a silent waterfall over the door, is like a mini-vacation from the Connecticut Avenue scurrying.

### Gourmet Snacks,

**1200 Wilson Boulevard, Arlington (528-5230).** Inexpensive.

The little underground luncheonette called Gourmet Snacks feels like a house party, with everybody seeming to know everybody else. The basement room is brightened with yellow paint and some of the owners' friend's oil paintings—for sale—propped against the wall. Service is cafeteria-style from a choice of sandwiches, soups, and daily special platters like braised lamb with spinach or zucchini baked with cheese. The marinated sliced steak platter is justifiably a bestseller. And nobody who had the choice would miss the desserts—meringue with strawberries and whipped cream, napoleon, chocolate royal pie, and a pie-shaped éclair.

### Harvey's,

**1001 18th Street, N.W. (833-1858).** Expensive.

The rules for getting the best out of Harvey's are simple: Order seafood, and order it simply prepared. Whatever oceanic delicacies are around, you will find the first quality at Harvey's; I could hardly imagine a better flounder, for instance. And overcooking is unheard of. But don't confuse the issue with fancy sauces or elaborate preparations, and be prepared to pay the price. A seafood salad here may hover around the $7 range, but it will consist of great quantities of top-of-the-line crab and lobster, simply dressed, tossed with faultless greens. The service is experienced, the drinks compete with the best in town (in fact, if you take along a child you will discover that the Shirley Temples are the best), vegetables may include extravagances like broccoli in a crêpe, and the desserts are in the American tradition that made strawberry shortcake the stuff of midwinter dreams.

## Il Giardino,
**1110 21st Street, N.W. (223-4555). Very expensive.**

The room is handsome, with decorative tiles on the floor and the walls lined with antique sideboards and fair-to-good modern paintings. Spacious tables are set with gorgeous flowers and tableware of admirable quality. The menu is so comprehensive, from hot and cold hors d'oeuvres to pastas to meats, fish, vegetables, salads and desserts, each with close to a dozen possibilities, that you will want to spend considerable time poring over it. Order pasta, of course, perhaps a half-portion of spinach-stuffed agnolotti to start. But then the mozzarella melting in a deep-fried bread boat and drizzled with anchovy butter is irresistible. Lamb chops are superb, veal flawless, fish exceptional —particularly with a powerful

fennel sauce piquant with vinegar. Vegetables receive special attention. And the desserts, from the chocolate-drenched profiteroles to the rum-drenched zuppa inglese, deserve serious attention even if you have already eaten your fill. The fly in this ointment is the price—very high, from the antipasto through the wine list. And the kitchen at lunchtime has no care for your working schedule. But the dinning room operates like a well-oiled machine, and the food is worth the wait.

## Jean-Pierre,
**1835 K Street, N.W. (466-2022). Very expensive.**

Among the things you can depend on in this life is Jean-Pierre. The cuisine is dependably good, the menu is dependably traditional, the dining room is dependably dull looking, and the service is dependably erratic. To start, as one should, with the food, Jean-Pierre does very well by its standards—rich, spicy lobster bisque, veal pale and elegant in rich cream-and-mushroom sauces, lamb chops beautifully trimmed and cooked and cleverly dressed with green peppercorn cream sauce. To their credit, the seasonings tend to be splashy—a great deal of mustard in the grilled rockfish with mustard cream. But they occasionally overreach, as in the slightly cloying venison grand-veneur. The timing of the heat turns out flawless fish, veal, grilled meats. But the timing in the dining room can leave you waiting for an hour for your appetizer or grabbing your waiter to ask what the day's specials are before he disappears at a run. Jean-Pierre is one of the only top French restaurants willing to take an 8 P.M. reservation rather than insisting on 7 and 9:30 P.M. seatings, and for that it may be worth putting up with the mid-evening rush to have a chance to linger over coffee without being pressured for your seat. I would recommend that a redecoration be considered, but the last one—plaid wallpaper in autumn colors—only made things worse. So it remains a graceless room with considerable bustle and little space between the tables. But usually the service is not only professional, but personable, and care is taken with details such as salads, cheeses and desserts. If the wine list—broad and fairly interesting, more expensive than average—does not tempt you, ask for the special list of red wines—mostly '66s—which are higher priced but better buys and exceedingly tempting. If Jean-Pierre has been upstaged by more extravagant competition, its prices are slightly less extravagant, and it remains as good as it has always been, which is very good.

### Kelley's Beef,

**629 Pennsylvania Avenue, S.E. (544-2100). Inexpensive.**

Some days you don't want to have to make choices. You don't want to face some food you've never heard of before. You want something familiar, uncomplicated. It's the day for Kelley's Beef. You don't have to look at the decor; it's just a house-brand Roy Rogers. You can skip all the accessories that are carefully labeled homemade—the macaroni and cheese, bread pudding, soup. Stick to the roast beef sandwich. It is carved just for you from a great big steamship round, and slurped into meat juices and piled on a pretty good roll. It's a classic.

### Kowloon,

**1105 H Street, N.W. (638-4243). Moderate.**

Typically Asian in a pretty, sedate way is Kowloon. It was one of the first Chinese restaurants around to serve dim sum every day, and the twenty-eight choices run from the familiar har gow (shrimp dumplings) to sow stomach and hot pepper chicken feet. Each order is ninety cents, and the best of those I tried were the har gow and the pillowy roast pork bows. Ordering from the dinner menu at lunch you can have a juicy, crisp-skinned half of a roast duck, fragrant with five-spices powder. Or venture into a unique taste, steamed pork with dried grapefruit peel. In crab season, the fried crabs with scallions and ginger are less peppery than American steamed crabs, and as much fun to eat.

### Kramer Book's Afterwords Café,

**1517 Connecticut Avenue, N.W. (387-1462). Inexpensive.**

Since it has become fashionable to read at state dinners, you may want to practice at Kramer-book's Afterwords Café, the city's first bookstore-café (one hopes only the first of many). It is not really a serious restaurant, as the meals are more collected than cooked, for there is no real kitchen in the place. But they serve well-chosen pâtés, quiches, salads and pastries, a few hot dishes and fruits in season. Like the books, there is usually something good on the shelves to fit your mood.

### Le Lion d'Or,

**1150 Connecticut Avenue, N.W. (296-7972). Very expensive.**

More than any other restaurant in the last half dozen years, Le Lion d'Or has moved Washington into the big leagues, and it just keeps getting better. No other in town serves fresh truffles in its sauces, fresh foie gras with its veal or beef. No other restaurant serves rare breast of duck. No pâté in town compares with its hot rabbit pâté. Le Lion d'Or serves fresh shrimp, perfectly cooked, in a warm, buttery dill sauce, and whole baby rockfish consummately baked in a flaky puff pastry. Its ingredients are impeccable, its daily specials increasingly unique. Trout stuffed with the most airy fish mousse, complemented by a froth of a champagne sauce. Wild boar heavily marinated and juniper scented, in a powerful winey sauce, arranged like a picture with browned apple quarters and lentils. Only gratin de homard has disappointed, the

lobster too chewy and the sauce less airy than the others. Le Lion d'Or seasons dishes—lamb with eggplant and fennel, for instance—with force, and carries that off valorously. The elaborate attention carries through to garnishes, to salads, to a cheese tray filled with seven in perfect condition, to some of the finest desserts this town sees. The orange soufflé is the lightest puff, bursting with orange bits and liqueur. Bittersweet chocolate mousse du chat is delicately sauced with mocha. Jean Pierre cake is a melt of nutted cake layers with butter creams and mousses, no flour at all. Even the tarts are, at last, quite good. This culinary grandeur is absorbed in a dining room of striped walls and soft chairs, handsome if not original, fairly close and noisy on a busy day (which is everyday). Service is as smooth as any in town. The wine list stands out, being an in-depth list with fair prices, many particularly tempting in the $12 to $14 range, and a smaller list that is in general more expensive but includes a good buy on occasion. Le Lion d'Or, when all its assets are totaled to make an evening that can be extraordinary, comes as close as we have to fine dining in the French tradition.

### Magic Pan Créperie,

**5252 Wisconsin Avenue, N.W. (686-5500). Montgomery Mall. (365-0500). Tysons Corner Shop-**

**ping Center. (790-8084).** Inexpensive.

Mass production has its assets, and the Magic Pan is one of them. These three restaurants are very pretty, hung with plants and washed with sunlight. And watching the crêpes go round the specially constructed stove is fun. The dozens of different fillings often sound better than they taste, for there seems to be an overzealous effort to be inoffensive. But the salads are appealing, the dessert crêpes gooey, the service cheerful. And, while prices are not as low as one might expect from a chain restaurant, the food is a bit better than what chains tend to serve. This is one of the area's few restaurants with a special nonsmoking section.

## Malabar,

**4934 Wisconsin Avenue, N.W. (363-8900).** Inexpensive to Moderate.

This is an unassuming neighborhood Indian restaurant, gracious, and decorated with restraint. The food is similarly pleasant and unassuming. Spicy but not overwhelming. The appetizers—triangular fried samosas, spicy shami kebabs, crisply battered pakoras—are very well made. Among the curries, the chicken korma is especially interesting, and they do kebabs well. Even better are their homemade breads, the puffy puri and flat, dense paratha and chapatis. Surprisingly, they do better meat

than vegetable curries, and not surprisingly, desserts are supersweet and soggy. This is a good choice for a casual, reasonably priced change of pace.

## Man in the Green Hat,

**3rd Street at Massachusetts Avenue, N.E. (546-5900).** Moderate.

New and trying hard, its menu is mostly salads, a few hot platters, and sandwiches, with special fetishes made of the homemade breads and the fried potatoes. Desserts can be as spectacular as the angular green-and-white two-story design of this Capitol Hill pub-restaurant.

## Market Inn,

**200 E Street, S.W. (554-2100, 554-7400).** Moderate.

Among the last remnants of the old market area is the Market Inn. And among the last remnants of Washington as a seafood capital are some of the Market Inn's specialties. New England clam chowder, for instance, is as thick with clams as it is with cream, and the crab Norfolk is a simple buttery dish of the backfin crab which has made the Chesapeake Bay a culinary legend. Fried seafoods crunch where they should and give where they should, and taste as fresh as they should. To wash these down, try a musty ale, which is a mug of ale mixed with beer. You can enjoy all this in a choice of dark, musty rooms, one decorated with portraits of classic cars, another with portraits of classic nudes. And if you hang around at the right time, live music will accompany your lunch. Pick through the menu with care, because you may get caught by the likes of she-crab soup, which tastes like thickened Newburg sauce and is topped by sweetened whipped topping, or a chef seafood salad which is studded with fine lobster and crab, but drowned in bacon which tastes, at best, as if it came from a can. It is certainly not necessary to bother with the stolid, soggy key lime pie or the anemic strawberry parfait.

### Mikado,

**4707 Wisconsin Avenue, N.W. (244-1740). Moderate.**

Inside this small restaurant on Wisconsin Avenue is another world, serene and quiet, the waitresses with gentle voices and graceful manner. Pale colors and bamboo make the room look very Japanese. The menu ranges from familiar tempura and sukiyaki to lesser known noodle and rice dishes. Sukiyaki for two, and a similar one-person dish cooked in the kitchen rather than at tableside, are here rich and fragrant, a far cry from the bland, mushy versions in less authentic restaurants. Try also the sukinabe, or any of the grilled dishes. Sushi and sashimi, too, are done well at the Mikado. Not only do they serve a good cross section of Japanese foods at moderate prices, they prepare them very well, serve them beautifully, and send you off feeling well cared for.

### The Monocle,

**107 D Street, N.E. (546-4488). Moderate.**

The Monocle is not as old as it looks, but it does hold a place in Washington's history and continues to draw heavily from the halls and caucus rooms of the Capitol. It is a meat-and-potatoes sort of place, meant to give stomachs a rest from exotic reception food, and plain is best. The crab cakes are little but crab and mayonnaise, not lump crab but fresh and sweet. The Greek salad is heavy with feta cheese and good Greek olives, blanketed with orégano and anchovies, the better to work up one's thirst for the evening's cocktail party. The rum pie, despite excessive gelatin and soggy crust, tasted pleasant.

### Napoleon's,

**2649 Connecticut Avenue, N.W. (265-8955). Moderate.**

In some cities, this would be the best French restaurant in town, but in the Washington context the fare is considered standard—primarily filet mignon with a choice of competent sauces. Also in the Washington context, it is a bargain, since a perfectly nice filet or rack of lamb, with ambitious potato puffs and fresh vegetables, an imaginative salad and a choice of pleasant desserts costs around $10 a person. The wine list is more ambitious and even more reasonable than the food. Service is more efficient than polished, but the curved banquettes and live guitar music add a romantic flair.

## Nathan's II,

**1211 Connecticut Avenue, N.W. (659-1211).** Expensive.

Washington has lately become heavily invested in very expensive northern Italian restaurants (probably the best being Il Giardino on 21st Street and Cantina d'Italia on Connecticut Avenue), but you can sample the genre with less of a dent in your bank account at Nathan's II (not to be confused with Georgetown's sibling Nathan's, which is now in flux). Pale blue velvet banquettes, a superb tape system for musical background, late-night dancing and attentive service would be enough incentive for some. For others, the food fills out the qualifications. The pastas, especially those with cream and parmesan, are excellent. Veal is a good choice, none better than the ricotta-stuffed ostriche di vitello. And appetizers and desserts are among the best in town.

## National Gallery Cafeteria,

**6th Street and Constitution Avenue, N.W. (737-4215).** Inexpensive.

Give them an A for effort. The buffet and café, side-by-side operations that are distinct, yet blend well are as stylish a setting as one could want for an art museum. The buffet works best because the usual steam table foods are here garnished prettily and taste about as you would expect from a cafeteria. The carved-to-order sandwich meats are even better than one might expect. But the café is a disappointment because service is spotty, and the food is not handled as well as the setting implies, tending to weary and bland, underheated or overthickened. The menu changes seasonally, and shows imagination, but the execution leaves a lot to be desired.

## Old Ebbitt,

**1427 F Street, N.W. (347-5560).** Moderate.

If Reeves looks like Boston, the Old Ebbitt could pass for a New York pub, with its Twenties-style chandeliers and dark wood, stuffed animal heads and high ceilings. On tap are Bass Ale, Guinness Stout and more everyday brews. On the plates are some pedestrian versions of pub food: club sandwiches, reubens with chewy corned beef, hamburgers, and crab cakes which taste like bread flavored with sea water. Even the homefried potato chips are overcooked and stale. Two redeeming features are fresh-tasting turkey and authentic whipped cream. But beer is the thing.

## Old Europe,

**2434 Wisconsin Avenue, N.W. (333-7600).** Moderate.

One of Washington's old standbys, Old Europe has long enhanced Washington's dining out. It celebrates the seasons European-style, with great bundles of asparagus and May wine in spring, weissbier mit schuss in summer, game in fall and winter. And it offers a wide variety of wursts, with tangy accompaniments like red cabbage and sauerkraut, year round. Surprisingly, the many veal dishes are not its best efforts; instead, try the spicy stewed dishes. And save room for real apple strudel.

### The Palm,

**1225 19th Street, N.W. (293-9091).** Very expensive.

If you have any doubt that the Palm is a meat and potatoes restaurant, try to order the linguine with clams. The waiter probably won't let you. But the warnings are even more evident. Ceiling fans whirring over green-and-white checked tablecloths, the walls covered with caricatures. All it needs is sawdust on the floor. The waiters may not be as old as the legendary New York steakhouse waiters, but they are well versed in the tough-but-efficient steakhouse manner, and they carry your silverware in their pockets as if they were born with a steak knife poised. Besides steak—filet has been best of late—and potatoes, order vegetables, particularly the zesty creamed spinach and thin, crisp fried onions. Either is a meal in itself. Clams—raw or casino with lemon butter and bacon—are a good start. As for their famed lobster, it tends to be over four pounds and plenty to share for two, is cooked exquisitely, but demands an outrageous price. When is a lobster worth nearly $50? On the other hand, nothing on the small wine list is over

$13.50. You won't have room —or maybe money—but end the meal anyway with the ultimate creamy cheesecake, which, like the wine, benefits from being served at the right temperature.

### Patent Pending,

**8th and G Streets, N.W. (638-6503).** Inexpensive.

An art museum should be tasteful from tip to toe, and so it is fitting that the National Collection–Portrait Gallery feeds its visitors at Patent Pending. Light, white and bright, as the saying goes, the small dining area displays parsley bouquets rather than flowers on the tables. The menu is sandwiches, salads, quiche and soups; the style is abbreviated cafeteria. There is wine and beer, and the second cup of coffee is free. More important, the food is fresh and appealing, nicely cooked. Soup or chili—both homemade—can be ordered with half a sandwich. Or you can get a hot dog—nitrite-free—piled with onions, mustard, pickles, relish, tomato and hot peppers. But whatever your choice, stick around for the buttery, cinnamony apple pan dowdy capped with thick whipped cream. All the art in this museum is not on the walls.

### Pawnshop,

**1911 North Fort Meyer Drive, Arlington. (522-7400).** Moderate.

It may be a Disneyland version of skid row, but the Pawnshop is fun. In decor terms, one might say that is has everything; windows with a view, park benches, mirrored walls, trumpets and rhino heads hanging from the ceiling. From the umbrellas suspended over the tables to the peacock blue wrought iron, the colors are flossy. The music is loud and nostalgic. The waitresses are spirited. As for the food, pawn your calorie allotment for the potato skins with sour cream and butter, as an appetizer. The burgers are big and lean, served rare if you want, best with both Swiss and American cheese and bacon, though the blue cheese and mushroom version sounds smashing. Otherwise, the dishes—salads, sandwiches and omelets—confuse quantity with quality. For dessert, Gifford's ice cream.

### Petitto's,

**2653 Connecticut Avenue, N.W. (667-5350). Expensive.**

A quick course in Washington restaurant trends (homemade pasta, liqueur-stoked cappuccino, small rooms with strong personalities). Petitto's is new and pretty, with eager service and food (pasta, pasta and more pasta, plus a few appetizers) that is fresh and imaginative. Dressing in this year's style is a costly indulgence, and the pasta and salad will average $6 before you even think about soup or wine or tax and tip.

### Prime Rib,

**2020 K Street, N.W. (466-8811). Very expensive.**

The trouble with doing something beautifully is that the disappointments stand in such vivid contrast. The Prime Rib is so stylish, with its black walls discreetly gold-trimmed and its lucite-topped piano, that you doubly resent being crushed into the doorway that serves as a waiting room. Elegant tables with brass lamps reflecting the black-and-gold rimmed china are so small that the waiter has to ask where he can put the bread basket. It is as smoky and noisy as a poker den, masking the pleasant dinner music. Though the menu is limited to three steaks, roast beef, lamb chops and three seafood dishes (which you could justifiably save for another restaurant), it is enough, for the beef is superb, well aged and carefully cooked, served in gargantuan portions. Appetizers—seafood cocktails, snails, clams casino and lobster bisque—are presentable if not memorable. Except for the buttery crisp potato skins, the vegetables are not more than pleasant. Desserts, too, include only one of note, a tall goblet of cold buttered rum, which tastes like melted ice cream with rum and nuts, a brilliant idea. If you enjoy what Prime Rib has to offer—handsome room, prime location, and the best of the beef that made America famous—and don't expect it to act Continental, the restaurant is well worth the money—as long as you have that much to spend.

### Le Provencal,

**1234 20th Street, N.W. (223-2420). Expensive.**

There is good news to report at Le Provencal, where this year the food has seemed better than ever. It has always managed competent service and a fresh, fairly grand look to the two-level dining room. And now one can find the likes of blanquette de veau succulent and mellow, scallops sautéed with garlic and herbs just long enough to retain their juiciness, mousse of scallops tender and smooth, sweetly scallop flavored, in a light cream sauce flecked with sorrel. Sauces have well-controlled seasoning, airy texture. Pâtés are fresh and lively, salads tossed with good oil and vinegar. Even the pastries are more crisp and rich than ever, the strawberry tart far above average. Of late, only a pallid coquille ocean with tough seafood, and a brie with almonds chilled and underripe have been cause for complaint. It seems as if Le Provencal has climbed back up to its former elevation.

**Reeves,**

**1209 F Street, N.W. (347-3781).** Inexpensive.

Over ninety years old and as spry as ever, Reeves looks as a lot of restaurants in Washington only try to look. The Tiffany lamps appear to be originals, and so do the waitresses. Long counters line both aisles, their mirrored walls punctuated with coat hooks. Noisy and efficient, it reminds one of Boston's historic market restaurants. Few other restaurants make their own mayonnaise, and even fewer serve peanut butter and jelly sandwiches, or potato salad (quite good, by the way) as a main dish. Reeves is a charming anachronism, with commendable but timid chili and tamales, and a long list of tea-roomy sandwiches. All that is prelude, however, to the desserts. Reeves' bakery counter, which lines the front, is a magnet, its strongest force being the strawberry pie. But the other pies are more than supporting cast, and any of them is sufficient reason for a stroll down F Street.

**Rive Gauche,**

**Wisconsin Avenue and M Street, N.W. (333-6440).** Very expensive.

Besides having one of the grandest dining rooms in Washington—whatever is not covered with red leather or velvet is covered with gold—Rive Gauche is capable of some of the grandest food served in Washington. Their young French chef is an innovator, and his scallops steamed with vegetables, moistened with a tart butter sauce, are an exquisite example of the new wave of French cooking. The best appetizers are the most elegant (fresh foie gras) and the most homely (potage St. Germain). Forget the onion soup. While salads are in general very fine like most French restaurants', Rive Gauche charges top prices ($7.50 for two) for Caesar salad, but so disdains it as to use packaged grated cheese on it. Skip it. Otherwise, ingredients are top quality, and the cooking is often inspired. Mistakes are made—

oversalted Nantua sauce, too-dry lobster in a $38 lobster soufflé for two. But these are aberrations. Sometimes there are delicacies such as imported fresh baby string beans, or fresh fish flown in from France, and the daily specials not only reflect what is best in the markets, but what new ideas the chef is trying. Dessert, for instance, can be an intensely perfumed sherbet of the season, made daily in the kitchen. The wine list is impressive, but priced so that you need a sense of abandon to take advantage of its breadth. But if you knew the old Rive Gauche, today it is a comparative breath of fresh air, not only because of its imaginative chef, but because the imperiousness is gone, and the polished staff serves everyone, from tourist to celebrity, with admirable competence.

## La Ruche,
**1206 30th Street, N.W. (965-2684). Also 239 Massachusetts Avenue, N.E. (596-9154).** Moderate.

New ownership doesn't seem to have changed this tiny café, thank goodness. We liked it the way it was—and is. The green-and-white room is as fresh as the food, which is wisely limited to a few quiches, salads, sandwiches, egg and vegetable dishes, and a handful of daily specials. Plus pastries, among them melting walnut and cream tortes, tarts which crunch and ooze, feathery cake rolls filled with whipped cream. Unlike most French pastry selections,

these taste as good as they look. So do the dark, moist coq au vin, the refreshing salads, the pâtés. Quiches would be spectacular if they were less often overcooked. With the pleasant service and the reasonable wine list, catching a seat at one of the small tile tables is worth the patience it usually requires.

## Sakura,
**7926 Georgia Avenue, Silver Spring. (587-7070).** Moderate.

The Sakura is an old-timer among local Japanese restaurants, and is commended by people who know Japan as authentic in its decor as well as its food. There are several rooms, which you choose depending on whether you like to sit on the floor or on chairs. And the menu is extensive, from seafoods to teriyakis to sukiyakis to noodle and rice dishes. Tempura is particularly good here, and as we have grown to expect in Japanese restaurants, the service lacks no small attention. But the most wonderful thing about the Sakura is its sushi bar, where several deft young men, scarves tied around their foreheads, put on a show of slicing raw fish, molding rice, rolling rice and fish in seaweed, and turning out a beautiful array of fish and rice combinations which make you want more—and more. Don't miss the noritake, a long seaweed-wrapped roll filled with egg, spinach, black mushrooms, pickled squash, and a touch of pink, surgary fluff. Sliced into discs, it is both pretty and delicious. And it provides a piquant contrast to the tuna, squid, abalone, sea urchins, salmon roe, scallops, shrimp, flounder—all perfectly fresh and glistening—which are the usual sushi choices.

### Sans Souci,
**726 17th Street, N.W. (298-7424).** Very expensive.

Notable for its celebrity clientele, noteworthy for its crystal-leather-gilt edged room, and notorious for its treatment of unknown women, Sans Souci is taken more seriously as a tourist site than as a dining room. The food can be excellent, particularly the simply sautéed sweetbreads or softshell crabs. Fish dishes such as trout stuffed with a fish soufflé and napped with sauce bercy can hit high notes. And at dinner some attention is paid to vegetables. But even the suave service and handsome presentation can't hide the indifferent appetizers and desserts. And main dishes seem to miss as often as they hit. At its best it can compete with Washington's top French restaurants, but not everyone has the patience to hang around just in case Sans Souci is doing its best.

### Sheraton-Carlton,
**16th and K Streets, N.W. (638-2626).** Expensive.

At the Sheraton-Carlton the lavishness of the arched windows and elaborately painted beams is matched by the lunch buffet's studiously garnished foods. It is a truly grand room, with service to match, and for the price one would not find a more impressive spread. What endears the careful observer is the freshness of the vegetables and fruits. Forbear the boring seafood and the sleazy curry. The green beans and the new potatoes, the turkey and ham salads, fruit mélange and even—surprisingly—very good egg salad suffice, and there may be hot corned beef carved to your measure. Coffee is the best finale, perhaps with ripe Persian melon. The cakes and pies and puddings taste as if they are strictly for show.

### Sholl's,
**1433 K Street, N.W. (783-4133).** Inexpensive.

High-priced French restaurants serve canned string beans, but Sholl's cafeteria serves fresh. Fancier restaurants bring their pies in from bakeries, while Sholl's makes its own. You can pay several dollars for a soggy salad at some of Washington's eating places, whereas a crisp one at Sholl's costs twenty-five cents or less. Where else can you get liver for fifty cents, homemade puddings for fifteen cents? These cafeterias look fresh and clean, and are kept that way through their crowded service hours. As steam tables will have it, the food is sometimes soggy. But if you choose carefully, you can collect a very satisfying meal for $2 or $3, from the freshest of vegetables, nicely fried seafood, excellent hamburger, and breads and pastries which include some of this city's best pies.

### Szechuan,
**615 I Street, N.W. (393-0130).** Moderate.

Szechuanese restaurants have opened all over the suburbs, and at last Chinatown has a Szechuan restaurant, a very ambitious one. It is elegant, after a fashion, its bright yellow fabric walls decorated with swirling three-dimensional abstract paintings and punctuated with elaborate draperies and keyhole-shaped doorways. The kitchen has had its ups and down, but seems to have settled into handling esoteric dishes very well, standard things like egg rolls and spareribs not very well. Sauces are intricate, vegetables crisp, peppery dishes properly so. The extensive menu lists rarities such as shower-fried chicken, lamb sautéed with garlic and honeyed ham. The appetizers are extensive, including tantalizing cold sesame-and-pepper flavored bon bon chicken, marinated jelly-fish-like crunchy noodles, and perfumy marinated beef. They handle fish expertly. But their lemon chicken is dry and sprinkled with lemon juice rather than lemon-sauced.

The most interesting time to dine at Szechuan is Sunday morning, when the Chinese community turns out for the dim sum. While their meat and seafood dumplings are, in general, not as good as those at some other local restaurants, they have a wide choice, and are the only restaurant to serve long crispy fried rolls that taste like unsweetened doughnuts, to dunk into almond tea. It is a delectable, subtle dish.

No restaurant in town attempts more than this Szechuan restaurant, and the disappointments are few.

### Taverna Cretekou,
**818 King Street, Alexandria. (548-8688).** Expensive.

Middle Eastern restaurants in the Washington area have been traditionally places where you eat cheaply but with little style. Taverna Cretekou changed that, with an elegant, simple white-washed setting that evokes Greek islands, and food presented with an eye for beauty. Try Sahanki, casseri cheese fried in butter so it is oozing and doubly rich. Besides the usual kebabs and moussaka, they have grilled lamb, squid, and lemon-basted rockfish (nicely flavored, but sometimes overcooked). It is not so much the breadth of the menu, but the attractiveness of the surroundings and competent cooking that set off Taverna Cretekou as a Middle Eastern restaurant which is worthy of a special evening out.

### Thai Room,
**527 13th Street, N.W. (638-2444). Connecticut Avenue at Nebraska Avenue.** Inexpensive.

The Thai Room is a long-needed downtown branch of Chevy Chase's jam-packed, bargain-priced Asian favorite.

Like the uptown version, the Thai Room serves fiery food such as pearly white but potent coconut milk soup, and beef, pork or chicken with hot chili and garlic. Not all the food is searing, though you can smell the garlic and peppers halfway through the door. On the mild side, and consistently delectable, is the Thai Room chicken, fried drumsticks stuffed with crab and mushrooms. And besides teasing your palate, this downtown branch tickles your ribs; where else can you eat Thai-style noodles in a forest of gilded Corinthian columns and Roman friezes, where timid Oriental waiters weave between draped goddesses. The old Caesars II restaurant lives on in Asian splendor.

**Tiberio,**
**1915 K Street, N.W. (452-1915).** Very expensive.

Tiberio has had its ups and downs, but through it all the pasta has been unfailingly superb—fragile noodles with soft, subtle meat stuffings and rich cream sauces. The cannelloni, tortellini, and agnolotti—it is hard to think of them as starchy dishes, so light are they. Desserts, too, at Tiberio are works of talent, though they are too often left to grow soggy through the day. Nevertheless, the zuppa inglese, sopping with rum, is a complex construction of meringue, custard, jam, candied fruit and sponge cake. The almond tart is crunchy from its cookie crust, profiteroles are laden with brandied chocolate sauce and whipped cream. But in between pasta and dessert? You take your chances, though lately your chances are good. The choice is difficult, but veal is usually excellent, especially in a brandied cream and mushroom sauce, or breaded and fried with a core of Parma ham and Fontina cheese. The menu extends from an Italian version of chicken Kiev to an Italian version of lobster Américaine, with Italian quenelles and Italian duck with orange sauce along the way. If you are reminded of French cuisine's Italian origins, that is only just. But there are the zesty touches of orégano, garlic, parmesan. Even the decor, a kind of whitewashed contemporary splendor, with pink roses on the tables, has a piquant touch of the electrical wiring used for a decorative effect. Like the pasta, the decor and the service benefit from a light, deft touch.

**Yenching Palace,**
**3524 Connecticut Avenue, N.W. (362-8200). 905 N. Washington Street, Alexandria. (836-3200).** Expensive.

The two Yenching Palace restaurants, at their best, compete favorably with any in town. The trick is to catch them at their best, no easy feat. Maybe the best way is to order a banquet, thus increasing the chances of the top cooks doing your food. For when they miss, the Yuling duck reeks of too much soy sauce, the lamb may include a chunk of gristle, while the tung ting shrimp may lack its chicken velvet. Usually, if something goes awry, it is the seasoning; the vegetables seem consistently crisp, and meats and seafoods are dependably juicy. Yenching Palace makes excellent dumplings, and their sauces are more interesting than extensive, and service is competent. If you are lucky, you will get a grand meal worthy of its price.

# *Lunching Around*

## By Christopher Dickey

It is with a sense of trepidation and a bottle of Alka-Seltzer that a visitor (and many a native) confronts lunch in Washington. For people interested in eating cheaply, there are a few good delicatessens and counters to be found, an occasional outpost of the national fried chicken and hamburger chains, several restaurants catering to businessmen with all-American tastes (and featuring a bar), others directed toward vegetarians, and at least one with mystical, messianic overtones in its menu. But Washington, especially near the Mall, is a cafeteria city. One might as well be resigned to standing in line; a vast number of Washingtonians spend their lunch hours that way every working day.

For those unaccustomed to cafeterias, a bit of advice: beware temptation. Basic cafeteria prices can be incredibly cheap, but it's not uncommon for people to run up very substan-

Christopher Dickey is a member of *The Washington Post* Metropolitan staff.

tial bills because they can't resist the lure of items on the rack they would not think of ordering off a menu; or because they don't realize that almost everything, including pats of butter, gets rung up on the tab.

**All States Cafeteria, 1750 Pennsylvania Avenue, N.W. 393-5615.** Bland food at reasonable prices. Gaudy orange vinyl décor in a fluorescent-lit subterranean setting. Room to accommodate large crowds, and yet, for those who dine alone, there are a number of small individual tables. Two serving lines operate at peak hours. No beer, wine, or liquor.

**Astor Restaurant, 1813 M Street, N.W. (223-5249; 331-7994).** Greek-American food at very low prices and of variable quality. If you stick to eating and avoid the drinking and entertainment offered here in the evenings, you may emerge satisfied with your meal and your bill.

**Barney's, 621 Pennsylvania Avenue, N.W. (737-2989).** Good but not great kosher food at a counter and to carry out. Prices are low and service cordial.

**Bassin's Downtown Cafeteria, 511 Fourteenth Street, N.W. (628-1441). Bassin's Restaurant, Fourteenth Street and Pennsylvania Avenue, N.W. (628-1441).** There is nothing special about the food, but the prices are low and the locations are convenient to the Mall, the White House, and the National Theatre, among other places. In the summer, outdoor tables are available at the restaurant.

**Bull 'n Bear and Chamberlin Cafeteria, 819 Fifteenth Street, N.W. (628-7680).** Next door to Merrill Lynch, Pierce, Fenner & Smith. The food is essentially the same upstairs and down, but the entrees are more varied up in the Bull 'n Bear. The cafeteria is smaller than most, the light is lower and the décor is pleasant. The food costs a little more than usual in such places.

**Fatted Calf Restaurant, 1432 K Street, N.W. (638-8856). 415 Twelfth Street, N.W. (638-7003). 1019 Nineteenth Street, N.W. (293-9681).** The hamburgers here are cooked to taste, and they can be ordered with any of a variety of toppings. The quality of the food is higher than in most hamburger chains, but then, so are the prices. Beer only, except at the Twelfth Street place where there are both beer and wine.

**Flagship, 900 Water Street, S.W. (488-8515).** Plenty of seafood at reasonable prices. Good for family meals.

**Golden Temple Conscious Cookery, 1521 Connecticut Avenue, N.W. (234-6134).** Mung beans, alfalfa sprouts, homemade breads, fruits, dates, nuts, and cheeses are brought eclectically and often excitingly together in cuisine mingling Chinese, Indian, Middle Eastern, and Mexican influences. The perfect diet for people conscious of living on a small planet. Prices are reasonable. No alcoholic beverages or smoking.

**Greenbrier Restaurant (in Garfinckel's downtown department store), Fourteenth and F Streets, N.W. (628-7730).** A favorite restaurant for shoppers and nearby office workers, it is owned and operated by a Continental chef. The menu is predominantly French, but dishes from other countries, as well as popular sandwiches and soups, are available at moderate prices. The preparation of chilled fruit salads and desserts is especially appealing.

**The Greenery, 1144 Eighteenth Street, N.W. (872-1658).** The plant store next door provides much of this restaurant's décor, and much of the menu is made of salads. The "Salamagundi," with chunks of fresh turkey and ham among the greens and herb dressing, is popular. The "Super Summer Salad" is awesomely ample. The "Cheese Board" is a meal, not an appetizer, and the "New Leaf Club"—with turkey, orange, spinach leaves, and pecans on Syrian bread—is a delightfully original sandwich. Burgers and roast beef are also available; there are crowds at lunch, and the prices are not terribly high.

**The Greenhouse, Loew's L'Enfant Plaza Hotel, 480 L'Enfant Plaza East, S.W. (484-1000).** Typical luncheon fare—hamburgers, salads and the like—at reasonable prices and in a pleasant setting.

**H &S Restaurant & Caterers, 1712 L Street, N.W. (293-5737).** Good fresh foods cooked simply but well on a grill. There is also a carry-out. Prices are moderate. No beer, wine, or liquor.

**Health's A'Poppin, 2020 K Street, N.W. (466-6616).** A fairly new natural foods restaurant and cafeteria. Lots of fruit, yoghurt, sprouts, nuts and the rest; homemade soups and healthy sandwiches. No alcoholic beverages.

**Hogates Spectacular Seafood Restaurant, Ninth Street and Maine Avenue, S.W. (484-6300).** This warehouse-size eatery goes in for big seafood platters, rum buns, and fairly long waits for a table.

**Hot Shoppes Cafeteria, 1621 H Street, N.W. (347-9485)** (and many other locations, including the Smithsonian's Museum of History & Technology). This particular branch of the Marriott chain is underground, cavernous, and depressing. The food is nothing special at all and neither is its price. What is nice, however, is the carry-out service, which is just across the corner from the statue of Von Steuben in Lafayette Park, convenient for an instant picnic any time the weather is right. No alcoholic beverages.

**The House of Rothschild, 1030 Fifteenth Street, N.W. (296-5797).** This cafeteria overcomes a sense of crowding and commotion by providing three different dining areas. Hot specials are featured daily but the sandwich line is the focus of attention. The separate carry-out serves prepackaged sandwiches and salads that are not as good as those in the cafeteria but remain a favorite for local office workers who eat in McPherson Square or Lafayette Park on sunny days. Prices are moderate. Beer is available in the cafeteria; but no wine or liquor.

**Iron Gate Inn, at the rear of 1734 N Street, N.W. (737-1370).** The food here tends toward the Greek, and not always with good results (occasional oil slicks). The service is frequently terrible. But the setting—in a courtyard near Connecticut Avenue—is delightful.

**Kay's Sandwich Shoppe, 1410 New York Avenue, N.W. (628-2323). 1733 G Street, N.W. (638-6200).** These restaurants, owned and run by the same people who operate Le Souperb, offer some of the best sandwiches and short-order meals in town. Though they are popular and often crowded, the wait for a table is not usually very long. Prices are reasonable. Beer is available.

**Kitcheteria, in the Harrington Hotel, Eleventh & E Streets, N.W. (628-8140).** Virtually a self-service food factory with low prices, decent food, and lots of people all around. No beer, wine, or liquor.

**Kramer Books & Afterwords, 1517 Connecticut Avenue, N.W. (387-1400).** This delightful bookstore and café is a place where you can spend several hours browsing and munching. Fare consists of soups, salads, quiche and patés. When weather permits, watch most of Dupont Circle come and go at the sidewalk café. The café, open until 2 P.M. on weekends, has a full-service bar and takes most charge cards. Prices are moderate.

**Loeb's Restaurant, 617 Fifteenth Street, N.W. (783-9306).** A popular counter and carry-out of a kind well-known in New York. Service is fast and efficient and sometimes, when business is really moving quickly, a virtuoso juggling act of water glasses, milk shakes, and sandwiches. The combination sandwiches are a specialty.

**Luigi's Pizzeria Restaurant, 1132 Nineteenth Street, N.W. (331-7574).** The best pizza in the city (some would say the best anywhere) at moderate prices. The fish is also excellent; and in the summer sidewalk tables are an added attraction.

**Old Ebbitt Grill, 1427 F Street, N.W. (347-5560).** Simple American fare, plus omelettes on the upper level, in this renowned saloon with a century-old mahogany bar. Same ownership and atmosphere as Clyde's bar in Georgetown.

**Professional Coffee Shop, 1726 I Street, N.W. (298-6462).** The flecked red plastic upholstery in the booths looks as if it belongs on a motorcycle helmet. No alcoholic beverages are available. But with its fast service and cheap, good sandwiches made from fresh meat and vegetables, this little lunch spot draws in crowds of office workers every day. Carry-out service is also available.

**Reeves Bakery & Restaurant, 1209 F Street, N.W. (347-3781).** The décor hasn't changed much since this restaurant opened in 1886; there are brass chandeliers and Tiffany lamps on the high ceilings and tiny wooden stools at the dark, polished counters. At the rear there are a few tables. Entrées and sandwiches are good enough for the moderate prices, not better than that—but they're only incidental anyway. The main course is dessert. The pastries are American, gooey and rich. It's a place to get fat. The waitresses help the cause with quick and courteous service. No alcoholic beverages.

**Sholl's Colonial Cafeteria, 1032 Connecticut Avenue, N.W. (296-3065).** The food is decent and basic and very, very inexpensive, though anything as exotic as eggplant may not be worth the price. Beef, fish, and French fries are values. The décor is clean, the carpet springy and soft on tired feet. On the walls and counters mottoes of religion and thrift act as prelude to the prayer between the salt and pepper on each table. There are no outside windows and the lights are dim to the point of dinginess, but not romance. No beer, wine, or liquor.

**Sholl's New Cafeteria, 1433 K Street, N.W. (783-4133).** The food is the same fresh, healthy fare as at the other Sholl's, but at this location there are large windows looking out on McPherson Square and neighboring office buildings. No alcoholic beverages here, either.

Both of the Sholl's cafeterias are popular with large tours and visiting schools because of the low prices and the fast processing of people as well as food. At lunch hours there are always crowds, and if you take a table with more seats than you can use you are liable to have company.

**Le Souperb, 1221 Connecticut Avenue, N.W. (347-7600).** Five varieties of soups are served every day in ample enough portions to satisfy any appetite. Though the prices may at first seem high for a cafeteria, the soups are thick with substantial foods, they're rich, and they're served at the right temperature (in the summer cold gazpacho and vichyssoise are often available). Pastrami and beef sandwiches, cheesecake and carrot cake, are also on sale. Beer and wine; no mixed drinks.

**YWCA Cafeteria, 1649 K Street, N.W. (638-2100, ext. 4).** The décor is institutional without being sterile, the prices are low, and the entrees are adequate, though predictably bland. But the soups are good. The main attractions are the cakes, cookies, pies, and muffins prepared by the YWCA's bakery in the same building. (There is, as one might expect, no bar at all.)

---

The U.S. government and the Smithsonian offer a number of cafeterias and restaurants in Washington. In almost all of them the food is good—or, at least, fair—and the prices are fairly low.

Most of these dining rooms are in or near the city's most popular tourist attractions, thus adding convenience to the list of their attractions (though crowds may be a real problem, and lines are inevitable throughout the summer). In most instances, alcoholic beverages are not available.

In the Capitol, on the first floor, there are two branches of the **United States Senate Restaurant** open to visitors: the **Public Dining Room,** with a very limited unreserved seating capacity, and the **Family Dining Room.** Go in through the Capitol's east entrance. If both of these are crowded you can take the special subway from the Capitol's basement to the identical **North and South Cafeterias** in the basement of the **New (Dirksen) Senate Office Building (224-3080), across Constitution Avenue from the Capitol.** The menu is changed daily in all the branches of the Senate Restaurant, but bean soup is always a feature on it. In the Capitol dining rooms a large helping is served in a tureen that holds two bowlfuls. The phone number for all restaurants on Capitol Hill is **224-3121.**

Not to be outdone by Congress, the **Supreme Court Cafeteria—1 First Street, N.E. (393-1528),** enter through north door beneath steps—has recently redecorated and streamlined its cafeteria and coffee shop. The menu here frequently features more exotic foods than at other government eating places (teriyaki, for instance).

Along Independence Avenue near the Air and Space Museum and the Hirshhorn, **Federal Office Building 10A (FAA) (783-0075), Federal Office Building 10B (783-0082),** and the **Forrestal Building (554-4400)** all have cafeterias open for breakfast and lunch.

On the Mall, the **Museum of History and Technology (381-5198)** has a huge cafeteria decorated with attractive carousel animals. Though it is situated in the basement, there are big windows looking out on an impressive black stabile by Alexander Calder. Also in the same building is a branch of the Hot Shoppes hamburger chain. The basement of the **National Gallery of Art, Constitution Avenue at Sixth Street, N.W. (737-4215)** features a good, new, cafeteria under the Fourth Street Plaza. And, if you are a Smithsonian Associate one of the benefits of membership ($10 nationally, $15 locally) is the opportunity to eat at **The Commons, 1000 Jefferson, S.W. (381-6291),** quite a nice buffet in the

Smithsonian's "Castle." The windows have leaded glass, the ceilings are vaulted (with stars painted on them), and there is little noise.

# Movable Feasts in Georgetown

### By William Rice and Marian Burros

If there is a lack of magnificent food in Washington, the variety and originality of food shops and restaurants, especially in the Georgetown area, has increased enormously in recent years. And they are getting better all the time.

An astonishing amount of good food can be found in establishments that sell food for off-premises consumption. The range of selection is surprising. You may wish for an ice cream to cool a sidewalk stroll along Wisconsin Avenue, or a picnic luncheon selection to consume in Montrose Park or beside the C&O Canal, and these days you can find both.

Most of these shops are on M Street and on Wisconsin Avenue; a few are tucked away on side streets. The quality of what they sell is uneven—therefore, the list includes featured items or those that our samplings have established as worthy of special mention. Listings within each category are made in descending order of preference.

There is a welcome informality in the French food at two cafés, La Ruche and Café de Paris, as well as the latter's offshoot, La Patisserie. La Ruche is one of the most attractive restaurants

William Rice and Marian Burros are food editors of *The Washington Post*'s Style section; both have written books.

in Georgetown and also serves some of the most outstanding food.

Current eating trends are reflected in the vegetable orientation of the menus at the attractive Gate Soup Kitchen and at Yes, which has a charming garden. Young people prepare food at Yes, the Gate, the popular Booeymonger, and elsewhere.

Alas, there is not a truly outstanding pizza to be found in Georgetown, in our opinion, nor is the best ice cream (at Swensen's) the finest in town. There is, however, the surprise of finding fine pastry items at reasonable prices in Maison des Crêpes.

More than anything else, it is a delight to be able to escape the boring sameness of franchise fast-food operations. Sometimes this means a loss of efficiency, and while some of the shops may look shabby, their food can be a pleasant surprise. For the most part, these are small-scale provisioners, and they reflect enterprise and a search for quality.

Washington's emergence from its sleepy Southern stereotype and growth toward recognition as a cosmopolitan world capital is not, by most accounts, complete as yet. (Peanuts are becoming more popular with corner vendors.) But, finally you can find something other than a hamburger to eat after 9 P.M., and an international sampling for casual eating day or night.

Unless otherwise noted, these establishments do *not* serve alcoholic beverages, and as a general rule, none "to go" unless they are package stores.

## INTERNATIONAL

**La Ruche, 1206 30th Street, N.W. 965-2684.** Top quality soups, quiche, fresh vegetables daily, delicious strawberry tarte, meringue maison, espresso and cappuccino. Beer and wine.

**Café de Paris, 3056 M Street, N.W. 965-2920.** Good pastries, fine empanada, pâté, espresso, cappuccino. Wine and light French cocktails.

**La Patisserie, 1340 Wisconsin Avenue. 338-4207.** Branch of Café de Paris.

**Macripodaris Gourmetisserie, 1624 Wisconsin Avenue. 338-1531.** Good cheesecake, Napoleon, interesting combination platter with five main dishes.

**Vietnam Georgetown Restaurant, 2934 M Street, N.W. 337-4536.** Good fish dishes and spring rolls. Bar.

**Ikaros, 3130 M Street, N.W. 333-5551.** Phyllo-wrapped cheese pastry, souvlaki, pizza, hero sandwich, fruit drinks.

## HEALTH FOODS

**Gate Soup Kitchen, 3338 M Street, N.W. 337-4283.** Excellent soups, delicious garden sandwiches. No smoking allowed.

**Yes, 1039 Thirty-first Street, N.W. 338-1700.** Soups, breads, desserts. No smoking allowed.

## ICE CREAM AND SWEETS

**Swensen's, 1254 Wisconsin Avenue. 333-3433.** Outstanding ice cream, sundaes, sodas, sandwiches.

**Maison des Crêpes, 1305 Wisconsin Avenue. 337-1723.** A variety of cakes and pastries of good quality. Wine, beer, and liquor.

**Crumpets, 1259 Wisconsin Avenue. 337-9629.** Pastries both good and indifferent, ice cream fair.

**The Parlor, 1531 Wisconsin Avenue. 337-9796.** Adequate ice cream, overly exotic sandwiches.

## MARKETS

**Neam's, 3217 P Street, N.W. 338-4694.** Excellent sandwiches, top-quality ingredients, top prices; cheeses, breads, salads. Beer and wine sold.

**Booeymonger, 3265 Prospect Street. 333-4810.** Inventive sandwiches with fanciful names, uneven execution. Beer and wine sold.

**French Market, 1632 Wisconsin Avenue. 338-4828.** Extensive assortment French charcuterie and sandwiches, expensive but high-quality; salads, breads, cheeses. Beers, wines, champagnes sold.

**Food Mart, 3075 M St., N.W. 333-3466.** Wide selection of

sandwiches, salads, cheeses, breads, beverages. Beer and wine sold.

**Wisemiller's Delicatessen, 1236¹/₂ Thirty-sixth Street, N.W. 333-8254.** Thick submarine sandwich, fresh and tasty sweet rolls, coffee. Beer and wine sold.

**Olde Georgetown Market, 1425 Twenty-eighth Street, N.W. (at P). 333-1570.** Sandwiches, pastries. Beer and wine sold.

**7-Eleven, 2617 P Street, N.W. 337-9822.** Barricini ice cream, coffee, pre-packed sandwiches.

---

## SANDWICH SPECIALTIES

**Harold's Delicatessen, 3011 M Street, N.W. 333-4373.** 28 sandwiches, good homemade salads and deviled eggs. Beer, wine, and liquor sold here.

**Hoya, Thirty-fifth Street, N.W. and Reservoir Road. 965-3621.** Turkey club, other sandwiches.

**Tony's G.T. Carryout and Luncheonette, 3308 M Street, N.W. 337-6927.** Sandwiches, homemade salads, chili beans.

**Good Old Phil's, 1353 Wisconsin Avenue. 337-0221.** Well-seasoned pizza, submarines, hot dogs.

**Le Gourmet, 3318 M Street, N.W. 333-5462.** Thick sandwiches, submarines, soup, salads. Beer and wine sold.

---

## FAST FOODS

**Hector's, 3207 M Street, N.W. 333-5073.** Souvlaki, hamburgers, hot dogs.

**Roy Rogers, Wisconsin and Prospect, N.W. 338-0146.** Fried chicken, hamburgers, French fries.

**Little Tavern(s), 3331 M Street, N.W., 337-9784, and 1301 Wisconsin Avenue, 333-9821.** Hamburgers, coffee.

**Peoples Drug Store, 1403 Wisconsin Avenue, 337-4848.** Sandwiches, hamburgers, soft drinks.

## OTHER

**Wine and Cheese Shop, 1413 Wisconsin Avenue. 333-8822.** Cheese, bread, pâté, chilled wines. Beer, wine, and liquor sold.

**Eagle Wine and Cheese, 3345 M Street, N.W. 333-6655.** Cheese, breads, quiche, cold wines and beer, liquor.

**Georgetown Coffee House, 1330 Wisconsin Avenue. 338-2366.** Breads, cheese, chilled beverages.

**Hudson Bros. Greengrocers, 3206 Grace Street, N.W. 337-8585.** Fresh fruits and vegetables.

**Paul Muir Cheeses, 3206 Grace Street, N.W. 337-8737.** Cheese.

**Cannon's Sea Food, 1065 Thirty-first Street, N.W. 337-8366.** Cooked and spiced shrimps.

# XII
# The Performing Arts

## By Tom Shales

That cultural life in Washington has improved in the past decade is the most blatant sort of truism. For one thing, ho-hum is not that hard to improve upon. For another, the John F. Kennedy Center for the Performing Arts opened in 1971 and, though widely derided as an architectural embarrassment (compared by one critic to the behemoth buildings of Nazi Germany), it gave the city something the performing arts inevitably require: a place to perform.

At first, in those hardly halcyon but hopeful days, it looked like a renaissance on the rise. The Center opened, the arts appeared to flourish, and it looked as though other theaters would not only survive the competition but thrive from it; arts awareness was increasing, and that spilled over from the lit-up Center to other theaters. We were even talking of overtaking New York as America's cultural capital.

We got carried away with ourselves.

Now, a leveling off has occurred. Some arts institutions fell by the wayside: the National Ballet (which could not afford to play the expensive Center), the Washington Theater Club, the American Theatre in L'Enfant Plaza—all dead. The proud old National Theatre, meanwhile, long the home of touring Broadway shows and pre-Broadway tryouts, found itself repeatedly bypassed for the more prestigious Center. It was snatched from the cliffs of calamity, ironically perhaps, by Center Chairman Roger L. Stevens, who took it over and set up an independent—at least on paper—board to run and book it. Since then, its health has improved, though the fancy Center still gets more attention and is considered *the* place in which to appear.

Tom Shales is a reporter and television critic for *The Washington Post* Style section.

Washington, then, is not New York or London or Paris —and the city's embassy or White House parties may still be, in the minds of the local establishment, the most important and entertaining shows in town—but the city has come of age as an arts center. Though it is said the only common value in this corrupt old capital is power, even the power-mad need diversions. And in its insidious way, the media adjunct of the power elite decides that certain shows are the ones to be seen at if one wants to appear to matter. If the motives for attendance by city residents are thus often questionable, the results may be nevertheless beneficial, to the city, to the people who visit it, and even to those powermongers themselves. They may even have souls like you and me.

---

### THE KENNEDY CENTER

**Adjacent to the Watergate complex, where New Hamphire and Virginia Avenues, N.W., meet.** Pay parking in the building. **General information: 254-3600.**

After one has been incalculaby enriched with the knowledge that its Grand Foyer is as long as two football fields and its chandeliers each weigh a ton, the Kennedy Center still has much to offer. In its three large theaters and one small movie house, something is almost always happening, and variety, within a certain spectrum, is rampant. About the only cultural stratum consistently absent is the trend-setting avant-garde. For that, you still have to go to New York.

Although the Center was built largely with public and federal funds, only the maintenance of the building itself is subsidized with government money now. The theaters are privately operated. Thus ticket prices are no lower than anywhere else. Specially priced seats are available for full-time students, persons over 65, certain military personnel, and people who can convince the folks behind the ticket windows that they have "limited incomes." (For information, call 254-3718.) All others pay full fare, except for some seats in the Concert Hall priced very low because, due to a designer's goof, they have obstructed views of the stage—which mainly amounts to no view at all. You must stand to see, but you can hear while seated. It is a qualified sort of bargain.

The first public performance at the Kennedy Center—a 1971 dress rehearsal of Leonard Bernstein's *Mass*.

In the airy seating under the canopy, viewers enjoy a performance at Wolf Trap Farm Park.

The Kennedy Center has made it fairly easy to buy tickets for most of its shows *if* you have one of several "major" credit cards. An "instant charge" phone number published in local newspaper advertising enables you to call and reserve a seat, then pay with your credit card when you pick up your ticket. Phone lines are often busy though, and the bigger the hit, the harder it will be to get through.

Unfortunately for Washington visitors and residents as well, sell-out attractions are frequent at the Center. Even if the show in question has laid or will lay a big fat egg elsewhere, it may be the hottest thing in town while playing the Center. Washington's international audience of embassy people eats up plays, dances, and music from abroad, and the appearance of a luminary like Ingrid Bergman or Yul Brynner in virtually anything almost guarantees SRO. Still, there is room for hope even when the sold-out sign goes up. In most cases, standing room is reserved for sale until the morning of a performance. In addition, "house seats" in prime locations are retained for most performances in the event that a VIP—and the city is crawling with them—suddenly gets a mad urge to see a certain show. If these house seats are not doled out one way or another, they may be available at the box office just before curtain time. It is a gamble, but some people find it worth loitering and hoping as the hour of performance approaches.

One is less likely in Washington to find "scalpers" peddling tickets at the door than to find people begging for extra seats. There is not yet a hefty trade here in what New Yorkers call "ice" (scalpers' sales at the door, with sizable mark-ups in price), except perhaps for superevents starring superstars.

Parking in the Center costs $2 a night, but a 50-cent rate is available in the daytime for dashing in and picking up tickets, with a half-hour limit. On heavily attended nights, especially weekends, the Center lot fills up, but other parking is available in nearby apartment and commercial developments like Watergate and Columbia Plaza. Street parking is free at night but in extremely short supply.

### The Opera House
**Recorded information: 254-3770; Instant-charge: 857-0900.**
The Opera House is ungodly red and discomfortingly decorated, but the sight of its huge Austrian chandelier dimming

before a performance makes newcomers and even some veterans say "ooh." The place is overly formal and stuffy, and since the wooden seat backs go all the way to the floor, performances are regularly punctuated with the sounds of shoes kicking wood, as people attempt, with futility, to stretch their legs. Opera actually occupies only a small part of the year here—performed usually by the Opera Society of Washington, known for inventive and off-beat productions that invariably sell out, or by visiting companies who tend to trot out the warhorses. Otherwise you can expect a full-scale musical on its way to or from Broadway, an occasional straight play looking very uncomfortable in the oversized surroundings, or a visiting dance or novelty group. Unusual offerings like the Chinese acrobats or the Moiseyev dancers will sell out early if it seems at all politically trendy to attend them. In the age of détente, almost anything from behind the Iron Curtain, as it used to be called, is likely to be considered chic in Washington, and to be overpraised. Tickets may become collectors' items quickly.

### The Eisenhower Theater
**Recorded information: 254-3670; Instant-charge: 857-0900.**

More musical comedies and straight plays here—some of them originate in Washington under the aegis of Kennedy Center Productions, a commercial outfit also helmed by Center Chairman Stevens. Such shows may or may not go on to Broadway or other cities where they may ("Pippin") or may not ("Outcry") succeed. Stevens, who earns no salary as Center chief, has proven not only shrewd but, for a commercial producer, mildly adventurous in what he has chosen to sponsor, and he is also a master of ballyhoo. The biggest undertakings ("Jumpers") are launched with social do's that inevitably attract what Washington considers glamour people (nearly any Kennedy, for example) and dominate the next day's newspaper society pages. With such a send-off, even a show that later flops in New York may prove a Washington sell-out.

Stevens further caters to and exploits the city's celebrities with his Golden Circle society, where the only requirement for membership is a thousand bucks' donation. For that you can sip intermission drinks in a private lounge off the Opera House with fellow luminaries. Mere mortals booze it up in the Grand Foyer.

The Eisenhower is more hospitable to live performances

than the Opera House, but its stage is so impractically oversized that most touring productions have to mask off large portions of it in black; their sets were designed for conventional stages. For that reason, one should sit as close as possible to, but not among, the first five rows of the orchestra section.

### The Concert Hall
**Recorded information: 254-3776; Instant-charge: 857-0900.**

The most aesthetically pleasing of the three main theaters, the Concert Hall, also has outstanding acoustics and an impressive pipe organ at the rear of its stage.

Concerts here often feature Washington's National Symphony Orchestra, which has increased in stature and quality in recent years under the direction of Mstislav Rostropovich. Seats are reasonably priced, and unless the program is spectacular, they are often available the day of the performance. Heavily subsidized by the National Endowment for the Arts and further blessed with hard-working fund-raising staff members and volunteers, the National Symphony has become one of the city's healthiest cultural institutions. And it probably has never sounded better.

Visiting orchestras and soloists also perform here, often under the auspices of the Washington Performing Arts Society. White-haired impresario Patrick Hayes, who thinks the Kennedy Center is the greatest thing since Mozart, is often at Performing Arts' productions and may even take a hand in arbitrating ticket snafus and other problems.

Pop stars (Burt Bacharach, Tony Bennett, Shirley Bassey) also turn up here; most of them leave raving about the hall's fine sound. Rock concerts are more infrequent, partly because rock audiences leave the place a mess and their funny little cigarettes burn holes in the rug (the grim-faced ushers huddle and despair at such events). Other novelties play here: Sally Rand has fan-danced and Rod McKuen has croaked his greeting-card "poetry."

### The American Film Institute Theater
**Recorded information: 785-4600.**

Located just inside the Hall of States, the small, 224-seat AFI Theater has twice-nightly showings, at 6:30 and 9 o'clock, of old and new movies grouped into concurrently running series:

"Cities on Film," "Shakespeare on Film," studio and director retrospectives, international cinema, and so on. Occasional special events—a super rarity or a pre-release commercial movie première—will be moved into the much larger Eisenhower, which also has projection facilities. The AFI Theater is tiny and tacky, supposedly temporary since AFI Director George Stevens, Jr., has said he eventually wants a bigger, better-equipped theater located elsewhere in the Center. That, however, is millions of dollars away, and for now, the primitive, to be polite, décor of the AFI Theater is pleasant relief from the glittering pomposity of the Center's main theaters.

During the summer, short and innocuous films are sometimes screened during the day, usually requiring less than an hour in time and little, if any, money. These are open to the public. In addition, there are semi-regular children's matinees of classic or recent "family" films, but the tickets for these go like, well, hotcakes, and you probably should not expect to be able to purchase a ticket just before the showing. Check with the box office.

---

## OTHER PLACES TO HEAR MUSIC

**Wolf Trap Farm Park for the Performing Arts, a half-hour's drive from Washington in Vienna, Virginia; 938-3800,** is now open only in summer months, though plans call for a year-round facility when the money is scrounged up. The open-air theater is popular—it attracts 500,000 people per summer, around 6,000 at a time, for performances by—among others—the Metropolitan Opera, the Preservation Hall Jazz Band, Sarah Vaughan, Alvin Ailey's dance company, and on one fine night in '74, the late Jack Benny, billed in the program as a "violinist." Even if its 3,500 sheltered but noticeably unpadded seats sell out, you can still sit cheaply on an unprotected grassy slope. Many bring blankets and picnic trappings and do just that. An overpriced but satisfactorily prepared meal is also available under a tent, but you have to reserve space in advance, and it is not really worth the trouble.

**DAR Constitution Hall, Eighteenth and D Streets, N.W., 638-2661,** cannot compare with the Kennedy Center Concert Hall acoustically or visually, but musical organizations still appear here, and for years, this homely, cavernous barn owned by the Daughters of the American Revolution was all Washington had. For years, too, in times people may want to forget, blacks were banned from appearing on its stage, which is why Marian Anderson sang at the Lincoln Memorial on Easter Sunday in 1939; she had been denied the use of the Hall. Today, such events are part of history, and music of all kinds and colors is performed at the Hall—even an occasional rock group as outrageous as, say, Sly and the Family Stone.

**Lisner Auditorium, at Twenty-First and H Streets, N.W., 676-6800,** on the campus of George Washington University, has a smaller audience capacity than Constitution Hall but a much warmer ambiance and better acoustics.

**The Library of Congress Coolidge Auditorium, First Street between East Capitol and Independence Avenue, S.E., 426-5000,** holds concerts by the Juilliard String Quartet, playing genuine Stradivarius instruments, Friday and Saturday evenings. Tickets are cheap but must be purchased in advance during the week.

**The National Gallery of Art, Constitution Avenue at Sixth Street, N.W., 737-4215,** is also the scene of specialized music programs, Sunday evenings at 8, September through June, in its 650-seat and very airy East Garden Court. Admission is free and not bookable in advance. The smaller **Corcoran Gallery of Art, Seventeenth Street and New York Avenue, N.W. (638-3211)** and the **Phillips Collection, 1600 Twenty-First Street, N.W. (387-2151)** also have chamber music programs, now and then, October through May.

Summer sends music outdoors, and each year more such music seems available. The Army, Navy, Marine Corps, and Air Force bands take turns playing outdoor nighttime concerts at the Jefferson Memorial—where the jets and the helicopters also play, overhead—and on the East Front steps of the Capitol Building. For the most part, the music is light as lemonade and the audiences polyglot and picturesque. Daily newspapers print the schedules. In addition, Washington's Summer in the Parks program dispatches the National Symphony Orchestra, sometimes for lunch-hour concerts to soothe the savage bureaucrat. Schedules, published as summer begins by National Capital Parks, are available at tourist information centers around town. The daily newspapers also try to keep up with these and other free events in their entertainment sections.

More music under the proverbial stars is available at the

**Carter Barron Amphitheatre,** which seats 4,500 for its classical, pop, and rock music, dance, and theater programs. A congenial spot in **Rock Creek Park on outer Sixteenth Street, N.W. (829-3202),** it is leased to entrepreneurs by the National Park Service.

If rock—in concert—is what you want, you may find it at the **Alexandria Roller Rink, 807 North St. Asaph Street, in Alexandria, Virginia (836-6167).** Occasionally a rock group will be confident enough of its drawing power to book itself into the huge **Robert F. Kennedy Stadium, East Capitol and Twenty-Second Streets, S.E., 546-222,** where it is difficult to hear and difficult to see but easy to feel a part of an event. The area's most favored rock palace is the mammoth, sports-oriented **Capital Centre, 1 Harry S Truman Drive, off the Beltway in Largo, Maryland,** about a 45-minute drive from downtown Washington **(350-3900).** There, 18,000 fans can convene to boogie, flip out, party or, conspicuously, consume drugs and alcohol of varying potency. Meanwhile, far-far-away onstage, Supergroup of the Moment is thrashing and gnashing wildly, its image brought closer and made slightly surreal by the huge TV system whose four screens hang down from center ceiling. Yes, some people come here to watch television (and they may even watch themselves if the camera happens upon them). Large corporations lease stratospheric "sky suites" high in the rafters where the very rich and their pals can hold private parties replete with catered liquor and snacks, and take in the mad panorama below. Of course, it is not always a madhouse with rock stars. The Centre has offered Lawrence Welk, too, and ice shows, traveling circus revues ("Disney on Parade"), as well as an actual, annual circus, and pop music events like the Frank Sinatra comeback of 1974.

---

### OTHER PLACES TO SEE PLAYS

**The National Theatre, 1321 E Street, N.W., 628-3393,** is a large, comfortable house that has been a city landmark for more than a century. The Booths, the Barrymores, and Bernhardt appeared on its stage, and Presidents Franklin D. Roosevelt, John F. Kennedy, and Lyndon B. Johnson appeared in its audience, with LBJ and Lady Bird coaxed onto the stage by Pearl Bailey for a "Hello, Dolly!" finale.

**Arena Stage, at Sixth and M Streets** in the urban-renewed southwest, **554-7890,** for more than 25 years has been the Washington theater most likely to intrigue and excite an audience—even during the days when its plays were mounted in a converted brewery. Old and new productions are staged, from "King Lear" to "Pueblo," plus such fated-for-Broadway works "Raisin" and "The Great White Hope." Arena has become one of America's top regional theaters. Production standards are high, the batting average enviable, and the highest priced individual ticket during its October-through-June season less than $7. Parking is available in a small lot or on surrounding streets. Because Arena is heavily subscribed every year (nearly 18,000 subscribers), weekend evening performances may be inaccessible.

**The Folger Theatre, 201 East Capitol Street, 546-4000,** in the Elizabethan Folger Shakespeare Library on Capitol Hill, has made giant leaps in reputation and number of regular subscribers in the past few years by presenting not only fresh stagings of Shakespeare plays ("Romeo and Juliet" set at a circus) but also by introducing worthwhile new plays and playwrights. Five plays a year are staged between October and June in its small, period playhouse, and tickets are relatively cheap. (*See* Chapter X, "Archives and Libraries.")

**Ford's Theatre,** the capital's most historic, at **511 Tenth Street, N.W., 554-7890,** is, of course, the very playhouse where Lincoln was assassinated while watching "Our American Cousin" (he had planned on going to the National that night to see a trained horse, as it happens, but Mrs. Lincoln wanted to go to Ford's). Beautifully restored to look the way it did then, the theater houses small-scale touring productions that range from proper classical theater to such romps as "Don't Bother Me, I Can't Cope," and "Godspell," which ran for more than a year. Frankie Hewitt, who runs the place, has one guiding rule: don't book plays that are too long, because the theater's cute but uncomfortable chairs cannot be endured for more than two hours. (Hint: If you flip the red cushion up behind your back rather than sitting on it, you may find yourself almost comfortable.) Parking lots are nearby and a Lincoln Museum is open in the basement. (*See* Chapter V, "Monuments and Memorials.")

**The American Society of Theater Arts** is a new and struggling theatrical group operating out of two converted movie houses at **507 8th Street, S.E., 543-7676.** Plays run from established works to original, untried productions.

**The Sylvan Theater,** on the Washington Monument grounds at **Fifteenth Street and Independence Avenue, N.W., 426-7724,** is the tree-surrounded scene for one play per summer, usually Shakespeare but often Shakespeare-for-fun, with the bard abetted by rock music or other updatings. Trouble is, airplanes landing at National Airport make so much noise overhead that the play is only intermittently the thing. Admission is free.

**Back Alley Theatre (1365 Kennedy Street, N.W., 723-2040)** offers drama for more specialized interests. Sometimes highly political or topical, sometimes qualifying as experimental, the plays are performed by actors who most definitely are not doing it for the money, since they are paid minimally. It is art for art's sake.

In addition, the Washington area's population of dinner theaters has grown to 12, all of them in a Maryland or Virginia suburb. Only three of the theaters, however, subscribe to Actors Equity, the professional actors' union: the **Garland** in **Columbia, Maryland, (301)730-8311;** the **Hayloft** in **Manassas, Virginia, 591-8040;** and the **Lazy Susan** in **Woodbridge, Virginia, 836-1259**—all considerable distances from the District. At non-Equity houses, acting standards are likely lower, and productions minimal and amateurish.

**Shady Grove Music Fair,** a 45-minute drive from Washington **in Gaithersburg, Maryland; 948-3400,** has an annual June-to-September season of touring summer-stockish musicals and comedies, plus occasional specialties of the Las Vegas revue genre. The audience surrounds a small, round stage, and lobby refreshments include steamed hot dogs and beer. Highly and deservedly informal.

---

### THE MOVIES

Washington has its distinctions, good and bad, as a movie town. Among the good: a local appetite for quality foreign films, and a few exhibitors willing to show them; fairly high standards of projection and presentation; substantial availability of old movies, from the classics to classic trash; and a considerable variety of houses.

Among the bad: the fact that an increasing number of first-run movies open only in the suburbs, not in the District. Downtown, once-grand houses like Loews Palace are given over to repetitious kung-fu or low-grade black action pictures. Other downtown theaters have either gone porno or gone out of business. One was converted to a burlesque joint.

Washington moviegoers are a fairly independent lot, not always obedient to the screaming notices from silly New York critics that clutter up movie ads. That can mean that a good movie that did not stand a chance in chancey Manhattan can find an audience here—a well-educated, youngish, and affluent one, as movie audiences go.

The theaters listed below do not show exclusively first-run commercial pictures; their programming and their loyalists indicate each is more than an in-a-rut moviehouse. They are likely to give screen space to the unusual and, therefore, the welcome.

**The American Film Institute Theater** (*see* Kennedy Center) shows two movies per night in its small Kennedy Center auditorium. Filmmakers' work shown ranges from Alfred Hitchcock's to Ed Emshwiller's, Luis Buñuel's to Chuck ("Looney Tunes" and "Merrie Melodies") Jones'. Box office phone: 785-4600.

**The Biograph, at 2819 M Street, N.W., 333-2696,** is a cozy Georgetown theater, transformed from a used-car showroom by five movie-loving young lawyers. It is now a popular haunt for the cinema generation, not only for regular nightly showings of youth-appealing pictures, from the Marx Brothers to Michelangelo Antonioni, but for off-beat, sometimes way off-beat, weekend midnight frolics. This might be a collection of old TV shows or the Biographs's long-run gross-out champ, "Pink Flamingos," a movie designed by Baltimore filmmaker John Waters to make an audience sick. Or your money back.

**The Circle Theatre, at 2105 Pennsylvania Avenue, N.W., 331-7480,** is the Parthenon of local moviehouses—which is not to say that it is falling apart, but that it is a shrine, a shrine whose double bills of golden (or aluminum) oldies for $2 or less admission lure hordes of worshippers. Ted and Jim Pedas have respect for their customers and a perpetual fear of becoming bored. In addition to the original and incomparable Circle, they have opened the **Inner Circle**—with peace-inducing rocking-chair seats—**next door (331-7480),** and the **Outer Circles 1 and 2 on outer (Number**

**4849) Wisconsin Avenue, N.W., 244-3116.** They have also acquired the **Dupont Circle, 1332 Connecticut Avenue, N.W., 785-2300** and the **West End Circle** at **Twenty-Third and L Streets, N.W., 293-3152.** At all these theaters, something better than ordinary is likely to be playing—a foreign film other theaters have ignored or would not risk, or the latest sensitive essay on human frailty by India's Satyajit Ray, whose movies invariably have their U.S. premières at a Circle. In addition to all these riches, the original Circle has a great, messy, buttered popcorn, though its fellow Circles dish it out only via vending machine.

# XIII
## Nightlife

### By Larry Rohter

"You can't tell the players without a scorecard," says an old baseball adage. The same thing can be said of Washington nightlife, a source of rich and varied entertainment which too often seems a confusing welter of clubs, bars, cafés, discotheques and cabarets of indeterminate price and quality.

The problem is not so much where to find nighttime diversion—the Washington area is dotted with scores of nightspots—as what to expect in the way of prices, opening and closing times, and type of entertainment at particular establishments. The guide below, which provides basic information on some major centers of nightlife for the District of Columbia and suburban Maryland and Virginia, is an attempt—admittedly selective—to point out the places that are most frequently turned to by tourists and area residents when the order of business is a night out on the town.

These nightspots have little in common. Some are major nightclubs where big-name acts on stage almost automatically mean a large tab at evening's end. Others are quiet, submerged spots with local and little-known talent, but with prices that are quite reasonable.

What unites this otherwise disparate selection of establishments is the presence of live entertainment. At the discos, much of the fun is generated by disc jockeys who use their electronic accessories to encourage the crowd's excitement, but in most nightspots listed below, live rather than recorded entertainment is synonymous with music. And what an array of music it is. It is safe to say that in Washington there is something for even the most demanding tastes. Jazz, rock, country, soul, pop, and

Larry Rohter wrote regularly for *The Washington Post* Style section on music and the area entertainment scene until he left to cover the same scene in Brazil.

bluegrass all have found havens here, and some truly eclectic spots manage to feature the whole gamut of musical styles.

**Where:** Most of the clubs are conveniently located, and many are clustered together in certain key areas. The soul-music clubs, including some not mentioned below, are mostly concentrated along Georgia Avenue, N.W. The bluegrass scene is strongest out in Maryland and Virginia, flourishing in clubs that are collectively known as "The Beltway Circuit" because of their proximity to Interstate 495.

Georgetown, however, remains the area where nightlife is the most active and the most varied. Whole blocks of Wisconsin Avenue and of M Street, N.W., are given over to the pursuit of after-dark amusement. Connecticut Avenue, N.W., south and just north of Dupont Circle, is another center of activity. (For example, the Junkanoo, where Wilbur Mills and Fanne Fox allegedly had some of their best-known adventures, is in this area.) And on, or just off, downtown 14th Street, N.W., is where, according to an old saying, "the girls get stripped and the customers get clipped"; money-minded entertainment seekers should be wary.

**When:** In most District of Columbia clubs, regardless of location, live entertainment starts between 9:00 and 9:30 P.M. and continues until 1:30 or 2:00 A.M. on weeknights, 2:30 or 3:00 A.M. on weekends. Stricter liquor and licensing laws in Virginia and especially Maryland mean that clubs in the suburbs open and close earlier than their D.C. counterparts; figure on an 8:00 P.M. starting time and a 12:00 or 1:00 A.M. closing time on both weeknights and weekends in Virginia and Prince George's County, Maryland. In Montgomery County, Maryland, hours of operation are roughly the same as in the District.

**How Much:** That perpetual bugaboo, prices, must be mentioned. Like every other economic sector, the entertainment field has been subject to spiraling costs and expenses. Also, the situation is fluid, so when talking about dollars and cents, there is no assurance that today's figures will hold true next week. Since prices and policies change so rapidly they are not given here. Call before you go.

Nevertheless, this survey classifies nightspots into three price categories: expensive, moderate, and inexpensive. Certain clubs, traditionally, have been more costly than others and are likely to remain so even as prices inflate all down the line.

## A BIT OF EVERYTHING

Consider, for instance some of the spots offering something for everyone:

The **Cellar Door (1201 Thirty-fourth Street, N.W., 337-3389)** is Washington's answer to New York's Bottom Line or Los Angeles' Troubador; a small (200-seat) club that regularly features top folk, rock, jazz, blues and comedy artists. The emphasis is as much on rising talents—Neil Young, Linda Ronstadt, and John Denver all made their first Washington appearances here—as on established club-circuit regulars such as Tom Rush, Les McCann, and Muddy Waters. This entertainment policy and a Georgetown location make the club especially popular with the under-30 crowd, but even their elders would probably agree that for variety and quality of live music presented on a regular basis, the Cellar Door cannot be beat. A substantial cover charge and minimum make this spot an expensive one. Be sure to bring cash; checks and credit cards are not accepted here. Reservations are necessary.

Even if you are not looking for a place to spend the evening you are likely to come across Mr. Henry's: four local nightspots share the name and the management. At all Mr. Henry's places, American Express and Visa are accepted. Each has, however, a slightly different pricing and entertainment policy. Mr. Henry's is best known, perhaps, as the place where jazz-pop singer Roberta Flack got her start. Its current entertainment standards are not quite that high, but the various locations offer relaxed settings for people who like to converse and sip drinks leisurely, with live music in the background.

The original **Mr. Henry's** is at **2134 Pennsylvania Avenue, N.W. (337-0222),** near the George Washington University. Two rooms feature live entertainment. For the economy-conscious, downstairs is probably the better bet: soft folk music is offered by singles and small groups for no cover charge or minimum. Upstairs tends to be considerably more expensive.

**Mr. Henry's Georgetown (1225 Wisconsin Avenue, N.W., 337-4334)** is in the heart of Washington's largest entertainment district. Its long-time "no cover, no minimum" policy attracts local college students and young singles, but live music has all but been eliminated. Still a good place for hanging out.

Not so at **Mr. Henry's Tenley Circle (4323 Wisconsin Avenue, N.W., 362-6079).** Here the emphasis is on the music, mostly soft rock and folk. Also notable is the Victorian pub decor. Again, there is no cover, no minimum.

Jazz is the keynote at **Mr. Henry's Upstairs,** of Roberta

Flack fame **(601 Pennsylvania Avenue, S.E., near Capitol Hill, 546-8412).** Piano trios and quartets are the rule here, although occasionally a slinky chanteuse slips in. This branch is more expensive than the others, with a substantial cover charge and minimum on weekends. Tiffany lamps and dark-wood furnishings provide the setting.

**Rocky Raccoon's, 1243 Twentieth Street, N.W., 872-1643, is a** bar-restaurant-nightspot serving up a Tex-Mex menu and a combination of country/folk/rock groups who perform on a small stage at the far end of the main room. Slickly cosy with gingham-covered tables, and a big fireplace with the requisite stuffed raccoon above it. Cover charge Thursdays and weekends.

## POP MUSIC PROSPECTS

In a somewhat different category are Washington's numerous small and independent nightspots that specialize in rock 'n' roll and related music styles. Local performers, almost exclusively, occupy their bandstands. These easygoing and casual clubs are scattered around the District.

**The Childe Harold is at 1610 Twentieth Street, N.W. (483-6702),** two blocks north of Dupont Circle. A gathering place for young Washington artists and craftsmen, it features consistently good rock, blues, country, and even some bluegrass. Cover charge depends on the performer's popularity; there's never a minimum. The talent is often the very best that Washington has to offer: country-rock singer Emmylou Harris is now a national star, but back in the days when she was just a local phenomenon, this was her home base. Even the food here is worth trying. Major

credit cards are accepted at this delightful and moderately-priced spot.

**Reading Gaol is off an alley between O and P Streets,** but its official address is the rear of **2120 P Street, N.W. (833-3882).** The club has an upstairs and a back room, but when one of the fine rock 'n' roll bands that are a regular feature here takes the stage on a Friday or Saturday night, the large crowd squeezes out into the aisles and begins—or at least tries to begin—to dance. A cover charge here, but a moderate one, and there is no minimum. Drinks are cheap and the oh-so-relaxed waiters very rarely pressure patrons to reorder. The result is one of the most friendly and enjoyable of the Washington area clubs catering to young singles. Major credit cards honored.

**Desperados (3350 M Street, N.W., 338-5220** is a recent addition to Georgetown's already teeming nightlife. Dancing here is seven nights a week, but the main attraction is always the live music, which regularly spotlights Washington's best rock 'n' roll bands or even an occasional up-and-coming group brought in from Boston or New York. Try and catch either The Nighthawks or D.C. Dog, two stalwarts who observers-of-the-local-rock-scene argue are the cream of the musical crop. There is a bit of the "swinging singles" ambiance at this tiny club, but it does not get in the way of the good music. Moderate in price—but finding a place to park nearby is extremely difficult.

## JAZZ AROUND TOWN

The Washington jazz scene has never been strong. It limps along from year to year, occasionally showing signs of making a comeback, but usually it just manages to hang on. A half-dozen clubs that attempted to bring nationally known jazz artists to Washington on a regular basis have failed in the last dozen years, so now most leading D.C. jazz clubs stick to home-grown talent:

**Blues Alley (1073 Wisconsin Avenue, N.W., 337-4141)** is aptly named. Comfortable, off a narrow passageway just south of the corner of Wisconsin and M Streets in Georgetown, it stresses mainstream jazz and Dixieland. Big names from the swing era, such as Teddy Wilson and Red Norvo, make Blues Alley a regular stop, but local performers also appear frequently. As much a restaurant as a nightclub, Blues Alley is also well known for its cuisine; the main entertainment room doubles as a dining area where good New Orleans-style food is served. All major credit cards are honored. Moderate-to-expensive.

**Harold's Rogue & Jar is at 1814 N Street, N.W., 296-3192,** a half-block off Connecticut Avenue. Billed as a "jazz pub," this somewhat cramped spot is the place where many Washington jazz musicians congregate and get together to jam on stage when the mood strikes. Every style of jazz, from the avant garde New Thing to bop, appears on the Rogue & Jar's rotating schedule. Call, not only to make a reservation, but also to be sure that the jazz being played suits your tastes. All the musicians, however, are professionals—they have played extensively with the likes of Buddy Rich and Doc Severinsen. The cover charge may vary from day to day, but prices always fall in the moderate-to-expensive range. No credit cards.

**Top O'Foolery** is a small place on the **second floor of 2131 Pennsylvania Avenue, N.W., 333-7784.** There is no cover charge on weeknights, when an assortment of singers and small jazz ensembles provide the musical fare. The best time to go to Top O'Foolery, though, is on a Sunday afternoon, for its famous Jazz Matinees. The prices are considerably steeper then. If you are in luck, you will see and hear saxophonist Andrew White, whom many consider one of the most brilliant of the young post-Coltrane players. Even when White is not around, the Sunday matinee features first-class musicians playing some of the best jazz in town. A bargain at any price.

## THE SOUL CLUBS

Most of the clubs listed above draw racially mixed audiences. It's not unusual for up to one quarter of the crowd at a rock club to black; the ratio is reversed at most jazz places. But there are also numerous nightclubs frequented almost exclusively by blacks:

**The Mark IV Supper Club (Thirteenth and F Streets, N.W., 638-0200)** is one of the few downtown spots featuring quality live musical entertainment. Its speciality is nationally known soul and rhythm 'n' blues acts, usually brought in for one-week engagements. There is dining and dancing, but for most patrons the main attraction is the live talent: performers like the Stylistics, Jerry Butler, the Dells, and Millie Jackson have played here on several occasions. The Mark IV frowns on casual dress and does not accept credit cards. The price for an evening is high, thanks to a hefty cover charge and a two-drinks-per-set minimum.

**Part III (3642 Georgia Avenue, N.W., 667-9339)** has live soul music seven days a week. The emphasis is on local groups that can lay down a funky beat. Dancing is encouraged, but the club is small and has only a tiny dance floor. That cramped feeling is somewhat compensated for by reasonably priced drinks and a minimal cover charge that applies on weekends only. Inexpensive in price and simple in design.

**Rand's (1416 I Street, N.W., 783-7541)** has a somewhat garish exterior, but is worth checking out for those who have even the slightest interest in dancing to funky sounds by polished local soul bands. Whatever dance steps are being performed by the young crowd that frequents Rand's, you can be sure they are the latest and the hippest. Parking is available. There is a cover charge, but not until after 10. Prices are moderate to expensive.

## DISCOS

Discos have popped up all over the country in recent years, and Washington, no exception to the national trend, has been watching its disco population multiply. The disco scene is booming here thanks to the adventurous spirit of young people, blacks, gays, and other groups looking for something other than traditional nightlife and entertainment. Most outstanding of the numerous Washington disco spots are:

**The Room is at 1200 New York Avenue, N.W. (393-0200).** Atmosphere and style here are similar to Rand's, but the cover charge is a bit cheaper. Disco music and energetic dancing dominate the scene in this 250-seat club, across the street from the Greyhound bus station.

**Pier 9, 1824 Half Street, S.W., 488-1205.** As the name indicates, this club was formerly a huge warehouse. It is now a dual-level nightspot that accommodates as many as 700 people. Pier 9 is particularly popular with members of the Washington gay community, but others also frequent the club, drawn perhaps by the top-flight live performers who come in and sing when the jukebox and sound system are silent. Gloria Gaynor and Carol Douglas appear here frequently. No cover charge, but on weekends there is a moderately priced minimum. Right nearby is **Lost and Found, at 56 L Street, S.E., 488-1200,** which appeals to a similar clientele.

**Tramps (1238 Wisconsin Avenue, N.W., 333-2230)** is an attractive and stylish disco, owned and operated by Michael O'Harro, fashionable young pioneer in Washington's singles world.

## TOP 40

Also appealing to audiences in a dancing mood are the Top 40 clubs:

**The Crazy Horse (3259 M Street, N.W., 333-0400)** bears the same name as the famous Paris strip club, but this Georgetown spot is actually a Top 40 club, and a pretty good one at that. The musicians may not be the world's most creative, but they know all the latest hits and a fair share of golden oldies, too. Dancing is encouraged as an icebreaker for those who want to meet attractive members of the opposite sex. Try to arrive by bus, taxi, or foot if at all possible: as in most of Georgetown, finding a parking place is next to impossible. Moderate in price. No credit cards.

**The Keg (2205 Wisconsin Avenue, N.W., 333-9840)** is on Georgetown's outskirts along a stretch that includes several discos, pubs, and singles bars. The Keg, however, is a spot specializing in rock 'n' roll of the Top 40 variety. Naturally there is a dance floor and plenty of people packed into its space. And, of course, someone is always willing to go out onto that floor and move around with you. Bands vary in quality, but then the bands are not why young people come here. Cover charge is reasonable, and limited parking is available. Moderate in price, so long as you do not go overboard on the drinks.

## BLUEGRASS/COUNTRY MUSIC HAVENS

Bluegrass music is one of the D.C. area's great specialties. Washington's closeness to the Appalachian foothills of West Virginia has made it a mecca for mountain musicians who want to make a living in the big city by playing the music they grew up with out in the country. With the general resurgence of interest in all forms of country music, the bluegrass scene has come into its own.

**The Birchmere, 2723 So. Wakefield Street, Arlington, Virginia, 932-5058.** Considered the best bluegrass club around. Linda Ronstadt stopped in and joined The Seldom Scene for a few numbers. Open mike Monday (no cover), live music Tuesday through Saturday. Be sure to call ahead. Groups like The Seldom Scene and The Country Gentlemen fill the club quickly. Cover varies with group.

**The Red Fox Inn (4940 Fairmont Avenue in Bethesda, Maryland, 652-4429)** is where Washington's bluegrass boom got its start a few years ago. This small club is still the headquarters of what is now a full-fledged movement. All of modern bluegrass' top names have played here. Sometimes they even show up on a night they are not scheduled for, just to jam a bit with friends and fellow performers. It is like "Dueling Banjos" every night of the week. Obviously, this makes the Red Fox Inn a great place to listen to music, even though it all closes down earlier than District nightspots. Thursday through Sunday is the best time. Reservations are advised if a well-known group is scheduled to appear; the Red Fox's 150 seats fill rapidly. Prices are moderate, but credit cards are not accepted.

# XIV
## Natural Life

### By Henry Mitchell

Nature lovers are people who suspect they are natural creatures, and if they visit Washington they naturally wish to make sure there are skies, rivers, bugs, and trees abounding. Given those natural assurances, they quickly make themselves at home and it is a long, long life that is long enough to get to the bottom of so many wonders.

Washington has no Grand Canyon, since gullies are under reasonable control, nor any Victoria Falls either, since the city has no high excrescences to speak of.

But it does have Rock Creek and Great Falls and, of course, the smooth Potomac. There are raccoons who will pull the leaves off your water lilies even in the middle of the city, and nowhere else in the world can you enjoy vultures, sea gulls and crows, none of them essentially urban fowl, so close to a Capitol Dome.

Geologically, the capital is interesting, as well as important, and the soils and formations, so variable, are a delight to the gardener or should be. Heavy clay, sandy loam, solid rock—there are surprises wherever you dig.

The first freeze of fall—and this will show the grand diversity of the climate and prepare you for some of the diversity of its life—comes on November 10 at National Airport near the center of the 10-mile square that was originally set aside for this capital. Yet in suburbs less than 10 miles distant, the first killing frost comes October 12, nearly a full month earlier.

Since the city's climatic zones run almost due east and west, instead of north and south, people in a northern part of town may have their tomatoes unfrozen long after they are killed in the more southern parts of town, and since the climatic zones or

Henry Mitchell, a reporter for *The Washington Post* Style section, writes a weekly article on gardening called "Earth Man."

bands are so close together, and of course not firmly fixed by Congress, you never quite know what will come.

Even the flowering of the cherry trees, which are in a rather climatically settled and sober part of the city, has varied in recent years from March 20 to April 17—let's say April 3 is the best average date for them; and while this is bad for pilgrims who have chartered buses and hotel reservations, it does make possible a kind of excitement. You never quite know.

Sometimes you think you are in Savannah. Again you think it is very like Toronto. But while there is ample room for subjective delight and outrage at the climate, you will see there is a pattern here: the heats and colds come within limits, things do not get out of bounds. It is moderate, it is mild, much milder than New York in winter, and yet more agreeable in summer than the basin of the Amazon or, for that matter, Omaha.

On two factors—the moderate climate tempered by nearness to the sea, and the drop from the Piedmont to the Coastal Plain—hang all the natural life and lore of the place. But far beyond natural endowments, Washington enjoys several political, economic, and cultural decisions of enormous importance to any visitor. Its museums and libraries, its remarkable parks (which might so easily have been devoted to commercial development instead of reserved for us), and its public gardens are not only rich, but are also available in daily life.

It is common here for lovers, bird watchers, and folk of that sort to stroll in the parks without making any great project of it, and even those of us who must work for a living are forever going down tree-lined boulevards and riding over bridges beneath which something like the primeval forest still flourishes. Here you know when it is spring, because the birds are all around you (and all night, in the case of the mockingbirds) even if you don't know a tufted tantamount from a bald orkin. And nowhere this side of Borneo are there so many trees, all equipped with leaves, and nowhere this side of Utah does one have such a sense of open space.

So much for the general setting which is, in a word, felicitous.

Let us go then, you and I, to the towpath. This is, of course, the little path that runs along the side of the **Chesapeake and Ohio Canal.** Boys led mules with hawsers attached to the canal boats, and as they moved along, so did the boat. Here we may walk where mules have trod, and it is a poetic feeling in the spring especially.

You get on the **towpath** a block south of **Thirtieth and M Streets, N.W.,** Georgetown, or just ask anybody, they will know. Picturesque hovels abut the path in parts of Georgetown, sometimes with wooden porches, a bit wobbly, with picturesque people sitting on them looking at the canal. These modest dwellings are now expensive; do not think it would be nice to buy one for $6,000. Here and there you see climbing roses abloom in late May; they are more or less propped up against the houses, but Watch Out for the Roses is always a sound warning.

George Washington was much interested in this canal to link the capital with the interior, and was an investor in the "Patowmack" Canal Company. Indeed he left his canal stock to found the George Washington University. The old company went bankrupt, but a successor company extended the canal all the way to Cumberland, Maryland, which is 184 miles northwest. The waterway, as we know it, dates largely from the period 1828–1850, and the chief cargo on it was coal, though in earlier days whiskey was important also. When the mules were not towing the canal boats along, they rode in them. So, presumably, did the canal boys.

What is chiefly fine now is the wild nature along the banks. Adventurous souls, from a Justice of the Supreme Court on down, hike the full route of the old canal, but less historical and robust visitors will content themselves with going only as far as **Great Falls,** where they may see the 76-foot drop mentioned earlier.

At Great Falls, though the whole distance from the towpath to the falls is only 14 miles, you will see wild, rugged scenery with ferny hills, the modest falls of the Potomac, such fine aquatic things as the pickerel weed with blue spikes or flowers off and on all summer, and a remarkable concentration of birds. They nest far more densely in the trees along the canal than elsewhere. As a rule, you find no more than 4 to 5 breeding birds per acre, but along the canal the density is 14 to 15.

Not everybody is mad about birds; some of us go through life guiltily calling everything that is not a buzzard a sparrow, and we are always therefore amazed when they turn out to be (as they do along the canal) whippoorwills, barred owls, Acadian flycatchers, redstarts, wood thrushes, wood ducks, scarlet tanagers, blackbilled cuckoos, and the Lord only knows what else. The canal is very strong in warblers, as everyone knows. The barred owl is supposed to say "who cooks for you?" which on the whole is as sensible as "to-whit, to-whoo," which is what owls say in sixteenth and seventeenth century poetry. This writer has heard owls at night saying "ooooogh," and missed the rest of it.

But of course the more you look into it, the more there is to see and hear, not only in the world of Washington birds, but all nature. It has never been clear whether the Audubon Society here is so influential because there are so many birds, or vice versa. In any case, bird walks must rank with cocktail parties as a prime occupation of the city, and it is said there are more binoculars in Washington than in all the rest of America put together.

I have myself been startled and pleased by a hummingbird at Dumbarton Oaks Gardens in the spring, exploring an excellent clump of yellow lady slippers, one of our most attrative wild orchids. It was a small thing, and as natural wonders go, not worth mentioning. Yet when you see such a thing, unscheduled and unannounced—a gratuitous command performance for you alone—it will quite make your day for you.

Louis J. Halle's *Spring in Washington* should introduce any bird lover to the better bowers around town, but even the most casual visitor, if he keeps his eyes open, may see a green heron, whether he recognizes it or not. Notable birds are like famous humans—the city is full of them, though we pass them unawares in our travels.

**Dumbarton Oaks,** where we saw the hummingbird, is an eighteenth and nineteenth century place, celebrated for its studies of Byzantine art (it is owned by Harvard and the library and its various collections attract scholars) and famous as the site of the Dumbarton Oaks Conference, but never mind all that. There are several acres of garden, open to the public free. It is remarkable to find a garden so meticulously maintained, yet open to all, though it closes during the main heat of the summer.

Not everybody knows of the great slope at Dumbarton planted solid with forsythia. In late March or early April this is a tangle of golden chrome, and it must be one of the great examples of using a common shrub boldly, to give a quite different look from the ordinary. There are formal parts, too. An offbeat pleasure is to visit the Ellipse, with its double row of hornbeams, in November, when the brown leaves tenaciously hold on, though other trees are bare. The absurd and wonderful contrast of the elegantly clipped trees holding their windbeaten sere foliage will move you strangely, for these hornbeams are holding on to a few standards, by golly, no matter what the rest of the dumb forest is up to.

More on the beaten track are the seasonal displays of chrysanthemums at the end of October, the daffodils and roses and clematis in due season in the spring. Always, at all seasons, there is the great beech, one of the noblest to be seen anywhere, the superb oaks and lawns, the polished tumbles of old boxwood, and the glorious creeping fig in the conservatory, which any year now will probably pull down the whole mansion. This is one of the best places in Washington to be quiet and happy in, and to enjoy the fruits of good gardening and design without being much of a gardener oneself.

## AROUND THE TOWN

As you go through Washington, and especially as you navigate its numerous circles at intersections of avenues (what style they give the town, and how rightly was their designer, L'Enfant, proud of them), it cannot be recommended that you admire their planting if you are driving a car. Survival comes first, after all.

Few cities of the world give such an impression of universal green, thanks to its trees. In August visitors often ask about the trees that are sprinkled through downtown like weeping matrons in jade feather boas clutching their beads. These are sophoras.

As you shudder past the pornography shops on Fourteenth Street in earliest spring, the trees with small white suede blooms are rather rare Oriental magnolias; later on, all over the city, the trees with pink tulips all over them are commoner garden-hybrid magnolias. The glossy ramparts of green with white blooms like fishbowls, which you see again and again by federal buildings, are the Southern magnolia, the bull bay.

If you go to the White House through **Lafayette Park,** the lime-green object that looks like a ferny Christmas tree is the bald cypress, which grows as well in Washington as in the bayous off the Mississippi River.

If you go to the National Gallery to see the art, don't miss the Chinese wisterias in a huge passion of bloom against the blush marble walls to the side of the north entrance. That's in early May.

On a winter day, drop in to see the orchids at the **Botanic Garden** conservatory on **Independence Avenue near the Rayburn House Office Building,** or in early summer or late spring note how cleverly the climbing hydrangeas are making their way up the joints in the massive retaining wall of that building.

On Olive Street the trees are, of course, ginkgoes, while the Russian olives perfume the L Street entrance of *The Washington Post* in November. They are not necessarily worth going to see but nice to know about when you're passing by.

Even in winter you can admire the goldfish in the little park across from **Octagon House (1799 New York Avenue, N.W.).** In summer, there are big tropical blue and rose waterlilies.

Speaking of goldfish, sooner or later you will be in the neighborhood of the **Department of Commerce (Fourteenth Street between E Street and Constitution Avenue, N.W.),** where they have an aquarium in the basement. They used to have goldfish, but not now. They have good displays of native fishes and of ornamental tropicals as well, to say nothing of the large tank of ornamental Japanese carp or koi. The tricolored ones are most esteemed, but even the least of them looks like a catfish gone to heaven.

I once knew an aquarium director who discovered his 6-foot plate-glass tank of native gar had been broken during the night. The glass was in smithereens and the gar had lain on the floor for several hours with bits of glass here and there in their hides. With heavy heart he put them back in water in a reserve tank. To his joy, every one of them pulled through the ordeal.

Nature is never more beguiling than when we "tame" and "mold" her, then turn our backs for a moment.

**The Kenilworth Aquatic Gardens** were meant to be 14 acres of ponds dappled with a most distinguished collection of aquatic plants, including especially the finest water lilies in bewildering variety. As it has turned out, however, its budget does not quite permit the vast labor of keeping a first-rate aquatic collection in first-rate shape. From time to time a fiery citizen writes a Letter to the Editor saying the place is run down. The dragonflies, the frogs and the lotuses would not think so, and they have got the upper hand.

Often there are no crowds at all, and as you walk about the

distrustful frogs splash just ahead of your feet. The garden is on **Kenilworth Avenue near Eastern Avenue, N.E.;** you have to mosey about and follow the signs to find it. It is as magical as any place in Washington for country boys from the South, some of whom hope the public at large will never discover it. Of course you either go ape when you see a pond with frogs, or you don't.

## PARKS

Any number of excursions can be made to the almost endless series of parks in Maryland and Virginia. Many of these are new, undeveloped, while others are almost in town. **Wheaton Regional Park,** which includes **Brookside Botanical Gardens,** for example, is a relatively little-known wonder with what must be one of the most beautifully manicured conservatories anywhere, and while not everything in the glass house is a great rarity, it is safe to say they have the largest, healthiest, fattest Boston fern in the world, to say nothing of a really fine reference library of garden books which few seem to know about. Outdoors, the large rose garden is taking shape, and the woods are filling up with witch-hazels from China. The plant lover will wish to explore, and even the most sedentary will gape at the superbly grown fuchsias.

The **American Horticultural Society** has moved into the old River Farm of George Washington's near Mount Vernon, and the gardens are being taken in hand. At **Mount Vernon** itself, there is still an assortment of trees Washington loved, and the pretty old orangery is intact and rare. You can buy seeds of Mount Vernon hollyhocks and other things, and they actually grow when you plant them.

A greenhouse northeast of the Bishop's Garden at the **Washington Cathedral,** by the way, is an excellent place to buy young plants of wormwood and lady's mantle and herbs in general; you never know what they may come up with. There is also an herb cottage nearby. Don't miss the orchids and dignified boxwood of the **Bishop's Garden,** and the rosemary, while you're there.

The **National Arboretum** in northeast Washington is best known for its riotous display of azaleas mid-April to mid-May. Less well known, and even more surprising, is a fine collection of camellias grown outdoors, and down in the glade of cryptomeria trees is a scarlet-lacquered garden house of no particular use that one knows of, yet one of the loveliest little structures in town.

Nothing much has been said of other remarkable azalea displays, but much of the city is awash with color when azaleas and dogwoods bloom. The dogwoods are especially fine on the Virginia side of the Potomac along the George Washington Memorial Parkway. There is also a new grove of pines in the making there in memory of President Johnson.

Lady Bird Johnson, when she was in the White House, provided a great stimulus to the planting of flowers, and one million daffodil bulbs (all carefully counted) now bloom in April in masses along the Parkway between Memorial Bridge and the Fourteenth Street Bridge. On a good day one can see citizens strolling among the flowers with Old Morley or similar personal hounds, who invariably avoid tromping the blooms but enjoy the excitements of spring.

The parks of the metropolitan districts are run by more than one agency, but a call to any one will set you on the track of any other. (*See* the list below.) **East Potomac Park** and **Hains Point,** jutting into the Potomac River almost downtown, as well as the new **Constitution Gardens** next to the Reflecting Pool, are great for bird lovers, joggers, and those in need of a cool breeze on a hot day. On any day **Rock Creek Park** is the showpiece of parks, its 1,754 acres running through the northwest sector of town. Many protested and howled when express roads were put in the park, but now that they are there they form a sort of paradise route for motorists. You can picnic in one of the 70 spots set aside for that purpose (phone the Recreation Department, 673-7660, for a reservation) or visit the Nature Center on Glover Road, N.W.

**Theodore Roosevelt Island** in the Potomac, approached by a little footbridge from the Virginia side, has a couple of miles of unspoiled walks. This is another spot that some hope will not become too widely known, and yet it would be a crime not to let people know it is thick with birds and wild beauty, and the large statue of Roosevelt is accepted by the wildlife as one more rook. No harm done.

---

## THE ZOO

The **National Zoological Park, Connecticut Avenue, N.W., west of Calvert Street,** is merely one arm of the Smithsonian Institution, that unique establishment with the Chief Justice heading its board, and which is into everything from Smokey the Bear to the Hope Diamond and Lindbergh's airplane and basalt fossils and Bess Truman's ball gown and Persian tiles and Sung sculpture. Indeed a lifetime could be spent without going even to the limits of the Smithsonian's boundaries. (*See* Chapter VII, "The Smithsonian.")

But back to the zoo. The original Smokey, a cub rescued from a forest fire, died after retiring from government service at the age of 25. There is now a new Smokey, no relation, to keep the name alive. The main attraction since they came to town have been the residents of the Panda House. Here you will find Ling-Ling and Hsing-Hsing, the rare gifts of the People's Republic of China and the only giant pandas in the Western Hemisphere.

There are now some 2,400 animals in 650 species, including about 30 kinds of animals almost extinct in the wild.

Two dorcas gazelles, given the zoo by the Eisenhowers, were not as hopelessly shy as many feared, after all, and the zoo now has a nice herd of them.

A glory of the zoo, and indeed of the world at large, is the little line of white tigers. Mohini, the first white tiger in our hemisphere, came to the zoo from India in 1960. Since white is a recessive genetic factor in tigers, as all tiger breeders know, it takes time to establish a good line of them when you start with just one white tiger. If you breed one with a yellow, the first generation gives yellow tigers, but with the recessive gene for white. As these are inter-bred or bred back to whites, the laws of chance insure that a certain percentage will be white tigers. In England they have bred some pretty primrose-colored tigers.

There is a big outdoor flight cage 90 feet high and 130 feet across. You may walk in and find no barriers at all between yourself and the birds.

Some people do not like zoos, just as some do not like dogs. People can be very strange.

There are ponds just below the zoo cafeteria where migrating ducks join the resident exotics for the winter. It is delightful in the spring to see them all swimming about, the new generation learning to paddle in the immemorially ancient style.

The world turns, as they say, and the mountains are being worn down and the sun is burning itself up and one never knows what will happen in the next billion years. It is well to notice that ducks are still learning to paddle: that much of the world seems sound and firm enough for the time being. Joggers still jog, daffodils still bloom in April, mockingbirds are more plentiful by far than they were the last century, and the seasons still follow in time. The gazelles are in good shape. Even the rhinoceroses are coming on well. The gulls still squeak; the herons cry toward night as they are flying, and the lover of nature still may say with some assurance that the sun is up and the light streams down in our capital, at least on sunny days, and the big bright daystar that sustains all life is megabrilliant still. Apart from fleas, in other words, a hound will find the natural world enough, and amply good.

---

### WHERE TO FIND IT

**Coming Park Events/National Capital Parks: 426-6700**
**Dial-A-Park: 426-6975**

**American Horticultural Society,** *at the River Farm, approximately 5 miles north of Mount Vernon, off the George Washington Memorial Parkway; 768-5700.* Open to members only, Monday-Friday 8:30–5 all year.

**Aquarium,** *Commerce Building, Fourteenth Street between E Street and Constitution Avenue, N.W.; 377-2000.* Open daily 9–5.

**Aquatic Gardens** (*see* Kenilworth Aquatic Gardens).

**Arboretum** (*see* National Arboretum).

**Bishop's Garden** (*see* Washington Cathedral).

**Botanic Gardens** (*see* U.S. Botanic Gardens).

**Brookside Botanical Gardens** (*see* Wheaton Regional Park).

**Cherry trees,** *surrounding the Tidal Basin and East Potomac Park.* For expected blooming dates and other information, call National Capital Parks, 426-6700.

**Chesapeake & Ohio Canal and the Towpath.** *Entrance to the towpath a block south of Thirtieth and M Streets, N.W.,* in Georgetown. (*See* Chapter XVI, "Sports," for recreational facilities, such as boat and bike rentals.) For special hikes and bird watchings, watch *The Washington Post's* "Calendar" in Friday's Style section, or call Great Falls Tavern visitors' center at 299-3613 or the C&O Canal office at 948-5641.

**Constitution Gardens,** *along Constitution Avenue between Seven-*

*teenth Street and Henry Bacon Drive.* Gracing the north side of the Lincoln Memorial Reflecting Pool, a natural habitat of flowering trees and meadows surrounding a pond, the informal gardens were a Bicentennial project. Have some beer and wurst in the beer garden setting amid the honey locust trees.

**Dumbarton Oaks Gardens** *on R Street between Thirty-first and Thirty-second Streets, N.W., in Georgetown: 232-3101.* The Gardens are open from 2 to 4:45 P.M. daily except legal holidays. Closed July 1 through Labor Day, and during inclement winter weather. Enter on R Street. The Dumbarton Oaks Byzantine and Pre-Columbian Collections have the same hours as the Gardens but are closed on Mondays; entrance to the Collections is at 1703 Thirty-second Street, N.W.

**East Potomac Park,** *the peninsula between the Washington Channel and the Potomac River, just south of Independence Avenue and east of the Tidal Basin; 426-6700.*

**Gunston Hall Plantation,** *off US 1, Lorton, Virginia; 550-9220.* See the boxwoods.

**Hains Point,** *the tip of East Potomac Park (see* East Potomac Park).

**Kenilworth Aquatic Gardens,** *Kenilworth Avenue and Douglas Street, N.E., near Eastern Avenue; 426-6905.* Owned by the National Park Service since 1938, it is open daily 7:30 A.M.–5:30 P.M.

**Lady Bird Johnson Park and the LBJ Memorial Grove,** *along the George Washington Memorial Parkway between Memorial and Fourteenth Street Bridges; 426-6700.*

**Lafayette Park,** *bounded by Pennsylvania Avenue, Jackson Place, H Street, and Madison Place, N.W.*

**Mount Vernon,** *George Washington Memorial Parkway, about 8 miles south of Alexandria, Virginia; 780-2000.* Admission charge to grounds and house. Open daily March through September 9–5; October through February 9–4. The Literature Sales Room, where seeds for hollyhocks and other flowers are sold, has the same hours and is located just outside the north flower garden gate.

**National Arboretum,** *Twenty-eighth and M Streets, N.E.; 399-5400.* April through October: Monday–Friday 8 A.M.–7 P.M., Saturday and Sunday 10–7. November through March: Monday–Friday 8–5, Saturday and Sunday 10–5.

**National Zoological Park,** *in Rock Creek Park.* Entrances at 3000 block of Connecticut Avenue, N.W.; 628-4422 and 381-7228. Guided tours: call Friends of the National Zoo (FONZ) at 232-7703. No admission; parking $1 per car. Gates open 6 A.M.–5:30 P.M., until 7 P.M. in April through September. Exhibit houses open 9 A.M.–4:30 P.M., until 6 P.M. in April through September. Restaurant, snack bars open 10 A.M.–5 P.M. at Harvard

Street and Adams Mill Road, and off Beach Drive. (Zoo police station next to the restaurant for first-aid, wheelchairs, lost children and belongings.) L2, L4, L6, and H2 and H6 buses serve the Zoo.

**Octagon House,** *1799 New York Avenue, N.W.; 638-3105.* Tuesday-Saturday 10–4, Sunday 1–4. Closed Monday.

**Rock Creek Park,** *extends north into Maryland along Rock Creek, beginning near the National Zoo.* For general information on the park call 426-6835. Most convenient entrances to the park are from Rock Creek Parkway, Military Road, or Tilden Street. The Nature Center is at Military and Glover Roads; 426-6829. For picnic reservations: 673-7646.

**Theodore Roosevelt Island,** *off the George Washington Memorial Parkway, just north of Theodore Roosevelt Bridge; 426-6922.* Opens daily at 6 A.M., closes at dusk.

**Towpath** *(see* Chesapeake & Ohio Canal).

**Tulip Library,** *south of Independence Avenue near the Tidal Basin Boating Center.* For specific information on the tulips, call the National Capital Parks horticulturists at 523-5555.

**U.S. Botanic Gardens,** *at the foot of Capitol Hill near the Rayburn House Office Building, on Maryland Avenue between First and Second Streets, S.W.; 224-3121.* Open daily 9–6.

**Washington Cathedral** (also known as the National Cathedral, or most properly, the Cathedral Church of SS. Peter and Paul), *Wisconsin and Massachusetts Avenue, N.W.; 966-3500.* The cathedral is open 10–4:30 (one chapel never closes); the Bishop's Garden 8–4:30 daily. The Greenhouse is open 8:30–4:30, the Herb Cottage 9:30–5 every day except Sunday.

**West Potomac Park,** *surrounding the Tidal Basin and along the Potomac River up to the Lincoln Memorial; 426-6700.*

**Wheaton Regional Park,** *in Montgomery County, Maryland.* For general information call 622-0056. The Park is open daily 10 A.M. until sunset; main picnic area entrance at Shorefield Avenue off Georgia Avenue. Park includes Brookside Botanical Gardens at 1500 Glenallan Avenue; 949-8231; open 9–5 daily. There is also a Nature Center at 1400 Glenallan Avenue; 946-9071.

**Zoo** *(see* National Zoological Park).

• Surprise Plot: Each spring and summer, in a small downtown sidewalk plot in front of The Grange headquarters at 1616 H Street, N.W., Mr. Elmore Miller plants for your pleasure a tidy vegetable patch complete with cabbage, corn and tomatoes.

# XV
# Of Special Interest to Children

### By Elizabeth Reilly

Visiting Washington can be an overwhelming experience for any child. Even well-behaved children get restless and bored with too much sightseeing. In the preceding chapters you will find many activities suited to children as well as adults: besides the national monuments on the Mall, children usually enjoy the Capitol, White House, and of course, the National Zoo. This chapter is intended to supplement that information with several places where children are easily amused, allowing parents an hour or two of relaxation. It includes both indoor and outdoor activities, plus some special events throughout the year.

At the top of the list are two Smithsonian museums' special exhibit rooms for youngsters: **the Discovery Room in the Museum of Natural History, Constitution Avenue at Tenth Street, N.W., 628-4422,** and the **Explore Gallery in the National Collection of Fine Arts, Eighth and G Streets, N.W., 628-4422.** Both exhibits are great fun for children, who are encouraged to touch and examine the objects on display. The Discovery Room is set up much like a classroom filled with objects for "show and tell." There are seashells, animal skins and pelts, fossil imprints, rocks and other specimens scattered about the room on shelves and waiting to be examined by young scientists. Upon entering they are given magnifying glasses attached to chains that can by hung around the neck. Children must be accompanied by an adult, but once inside, the room is theirs. All the exhibits are carefully labeled in big block print and a staff member is ready to answer questions. A child may request one of the many boxes filled with shells, animal

Elizabeth Reilly is a free-lance writer.

teeth and so forth to take to a table for examination. Even children who can't read yet will enjoy touching all the objects found here.

The Explore Gallery, a bright and colorful room filled with different textures, shapes, and colors, is designed to give youngsters a feel for the tools used in the fine arts. Children crawl through a hole at the bottom of the door and enter an exciting world of sight and sound. Who can resist running up and down the multi-patterned rug ramp, or swinging on a jungle gym that is draped with a striped snake? The children are free to roam at will and discover a private light show under the ramp, an antique toy carousel, an illuminated globe with unusual shapes floating inside, and other exhibits. Certainly this gallery and the Discovery Room are great discoveries for parents, too.

The Discovery Room is open noon to 2:30 Monday through Thursday; 10:30–3:30 Friday, Saturday, and Sunday. On Saturdays and Sundays, pick up tickets for the room when you enter the building. Also, never a group of more than seven, with one adult. The Explore Gallery is open 10–5:30 seven days a week.

For any child who has dreamed of exploring the Arctic, unearthing the remains of an ancient civilization, or diving into an underwater expedition, **Explorers Hall at the National Geographic, Seventeenth and M Streets, N.W., 857-7000,** is the place to let fantasies run wild. The exhibits emphasize some important accomplishments of National Geographic-sponsored expeditions and research studies. On display are the dogsled used by Admiral Peary on his trip to the North Pole, the Aqua-Lung and Diving Saucer used by Jacques Cousteau in underseas expeditions, and ever-changing photographic displays from every corner of the world. Budding archeologists will enjoy visiting the exhibit on man's origins, the beautifully reconstructed kiva belonging to the cliff dwellers of the Southwest, and the solemn Olmec head unearthed in 1939. Most of the exhibits are accompanied by taped recordings offering detailed explanations of the exhibits. There are also free educational films, which run continually throughout the day.

The Hall is open 9 to 6 Monday through Friday; 9 to 5 Saturday, and noon to 5 Sunday.

Any child who plays with dolls or has a doll collection of his/her own will be fascinated by two museums in Washington.

The first is the **Children's Attic in the DAR Headquarters, 1776 D Street, N.W., 628-1776.** The doll collection here dates back almost one hundred years. Tours are given on an individual basis by volunteers who explain how the dolls were made. The earliest models on display are made with simple materials such as corncobs, rags or wood. Later, as dolls became more sophisticated, they are of papier mâché, or with wax and china heads that could be painted to look realistic. For groups of 15 or more children, the DAR offers a "touch it" tour, where they demonstrate the use of early American implements such as a spinning wheel, an old toaster, which was placed over the hearth, and a foot warmer.

Open from 9 to 4 Monday through Friday. Tours are available between 10 and 3.

Among the most delightful new additions to the small world of Washington is the **Dolls' House and Toy Museum, 5236 Forty-fourth Street, N.W., 244-0024,** right behind the Lord & Taylor parking lot.

The museum is built around Flora Gill Jacobs' collection of antique doll houses, completely furnished, plus a toyland of antique treats such as building blocks, a Noah's Ark, Mount Vernon replica, Sunday "parlor toys," vintage baseball games and cards, and old-fashioned wind-up toys. The museum is open Tuesday through Saturday 11 to 5, on Sunday from noon to 5. If plans are made well in advance, birthday parties can be held in the museum. The museum is opened an hour early for the festivities—at 11 A.M.—and these parties include treasure hunts, tours of the museum, and sandwiches, ice cream, birthday cake, and punch served in a room set up to resemble an old ice cream parlor. Call at least a month in advance to make plans and work out a party contract. Cost should be $1.00 per child and $2.00 per adult.

Just a block from the DAR is a small **museum** in the **Department of the Interior building, C Street between Eighteenth and Nineteenth Streets, N.W., 343-5016.** Various exhibits illustrate the activities of the department in areas such as wildlife preservation, the national parks, and Indian affairs. On display are exhibits of Indian life, past and present, paintings of historic events, the illustrated story of the opening of the West, and more. It is open from 8 to 4, Monday through Friday.

Children interested in the American Indian exhibits are

likely to want to continue their studies of ethnic cultures with a visit to the **Museum of African Art, 318 A Street, N.E.** Housed in the townhouse where Frederick Douglass lived is a great collection of traditional African sculpture, textiles and musical instruments. If you call in advance **(547-7424)** you can arrange to have your children join one of the scheduled daily tours. The Museum of African Art is open 11 to 5 Monday through Friday, and noon to 5 on Saturday and Sunday.

History doesn't exactly leap to life, but it may seem more three-dimensional to children at the **Wax Museum, Fourth and E Streets, S.W., 554-2600.** They can meet Ben Franklin, Betsy Ross, Ponce de Leon, and other favorites, and take in entire scenes from "Great Moments in American History," such as the signing of the Declaration of Independence and man's first step on the moon.

The Wax Museum is open daily from 9 to 8 (from March 15 until Labor Day the museum is open until 10 P.M.).

In a different vein but also a great favorite for kids is the **U.S. Navy Memorial Museum in the Navy Yard, Eighth and M Streets, S.E., 433-2651.** (*See* Chapter IV, "The Defense Establishment.") There are two parts to the museum, one indoors and one out. The exhibits inside trace the role of the Navy in American history dating back to the Revolutionary War. Children like to man the periscopes and scan their surroundings. Outside there are numerous ship and anti-aircraft guns where children can stage their own make-believe battles. The Navy Museum is open 9 to 4 Monday through Friday, and 10 to 5 on Saturday and Sunday.

All kids love detective stories, so it is only natural that they may want to visit the **F.B.I.** The agency operates 90-minute tours of the building from 9:15 to 4 Monday through Friday. It is at the **J. Edgar Hoover Building, E between Ninth and Tenth Streets, N.W., 324-3000.**

More peaceful is the **National Aquarium** in the basement of the **Department of Commerce, Fourteenth Street between Constitution Avenue and E Street, N.W., 377-2000.** (*See* Chapter XIV, "Natural Life.") Children enjoy watching the electric eel, sharks, snapping turtles, and other aquatic species. There are exotic looking butterfly fish and batfish in the Atlantic and Pacific coral reef communities. The Aquarium has approximately sixty tanks, and many are designated according to different underwater habitats. Open 9 to 5 Monday through Friday.

Not all your time should be spent indoors, however. Washington's large and beautiful Rock Creek Park runs right through the city and offers several exciting activities for children. Pay a visit to the **National Zoo, 3001 Connecticut Avenue, N.W.,** where the famous pandas reside. *(For more detailed information on the Zoo see* Chapter XIV: "Natural Life.") Watch the miller grind wheat and corn between two great stone slabs at the old **Pierce Mill, at Beach Drive and Tilden Street, N.W.** The mill is open between 9 and 5 Wednesday through Sunday. It is best to come in the morning during the week or on Sunday afternoon when the miller does most ot his work. Another place of interest is the **Rock Creek Nature Center, at the intersection of Military and Glover Roads, N.W.** Inside there are exhibits on insects, birds, rocks, and plants. The planetarium is extremely popular with children of all ages. Outside there is a well-marked nature trail for those who wish to explore on their own. The Nature Center is open from 9:30 to 5 Tuesday through Friday, and noon to 6 on Saturday and Sunday. Rock Creek Park is also the perfect spot for a family picnic or bicycle outing.

## SPECIAL EVENTS

Throughout the year there are many special activities planned for children—puppet shows, music concerts, plays, plus some once-a-year events that are certain to highlight any child's visit to Washington.

In May of every year, the National Collection of Fine Arts sponsors Children's Day at the museum. The general theme changes from year to year but its basic concept remains the same. This is a chance for kids to meet with artists first-hand and dabble in simple sculpture, painting, drawing, and other mediums. Artists demonstrate how to use special tools and explain their work to the children. There are usually music and dance programs, too.

In the month of July, the Mall area resounds with activity. On Independence Day, a spectacular fireworks display begins at dusk. Another main event this month is the Festival of American Folklore, which normally runs for 10 days. Craftsmen and musicians come from all over the country. The idea is to show the diversity of ethnic backgrounds found within our country and see how they have shaped our cultural heritage. There are different groups from year to year. Good music, folk dancing, and delicious things to eat.

To keep posted on upcoming events for children of all ages consult *The Washington Post's* Weekend, the tabloid that appears every Friday.

### ADDITIONAL READING

For a more detailed look at what Washington has to offer children, see *Going Places With Children,* published by the Green Acres School, and *Washington for Children,* by Ray Shaw.

# XVI
## Sports

### By Don Bread

In Washington residents are joined by tourists from across the country and around the world. Other than politics, nothing reflects this melting pot of cultures as well as sports.

If you've heard of a sport, someone in Washington undoubtedly plays it. Washingtonians, both permanent and transient, can fill their leisure time in the woodlands or on the water, in the stadium or at the track, as spectators or participants.

The wide-ranging and constantly changing aspects of the area sports scene prohibit a complete listing of all available activities. But what is not found in this guide probably can be obtained from one of the following general information numbers:

Dial-a-Park activities.............................426-6975
National Capital Parks ...........................426-6700
D.C. Department of Recreation ...................673-7660
Northern Virginia Parks..........................278-8880
Smithsonian Associates ..........................381-5157
Capital Centre Activities .......................350-3900

In addition, both *The Washington Post* Sports section (daily) and Weekend section (Fridays) provide listings of various events.

Once you've located a prospective activity, check on the weather with the numbers:

Washington and vicinity ..........................936-1212
Md., Va., Del. extended outlook ..................899-3240
Chesapeake Bay boating report ....................899-3210
Aviation weather .................................347-4950
Extended mountain weather ........................920-3820

The prime mover of tickets for sporting events is Ticketron. Their main local outlet is at 1101 17th Street, N.W. For information, call 659-2601.

## BASEBALL

The National Pastime has been missing from the nation's capital at the major league level since the Washington Senators made their exodus to Arlington, Tex., after the 1971 season.

Washington-area fans are not without access to the summer game, however. Baltimore's Memorial Stadium (1000 block of East 33rd Street) is approximately 50 minutes away and houses the Baltimore Orioles, consistent contenders in the American League East.

From mid-April until September or October (depending on playoff and World Series participation) a price of from $1 to $6 will put you in one of the stadium's 52,137 seats. Tickets for all Oriole home games are available at area Ticketron locations or by calling (301) 338-1300.

Game times are 2 P.M. for day games and doubleheaders, 7:30 for night games and 5:30 for twilight doubleheaders.

If a drive to Baltimore does not appeal to you, minor-league baseball is available just across the Potomac River in Alexandria, Va. The Alexandria Dukes will perform at Four Mile Run Park, 3600 Commonwealth, ticketed from $2 to $3. Game times are 7:30 for night games and 6:30 for doubleheaders. For information call HOMERUN.

## BASKETBALL

Washington abounds with hoop activity throughout the winter with every level of play from schoolyard to professional amply represented.

The Washington Bullets are the kings of the area courts and perennial contenders in the Central Division of the National Basketball Association. An outlay of from $4 to $9 gives you one of the 19,035 Capital Centre seats. Tickets are procurable through Ticketron or by calling 350-3400.

The Centre is located just outside the Capital Beltway and can by easily reached from Beltway exits 32E or 33E.

A second professional franchise now exists, the Washington Metros of the Eastern Basketball Association. The Metros' roster is liberally sprinkled with former area college stars. Ticket information is available at 459-6584.

The play-for-pay squads are supplemented by a fine aggregation of college and high school teams. The University of Maryland competes in the strong Atlantic Coast Conference and combines with American, Catholic, Georgetown, George Washington and Howard universities to offer a wide variety of well-played basketball. Call the athletic departments of the respective schools for ticket and schedule information.

Washington also boasts some of the best year-in-year-out prep play. *The Post* ranks the top twenty boy's and girl's high school teams each week and a check of the daily events column in *The Post* should reveal an attractive matchup.

## CANOEING AND ROWING

Should sultry summer weather inspire you to leave your land legs behind, relief is as close as the historic Potomac River. The Potomac offers a full range of river conditions, from the placid waters opposite the city to the completely impassable stretch of Great Falls.

Should you find an area to your liking, canoes and rowboats can be rented at the following locations:

Thompson Boat Center, Virginia Ave. and Rock Creek Parkway, NW, 333-4861; Fletcher's Boat House, Canal and Reservoir Roads, NW, 244-0461; Swain's Boat House, 10700 Swain's Lock Road, Potomac, 299-9006; and the Tidal Basin Boating Center, on Maine Ave. behind the Bureau of Engraving and Printing, 783-9562.

## CYCLING

The popularity of cycling in the area has increased steadily since the District became the site of the first commuter bike path in the nation. Bike paths are now located throughout the city and the suburbs and efforts continue to expand the network.

Races and rallies are sponsored in the area by several groups, most notably the National Capital Parks. For information, call Dial-a-Park. An even better source for everything from activities to pro-biker legislation is the Washington Area Bicyclist Association at 265-4317.

If you need to rent some wheels, check Thompson Boat Center, Swain's Boat House and Fletcher's Boat House (*see* Canoeing and Rowing for addresses and phone numbers) or Hains

Point, 554-9049; Big Wheel Bikes, 1034 33rd Street, NW, 337-0254; The Bicycle Rack, 1114 S. Washington Street, Alexandria, 549-4900; or the Arlington Park Department, 558-2426.

## EQUESTRIAN SPORTS

Washington's location betwixt Maryland and Virginia puts it almost in the heart of hunt country and, consequently, horse country. Be you rider or observer, there is something here for everyone.

### Riding

Mounts for rent are available at several locations in the area. But if you are limited in your experience or funds, here are some suggested starting places.

The Rock Creek Park Horse Center at Military and Glover roads, NW (362-0117), is the only riding facility in the District. It offers trail riding, pony rides, ring lessons, boarding and training.

The Meadowbrook Stables at the Rock Creek Recreation Center at 8200 Meadowbrook Lane in Chevy Chase (Md.) (558-6935) offers courses in riding and jumping.

The Arlington County (Virginia) Department of Environmental Affairs at 300 North Park Drive (558-2700) offers riding classes.

### Horseback Pack Trips

Several organizations undertake pack trips into the mountains of West Virginia and as far away as the Great Smokies. For information, check the Friday editions of Weekend in *The Post.*

### Polo

Should you wish to check out a chukker, head for the Lincoln Memorial Polo Field at 23rd and Independence Ave., SW, on any Sunday during May–July or September–October. Local clubs representing Reston, Woodlawn, Lincoln Mall and Potomac compete regularly. Call Dial-a-Park to confirm dates and times.

### Steeplechase

Fall and spring are the prime times for the cross-country run-and-jump variety of horsemanship. The Virginia Gold Cup, the

Maryland Hunt Cup and the Middleburg (Va.) Hunt Cup highlight the spring season. In the fall, Fairfax, Middleburg and Montpelier (all in Virginia) host the major meets.

The Fair Hill meetings in Maryland, two days in May and two in September, are the only events with pari-mutuel betting.

Point-to-point races are a specialty of Maryland and Virginia. Virginia has nine days of point-to-point in the spring and Maryland has seven days. Check *The Post* Sports and Weekend sections for listings.

### Horse Shows

The Washington International Horse Show, held each fall at the Capital Centre, is one of the two shows in the nation rating Nations Cup competition. The Warrenton (Va.) Horse Show highlights the Labor Day weekend. The Upperville Colt and Horse Show has been a summer fixture in Virginia for more than 120 years, making it "the oldest continuing sporting event in the country."

### Race Tracks

For those who like to put their money where their mount is, the Washington area is a bettor's delight. At least one local track is in operation nearly all year with the high point coming the third saturday in May when the Preakness, the second jewel in thoroughbred racing's Triple Crown, is run at Pimlico.

To confirm meet schedules and racing days check with:

Harness racing: April–September; Rosecroft Raceway, Oxon Hill (Md.), 567-4000; Ocean Downs, Berlin (Md.), (301) 641-0680; Laurel (Md.) Raceway, (301) 725-1800.

Thoroughbred racing: All year round; Shenandoah Downs, Charleston (W.Va.), (304) 725-2021; Bowie (Md.) Race Course, 262-8111; Pimlico Race Course, Baltimore, (301) 542-9500; Laurel (Md.) Race Course, (301) 725-0400.

### FISHING

The Chesapeake Bay area offers an angler a delightful variety of waters in which to cast for his fate. From the salty waters of the bay to the freshwater streams, rivers and reservoirs, a wide selection of finny catches awaits.

Make sure you check with the local game warden for seasons, licenses and limits before you drop your line. For further information check with Virginia's Commission of Game and Inland Fisheries, Box 11104, Richmond, Va., 23230 or the Maryland Wildlife Administration, State Office Building, Annapolis, Md., 21404.

## FOOTBALL

The Washington Redskins have captured the fancy of area residents on a scale unapproached by any of the other local professional teams. All 54,395 seats at Robert F. Kennedy Stadium, East Capital and 22nd Streets, are sold on a season-ticket basis. And the waiting list for season tickets is several years long.

So, should you want to check out the National Football League franchise, your best chance is during the exhibition season when tickets are sold on a game-by-game basis. Otherwise, well, check your televison listings and try the Baltimore Colts.

For those who want to see their footballers in the flesh, try the University of Maryland, Howard or the U.S. Naval Academy. Tickets are usually available. Check the sports section for schedules.

## GOLF

A duffer with a full bag of clubs and a full tank of gas can choose from among some 70 courses within a 40-minute ride of the Beltway. Here is a list of some of the best public courses in the area. Call ahead to check fees and starting times.

In the District: East Potomac, Hains Point, 554-9813; Langston, 2540 Benning Road, NE, 398-6005; Rock Creek, 16th and Rittenhouse, NW, 723-9832.

In Maryland: Allview, Columbia, 730-6060; Enterprise, Mitchellville, 262-4730; Falls Road, Rockville, 299-5156; Henson Creek, Oxon Hill, 567-4646; Laytonsville, 948-5288; Needwood, Rockville, 948-1075; Northhampton, Largo, 336-7771; Northwest Park, Weaton, 598-6100; Oxon Run, 894-2200; Paint Branch, College Park, 935-0330; Laurel Pines, 490-6261;

Redgate, Rockville, 340-2404; Sligo Creek, Silver Spring, 585-6006; White Plains, Waldorf, 645-1300.

In Virginia: Algonkian, Sterling, 450-4655; Burke Lake, Fairfax, 323-6600; Greendale, Alexandria, 971-6170; Pinecrest I, Alexandria, 354-8850; Pinecrest II, Fairfax, 278-8555; Reston South, 620-9333; Shannon Green, Fredericksburg, (703) 786-8385; South Wales, Jeffersonton, 451-1344; Twin Lakes, Clifton, 631-9009.

## HIKING

When you have assembled your hiking boots, canteen, bird-identification book and what have you, call one of the following numbers to learn about scheduled outings: Dial-a-Park, the Rock Creek Nature Center (426-6829), the Potomac Appalachian Trail Club (638-5306) or the Washington chapter of the Sierra Club (547-2326).

Should you wish to organize your own trek, opportunities abound from the C&O Canal towpath to the battlefield site in Gettysburg, Pa.

## HOCKEY

The Washington Capitals are a rather recent addition to the metropolitan sports scene. And the first few seasons have been record-breaking, in a negative sense. But the Caps have continually upgraded their performance and National Hockey League excitement is available at Capital Centre from $4.50 to $9.50 for the 18,130 seats. Call 350-3400 for ticket and schedule information.

## MOTOR SPORTS

Fast-flying vehicles first entered the area in 1906 with the formation of a half-mile dirt track at Brightwood Driving Park in Northwest Washington. Nowdays the District has no racing but auto buffs have a wide choice of tracks in the suburbs. Call the track for schedules.

Stock cars: Old Dominion Speedway, Manassas, Va., (703)

361-7753; Beltsville (Md.) Speedway, (301) 490-2300; Hagerstown (Md.) Speedway, (301) 582-0640. Grand Nationals are held in May and September at Dover Downs (Del.) Speedway, (302) 674-4600.

Sports Cars: Summit Point (W.Va.) Raceway, weekends from June to October, (304) 725-4071.

Motorcycles: Call the American Motorcycle Association Hotline (301) 922-2211.

Drag Races: Another hotline, 759-3685.

---

### RUNNING

The advent of the jogging craze has given new impetus to the various running groups in the area. The Potomac Valley AAU, D.C. Roadrunners, D.C. Harriers, D.C. RunHers, D.C. Striders and others all conduct events. Check *The Post* Events listings for information.

---

### SAILING

Believe it or not, Washington once had a thriving waterfront, particularly along the Potomac in Alexandria. Although those days are gone, sailing remains.

If your interest exceeds your experience, check with one of the following organizations for instruction: The American Red Cross, 857-3642; United States Coast Guard Auxiliary, 426-1079; and the Annapolis Sailing School, (301) 267-7205.

If you already have a craft to call your own, there are three marinas in the Washington area: Columbia Island, George Washington Parkway opposite the Pentagon, (347-0173) has 464 permanent and transient slips; Fort McNair Yacht Basin, 2nd and V Streets, SW (488-7322), has 165 slips up to 65 feet; and the Washington Sailing Marina, GW Parkway south of National Airport (548-0001) has 185 wet and 384 dry slips plus 72 rack spaces for small craft.

Fort McNair rents Oday Sprites; Washington Sailing Marina rents Oday Widgeons.

For a complete list of Chesapeake area clubs, write the Chesapeake Bay Yacht Racing Association, PO Box 1989, Annapolis, Md., 21404.

If your interest is more on the specatator level, check *The Post* events listings for regattas and races.

## SHOOTING

If you want to go hunting, contact the state departments of Maryland or Virginia for seasons and regulations; Wildlife Game Administration, State Office Building, Annapolis, MD., 21404 or Commission of Game and Inland Fisheries, Box 11104, Richmond, VA., 23230.

If your targets are made of paper, check with the National Rifle Association, 1600 Rhode Island Ave., NW, Washington, D.C. 10036.

## SKATING

A fine new ice rink now graces the Mall between 7th and 9th Streets, NW. It is open daily from late November to April 1, weather permitting. Call 347-9041 for information.

Other skating arenas are scattered about the metropolitan area. Check the Yellow Pages under "Skating Rinks" and phone ahead for dates, hours, and fees.

## SKIING

Winter weekends often result in mass migration from home to slope. There are several choice locations within driving distance. Check the Friday editions of *The Post* Sports section for the latest conditions.

Maryland: Wisp, (301) 387-5503; Braddock Heights, (301) 371-7131.

Virginia: Bryce Mountain, (703) 856-2121; Massanutten, (703) 289-2711; Wintergreen (804) 361-2200.

Pennsylvania: Ski Roundtop, (717) 432-9631; Ski Liberty, (717) 642-8282; Camelback, (717) 629-1661; Jack Frost, (717) 443-8425; Big Boulder, (717) 722-0101; Blue Knob, (814) 239-5111; Elk, (717) 679-2611; Seven Springs, (814) 352-7777.

West Virginia: Snowshoe, (304) 799-6600; Canaan, Valley, (304) 866-4121.

If you prefer a (relatively) flat track, cross-country skiing is

available at Catoctin National Park in Thurmont, Md.,
(301) 271-7447, or New Germany State Park in Grantsville, Md.,
(301) 895-5453.

## SOCCER AND RUGBY

The Washington Diplomats of the North American Soccer
League play two seasons' worth of soccer each year. A brief indoor season runs from January to March followed by the outdoor
season from April through August. For schedule and ticket information call 544-KICK.

Various amateur soccer and rugby groups hold games and
tournaments through much of the year highlighted by the Annual
Cherry Blossom Rugby Tournament each April. For information,
call Dial-a-Park.

## SWIMMING

Year-round swimming is available at two locations in the District; East Capitol Natatorium (724-4495) at 635 North Carolina
Ave., SE, and the Washington Highlands Community Pool
(767-7449) at 8th and Yuma, SE.

Nineteen other pools are open in the summer. Check with
the D.C. Dept. of Recreation for locations and schedules.

## TENNIS

The tennis boom that has swept the country in the last few years
has hit as hard in Washington as anywhere. Many vacant lots
have turned into tennis courts and many heretofore vacant tennis
courts are now filled from sunrise to sunset in all seasons.

Courts in the District require a permit, obtainable without
cost from the D.C. Department of Recreation Tennis Permit Section, 3149 16th Street, NW, 20010.

Information on public courts in the suburbs is available by
contacting the respective Departments of Recreation. Check the
phone book for listings.

Should you pass a newsstand, look for the *Washington Tennis
Guide*. It lists more than 1,000 courts and provides specific infor-
mation on most. The book is also available from Rock Creek
Publishing Co., Box 19278, Washington, D.C. 20036.

Activity in other racquet sports takes place mainly within private clubs, but there are some public courts. The Wakefield Recreation Center (321-7080) at 8100 Braddock Road in Annandale, Virginia, has four racquetball and two squash indoor courts. Olney Regional Park on Georgia Avenue in Olney, Maryland, has outdoor racquetball courts. For information, call Montgomery County, Maryland, Recreation Department at 468-4176.

---

### ON THE MALL

Just about any activity that requires large amounts of area and energy can be found on the Mall at one time or another.

The Smithsonian sponsors an annual Spring Kite Carnival in March and a Boomerang Tournament in early May. Field hockey and jousting take place in October and cricket from September to November.

For information on these and other Mall sports, call Dial-a-Park or the Smithsonian.

# XVII
# Shopping

## The Washington Agora

Some people make a vocation out of shopping; some find it a total bore. But practically everybody shops in another town—domestic or foreign—where excuses to buy something always emerge. A gift for a friend, a dress not just to wear but to show off back home, or an extra pair of tennis socks from the same shop where Senator So-and-so buys his. You see, we all need proof that we were there.

But for non-essential shopping, the natives here easily outclass the newcomers. Local specialty shops abound to satisfy the well-off tastes of Washingtonians, who rank third nationally in per capita income and sixth in retail sales.

As the Capital Beltway continues to encourage massive shopping complexes in suburbia, the METRO has given a new boost to downtown. In plain and simple fact, Washngton is a town of "shopaholics"—comparative and complusive. So in the city's decentralized agora, there's an assuaging goodie for you, too. If you're looking—as sooner or later you're bound to be—here are a few paths to the marketplace.

**Georgetown**—the city's unparalleled emporium—is famed for its divers customwares designed to indulge the studied tastes of its decidedly fashionable dwellers, who now share a separate peace with an influx of street vendors and hippie habitués. Shops on M Street extend from Twenty-eighth to Thirty-fifth Street, N.W., and on Wisconsin from the Towpath below M up as far as R Street, N.W. Parking is bothersome, but the street and shop scene is a shopper's walking pleasure paradise.

**Capitol Hill:** a city community with the slower paced ambiance of a small southern town and some unique gems, like the Eastern Market. Shopping on the south side of Pennsylvania Avenue between Second and Seventh Streets, S.E. A few boutiques on Seventh between Pennsylvania and North Carolina Avenues, close to a METRO stop, will surely increase in numbers because travel to the Hill is now a breeze. And at Seventh Street at North Carolina Avenue is Eastern Market; don't miss it.

**Connecticut Avenue.** With a slightly more continental flair, this employment/restaurant/hotel hub of the city offers everything, from art galleries to haberdasheries. The shopping district on Connecticut stretches from K Street, N.W., beyond Dupont Circle to Florida Avenue, N.W., with more and more branches of Georgetown shops opening here.

**Downtown** is the ancestral domicile of the F Street retail giants—Washington's own home-grown department stores, who sprouted numerous branches in suburban marketplaces but maintain strong downtown matriarchal stores. Beginning with Garfinckel's at Fourteenth and F Streets, N.W., past Woodward & Lothrop at Eleventh, the downtown agora stretches to Hecht's at Seventh and F Streets, N.W., and is well served by METRO.

**The Mall and Environs.** Some of the best buys in town are in the museum and government shops spread around the Mall. You'll find cards at Freer Gallery, molas by the Panamanian San Blas Indians at the Pan American Union, inexpensive but famous art reproductions (framed or unframed) at the National Gallery of Art, Navajo squash-blossom silver and turquoise necklaces at the Department of Interior Indian Craft Shop. So when you're museum-meandering and you're in the market for a memento or two, keep your eyes peeled.

**Upper Wisconsin Avenue:** homestead of the outside retail giants where the inflow of national retail chains first began. Here, Lord & Taylor and Saks Fifth Avenue challenged the local department store giants, having market-researched enough to know the retail opportunities were ample for all. The result—the quality of shopping was raised all around as Neiman Marcus joined the national chains here in 1977. At the intersection of Wisconsin and Western Avenues, N.W., in Friendship Heights.

**Watergate.** A mini-city unto its own, the shopping bazaar at the Watergate office-apartment complex—of recent notoriety—draws shoppers from all over the city. The shopping range is expansive, from the 30 exclusive boutiques of the Les Champs arcade (Pierre Cardin, Yves St. Laurent, antiques, crystal, oriental rugs), to the crafts and specialty shops of Watergate Mall, to Saks Fifth Avenue facing Virginia Avenue, N.W. Where Virginia and New Hampshire Avenues meet, just before you get to Kennedy Center.

A special note: If you plan to use a bank-issued credit card, such as Visa or Master Charge, as identification for cashing a personal check, it's wise to do it at a bank in the Maryland or Virginia suburbs that participates in the card business. No bank in Washington is affiliated with a national bank-card organization. However, many establishments in Washington honor the cards for credit purchases, accommodations, and meals.

So, those are the marketplaces. Of the shiny spectrum of wares you'll find there, here are a few "for examples."

*—Anna Karavangelos*

## Antiques

**Arpad Antiques, 3125 M Street, N.W. (Georgetown), 337-3424.** Luxury shop of seventeenth, eighteenth, and nineteenth century American and Continental furnishings.

**Old Antique House, 817 Pennsylvania Avenue, N.W. (downtown), 628-5699.** Browse through seventeenth to nineteenth century furniture in this third-generation shop, the oldest and largest of Washington's antique stores.

**Peter Mack Brown, 1525 Wisconsin Avenue, N.W. (Georgetown), 338-8484.** Chinese export, eighteenth century French, English, and American furniture.

**The Thieves Market, 7704 Richmond Highway (Route 1, 3½ miles south of Alexandria, Virginia), 360-4200.** With 32 antique dealers in a 75,000 square foot marketplace, the selection is bound to have something for everyone. Dealers specialize in china, silver, furniture, glass, porcelain, paintings.

**Wm. Blair Ltd., 4839 Del Ray Avenue, Bethesda, Maryland, 654-6665.** One of the finest stocks in America of English period furniture.

## Boutiques

**Ann Taylor, 1415 Wisconsin Avenue, N.W. (Georgetown), 338-5290.** Chic modern fashions for young women. Separate shoe department.

**Elizabeth Arden, 1147 Connecticut Avenue, N.W., 638-6212.** Small boutique with elegant clothes, accessories, perfumes and the entire line of Elizabeth Arden cosmetics. Also at 5225 Wisconsin Avenue, N.W.

**Saint-Aubin de Paris, 1661 Wisconsin Avenue, N.W. (Georgetown), 338-8845.** Complementing

Madame Paul's haute couture is an expanded collection of ready-to-wear.

**Vogue Madame, 1657 Wisconsin Avenue, N.W. (Georgetown), 338-1914.** The latest European lines and styles, designed by Felix Alonso, manufactured in Spain. Sportswear, suits, dresses, party clothes.

## Children

**Granny's Place, 303 Cameron Street (Alexandria, Virginia), 549-0119.** A browsing bazaar for kids, parents too. Big on imported toys—Brio from Sweden, Stieff from Germany, Lego, Denmark—but also Creative Playthings, Madame Alexander dolls, and Eden stuffed animals, all from the U.S.A.

**The Red Balloon, 1073 Wisconsin Avenue, N.W. (Georgetown), 965-1200.** Oshkosh (b'gosh) overalls for small children. Toys, puzzles, stuffed animals, and games to amuse a child weary with sightseeing. Also at Les Camps, Watergate.

## Men's Shops

**Britches of Georgetowne, 1247 Wisconsin Avenue, N.W. (Georgetown), 338-3330.** Founded in 1967 by two local entrepreneurs, David Pensky and Rick Hindin, this elegant men's clothiers has become one of Washington's most respectable and popular stores, with several branches in the area. Its merchandise is geared toward young professionals with expensive tastes. Other offshoots: Britches

Slack Shop, Britches Western, and Britches Sale Shop, all on Wisconsin Avenue in Georgetown. Also on Connecticut Avenue, N.W., and in Tysons Corner Centre, Springfield Mall, in Virginia, and Montgomery Mall in Maryland.

**Brooks Brothers, 1728 L Street, N.W. (off Connecticut Avenue), 659-4650.** If you make it to the second floor at 1728 L Street, you could be in the New York store of this nationally known men's-wear manufacturer. High quality classic and conservative Brooks Brothers lines that stay in style. Stock up at their authentic and extremely good shirt sales.

**Georgetown University Shop, 1248 Thirty-sixth Street, N.W. (Georgetown), 337-8100.** Avowedly preppy, but some of the best names in men's wear; between the campus and Georgetown shopping district.

**Lewis & Thomas Saltz, 1409 G Street, N.W. (downtown); 1009 Connecticut Avenue, N.W.; 5500 Wisconsin Avenue, N.W. 393-4400.** Well-established Washington store known for its quality men's wear.

**Raleigh's, 1133 Connecticut Avenue, N.W., 785-7071.** Up-to-date suitings and furnishings in a large, modern store. Also at 1310 F Street, N.W., and in suburban centers.

**William Fox & Co., 2136 Pennsylvania Avenue, N.W., 337-7080.** Just a few blocks from the Connecticut Avenue strip close to G.W. Traditional, natural-shouldered suits and jackets, varied selection of slacks; all in a renovated brick townhouse.

## Crafts and Craftsmen

**The American Hand, 2904 M Street, N.W. (Georgetown), 965-3273.** Contemporary pottery and ceramics, functional and funky, made by American hands from all over the country.

**Appalachian Spring, 1665 Wisconsin Avenue, N.W. (Georgetown), 337-5780.** Patchwork quilts, potholders, pillows, and stuffed animals. Ceramic pots for hanging plants, and whiskbrooms in different colors and sizes.

**The Craftsmen of Chelsea Court, 2551 Virginia Avenue, N.W. (Watergate), 337-6650; 1311 Connecticut Avenue, N.W., 466-3142.** Unusual ceramics, handblown glassware, leatherwork, and jewelry. Craftspeople work in open for the curious shopper.

**Indian Country, 3207 O Street, N.W. (Georgetown), 333-5009.** Silver and turquoise jewelry made by Navajo, Zuni, and Hopi Indians.

**The Torpedo Factory, King and Union Streets at the Potomac River (Alexandria, Virginia), 836-8564.** The working studio of 180 artists and artisans, the Torpedo Factory, once manufacturer of World War I and II torpedoes, is a Bicentennial investment of the city of Alexandria. The 50,000 square factory-feet were purchased, renovated, and opened (1974) with city seed money. Painters, sculptors, print-

makers, potters, and fiber artists work at their crafts in the giant atelier and sell only works created on the premises.

## Gifts and Imports

**Camalier & Buckley, 1141 Connecticut Avenue, N.W., 783-1431.** Quality leather goods —wallets, handbags, briefcases. Separate luggage department upstairs. Also, Chevy Chase location.

**Little Caledonia, 1419 Wisconsin Avenue, N.W. (Georgetown), 333-4700.** A quaint shop housed on the ground floor of a Georgetown townhouse. Little Caledonia is synonymous with gift shopping for many Washingtonians. A miniature department store, bulging with functional bibelots, one could totally decorate one's house here.

**Nuevo Mundo, 313 Cameron Street (Alexandria, Virginia), 549-0040.** Nuevo Mundo, a misnomer according to Maria O'Leary, started out with an emphasis on Latin America. Now she and Cornelia Noland travel through the whole world to bring you: masks from New Guinea and Africa, Coptic textiles, primitive folk paintings from Sicily, antique ceramics from China, or a Macedonian silver breastplate.

**The Phoenix, 1514 Wisconsin Avenue, N.W. (Georgetown), 338-4404.** Jewelry, pottery, clothing and handwoven fabrics all imported from Mexico. Alexandria location, also.

**YWCA Gift Shop, 1649 K Street, N.W., 638-2100.** Pleasant

shop with greeting cards, gift wraps, dishtowels, placemats. Best chocolate chip cookies in town at the bakery down the hall.

**For the Home**

**The Design Store, 1258 Wisconsin Avenue, N.W. (Georgetown), 337-5800.** Scandinavian influence evident in fine crystal, ceramic and stoneware. Also, English crockery, copper pots, hanging planters, Marimekko fabrics. Suburban mall locations.

**Peterson's Warehouse, 1533 Wisconsin Avenue, N.W. (Georgetown), 337-1441.** Straw baskets, placemats, trivets, and coasters imported from the Far East. Good selection of wooden cutting boards. Suburban mall locations.

**W & J Sloane, 1130 Connecticut Avenue, N.W., 659-9200.** National furniture retailer whose special-item sales, based on volume purchases, offer some hard-to-beat buys. Traditional, modern, and summer furniture. Unusually elegant Oriental rug selection. Other stores: Bethesda, Alexandria, Seven Corners.

**Museum Shops**

**Folger Shakespeare Library, 201 East Capitol Street, S.E., 546-4800.** Books, posters, maps, and sundry items related to Shakespeare and the Elizabethan era, also the Renaissance, are sold in this corner cubbyhole off the main library.

**Museum of History and Technology, Constitution Avenue between Twelfth and Fourteenth Streets, N.W., 628-4422.** Two shops on the Mall level. One, specifically for children, stocks coloring books, model ships, hobby kits, paper dolls, patchwork dolls and animals, merchandise related to exhibits.

The adult museum shop, directly across the hall, offers collectible items also reflecting museum exhibits: costume dolls, Waterford crystal, Royal Copenhagen china, brass candlesticks, needlepoint kits of U.S. flags from different historical periods.

On the Constitution Avenue level, the Smithsonian Book Store (also the McGraw-Hill Book Store) presents an Americana collection . . . books about politics, culture, technology, arts and crafts of American life. From an ethnographic study of Black Foot Indians to details about specific museum exhibits. Also, folklore, trains and locomotives. Definitely worth a browsing turn.

**Museum of Natural History, Tenth and Constitution, N.W., 628-4422.** Stirring American Indian photographs taken by Edward Curtis in the late nineteenth century. Kits to reconstruct prehistoric scenes or animals; multicolored rope bags from Mexico; Sierra Club posters; and more.

**National Gallery of Art, Constitution Avenue at Sixth Street, N.W., 737-4215.** Among the best buys in town—the well-designed-for-browsing museum shop on the ground floor holds a treasure of inexpensive art reproductions.

**National Geographic Society, Seventeenth and M Streets, N.W.,**

**857-7000.** The sales counter in Explorer's Hall sells *National Geographic* books, maps, posters, globes, atlases, mural maps printed on heavy chart paper, and recordings of music from around the world.

**Pan American Union, Seventeenth and Constitution Avenue, N.W., 331-1010.** The gift shop, its wares brimming over into the verdant interior courtyard, sells jewelry, ponchos, hand-knitted sweaters, woven bags, belts, and skirts, and other articles from Latin American artisans.

**The Renwick Gallery, 1661 Pennsylvania Avenue, N.W., 628-4422.** This Smithsonian gallery is devoted to American crafts, design and the decorative arts. The gift shop is a mini-reference library for such subjects as pottery, weaving, cabinet-making, architecture, cooking, and gardening.

**Government Shops**

**Army Map Service, 6500 Brooks Lane, Bethesda, Maryland, 227-2496.** Plastic relief maps of different sections of the United States.

**Department of Commerce, Constitution Avenue at Fourteenth Street, 377-2000.** The Commerce Department bookstore offers books and pamphlets on almost any subject you can name: space exploration, mental health, foreign languages (including Swahili), and American history are some of the more common topics. Follow the signs to Room 1605.

**Department of Interior, C Street between Eighteenth and Nineteenth Streets, N.W., 343-1100.** A small, distinctive Indian-crafts shop displays a fine selection of crafts from the hands of American Indians. Hopi Kachina dolls, Navajo woven rugs, silver and turquoise jewelry from the Hopi, Zuni, and Navajo tribes. Beaded work, basketry, and pottery.

**Library of Congress, East Capitol and First Street, S.E., 426-5000.** Near the information desk, a small gift shop sells reproduction turn-of-the-century advertising posters, unusual greeting cards, book plates, and some bibliographic pamphlets.

But follow a long maze-like corridor to Room 153 to discover the Recorded Sound Division, an adventure in itself. Ask for the catalogues of Folk Recordings and Spoken Recordings. You'll find: folk music from America's past beginning with the American Indian; poetry readings by twentieth century poets; Pennsylvania coal miner and Michigan lumberjack working songs; Negro spirituals; and more. Also, folk music from foreign countries—Morocco, Mexico, Venezuela and Brazil. Poetry readings by T. S. Eliot, e. e. cummings, Robert Frost, and Archibald MacLeish. And for H. L. Mencken fans there is an off-the-cuff interview with the caustic critic taped in 1948 (a two-record set at $10.00). Other single LP's, $6.50. For catalogues of Folk Recordings and Spoken

Recordings write:
The Library of Congress
Music Division
Recorded Sound Division
Washington, D.C. 20540

**National Archives, Pennsylvania Avenue at Eighth Street, N.W., 523-3000.** As might be expected, the National Archives sells facsimiles of documents from America's past, posters, old maps, pamphlets on American heritage. Also, reproductions of FDR's print collection of old Navy ships—for purchase individually, or in sets of ten, very reasonably priced. Or, from the John F. Kennedy Library, a small portfolio of letters, facsimiles of handwritten notes, speeches belonging to the late President.

**Treasury Department, Pennsylvania Avenue at Fifteenth Street, N.W., 566-2000.** Enter on East Executive Avenue, across from the White House. The Exhibit Hall features souvenir coin sets from the Denver and Philadelphia mints. Presidential and National Historical commemorative bronze medals. From the Bureau of Engraving and Printing (but only sold here or through the mail), portraits of U.S. Presidents and Chief Justices, and vignettes of historical buildings.

*—Anna Karavangelos and Elizabeth Reilly*

---

## Books

Washington's bookstores aren't what you might expect. They are islands in the stream—surprising and startling in their variety, in how well they do what they set out to, and, most important, in how, like the very best of bookstores anywhere, they manage to create their own little worlds—cool oases.

Most of Washington buys most of its books at two places: the yeasty, determined **Discount Book Shop at 1324 Connecticut Avenue, N.W., 785-1133,** just below Dupont Circle, which really does offer discounts of up to 20 percent; or at the more genteel **Savile Book Shop at 3236 P Street, N.W., in Georgetown, 338-3321.**

Of more interest, however, are the close to half a dozen very special stores, each with its distinct aim and distinctive atmosphere, any one of which can happily use up as much of a browser's time as he wants to give:

**Booked Up, 1209 Thirty-first Street, N.W., in Georgetown, 965-3244.** More like a sumptuous private library than a place of business, this small, charming store, run by author Larry McMurtry and Marcia Carter, specializes in general antiquarian books, which means first editions, prize sets, rare collector's items, and all kinds of marvelous old books in equally marvelous bindings.

**Kramer Books, 1347 Connecticut Avenue, N.W.,** across the street from Discount, **293-2072.** Filled to bursting with remaindered books, special-sale books, publishers' overstock and damaged books, none of which are sold at anything like the original cost.

**Kramer Afterwords, 1517 Connecticut Avenue, N.W., 387-1400.** This bookstore *cum* coffee house has a wonderful selection of hardcover books, paperbacks, magazines, and a colorful array of calendars.

**Park-Reifsneider Antiquarian Book Gallery and Museum, 1310 Nineteenth Street, N.W., between N Street and Dupont Circle, 833-8082.** A mouthful of a name and a mouthful of a store, with well over 100,000 books located in a quiet, four-story townhouse that is easily the biggest used-book store in Washington. Of the same type are **Estate Book Sales, 1724 H Street, N.W., 298-7355.** A used-book shop with a large *National Geographic* selection and a room full of old picture postcards, and **Second-Story Books, 5016 Connecticut Avenue, N.W., 244-5550.**

**Yes!, 1035 Thirty-first Street, N.W.,** in Georgetown, **338-7874.** Next door to a health food store of the same name, this quiet, restful, human-scaled place is one of the most comprehensive metaphysical bookstores in the entire country.

Though not quite so very special, no listing of Washington bookstores would be complete without mention of the following:

**Government Printing Office,** the world's largest printer, in a mammoth red brick building at **710 North Capitol Street, N.W., between G and H, 275-2091.** The GPO offers access to its 25,000 volume backlist as well as an opportunity to browse through items like the government telephone directory and bound volumes of Supreme Court decisions. Very definitely offbeat.

**Smithsonian Bookstore (a McGraw-Hill enterprise), Fourteenth Street and Constitution Avenue, N.W., 347-7587.** Set up in the Museum of History and Technology, this is purely, as the sign says, "A Store of American Civilization." Especially strong in handicrafts and American history.

**Sidney Kramer Books, 1722 H Street, N.W., 298-8010.** One of the country's largest economics and social sciences bookstores, and a refuge for the academics.

**Francis Scott Key Book Shop, Twenty-eighth and O Streets, N.W.,** in Georgetown, **337-4144.** A small, quaint throwback to more leisurely days, this store will search out any and all out-of-print books. Special orders are their specialty.

**Earthworks, 1724 Twentieth Street, N.W., 387-6688.** Features the biggest collection of definitely-not-for-minors underground comics on the East Coast, titles of the "Zap," "Mr. Natural," and

"Slow Death" variety. **Lambda Rising, 2012 S Street, N.W., 462-6969,** is a small bookstore emphasizing homosexual-oriented literature.

**Universal News—Store Number 1, Fourteenth Street and New York Avenue, N.W., 638-1852.** The city's largest newsstand, boasting several dozen newspapers and close to 2,000 different foreign and domestic magazines, everything from *Needlepoint* to *The Bulletin of Atomic Scientists.*

**Vassar Book Sale.** Every April Vassar alumnae run a gigantic used-book sale that is a veritable saturnalia of literary delights, with bargains and surprises for all. Watch newspapers for dates and locations, or call **244-4667.**

National chain stores selling popular books are represented well in Washington: by **Bren-** **tano's** with three stores (downtown at **1326 F Street, N.W., 737-3913; and in Chevy Chase and Georgetown);** by **Doubleday (at 1331 E Street, N.W.,** near the National Theatre, **737-3646);** and by two **Walden Book Stores (downtown, 409 Twelfth Street, N.W., 638-0225, and out near American University).** Brentano's and Walden each has about four stores in suburban shopping centers.

**Trover Shop,** with a sprinkling of three downtown locations **(1031 Connecticut Avenue, N.W., 659-8138; 1751 Pennsylvania Avenue, N.W., 833-2855; 800 Fifteenth Street, N.W., 347-2177)** and one Capitol Hill store **(227 Pennsylvania Ave., S.E., 543-8006),** is Washington's own thriving local chain of popular books. Offering mostly paperbacks, it has a current selection of hardbacks.

*—Kenneth Turan*

Anna Karavangelos, a Washington writer and editor, is an assistant editor in *The Washington Post* Writers Group.

Elizabeth Reilly, a free-lance writer, worked as a special research assistant on this book.

Kenneth Turan is a staff writer of *The Washington Post*'s Style section.

# Where to Find
# the Best (Whatever) in Washington

## Compiled by William B. Dickinson, Jr.

Where is the best place in Washington to find some off-beat things when the yen strikes? *Washington Post* staffers who contributed articles for this book were asked to nominate their favorite places for everything from pizza to bluegrass music. In some cases two or more places qualified. In few cases will you be disappointed.

---

*POPCORN*
**Circle Theatre, 2105 Pennsylvania Avenue, N.W.**

*ICE CREAM PARLOR*
**Giffords's, 7623 Wisconsin Avenue, Bethesda, Maryland**
**Swenson's Ice Cream Factory and Parlor, 1254 Wisconsin Avenue, N.W. (Georgetown)**

*HAMBURGERS*
**Clyde's, 3236 M Street, N.W. (Georgetown)**
**Hamburger Hamlet, 5225 Wisconsin Avenue, N.W.**
**Golden Booeymonger, 1701 Twentieth Street, N.W.**

*BARBER*
**Mayflower Hotel Barber Shop, 1127 Connecticut Avenue, N.W.**
**Headstartt Hair Studio, 1802 Wisconsin Avenue, N.W.**

**Hairport Ltd., 1614 Wisconsin Avenue, N.W. (Georgetown)**

*PIZZA*
**Luigi's Pizzeria, 1132 Nineteenth Street, N.W. Zebra Room, 3238 Wisconsin Avenue, N.W. (Half price Tuesdays and Thursdays.)**

*PASTRIES*
**Watergate Pastry, 2650 Virginia Avenue, N.W.**
**University Pastry Shop, 3234 Wisconsin Avenue, N.W.**
**La Ruche, 1206 Thirtieth Street, N.W. (Georgetown; table or carry-out)**
**Shuman's Bakery, 430 South Washington Street, Alexandria, Virginia**

*ANTIQUES*
**Gonzalez Antiques, 2601 Connecticut Avenue, N.W.**

William B. Dickinson, Jr., is editorial director and general manager of *The Washington Post* Writers Group.

The Thieves Market, 7704 Richmond Highway, south of Alexandria, Virginia

*HAIRDRESSER*
Elizabeth Arden, 1147 Connecticut Avenue, N.W.
Charles the First, 2602 Connecticut Avenue, N.W.
Daniel's Hair Design, 1514 Connecticut Avenue, N.W. (Open Sundays)

*DOUBLE FEATURE*
Biograph Theatre, 2819 M Street, N.W. (Georgetown)
Circle Theatre, 2105 Pennsylvania Avenue, N.W.

*OLD BOOKS*
Park-Reifsneider Antiquarian Book Gallery and Museum, 1310 Nineteenth Street, N.W.
Booked Up, 1209 and 1214 Thirty-first Street, N.W. (Georgetown)

*SHOESHINE*
Mayflower Hotel, 1127 Connecticut Avenue, N.W.

*DISCOTHEQUE*
East India Sporting Club, 2915 M Street, N.W. (Georgetown)
TRAMPS, 1238 Wisconsin Avenue, N.W. (Georgetown)

*BIKE TRAIL*
George Washington Parkway to Mount Vernon
C&O Canal
Rock Creek Park

*PICNIC SPOT*
Turkey Run, on George Washington Parkway

Wolf Trap Farm Park, Vienna, Virginia
Battery Kemble Park, between MacArthur Boulevard and American University, off Chain Bridge Road
Rock Creek Park

*DELICATESSEN*
Booeymonger, 3265 Prospect Street, N.W. (Georgetown)
Loeb's, 617 Fifteenth Street, N.W.
Shirlington, 4015 Twenty-eighth South, Arlington, Virginia

*ADDRESS*
1600 Pennsylvania Avenue, N.W.
Chevy Chase
Cleveland Park
Georgetown
Alexandria (Old Town)
Capitol Hill

*DOUGHNUTS*
Crumpets, 1259 Wisconisn Avenue, N.W. (Georgetown)

*ENGLISH PUB*
Martin's Tavern, 1264 Wisconsin Avenue, N.W. (Georgetown)

*SINGLES BAR*
Nathan's, 3150 M Street, N.W. (Georgetown)
Clyde's, 3236 M Street, N.W. (Georgetown)
Fran O'Brien's, 1823 L Street, N.W.
Nathan's II, 1211 Connecticut Avenue, N.W.

*INTIMATE BAR*
Jefferson Hotel, Sixteenth and M Streets, N.W.

Harvey's, 1001 Eighteenth Street, N.W.

Four Georges, 1310 Wisconsin Avenue, N.W. (Georgetown)

Tabard Inn, 1739 N Street, N.W. (Upstairs Parlor)

*EGGS BENEDICT/BRUNCH*

Clyde's, 3236 M Street, N.W. (Georgetown)

Hay-Adams Hotel, 800 Sixteenth Street, N.W.

Billy Martin's Carriage House, 1238 Wisconsin Avenue, N.W. (Georgetown)

*PLACE TO THINK*

Bonnard room, Phillips Collection, 1612 Twenty-first Street, N.W.

Freer Gallery of Art, Twelfth Street and Jefferson Drive, S.W.

Roosevelt Island

The steps between Twenty-second and Twenty-third Streets, N.W., at S Street

Christ Church, 118 North Washington Street, Alexandria (Old Town)

Memorial to District of Columbia war dead, in the trees south of the Reflecting Pool on the Mall

*PUBLIC GARDEN*

Dumbarton Oaks Garden, 1703 Thirty-second Street, N.W. (Georgetown)

*LIBRARY*

Library of Congress, Capitol Hill at First Street and Independence Avenue, S.E.

Martin Luther King Memorial Library, 901 G Street, N.W.

Georgetown Public Library, Wisconsin Avenue and R Street, N.W. (Georgetown)

*SMALL MUSEUM*

Dumbarton Oaks Museum of Pre-Columbian Art, 1703 Thirty-second Street, N.W. (Georgetown)

*BLUEGRASS*

Birchmere, 2723 S. Wakefield Street, Arlington, Virginia

Red Fox Inn, 4940 Fairmont Avenue, Bethesda, Maryland

*FREE ENTERTAINMENT*

Congressional hearings, various buildings on Capitol Hill

Sylvan Theater, Washington Monument grounds on the mall (plays and concerts)

Oral arguments at the Supreme Court, First and East Capitol Streets, N.E.

Sunset parade at Marine Corps Barracks, Eighth and I Streets, S.E.

*LIVE ROCK MUSIC*

Desperados, 3350 M Street, N.W. (Georgetown)

Childe Harold, 1610 Twentieth Streets, N.E.

*JAZZ*

Blues Alley, 1073 Wisconsin Avenue, N.W. (Georgetown)

Harold's Rogue and Jar, 1814 N Street, N.W.

*MILITARY BAND*

Marine Corps Band

*BOAT RENTAL*
Fletcher's Boat House, 4940 Canal Road, N.W.
Paddle boats at the Tidal Basin near Jefferson Monument on the Mall

*MONUMENT*
Lincoln Memorial, on the Mall

*STATUE*
Saint-Gaudens' memorial called "Grief," Rock Creek Cemetery, Rock Creek Church Road and Webster Street, N.W. (northwest corner of Soldiers' Home)

*CITY SQUARE*
Lafayette Park, across from White House
Farragut Square, Connecticut Avenue and K Street, N.W.
Lincoln Park, East Capitol Street between Eleventh and Thirteenth Streets, S.E. (Capitol Hill)

**BIRD WATCHING**
Theodore Roosevelt Island
Pan American Union Plaza, Seventeenth and Constitution Avenue, N.W.
Mt. Vernon College

*COFFEE HOUSE*
Cafe de Paris, 3056 M Street, N.W. (Georgetown)
Potter's House, 1658 Columbia Road, N.W.

*CRAFTS*
Torpedo Factory, 101 North Union Street, Alexandria, Virginia

*NATURAL FOOD STORE*
Yes Inc., 1039 Thirty-first Street, N.W. (Georgetown)
Stone Soup, 1801 Eighteenth Street, N.W.

*SOUP KITCHEN*
The Gate, 3338 M Street, N.W. (Georgetown)

*STRIP JOINT*
Silver Slipper, 815 Thirteenth Street, N.W.

*PORNO MOVIE HOUSE*
D.C. Playhouse, Fifteenth Street between New York Avenue and H Street, N.W.

*BEER ON TAP*
Dubliner, 4 F Street, N.W. (Across from Union Station)
Jenkins Hill, 223 Pennsylvania Avenue, S.E.
The Tombs, 1226 Thirty-sixth Street, N.W. (Georgetown)

*EMBASSY ARCHITECTURE*
Brazilian; 3006 Massachusetts Avenue, N.W.
French; Ambassador's Residence, 2221 Kalorama Road, N.W.
British; 3100 Massachusetts Avenue, N.W.

*WALKING*
Georgetown
The Mall
Old Town Alexandria
Down Pennsylvania Avenue from the Capitol to the White House.

*HIKING*
**C&O Canal**
**Rock Creek Park near the Nature Center**
**Glover Park**

*MONTH TO BE IN WASH-INGTON*
**October**
**April**

*MONTH NOT TO BE IN WASHINGTON*
**August**

*SMITHSONIAN ARTIFACT*
**Hope Diamond**
**George Washington's false teeth**

*VIEW*
**Of the Potomac from the Kennedy Center balcony**
**Or, of the Potomac and the city, coming south from Cabin John Bridge on the George Washington Memorial Parkway**

*MARKET*
**Eastern Market, Seventh Street and North Carolina Avenue, S.E.**

*PLACE TO HAVE LUNCH*
**Sandwich bar and garden at the National Portrait Gallery, Seventh and F Streets, N.W.**

# Navigation
# &
# Accommodation

# XVIII
## Getting Here
## and Getting Around

### By Jack Eisen

### GETTING HERE

#### Driving to Washington

If you are driving to Washington, by all means try to schedule yourself to avoid arriving in the downtown area during rush hours—generally 7 to 9 A.M. and 4 to 6 P.M. A street layout that already is confusing is made more frustrating by hundreds of thousands of cars driven by commuters who tend to be impatient with perplexed, hesitant visitors.

Here are a few tips if you are coming by car:

Be sure your road map is up to date. Highway officials have renumbered several interstate freeways in and around the city, making old maps out of date. This occurred because plans to extend Interstate 95 through the center of Washington were dropped and officials want a continuous road with that number from Maine to Florida.

With the single exception of Interstate 95/395 from the south, all interstate freeways leading to Washington end at the Capital Beltway, currently designated Interstate 495/95. The Beltway is a loop road around Washington. It is 67 miles long and averages 10 miles' distance from the Capitol. There are interchanges an average of every 2 miles, providing access to other roads leading downtown and to areas with tourist accommodations.

Jack Eisen reports on transportation for *The Washington Post* Metropolitan staff.

Inside the District of Columbia, interstate and U.S. highway routes are marked by number. Virginia and Maryland state highway route numbers stop at the D.C. border, however, so be sure to remember the name of the street you use once inside the city.

**From New England or New York.** If you come from New England or New York via Interstate 95, decide on an approach to Washington before you reach Baltimore. You can take either:

• The Harbor Tunnel Thruway (toll) and the Baltimore-Washington Parkway. This leads to an interchange with U.S. 50 and brings you into downtown Washington along New York Avenue, N.E. If and when special tourist parking and shuttle bus service is provided, signs along the parkway as you approach Washington will direct you to it.

• Interstate 695 around the west side of Baltimore, to interchange 11, then south again on Interstate 95. Since I-95 terminates at Interstate 495, this route is useful if you plan to stay in the northern suburbs, or to use the Capital Beltway to reach the suburban home of friends or relatives.

Or, for an alternative, almost equally speedy and more scenic trip to Washington, travel U.S. 301 south from Wilmington, Delaware, picking up U.S. 50 for the trip across the Chesapeake Bay Bridge (toll) to Washington by way of Annapolis.

**From the Middle West and Western Pennsylvania.** If you come from the Middle West and Western Pennsylvania by Interstate 70, watch for the junction with Interstate 270 at Frederick, Maryland. Follow Interstate 270 to reach the Washington area.

Before you reach the Washington suburb of Gaithersburg, check your map to determine where in the area you will stay. Check the accommodations listings under various communities and major routes in the next chapter. If your accommodations are in the northern suburbs close to Washington, keep going on Interstate 270 to its junction with Interstate 495 (the Capital Beltway). Then go to an interchange convenient to where you will stay.

If you want to go downtown, follow the signs for Interstate 495 to Virginia, cross the Potomac River, turn east at interchange 14 onto the George Washington Memorial Parkway. The next 8 miles is by far the most scenic approach to Washington, following the Potomac River palisades. Several bridges are available to take you back across the river into Washington. Probably the

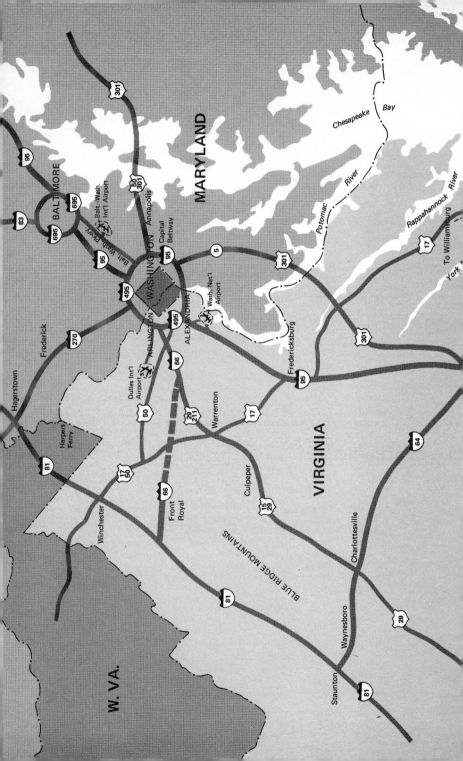

most convenient is the Theodore Roosevelt Bridge, which leads directly into the Lincoln Memorial and Mall area.

**From the Southwest.** If you are coming from the southwest by Interstate 66, check your road map before you reach the city of Fairfax to locate your accommodations.

If you want to go downtown by the shortest route, follow Interstate 66 to Interstate 495. Turn south. At interchange 8, turn east onto U.S. 50 (also known as Arlington Boulevard). This leads to Memorial Bridge and the Mall area.

For the scenic approach described earlier for those who arrive from the west via Interstate 70/270, follow Interstate 66 to Interstate 495. Turn north. At interchange 14, turn east onto the George Washington Memorial Parkway.

**From the South.** If you are coming from the south by Interstate 95/395, simply follow the road and the signs into Washington.

### For Airline Travelers

Washington has three commercial airports. Shorter flights are concentrated at **Washington National Airport,** usually called simply **National Airport,** only three miles from downtown.

Taxicabs from National in Virginia to destinations in central Washington are relatively inexpensive, especially when one person pays the fare for a family or other group. Be watchful, however; there have been numerous complaints of overcharges by unregulated "gypsy" cabs. If you have problems, be sure to get the cab number or other identification and call the airport manager's office at 557-2045, or the Washington Metropolitan Area Transit Commission at 331-1671.

The best local travel bargain from National is the rail rapid-transit service. The station is on an elevated structure opposite the airport's North Terminal building. The 50-cent fare entitles you to a free bus transfer anywhere in Washington. Ask the station attendant for instructions.

Longer flights operate in and out of **Dulles International Airport,** in Virginia about 27 miles west of Washington, and **Baltimore-Washington International Airport,** in Maryland about the same distance to the northeast. (Baltimore-Washington Airport was formerly called Friendship Airport.)

The cheapest way into downtown Washington or into certain suburbs from either airport is the franchised limousines, or buses.

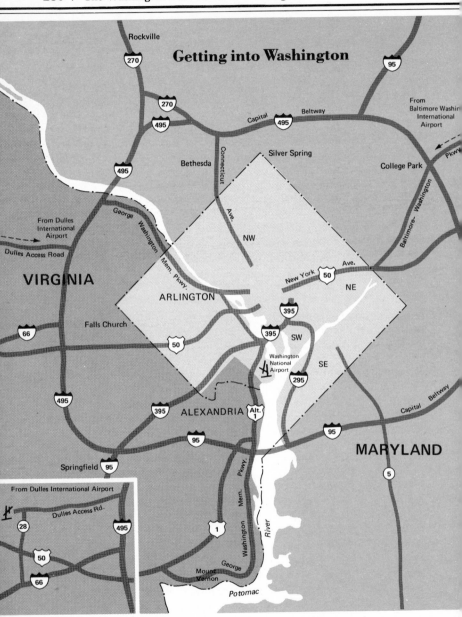

Getting into Washington

Depending on the time of day, the buses leave every 30 minutes or every hour. The downtown terminal for both airports is on the K Street side of the Statler-Hilton Hotel, Sixteenth and K Streets, N.W. Most major airlines maintain ticket offices in or near the Statler-Hilton.

Cab rides to and from these airports can cost as much as $20.

One word of caution: don't confuse the names of Washington National Airport and Baltimore-Washington International Airport. Out-of-town airline agents have been known to do so, with much confusion resulting.

### For Railroad Travelers

All railroad passenger trains into and out of Washington stop or terminate at Union Station, about four blocks north of the Capitol and on the eastern edge of downtown. The station's interior is a National Visitor Center, where tourists can come for an orientation to Washington and information about attractions and accommodations.

The best all-purpose transportation from Union Station is the taxicab. METRO subway service is also availabe to downtown and suburban Silver Spring, Maryland.

Numerous bus routes connect Union Station with downtown. The most direct are the 40 and 42, marked Mt. Pleasant; the D-2, marked Glover Park; and the D-4, marked MacArthur Blvd. The fare is 40 cents except in rush hours, when it is 50 cents (exact change is necessary)—free transfers are available anywhere in Washington.

Union Station also is served by Virginia bus routes. Be sure you know where the bus is going before you get aboard.

Many trains also stop at suburban stations—the Capital Beltway for trains from New York; Alexandria, Virginia, for trains from the south. These stations may be useful if you are going to be met by friends or relatives who live conveniently close to them. Otherwise they are remote from downtown.

### For Intercity Bus Travelers

Both downtown Washington bus stations, Greyhound and Trailways, are located at Twelfth Street and New York Avenue, N.W., facing each other on opposite corners. Although the location is only four blocks from the White House, it is the seediest part of downtown Washington—although not especially dangerous. Panhandlers, pornographic shops, cheap bars, and flop-houses abound. Unless you plan to walk two blocks south into the commercial downtown, the best advice is to take a cab promptly to your destination. The bus companies also maintain several suburban stations for intercity travel.

## GETTING AROUND

### Washington and Its Geography

Washington is a relatively small, compact city. It is little more than 10 miles across at its widest point. Downtown Washington, and most of the tourist attractions such as the Capitol, the White House and the museums on the Mall, are near the Potomac River, which forms the boundary with Virginia. If you are entering Washington by car from Maryland, a drive of about 5 miles on city streets is needed to get downtown. There are only a few freeways, and none of those from the north.

Don't be surprised to hear local people call Washington "the District" or "DC" more often than they call it Washington. The city is run by the Government of the District of Columbia, which combines the functions of a state, a county, and a city.

Washington is divided into four of what are called "quadrants," or quarters, with the Capitol at the center. Northwest is often abbreviated NW; Northeast, NE; Southwest, SW; and Southeast, SE. *See* Taxi Fare Zones/Quadrants map on page 284.

When you are trying to find an address (including one in a newspaper or a telephone directory), be sure to note what quadrant it is in. Looking for an address in the wrong quadrant is as confusing as trying to grope your way through the mirror maze at a carnival.

Since Washington's commercial downtown, the largest concentration of government offices, most foreign embassies, and the most fashionable residential neighborhoods are in the Northwest, the quadrant is often omitted from addresses. If you are in doubt, ask for help.

Washington's basic street layout is a grid system that is relatively simple. What makes it confusing are the avenues, roads, freeways, and parkways that seem to meander across the map. Here are a few tips to remember:
- Streets that are numbered run north-south. There are two

sets of numbered streets, those east of the Capitol and those west of the Capitol.

- Streets that bear letters (like K Street) or names (like Harvard Street) generally run east-west. In many cases, lettered streets north of the Capitol are duplicated south of the Capitol.
- Avenues that bear the names of states slice at angles across the grid pattern, creating many numerous odd intersections. Washington's infamous circles are located generally where the avenues cross each other, or where they intersect with important streets.
- There are two important thoroughfares that logically should be called streets but are avenues—they are Constitution Avenue, which forms the northern boundary of the Mall, and Independence Avenue, which forms its southern boundary.
- Washington also has roads, boulevards, parkways, and a few freeways, which crisscross the landscape at random. The roads were the country roads that existed before the city was settled.

### Taxicabs in Washington

There are about 8,000 taxicabs in Washington, in addition to those in the suburbs. Suburban cabs can take you into Washington, or pick you up in the city and take you back to the suburbs, but they cannot provide transportation within the city.

Fares for city cabs are collected by an unusual zone system, so it is possible to learn in advance how much a trip will cost. Washingtonians are not big tippers, so any tip from 25 cents up is usually appreciated by the driver. Cab rates in the city are relatively cheap, especially in the large downtown zone and for families (or other prearranged groups) riding together. In many instances, cab riding for family groups can be nearly as economical as riding a city bus. Many cab drivers in Washington also will provide sightseeing service by the hour. The prices are regulated.

The easiest way to get a cab in Washington is simply to hail it from the sidewalk (although the experience can be frustrating in rush hours). A few hotels and transportation terminals have stands where cabs line up and wait for riders. Several companies dispatch cabs by radio, but this service is not always reliable.

Cab drivers are permitted to pick up additional passengers who are not part of a group. This is supposed to be done only if it does not take the first passenger far out of his way. Don't be

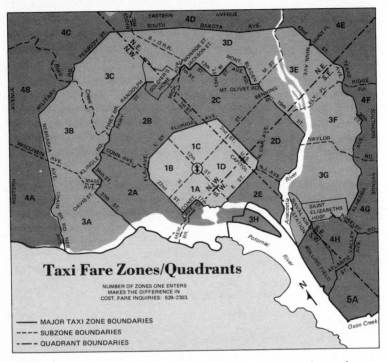

## Taxi Fare Zones/Quadrants

NUMBER OF ZONES ONE ENTERS
MAKES THE DIFFERENCE IN
COST. FARE INQUIRIES: 629-2303.

—— MAJOR TAXI ZONE BOUNDARIES

---- SUBZONE BOUNDARIES

—-— QUADRANT BOUNDARIES

surprised if your riding companion is a senator, an ambassador, or a noted journalist—it sometimes happens.

If a District of Columbia cab takes you into the suburbs, or picks you up at the airport and brings you into the city, the fare is based on the mileage traveled. Suburban cabs use meters. For fare inquiries in the District, call 629-2303.

If you experience problems with a cab in the city or want Lost-and-Found, call the D.C. Transportation Department taxicab office at 347-1398. If you have problems with a cab that travels between the city and the suburbs, call the Washington Metropolitan Area Transit Commission at 331-1671. If you have a problem with a suburban cab, try to determine the city or county in which it is licensed (it usually is painted on the cab door), and call the local police department.

### The Metro Subway

The Metro, Washington's subway, is now a reality. One line connects Silver Spring, Maryland, Union Station and its Visitor Center with the commercial downtown area along G Street,

N.W., the section of town just north of the White House as far as DuPont Circle. Clean and modern, with sleek, quiet cars, it's worth a ride just for the experience. A second line that interconnects National Airport, the Pentagon, Arlington National Cemetery, Washington's Foggy Bottom neighborhood, downtown, the Mall, Capitol Hill, and the Kennedy Stadium parking facilities is a boon for visitors and residents alike. Service halts at 8 P.M. and does not operate on Saturdays, Sundays and most holidays.

Eventually, plans call for a rail rapid transit system totaling about 100 miles of routes, several of them extending to and beyond the Capital Beltway in Maryland and Virginia.

Both the subway and the Washington area's public bus system are operated by the Washington Metropolitan Area Transit Authority. Somewhat confusingly, the transit authority is generally called Metro while the rail system is called The Metro. The bus system is called the Metrobus system. You can also transfer from the subway to a bus, enabling quick trips across town in a city already known for its compact nature.

### The Metrobus System

There are about 400 city and suburban routes, but many of them operate only in rush hours. The layout is so Byzantine that few Washingtonians know how to use more than a few personally familiar routes. So don't try to master it. That is not to say that it will not be useful to you, either to travel to and from your hotel or motel, or to get around downtown Washington: schedule and route information are available by telephone from 637-2437. If you contact the Metrobus marketing office, 600 Fifth Street, N.W., Washington, D.C. 20001, in advance of your trip, they'll send you a route map and information specially tailored for the place you'll be staying.

The city bus fare is 40 cents most of the time, but 50 cents in rush hour (have the exact change!); transfers are available. People over 65 and handicapped persons pay half fare except during rush hours, but special identification cards are needed. (For the elderly, a Medicaid card will do.) The fare to travel to and from the suburbs—except during rush hours—is 60 cents one way; in rush hours, a higher fare is charged on suburban lines, calculated on a zone system. If you must travel in rush periods, ask the driver what it costs.

There are no half fares for children, and no special low-cost tourist passes. The Metrobus system is prohibited by law, in fact, from running low-cost service to benefit tourists.

The Metrobus system operates both local and express buses. Outside the rush hours, most buses are local. Beware of express buses unless you are sure in advance that they will stop where you want to get off. *Most express buses are not labeled "express"—if the route number on the front of the bus has a red background instead of a black one, it is an express.*

The Metrobus route-numbering system (if you can call it that) is a confusing jumble. Here is how it works:

• City routes in Washington and routes in suburban Maryland are either two-digit numbers (for example, 54) or a letter followed by a number (for example, L4).

• Routes extending into Virginia are numbers followed by a letter (for example, 11A). One exception is the R4, which goes through downtown Washington to the Crystal City area of Arlington, where many hotels and motels are located. "Express" and "Limited" buses that go to Virginia carry signs that say so.

The destination signs on the fronts and sides of Washington buses show only the end of the line, but do not indicate what streets they follow to get there or places of interest the routes serve. There are a few exceptions, notably Virginia buses marked "via Memorial Bridge," "via Pentagon," or "via National Airport."

A caution: all manner of construction may cause detours a block or two off the streets shown on the maps.

For tourists, the best all-purpose route to know is the 30 series—bus lines No. 30, 32, 34, and 36. (*See* page 287.) These lines run from far southeast Washington to far northwest Washington, chiefly by way of Pennsylvania and Wisconsin Avenues. Along the way they pass the Library of Congress, the Capitol, the Smithsonian Institution, the Archives, the National Gallery of Art, the FBI, the Treasury, the White House, Georgetown, and the Washington National Cathedral. The line is supposed to run every $7^1/_2$ minutes throughout the day, more frequently during rush hours, but you'll often have to wait longer than that.

Here are some other useful Metrobus routes:

• M6 leaves Union Station and goes through Georgetown, then over Key Bridge to the Rosslyn section of Arlington.

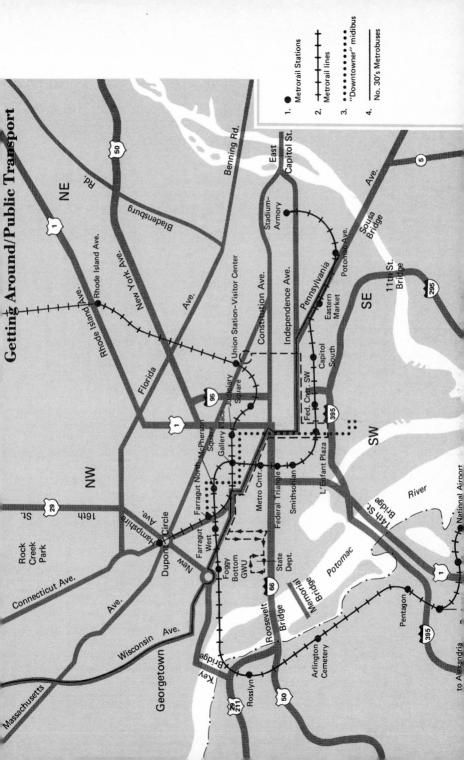

# Getting Around/Public Transport

| | |
|---|---|
| 1. | ● Metrorail Stations |
| 2. | —— Metrorail lines |
| 3. | •••• "Downtowner" midibus |
| 4. | —— No. 30's Metrobuses |

• 7E, 7X and 16B leave Union Station and travel along Constitution Avenue, portions of Independence Avenue, past the Lincoln Memorial, and over Memorial Bridge to (and beyond) Arlington National Cemetery.

• The M8 "midibus" (*see* map, this chapter), a medium-sized vehicle that links the government office area of southwest Washington with downtown and the Farragut Square–Dupont Circle area north of the White House. This line has bargain fares: either 10 cents or 25 cents, depending on where you catch the bus. It takes transfers from other routes, but doesn't give them.

• The group of No. 11 lines that run from Tenth Street and Constitution Avenue, N.W., to (and beyond) the Old Town area of Alexandria. Probably the biggest bargain in town, if you don't have a car available, is the 11A to Mount Vernon and back. Buses leave every 60 minutes at 25 minutes before the hour. The last bus you can catch and have enough time to spend at Mount Vernon before closing leaves at 2:35 P.M.

• The 42 bus that runs from the section of Connecticut Avenue just north of the White House to Union Station and Capitol Hill.

### Sightseeing Buses, Boats, Limousines

Many reputable sightseeing bus companies are operated in Washington. Check the Yellow Pages or ask your hotel or motel desk clerk. You should be aware, however, that many hotels and motels are agents for the sightseeing companies, and will try to sell you tickets.

If you're driving near the White House or another tourist attraction and a man wearing a police-style peaked cap waves you rather officiously to the side of the street, chances are he's a sightseeing-tour salesman.

A company called **Landmark Services, Inc., 554-5100,** has a franchise from the National Park Service to run "Tourmobile" buses from Capitol Hill, along the Mall, around the Jefferson, Washington, and Lincoln memorials, and across Memorial Bridge to Arlington National Cemetery. An all-day ticket, good for unlimited reboarding, costs $4 for adults and $2 for children. It's no bargain, but the convenience of escaping from your car may make it worthwhile.

There are also two sightseeing boat organizations running

public tours on the Potomac. The oldest, the **Wilson Boat Line, 554-8000,** has 394-passenger catamarans that cruise from the pier at Sixth and Water Streets, S.W., to Mount Vernon, and back. Call them for sailing times and current rates.

**Potomac Boat Tours, 548-5010,** operates a shallow-draft, canopy-covered vessel between Georgetown and Hains Point, departing from the Lincoln Memorial Dock, just south of the Lincoln Memorial, every hour on the hour from 9 A.M. daily. Last departure time in the early evening has been known to change due to special charters. Call ahead.

Limousine companies in the area tend to have one rate for business driving, another—slightly more ($1 or so)—for sightseeing. The average rate is $15 an hour, usually with a three-hour minimum for sightseeing. Most of the cars will seat seven passengers, plus the driver. Among the better known firms are: **Admiral, 638-3006; Capitol, 333-0383; Carey, 892-2000; Gray Line Limousine Service, 393-2227;** and **Orr's, 265-4888.** But it's always best to check the Yellow Pages and call for competitive rates and arrangements, as someone might have a new special tour or group deal. Also, a number of firms have added mini-buses to their fleet to accommodate more people.

### Driving: Rush Hours/Traffic Regulations

From 7–9:30 A.M. and 4–6:30 P.M., try to stay out of traffic. These are Washington's rush hours and not only will you find congested traffic, but traffic direction totally reversed on some major streets. Normal two-way streets are turned into one-way, or worse.

Left turns are banned during rush hours at many intersections where they are permitted during the rest of the day. Also, curbside lanes on several busy arterials are reserved for buses in rush hours. An exception is made if you are maneuvering to turn onto a cross street.

When you are driving out of a parking lot or garage during rush hours, you must turn right and cannot cut across the lanes of traffic to make a left turn. (The obvious exception is a one-way street where all the traffic is going left.)

With proper hand or turn signals, U-turns are permitted in the middle of a block. They are prohibited in intersections.

This is not an area that permits right turns on red signals

(unless, as in some Virginia communities, a sign tells you otherwise). Wait for the green. When making the turn, you must yield the right-of-way to any pedestrians in a crosswalk that is regulated by the same signal.

However, there is no law requiring a motorist to stop for pedestrians in crosswalks under other conditions.

A flashing red signal at an intersection is the same as a stop sign. Make a full stop, be sure your way is clear, then proceed. (Many signals are set for flashing late at night.)

A traffic or parking citation in Washington itself is enforced by the District of Columbia government as a local offense. For minor infractions, the fine (it's called "posting collateral") can be mailed with a check to the address shown on the ticket.

Be especially observant of traffic, speeding, and parking rules on federal reservations and parkways in the suburbs—the Baltimore-Washington, Suitland, and George Washington Memorial parkways (including the boulevard to Mount Vernon), the Pentagon area, Washington National Airport, and Dulles International Airport and its access road. The laws and penalties are enforced nationwide by the federal courts system and, in a severe case, you can be required to stay or to return to the Washington area to face trial.

Unless otherwise posted, the speed limit on Washington city streets is 25 miles per hour.

### Traffic Circles

Washington has many traffic circles. Generally they are where the diagonal avenues cross each other. Each circle has its own personality. Some, for instance, have traffic channelization, while others have underpasses for the traffic of one of the intersecting streets. Dupont Circle, north of the White House, has both. So no all-purpose advice can be given on driving through them.

When traveling through Dupont Circle, the *inside* lanes (closest to the hub of the circle) carry the Massachusetts Avenue traffic. The *outside* lanes carry traffic that will peel off onto side streets. The *underpass* carries the through traffic of Connecticut Avenue north and south beneath the circle.

As for other circles, generally: if you want to continue straight ahead on the avenue on which you are driving, your best bet is (1) stay in the right-hand lane or the one next to it, and (2) pick out something on the opposite side of the circle, such as a building or a large tree, and use it as a point of reference for peeling off from the circle's traffic flow.

Two bits of advice:

• Don't try any drastic maneuver from lane to lane once you're in a circle's traffic pattern. Go to the next intersection and work your way back.

• Never stop in a traffic circle to ponder where you're going or to consult a road map. It's a clear invitation to get smashed from the rear. Go into the next block and park, or turn off at the next side street.

### Lincoln Memorial Circle

The traffic circle around the Lincoln Memorial deserves special attention because it confuses almost every tourist who drives through it to get to and from Memorial Bridge and Arlington National Cemetery.

Going south from Constitution Avenue, you will enter the circle either from Twenty-third Street, N.W., or from Bacon Drive, a diagonal street that is only one block long. Bear right. The end of the bridge is marked by the SECOND group of large bronze statuary.

Returning to Washington, Memorial Bridge brings you to the back side of the Lincoln Memorial. Now you must go opposite what it used to be, and prepare to peel off to the left. The first turnoff is to Rock Creek Parkway, the second is Twenty-third Street, N.W.

A caution: in busy tourist periods, the circle is blocked off to Washington-bound traffic. Detours will lead you onto park roads and you'll have to puzzle your way downtown.

### Insurance

There is no law in the District of Columbia that requires automobile owners to carry liability insurance on their cars. You're well advised to check with your insurance agent before visiting, to see that you have adequate coverage against uninsured drivers. Both Maryland and Virginia, on the other hand, have tough laws that enforce insurance requirements. If you're caught without proper insurance in Maryland, you can get a police citation.

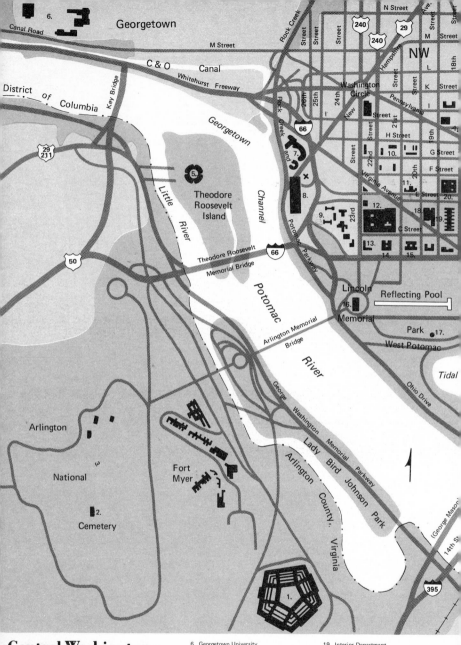

# Central Washington

Buildings, key sites, are numbered clockwise starting with the Pentagon.

1. Pentagon.
2. Tomb of the Unknowns
3. Arlington House (Custis-Lee Mansion), and the graves of John F. Kennedy, Robert F. Kennedy, L'Enfant.
4. U.S. Marine Memorial (Iwo Jima)
5. Roosevelt Memorial

6. Georgetown University
7. Watergate
8. John F. Kennedy Center for the Performing Arts
9. Navy Bureau of Medicine and Surgery
10. The George Washington University
11. American Red Cross
12. State Department
13. American Pharmaceutical Association
14. National Academy of Sciences
15. Federal Reserve Board
16. Lincoln Memorial
17. D.C. World War II Memorial
18. Civil Service Commission

19. Interior Department
20. General Services Administration
21. Pan American Union
22. D.A.R. Constitution Hall
23. Red Cross
24. Corcoran Gallery of Art
25. Octagon House
26. Old Executive Office Building
27. Renwick Gallery and Blair House
28. New Executive Office Building
29. Decatur House
30. St. John's Church (The Church of the Presidents)
31. Public Citizens Visitor's Center
32. Lafayette Park

### Service Stations

Partly because of the monumental character of the Mall area, gasoline service stations are extremely scarce in downtown Washington; most operate only during daytime. There are many stations on arterials entering the downtown area. The best advice is to have a full tank before you start touring. If you need service, here are a few areas or locations where stations may be found:

**Northwest—Downtown**
- L Street, N.W., at Thirteenth, Fourteenth, and Eighteenth Streets.
- Ninth and I Streets, N.W.
- Twelfth and E Streets, N.W.
- New Hampshire Avenue and M Street, N.W.

**Southwest Mall Area**
- Lower level of L'Enfant Plaza, Tenth and D Streets, S.W. (Tenth Street is also known as L'Enfant Promenade.)
- Fourth and G Streets, S.W.

**Foggy Bottom—Watergate Area**
- Virginia Avenue, N.W., at Twenty-second; and Sixteenth Street and Rock Creek Parkway.

**Capitol Hill Area**
- North Capitol Street north of Massachusetts Avenue, north of the Capitol.
- New Jersey Avenue, N.W., north of the Capitol.
- Second Street and Massachusetts Avenue, N.E.
- South Capitol Street south of the Capitol.
- New Jersey Avenue and E Street, S.E.

**Georgetown**
- Several stations on M Street and Pennsylvania Avenue, N.W., from Twenty-fifth Street west to Key Bridge.
- Wisconsin Avenue and Q Street, N.W.

### Parking

Downtown Washington is so congested on weekdays with commuters' automobiles that there is little parking space left over for visitors. So you are advised, if at all possible, to park your car on the fringes and use some form of public transportation—if it is available—to get into town.

Unfortunately, there are few suburban bus routes that get downtown very fast. Ask for suggestions from the manager of your hotel or motel, or from the friends or relatives you're visiting. One possibility is parking on a side street near an arterial that has a bus route into town. The people in the neighborhood won't like it, but it's a way of solving the problem. In general, it's easier to use the bus from Virginia than from Maryland. Subway service is available from Silver Spring, Maryland.

If you park on a street, carefully note the parking restrictions. Some areas are towaway zones where all parked cars are hauled away in rush hours. If this happens to you, call 626-2421, the police teletype office; they'll tell you where you can find your car. Be prepared to pay both a towing charge and a fine.

If you do drive all the way downtown on a weekday, you will find very few if any parking spaces in the Mall, Capitol Hill, and White House areas. There are some near the Washington Monument and the Lincoln Memorial, but they are usually filled to capacity. Of all the tourist-oriented buildings, only two have visitor parking—the new annex of the National Gallery of Art at Fourth Street and Pennsylvania Avenue, N.W., and the new National Air and Space Museum at Seventh Street and Independence Avenue, S.W. But it's expensive. All-day parking will cost $7 or more.

In looking for a paid parking lot or garage, it is best to stay away from the south side of the Mall. The area is crowded with commuters. Probably the best bet is the commercial area north of the Mall and the White House. All-day parking may range from $2 to around $5. Be sure to note the garage closing time. It is frustrating to return after dinner and find the garage locked up for the night or—and this has happened—for the weekend!

### A Driving Tour of Downtown

Although traveling around Washington by automobile is generally discouraged, a pleasant trip can be made in the evening or during a slack traffic period, such as early on a Sunday morning.

Start on Constitution Avenue at Sixth Street, N.W. (in back of the National Gallery of Art), heading west. Go west on Constitution Avenue. At Fifteenth Street, turn left (south). After the second signal (at Maine Avenue), bear right, and continue to bear right as you pass the Jefferson Memorial. Continue along the Potomac River shore on Ohio Drive.

You will encounter a signal at Independence Avenue. Go straight ahead (north) along the Lincoln Memorial circle to Constitution Avenue.

At Constitution Avenue, turn right (east). At Seventeenth Street, N.W., turn left (north). The Ellipse (sometimes called the President's Park) is on the right. At Pennsylvania Avenue, turn right (east), passing the front of the White House and the Treasury. At Fifteenth Street, N.W., turn right (south).

At the third signal, turn left—toward the southeast—on Pennsylvania Avenue, N.W. The rows of buildings on either side frame the Capitol dome. Just beyond Fourth Street, N.W., bear left and go east on Constitution Avenue. Pass the Capitol and at First Street, N.E., turn right (south), passing the Supreme Court and Library of Congress.

At Independence Avenue, S.E., turn right (west). At the next signal, turn right (north) and park in front of the Capitol. If you have time, get out and walk around the building's terraces. The panorama on a moonlit night or on a clear day is breathtaking.

Leaving the Capitol, return to Independence Avenue and turn right (west). At Fourteenth Street, S.W., turn right (north). (You enter Washington's northwest quadrant in the middle of the Mall.) At Thomas Circle, Fourteenth Street and Massachusetts Avenue, N.W., go around the outer edge and get onto Massachusetts Avenue going northwestward.

Embassies, fashionable old residences, and now the official residence of the Vice President line Massachusetts Avenue for much of the 3 miles you will travel before reaching Wisconsin Avenue. You might end the trip here, with a visit to the Washington Cathedral and its grounds—or follow signs and turn left (south) onto Wisconsin Avenue to end the trip in Georgetown.

For a much shortened version of this trip, start at Seventeenth Street and Constitution Avenue, N.W., heading north; end it at the Capitol.

### Bicycle Rentals

A good way to get around town is by bike, especially around the Mall and in the parks. For where to rent bikes, see the listing under Cycling, in the Sports chapter.

### Walking

It's still the best and most natural way to get around. In Washington, walk until your arches ache and you'll probably see more, enjoy more, for more than any other city in the U.S. it is a pedestrian's paradise.

# XIX
## Staying Here:
## Hotels, Motels, Hostels,
## and Campgrounds

Where you stay in Washington will probably depend on your preferred style of accommodation, your personal cache or company assets, the location of your business or pleasure pursuits, even whether you bring the car, children, or family pet. A lot of factors to consider—which we've tried to cover in the list below.

To stay well in Washington you need not stay *in* Washington, at least not right downtown. As pointed out in Chapter XVIII, there are many major routes to zip you into the city, via public transit system or, if you insist, your private car.

There are dense clusters of hotels and motels along these arteries, and the majority are clean, well-lighted places. Also, if you commit the cardinal visitor sin and arrive without reservation, you might head to these areas: if there's no room at one inn, you might luck out next door.

So we group accommodations by location rather than by price. But price is the lead-off factor in each listing. And we indicate price—for the minimum double room occupied by two people—by the following categories:

| | |
|---|---|
| Luxury: | $55 and up |
| Expensive: | $35 to $54 |
| Moderate: | $20 to $34 |
| Budget: | Less than $20 |

If children (usually the limit is two) are allowed to stay in their parents' room at no additional charge, or if a cot is provided free, we indicate "children free." And children means *under 12*. However, if the hotel will accept older offspring free, the age is noted. If there is no note about children, figure to pay extra for them.

We also tell whether the hotel permits pets, although it's good to know that the local police try to discourage visitors from bringing pets to Washington's beastly summers.

Besides hotels and motels, you will also find below a number of hostels, tourist homes, and community facilities such as the YWCA. And at the end of this chapter there's a list of campgrounds close enough to commute to Washington.

We've tried to be as complete as possible in the listing. But there are sure to be some establishments left out by, simply, oversight. Others, of course, have not been included because they aren't up to snuff on cleanliness and service.

All hotels here, unless otherwise noted, have air conditioning (and in Washington that's a virtual must in the summer), room television set and telephone, private bathroom.

Most lodgings offer facilities for the handicapped, but it's still wise to call ahead and check on arrangements.

About calls. If you're phoning long distance to make a reservation, the area codes are 202 for the District of Columbia; 301 for Maryland; and 703 for northern Virginia. But when you're in the metropolitan area, you seldom need to use the code.

Parking in central DC is scarce and costly, so watch the fine print on that. If it's "parking at charge" at the hotel, better figure an extra $2 to $3 a day at least just to board your vehicle.

*Regarding Holiday Inns:* There are some 25 in the area; all but one or two are franchised. Still, they all maintain the following facilities and policies: children under 12 in room with parents free, restaurant and cocktail lounge on the premises, televisions and telephones in all rooms, air conditioning, pool, free parking, kennels for pets. So, for each Holiday Inn listing below, we indicate only address, phone number, price range, and number of rooms.

*—Laura Longley Babb*

## DISTRICT OF COLUMBIA (AREA CODE 202):
## DOWNTOWN/CITY CENTER

**Annapolis Towers, 1111 H Street, N.W. 628-9222.** Budget. 42 rooms. Carry-out food service in building. No parking, no pets.

**Anthony House, 1823 L Street, N.W. 223-4320.** Expensive. 100 rooms. Restaurant. No parking, no pets.

**Barbizon Terrace, 2118 Wyoming Avenue, N.W. 483-1350.** Moderate. 77 rooms. No parking, no pets.

**Burlington Hotel, 1120 Vermont Avenue, N.W. 785-2222.** Moderate. 300 rooms. Children free—under 14. Restaurant. Parking free. Small pets permitted.

**Capital Hilton, Sixteenth and K Streets, N.W. 393-1000.** Luxury. 816 rooms. Children free. Several restaurants, including Trader Vic's. Parking at a charge. Pets permitted upon signing release. Bustly, noisy commercial hotel three blocks from the White House.

**Christian Inn, 1509 Sixteenth Street, N.W. 483-6116.** Budget. 72 rooms—8 with baths, not all air-conditioned. Carry-out restaurant. TV lounge. No parking or pets.

**Dupont Plaza, 1500 New Hampshire Avenue, N.W., on Dupont Circle. 483-6000.** Expensive. 312 rooms. Children free—under 14. Restaurant. All rooms equipped with refrigerator, wet bar, color TV. Parking at charge. Small pets permitted.

**Ebbitt Hotel, 1000 H Street, N.W. 628-5034.** Budget. 150 rooms. Children free. Recently remodeled; two restaurants. TVs can be rented. No parking. Housebroken pets permitted.

**Embassy Row, 2015 Massachusetts Avenue, N.W. 265-1600.** Luxury. 222 rooms. Children free. Fine restaurant (Le Consulat), pool. Parking (valet) at charge. Pets permitted if you notify hotel in advance. Posh, with a decidedly international flavor. Personnel multilingual—a big plus for foreign visitors.

**Executive House, 1515 Rhode Island Avenue, N.W. 232-7000.** Expensive. 200 rooms. Children free. Restaurant, coffee shop; refrigerators in the rooms. Pool. Parking free. Pets permitted but not particularly welcome.

**Fairfax Hotel, 2100 Massachusetts Avenue, N.W. 293-2100.** Expensive. 147 rooms. Children free. Two distinguished restaurants—The Jockey Club and Sea Catch. Parking (valet) at charge. No pets. Tasteful, residential establishment.

**Gramercy Inn, 1616 Rhode Island Avenue, N.W. 347-9550.** Expensive. 320 rooms. Children free—under 14. Restaurant, pool. Parking free. Pets permitted, but only with release for damages.

**Gralyn Hotel, 1745 N Street,**

N.W. 785-1515. Moderate. 34 rooms—15 with air conditioning and private baths. But all rooms in this cozy European-style hotel, once the Persian embassy, have huge Victorian beds and dressers. No restaurant but breakfast is served in a room with a view of the terraced garden, or in the garden. No elevator, but you can request a low floor. Parking free. No pets.

**Harrington Hotel, Eleventh and E Streets, N.W. 628-8140.** Budget. 300 rooms. Flat 4-person family rate of $20. Cafeteria and snack shop. Parking free overnight. Pets permitted.

**Hartnett Hall, 1426 Twenty-first Street, N.W. 293-1111.** Budget. A rooming "house" of 25 residence houses with 477 singles, 53 doubles, near Dupont Circle. Some buildings for men only, some for women, a few rooms for couples. No children allowed. No air conditioning or room phones; TV lounge. No parking, no pets. Daily, weekly and monthly rates.

**Hay-Adams, 800 Sixteenth Street, N.W. 638-2260.** Luxury. 165 rooms. Children free—under 14. Restaurants. Parking (valet) at charge. No pets. Dignified and exclusive. On Lafayette Park, opposite the White House.

**Holiday Inn—Central, 1501 Rhode Island Avenue, N.W. 483-2000.** Expensive. 214 rooms. (*See* introduction to this chapter.)

**Holiday Inn—Connecticut Avenue, 1900 Connecticut Ave-** nue, N.W. 332-9300. Expensive. 145 rooms. (*See* introduction to this chapter.)

**Holiday Inn—Downtown, 1615 Rhode Island Avenue, N.W. 296-2100.** Expensive. 161 rooms. (*See* introduction to this chapter.)

**Hotel 1440, 1440 Rhode Island Avenue, N.W. 232-7800.** Budget. 86 rooms—30 with bath. TVs to rent. No parking or pets.

**Hotel John Kilpen, 2310 Ashmead Place, N.W. 462-4336.** Moderate. 80 rooms. Children free. Some rooms have TV, most have air conditioning. Breakfast served in dining room. No parking; dogs permitted.

**International Inn, 10 Thomas Circle, N.W. 783-4600.** Expensive. 343 rooms. Children free. Pool, two restaurants. Parking free, and pets permitted if you'll sign a release against damages.

**Jefferson Hotel, 1200 Sixteenth Street, N.W. 347-4707.** Expensive. 150 rooms. Children free—under 14. No parking but plenty of Old World service. Intimate bar and restaurant. No pets.

**Madison Hotel, Fifteenth and M Streets, N.W. 785-1000.** Luxury. 374 rooms. Charge for children, parking, pets. Restaurants, including chic Montpelier Room buffet. For the expense-account trade. Up-to-the-minute amenities, excellent service.

**Manchester Inn, 1426 M Street, N.W. 785-2770.** Budget. 110 rooms—27 singles without private bath, 67 efficiency apartments with kitchenettes. Children free. No TVs. Small restaurant. Charge for parking, pets. Down the block from the Madison.

**Mayflower, 1127 Connecticut Avenue, N.W. 347-3000.** Luxury. 701 rooms. Children free—under 18. Restaurants. Parking at charge, pets permitted. Big, busy convention hotel with a big history: here Calvin Coolidge had his inaugural ball, Harry Truman declared he'd win in '48, Gene Autry rode his horse in the banquet room, J. Edgar Hoover dined daily for 20 years, and here some of his boys even caught a couple of gangsters.

**Mid-Town Motor Inn, 1201 K Street, N.W. 783-3040.** Moderate. Children free. Restaurant. Parking free, charge for pets.

**National, 1809 I Street, N.W. 628-5566.** Budget. 76 rooms. Children free—under 14. Coffee shop. Parking adjacent at charge. No pets.

**Park Central Hotel, 705 Eighteenth Street, N.W. 393-4700.** Moderate. 250 rooms. Children free (limit 2, under 12). Restaurant in the building; roof garden with barbecue facility. Adjacent parking with charge. No pets.

**Pick-Lee House, 1100 Fifteenth Street, N.W. 347-4800.** Moderate. 201 rooms. Children free. Restaurant, bar. No parking. Small, well-mannered pets permitted.

**Presidential, 900 Nineteenth Street, N.W. 331-9020.** Budget. 130 rooms. Children free—under 14. No restaurant, parking or pets. Clean lodging in converted apartment building. Many international visitors on a budget.

**Quality Inn—Thomas Circle, Massachusetts Avenue and Thomas Circle, N.W. 737-1200.** Expensive. 224 rooms. Children free—under 16. Pool, restaurant, oyster bar. Parking free. No pets.

**Rock Creek Hotel, 1925 Belmont Road and Twentieth Street, N.W. 462-6007.** Budget. 52 rooms. Coffee shop for breakfast, lunch. Free parking; no pets permitted.

**Sheraton Carlton, 923 Sixteenth Street, N.W. 638-2626.** Luxury. 250 rooms. Children free—under 17. Two dining rooms. Parking (valet) at charge. No pets. Grand old place with gracious ways. The Federal City Club makes its home here.

**Tabard Inn, 1739 N Street, N.W. 785-1277.** Moderate. 45 rooms. No TV. Nine singles lack private bath. Continental breakfast included. No elevator, but you can request a low floor. Limited free parking. In 1863, Edward Everett Hale wrote his "Man Without a Country" in one of the three fine townhouses that make up this handsome residential hostel. Bar, restaurant during the week.

**Washington Hotel, Fifteenth Street and Pennsylvania Avenue, N.W. 638-5900.** Expensive. 370 rooms. Children free—under 14. Restaurant, rooftop bar with a spectacular view. Parking at a charge. Small, housebroken pets permitted. Good location opposite Treasury Building, one block from the White House.

**Washington Hilton, 1919 Connecticut Avenue, N.W. 483-3000.** Luxury. 1200 rooms. Children free. Closest thing to a swish resort close to downtown. Several restaurants, pools, tennis courts, shops. Various special weekend and family plans. Pets permitted upon signing release.

**Washington International Youth Hostel, 1332 I Street, N.W. 387-3169.** Budget—$4.50 a night. But open to members only (over 18—$11 for Americans, $9 for others, a year; under 18—$5, families—$12), though a three-day membership is available for $1. There's room for about 65 people in dorm-type rooms. Kitchen for cooking your own meals. No parking. No pets.

**YMCA, 1736 Ninth Street, N.W. 737-7900.** Budget, 60 rooms. Children free. Single room, one person rate is less than $13. There's a floor reserved for women, and a couple may take a room with bath at about $21. Doubles run around $10 per person with bath. No restaurant. No parking. No pets. Just adequate.

**YWCA Strong Residence, 1011 Seventeenth Street, N.W. 638-2100.** Budget. 160 rooms. No small children. Singles run $12 to $14; doubles with running water about $20. There are two rooms, with private bath, for use by couples for less than $22. Pool, gym, cafeteria in YWCA next door open Monday through Friday for breakfast and lunch. No parking. Excellent location near Connecticut Avenue shops, four blocks north of the White House.

## DISTRICT OF COLUMBIA (AREA CODE 202): OTHER SECTIONS

**Capitol Hill**

**Bellevue, 15 E Street, N.W. 638-0900.** Budget. 280 rooms. Cafeteria. Parking free. No pets.

**Commodore, 520 North Capitol Street, N.W. 628-2300.** Moderate. 140 rooms. Children free—under 14. Restaurant. Parking at charge nearby. No pets.

**Hyatt Regency, 400 New Jersey Avenue, N.W. 737-1234.** Expensive. 900 rooms. Children free—under 14. Restaurants, lounge, nightclub. Parking (valet) at charge. No pets. The newest, slickest hotel on the Hill.

**Quality Inn-Capitol Hill, 415 New Jersey Avenue, N.W. 638-1616.** Moderate. 350 rooms. Children free. Restaurant. Parking free, pets permitted.

**Foggy Bottom**

**Allen Lee, 2224 F Street, N.W. 331-1224.** Budget. 100 rooms. Not far from the Kennedy Center but short on amenities and baths. No parking, no pets.

**Guest Quarters—District, 801 New Hampshire Avenue, N.W. 785-2000.** Luxury. 107

rooms, all with fully equipped kitchens. Pool. No restaurant. but breakfast in rooms. Billing privileges at restaurant across the street. Charge for parking and for small pets (weighing in at 25 pounds or less). Quiet, convenient, personalized.

**Howard Johnson's, 2601 Virginia Avenue, N.W. 965-2700.** Expensive. 190 rooms. Children free. Restaurant, room refrigerators, pool. Parking free. No pets. Directly opposite Watergate.

**Watergate, 2650 Virginia Avenue, N.W. 965-2300.** Luxury. 238 rooms (most suites). Children free, if no extra bed is required. Restaurant, pool, health club. Pets permitted. *The place where "Watergate" started.* Terrific views of Potomac; next door to the Kennedy Center.

### Georgetown Area

**Georgetown Dutch Inn, 1075 Thomas Jefferson Street, N.W. 337-0900.** Expensive. 54 rooms (some with kitchens). Children free—under 15. Restaurant, pool. Parking free, pets permitted. Comfortable lodging on historic sidestreet.

**Georgetown Inn, 1310 Wisconsin Avenue, N.W. 333-8900.** Luxury. 95 rooms. Restaurant (Four Georges). Parking free. No pets. In the heart of the shopping-nightlife strip.

**Wellington, 2505 Wisconsin Avenue, N.W. 337-7400.** Luxury. 150 rooms. Children free. Restaurant, pool. Parking at charge.

No pets. Above Georgetown's hurly-burly—by a few blocks.

### Upper Northwest (Connecticut Avenue above Rock Creek Parkway)

**Connecticut Inn Motel, 4400 Connecticut Avenue, N.W. 244-5600.** Moderate. 151 rooms. Children free. Restaurant adjacent. Parking free. Small pets permitted, with some restrictions.

**Sheraton Park Hotel and Motor Inn, 2660 Woodley Road, N.W. 265-2000.** Expensive. 1600 rooms. Several restaurants, pool, ice skating rink. Parking at charge. Pets permitted. Washington's largest hotel complex, with great character and sylvan setting; above Rock Creek.

**Shoreham Americana Hotel and Motel, 2500 Calvert Street, N.W. 234-0700.** Luxury. 800 rooms. Children free—under 14. Restaurants, pool, sauna. Parking at charge. Pets permitted. Plush, pricey.

### Southwest

**Channel Inn Motel, 650 Water Street, S.W. 554-2400.** Expensive. 100 rooms. Children free. Several restaurants, pool. boat docks. No pets permitted.

**Loews L'Enfant Plaza, 480 L'Enfant Plaza East, S.W. 484-1000.** Luxury. 372 rooms. Children free—under 14. Two restaurants. Parking charge. Pets permitted. Nice and new and fairly isolated from the city in the L'Enfant Plaza development.

**Skyline Inn, 10 I Street, S.E. 488-7500.** Expensive. 203 rooms.

Children free—under 11 only. Restaurant. Parking free. Pets permitted.

**Northeast Corridor**

**Envoy Motel (Best Western), 501 New York Avenue, N.E. 543-7400.** Moderate. 73 rooms. Children free. Restaurant, pool. Parking free, pets permitted.

**Holiday Inn—Shrine (near Catholic University), 730 Monroe Street, N.E. 529-8100.** Moderate. 147 rooms. (*See* introduction to this chapter.)

**Regency Congress Inn (Best Western), 600 New York Avenue, N.E. 546-9200.** Moderate. 50 rooms. Restaurant, pool, sauna. Parking free, pets permitted

**Royal Motel, 1917 Bladensburg Road, N.E. 526-7500.** Moderate. 150 rooms. Children free —under 12. Restaurant, pool. Parking free, pets permitted.

**Travelodge, 1615 New York Avenue, N.E. 529-3900.** Moderate. 52 rooms. Special family rates. Restaurant, pool. Parking free, pets permitted.

---

**MARYLAND (AREA CODE 301)**

**Baltimore-Washington International Airport**

**Friendship International Hotel, Baltimore-Washington International Airport. (301) 761-7700.** (Use area code from Washington.) Expensive. 198 rooms. Children free. Restaurant, pool. Parking free. No pets.

**Holiday Inn—Airport, 6500 Elkridge Landing Road. (301) 796-8400.** (Use area code.) Moderate. 157 rooms. (*See* introduction to this chapter.)

**Bethesda/Chevy Chase**

**Bethesdan Motor Hotel, 7740 Wisconsin Avenue. 656-2100.** Moderate. 73 rooms. Children free. No restaurant. Pool. Free parking. Pets permitted.

**Colonial Manor Motel, 11410 Rockville Pike. 881-5200.** Moderate. 115 rooms. Children free. Restaurant, pool. Parking free, pets permitted in some rooms.

**Holiday Inn—Bethesda, 8120 Wisconsin Avenue. 652-2000.** Moderate. 267 rooms. (*See* introduction to this chapter.)

**Holiday Inn—Chevy Chase, 5520 Wisconsin Avenue. 656-1500.** Moderate. 233 rooms. (*See* introduction to this chapter.)

**Linden Hill Hotel, 5400 Pooks Hill Road. 530-0300.** Moderate. 155 rooms. Restaurant, pool, sauna; also pay indoor tennis. Parking free. No pets.

**Ramada Inn—Bethesda, 8400 Wisconsin Avenue. 654-1000.** Expensive. 144 rooms. Children free—under 18. Restaurant, pool. Parking free. Pets permitted.

**United Inn of America, 8130 Wisconsin Avenue. 656-9300.** Moderate. 72 rooms. Children free, also free continental breakfast and parking. Pets permitted.

## College Park—US 1 North (Baltimore Boulevard)

**Colonial Plaza Motel & Dormitories, 10203 Baltimore Boulevard. 474-5678.** Budget. 50 motel units, 6 air-conditioned dorms with beds for 116, hotel with 21 rooms and two apartments. Good group lodging—minimum booking for dorms of $60. TV in game room. Pool. Free parking. Small, housebroken pets.

**Del Haven White House Motel, 10260 Baltimore Boulevard. 474-6565.** Budget. 49 motel-cottage units, including 15 family suites. Free parking. Pets permitted.

**Holiday Inn—Beltway, 10000 Baltimore Boulevard. 345-6700.** Expensive. 123 rooms. (*See* introduction to this chapter.)

**Holiday Inn—University of Maryland, 9137 Baltimore Boulevard. 345-5000.** Moderate. 68 rooms. (*See* introduction to this chapter.)

**Royal Pine Motel, 9113 Baltimore Boulevard. 345-4900.** Moderate. 62 rooms. Pool. Restaurants nearby. Parking free. No pets.

## Lanham/New Carrollton

**Ramada Inn, 5910 Princess Garden Parkway just off Annapolis Road at I-495, Lanham. 459-1000.** Moderate. 168 rooms. Children free—18 and under. Restaurant. Pool. Free parking. Pets permitted.

**Sheraton Inn, 8500 Annapolis Road at I-495, New Carrollton. 459-6700.** Moderate. 250 rooms. Children free—under 17. Restaurants. Pool. Free parking. Pets permitted.

## Silver Spring

**Georgian Motel, 7990 Georgia Avenue. 588-8520.** Budget. 118 rooms. Children free. Restaurant. Parking free. No pets.

**Holiday Inn—Silver Spring, 8777 Georgia Avenue. 589-0800.** Moderate. 231 rooms. (*See* introduction to this chapter.)

**Quality Inn, 8040 Thirteenth Street. 588-4400.** Moderate. 145 rooms. Children free—under 16. Restaurant, pool. Parking free. Small pets permitted.

**Sheraton Motor Inn—Silver Spring, 8727 Colesville Road. 589-5200.** Expensive. 218 rooms. Children free—under 18. Two restaurants, pool. Parking free. Small pets permitted.

**Silver Spring Motel, 7927 Georgia Avenue. 587-3200.** Budget. 50 rooms. Restaurant nearby. Free parking. Small pets permitted.

## VIRGINIA (AREA CODE 703)

**Alexandria**

Holiday Inn of Old Town, 480 King Street. 549-6080. Expensive. 228 rooms. (*See* introduction to this chapter.)

Olde Colony Motor Lodge and Convention Center (Best Western), North Washington and First Streets. 548-6300. Moderate. 153 rooms. Children free. Free continental breakfast, but no restaurant. Pool. Parking free. No pets.

Quality Inn—Towne Motel, 808 North Washington Street. 548-3500. Moderate. 25 rooms. Children free—16 and under. No restaurant. Pets permitted.

Ramada Inn—Alexandria, 901 North Fairfax Street. 683-6000. Moderate. 252 rooms. Children. Restaurant, pool. Free parking. Pets permitted.

Virginia Motel, 700 North Washington Street. 836-5100. Budget. 40 rooms. No restaurant. Parking free. Pets permitted, under guarantee.

**Alexandria—US 1 South (Richmond Highway)**

Brookside Motel, 6001 Richmond Highway. 765-5100. Budget. 60 rooms. Restaurant nearby. Pool. Free parking. Pets permitted.

Holiday Inn, 6100 Richmond Highway. 765-0500. Moderate. 108 rooms. (*See* introduction to this chapter.)

Holiday Inn—No. 2, 2460 Eisenhower Drive. 960-3400.

Moderate. 260 rooms. (*See* introduction to this chapter.)

Howard Johnson's, 5821 Richmond Highway. 768-3300. Moderate. 150 rooms. Restaurant next door. Pool. Parking free. Pets permitted.

Keystone Motel, 8588 Richmond Highway. 780-5210. Budget. 31 rooms. Pool. Parking free. Pets permitted.

Travelers Motel, 5916 Richmond Highway. 768-2510. Moderate. 30 rooms. Restaurant nearby. Pool. Free parking. No pets.

Virginia Lodge, 6027 Richmond Highway. 765-7000. Budget. 79 rooms. Restaurant next door. Pool. Free parking. Pets permitted with small deposit.

Wagon Wheel Motel, 7212 Richmond Highway. 765-9000. Moderate. 140 rooms. Restaurant, pool. Free parking. No pets permitted.

**Arlington Boulevard/Columbia Pike/I-95**

Arva Motor Hotel, 2201 Arlington Boulevard. 525-0300. Budget. 131 rooms. Restaurant, pool. Parking free. No pets.

Cherry Blossom Motor Inn, 3030 Columbia Pike. 521-5570. Moderate. 76 rooms. Children free. Restaurant adjacent. Pool. Parking free. Pets permitted.

Guest Quarters, 100 South Reynolds Street. 370-9600. Moderate. 215 rooms (suites with kitchens). Children free—if both parents accompany. With one parent, it's the double rate. Free parking. No restaurant. Pool. No pets. Suburban-style relative of District Guest Quarters.

**Hillwood Motor Court, 6301 Arlington Boulevard. 534-2005.** Budget. 19 rooms. Children free—under 10. Parking free. Small, housebroken pets permitted.

**Holiday Inn—Falls Church, 6633 Arlington Boulevard. 532-9000.** Moderate. 104 rooms. *(See* introduction to this chapter.)

**Holiday Inn—I-95, at 2485 South Glebe Road. 979-4100.** Expensive. 163 rooms *(See* introduction to this chapter.)

**Quality Inn—Central, Arlington Boulevard and North Court House Road. 524-4000.** Moderate. 74 rooms. Children free—under 16. Restaurant, pool. Parking free. Pets permitted.

**Quality Inn—Governor, 6650 Arlington Boulevard. 532-8900.** Moderate. 124 rooms. Children free—under 17. Restaurant, pool. Parking free. Pets permitted.

**South Gate (Best Western), I-95 and South Glebe Road. 979-4400.** Moderate. 208 rooms. Children free. Restaurant. Pool, shuffleboard. Parking free. Pets permitted—kennels available. Fine facilities for the handicapped, including wheelchairs.

**Spring Hill Motor Lodge, 5666 Columbia Pike. 820-5600.** Moderate. 60 rooms. Children free. Coffee shop on grounds.

Pool. Parking free. Pets permitted.

**Crystal City/National Airport Area** (Note: this area has easy access to the District via Fourteenth Street Bridge.)

**Americana, 1400 Jefferson Davis Highway. 979-3772.** Moderate. 102 rooms. Restaurant nearby. Free parking. Pets permitted.

**Holiday Inn—National Airport, 1489 Jefferson Davis Highway. 521-1600.** Moderate. 308 rooms. *(See* introduction to this chapter.)

**Hospitality House Motor Inn, 2000 Jefferson Davis Highway. 920-8600.** Moderate. 250 rooms. Children free. Restaurant. Pool. Parking free. Pets permitted.

**Howard Johnson's, 2650 Jefferson Davis Highway. 684-7200.** Moderate. 276 rooms. Children free—under 18. Restaurants, pool. Parking free. No pets.

**Marriott—Crystal City, 1999 Jefferson Davis Highway. 521-5500.** Expensive. 301 rooms. Children free. Restaurants, pool. Parking at charge. Pets permitted.

**Marriott—Twin Bridges. US 1 (Jefferson Davis Highway) at Interstate 95. 628-4200.** Expensive. 500 rooms. Children free. Restaurants. Pool. Winter ice skating. Parking free. Pets permitted. (The flagship of the Marriott fleet.)

**Presidential Gardens Motor Hotel, Mount Vernon Avenue and Russell Road, Alexandria.**

**836-4400.** More than 230 rooms, actually complete apartments with one or two bedrooms of various sizes, sitting rooms, completely equipped kitchens. Grocery, shops across the street. All in 21 two-story apartment buildings, vintage 1940s. Rates range from single one-bedroom suites at $14 a night to "senior" two-bedroom suites for four people at $30. Weekly, monthly, special group rates, too. Parking free. Small pets at a fee.

**Sheraton National Motor Hotel, Washington Boulevard and Columbia Pike. 521-1900.** Expensive. 336 rooms. Children free—under 17. Restaurants, pool. Free parking. Small pets permitted.

**Stouffer's National Inn, 2399 Jefferson Davis Highway. 979-6800.** Expensive. 400 rooms. Children free—under 16. Restaurant. Pool. Free parking. Pets permitted.

**Lee Highway**

**All State Motel, 11936 Lee Highway. 631-1414.** Budget. 12 rooms. Free parking. Small pets permitted. $18 double.

**Breezeway Motel, 10829 Lee Highway. 591-8450.** Budget. 50 rooms. Restaurant nearby. Pool. Free parking. Small pets permitted.

**Village House (Best Western), 245 North Washington. 534-8000.** Moderate. 65 units. Restaurant. Pool. Free parking. Pets permitted.

**White House Motel, 9700 Lee Highway. 273-1160.** Budget. 56 rooms. Children free. Restaurant nearby. Pool. Free parking. Well-trained pets permitted.

**Reston/Dulles International Airport**

**Holiday Inn, 1000 Sully Road. 471-7411.** Moderate. 124 rooms. *(See* introduction, this chapter.)

**Marriott—Dulles, Dulles International Airport. 471-9500.** Expensive. 210 rooms. Children free. Restaurant, pool. Free parking. Pets permited.

**Sheraton Inn and International Conference Center, 11810 Sunrise Valley Drive. 620-9000.** Expensive. 302 rooms. Children free—under 17. Restaurant, pool, free parking. Pets permitted.

**Rosslyn Area** (Note: this area has easy access via Key Bridge to Georgetown and the District.)

**Holiday Inn—Key Bridge, 1850 North Fort Myer Drive. 522-0400.** Moderate. 178 rooms. *(See* introduction to this chapter.)

**Marriott—Key Bridge, 1401 Lee Highway. 524-6400.** Expensive. 372 rooms. Children free. Restaurants, pool, parking. Pets permitted.

**Ramada Inn—Rosslyn, 1900 North Fort Myer Drive. 527-4814.** Expensive. 365 rooms. Children free—under 18. Restaurants, pool. Pets permitted—kennels.

Quality Inn—Iwo Jima, 1501 Arlington Boulevard. 524-5000. Moderate. 73 rooms. Children free—16 and under. Restaurant. Pool. Parking free. Small pets permitted.

## CAMPING NEAR WASHINGTON

Listed below are places to camp with tent or trailer that are close enough to Washington for regular commuting as a visitor.

**In Maryland**

**Greenbelt National Park, Greenbelt;** 12 miles northeast of Washington **via the Baltimore-Washington Parkway and Route 193.** Open year round. Five-day limit, late May to September; 14-day limit September to May. No reservations. 178 spaces for tents and camping trailers; maximum trailer length of 30 feet. Family camping. No hookups, no group camping. Operated by the National Park Service. For information on site availability, facilities, call the Park Ranger headquarters: 426-6819.

*The campsites below are administered by the State of Maryland. For more information on these or other Maryland parks, contact the Maryland Department of Forests and Parks, State Office Building, Annapolis, Maryland 21404; phone (301) 267-5776.*

**Cedarville Natural Resources Area, Brandywine;** 20 miles from Washington **off Route 301** five miles east of Townsend. Open all year. Two-week limit. Daily reservations. 90 campsites for families and youth groups. Water,

showers, fireplaces, picnic tables, playground, hiking, fishing. (301) 888-1622.

**Patapsco State Park, 78 Gun Road, Baltimore,** 10 miles from Baltimore, 32 miles from Washington, on the Patapsco River at River Road. Open all year. Two-week limit. Daily reservations. Two camping areas: **Glen Artney area, off Route 1 via Levering Avenue.** 98 unimproved campsites, meaning some without tables or grills, etc. Fireplaces, hiking, fishing. **Hollofield area, off Route 40,** 6 miles west of Baltimore. 60 improved campsites. Fireplaces, picnic tables, playground, hiking, fishing, interpretive program. For information and reservations call (301) 747-6602.

**In Virginia**

**Prince William Forest Park, Triangle,** 32 miles south of Washington and one mile west of Triangle, **via Route 1 or I-95 to Route 619.** Oak Ridge Campground has 120 sites. Open all year. 7-consecutive-days limit. No reservations. Picnic tables, fireplaces, firewood, toilets, water. No hookups. For information call

(703) 221-7181 or (703) 221-4840. **Prince William Trailer Village** is located at **16058 Dumfries Road, Dumfries.** Entrance is on Route 234. Open all year. 7-consecutive-days limit. No reservations. Approximately 90 trailer sites, some with water, electricity and sewer, others only electricity. For further information call (703) 221-2474. Operated by the National Park Service.

**Burke Lake, Burke,** 20 miles southwest of Washington, 6 miles south of Fairfax, on **Route 123.** Open all year. Two-week limit. No reservations. 163 campsites with no electrical units. All types of camping units are acceptable; maximum trailer length is 20 feet. Showerhouses, toilets, water. (703) 323-6600. Operated by the Fairfax County Park Authority, 4030 Hummer Road, Annandale.

**Lake Fairfax, Vienna,** about 20 miles west of Washington via the **George Washington Memorial Parkway, I-495, Route 7 and 6 miles to Route 606.** Open April–October. Seven-consecutive-days limit. No reservations. About 300 campsites, some electrical units for trailers. Picnic areas, 500 wooded acres, showers. No group camping. Call (703) 471-5414. Operated by the Fairfax County Park Authority.

*The following two parks are operated by the Northern Virginia Regional Park Authority, 11001 Pope's Head Road, Fairfax; (703) 278-8880.*

**Bull Run Regional Park, Centreville,** 28 miles west of Washington. Follow **US Routes 29-211** for 2.2 miles beyond Centreville, then left on **Virginia Route 621** at park sign, go 3 miles to park entrance. Open all year. 7-consecutive-days limit. No reservations. 150 pull-through campsites, electrical units on 40. Maximum trailer length of 30 feet. Restrooms, toilets, water, swimming, nature trails, concession, laundry room, picnic shelters, miniature golf. Call (703) 631-0550 for additional park information.

**Pohick Bay Regional Park, Lorton,** 25 miles south of Washington via **I-95 to Lorton exit.** Open all year. Seven-consecutive-days limit. No reservations. 150 campsites (not pull through). Electricity for 100. Same basic facilities as Bull Run. Swimming pool. Call (703) 339-6104.

# XX
# Walking Tours

## *Watergate Revisited*
### By Bob Woodward and Carl Bernstein

One of the few remaining signs of the Watergate break-in is a small engraved plaque on the door of a sixth-floor suite of offices in the **Watergate** office complex at **2600 Virginia Avenue, N.W.** It says that five men in business suits—James McCord, then a security adviser to the Committee to Re-Elect the President, Frank Sturgis, and Cubans Bernard Barker, Eugenio Martinez, and Virgilio Gonzales—were arrested there in the early morning hours of the Washington summer, June 17, 1972.

The Democratic National Committee no longer has its offices there. A consulting firm has moved in.

The Watergate scandals physically changed very little of the Washington landscape as it might be seen by a visitor. Instead, Watergate happened on what was here. The seventh-floor room in the **Howard Johnson Motor Hotel (2601 Virginia Avenue, N.W.)**, across from the Watergate, used as a listening post to monitor the electronic bug, is still the same. There is no plaque. Anyone can still rent room 723. Watergate conspirators E. Howard Hunt, Jr., and G. Gordon Liddy would have preferred one of Washington's posh hotels—say, the Madison—but they had to use the hotel closest to the Democratic headquarters.

The other memorials of Watergate are the hundreds of thousands of pages of files and records locked away now in the **U.S. District Courthouse,** where Chief Judge John J. Sirica presided over the major Watergate trials; in the U.S. Capitol—the Senate after the Watergate committee hearings, the

Carl Bernstein and Bob Woodward covered Watergate for *The Washington Post* and are co-authors of *All the President's Men* and *The Final Days* (Simon & Schuster).

House after the impeachment investigation; in the unmarked office on the ninth floor of **1425 K Street, N.W.**, used by the **Watergate Special Prosecutor** (first Archibald Cox, then, after the "Saturday Night Massacre," Leon Jaworski); and in the **White House.** Some of these records are open to the public. A visitor interested in the Watergate history might try the clerk of the U.S. District Courthouse, Constitution Avenue and John Marshall Place, N.W., between the White House and the Capitol. The House and Senate will make some records available to researchers.

On a regular tour of Washington, a visitor might want to take note of the following:

• The Watergate apartment buildings, some of the most expensive in the city, and part of the same complex as the burgled Watergate office building. Former tenants include John and Martha Mitchell and former President Nixon's personal secretary, Rose Mary Woods.

• The headquarters of the Committee to Re-Elect the President (CRP) were at 1701 Pennsylvania Avenue, N.W., a block from the White House.

• The **Old Executive Office Building,** next to the White House, at Seventeenth Street and Pennsylvania Avenue, N.W. This is one of the greatest office buildings in Washington, with its high ceilings, ornate black and white tiled corridors, and fantastically comfortable offices. Included are the former offices of such Watergate figures as John Dean, Charles W. Colson, and E. Howard Hunt, Jr. Room 16 in the basement was used by the "Plumbers"—Hunt, G. Gordon Liddy, David Young, Egil "Bud" Krogh—who planned and executed the 1971 burglary of the office of Daniel Ellsberg's psychiatrist.

• The White House itself, and the offices in the West Wing of Richard Nixon, and his chief aides H. R. Haldeman and John D. Erlichman.

• On Capitol Hill there are a great many Watergate landmarks: the Senate Caucus room of the **Old Senate** (Russell) **Office Building,** where the Watergate committee held public hearings in the spring and summer of 1973; room 2141 in the **Rayburn House Office Building** where the House Judiciary Committee had the impeachment inquiry; the **Supreme Court** where the famous Nixon tapes case was decided July 24, 1974. (Also, while on the Hill, the Library of Congress main reading room is worth a visit.)

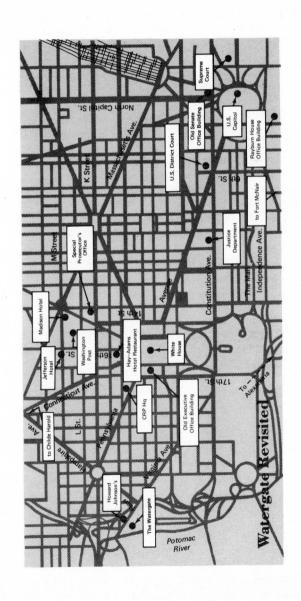

Supreme Court

North Capitol St.

Old Senate Office Building

U.S. Capitol

U.S. District Court

Rayburn House Office Building

Massachusetts Ave.

K Street

6th St.

to Fort McNair

M Street

Special Prosecutor's Office

Justice Department

Constitution Ave.

Independence Ave.

The Mall

Madison Hotel

Avenue

15th St.

Jefferson Hotel

Washington Post

16th St.

Hay–Adams Hotel Restaurant

White House

17th St.

Connecticut Ave.

St.

L St.

CRP Hq

Old Executive Office Building

Ave.

to Childe Harold

Pennsylvania

To Alexandria

Hampshire

Virginia Ave.

Howard Johnson's

The Watergate

Potomac River

**Watergate Revisited**

A tourist in Washington taking one of the Wilson Line tours on the Potomac, which depart from Sixth and Water Streets, S.W., might also want to visit nearby **Fort McNair,** at Fourth and P Streets, S. W. The sentries will let visitors on the post. The top Army brass have homes along the river. Quarters Seven was occupied in 1973 by General Alexander M. Haig, Jr., the former Nixon White House chief of staff.

Tourists who cross the river to **Alexandria**—the Old Town section—can find John Dean's old house at 100 Quay. Senator Lowell P. Weicker, the Connecticut Republican who served on the Watergate committee, later bought the house from Dean.

Washington is one of the best cities for a newspaper reporter for more reasons than just the location of the nation's capital here. It is a good city for doing investigative work. There is a big bureaucracy and no news organization can follow it all. But there are many places to meet news sources in private—the many monuments and parks. Many restaurants provide out-of-the-way tables for those who want to have private talks. Particularly private places (where the food is good) include the dining room in the **Jefferson Hotel,** on the corner of Sixteenth and M Streets, N.W.; the **Childe Harold** near Dupont Circle; the **Hay-Adams Hotel,** Sixteenth and H Streets, N.W.; and the coffee shop in the **Madison Hotel,** at Fifteenth and M Streets, N.W., opposite *The Washington Post.*

Washington is also full of public telephone booths. Reporters have their favorites—but that is a trade secret.

*Ed. note:* Not shown on map or revealed to this date is the location of the parking garage where Bob Woodward met his secret source, "Deep Throat."

# *Capitol Hill*
## By Ken Ringle

When all the monuments begin to look alike and the government seems too remote and complex; when you're tired of standing in line and the sight of one more Smithsonian artifact could move you to homicide; when Washington seems just too too big, too busy and too expensive—then come to Capitol Hill and relax.

Not the Capitol Hill of congressmen and lobbyists—you've already seen that—but residential Capitol Hill: the neighborhood of parks, houses and tree-lined streets that begins just behind the Capitol and the nearby Supreme Court. Stroll around. Sample a canolli or a doughnut from the Eastern Market or a Sunday champagne brunch at the bar called Jenkins Hill. You've learned something about how Washington works. Now learn something about how Washingtonians live.

Stretching eastward from the Capitol for 15 blocks or so is a microcosm of the social, cultural, architectural and historical life of the nation's capital, laid out in a setting you can happily lose yourself in for half a day or half a lifetime.

Now in the midst of a frenzy of restoration, it houses the city's most heterogeneous community in a collection of marvelous old houses—flat-fronted federal-style houses, turreted Victorians and bay-fronted frame Edwardians hung with ferns. Senators and mailmen, journalists and spies, lobbyists and plumbers live there. So do Renaissance scholars and photographers, lawyers and cabinetmakers, plus actresses, schoolteachers, and maids.

Their location entitles them to perhaps more of the city's amenities than the residents of any other neighborhood enjoy, and with very little effort. They can walk to plays at the Folger Shakespeare Library, take a lengthy walk to Redskins games at Kennedy Stadium—which shows, perhaps, the wide range of cul-

Ken Ringle is a writer on *The Washington Post* metropolitan staff and a Capitol Hill resident.

ture one can easily pursue in this neighborhood. The President gets inaugurated just around the corner, and the neighborhood library is the Library of Congress.

Three nights a week in the summer they can stroll up to the Capitol grounds, picnic on the grass, and listen to free concerts by the Army, Navy, Air Force, or Marine bands. On pleasant Friday evenings in the summertime, they can wander over to the Marine Corps Barracks for one of the most spectacular free shows in town: the weekly sunset parade, complete with drum and bugle corps, silent drill teams tossing bayonetted rifles and trumpeters ta-rahing on the parapets.

Capitol Hill, in short, is a microcosm of the Washington experience, easily sampled by the visitor, usually free, but often overlooked in the race from one monument to the other.

Like most neighborhoods that are primarily residential, the Hill is at its best in the morning and the evening and on the long, lazy weekends of the spring and fall. The early-bird tourist can hop the METRO to Capitol Hill (or outwit it by staying there at one of the old tourist houses) and watch the city wake up while enjoying a strolling breakfast at one of its friendliest institutions, the **Eastern Market** (*1*), **Seventh Street and North Carolina Avenue, S.E.**

The Eastern, sporting a recent face-lift, is the sole survivor of a network of farmers' markets once spread throughout the District of Columbia. The others fell victim to some unhappy concept of progress, but the people of Capitol Hill, in a continued spirit of feisty independence, saved the Eastern from deterioration and destruction. In the era of the chopped and frozen carrot and the plastic-wrapped strawberry, the Eastern survives as a joyful monument to freshness. It offers its visitors the soft, creamy beauty of a perfect mushroom and the rosy August perfume of the ultimate peach. You can buy an ox tail at the Eastern Market or a striped bass, discuss the advantages of North Carolina air-dried hams with an expert who cares about the subject, or select your favorite size brown eggs from a farmer who knows the chicken. If the doughnuts at the Eastern's bakery *are* 15 cents, they are the richest and chewiest in town. And a few stalls away you can beg a taste of cheddars from the straw-hatted cheese vendor, a Market fixture.

Flanked by Market Row, a busy collection of boutiques, the Eastern is at its richest and most colorful on Fridays and Satur-

# Capitol Hill Walking Tour

1. Eastern Market
2. Lincoln Park
3. 600 block, East Capitol Street
4. 617 A Street, N.E.
5. 407 A. Street, N.E.
6. 420 Constitution Avenue, N.E.
7. Museum of African Art
8. National Woman's Party
9. Supreme Court
10. Library of Congress
11. Folger Shakespeare Library
12. American Historical Association
13. Liberty Lobby
14. Mr. Henry's
15. Hawk and Dove
16. Jenkins Hill Saloon
17. Taverna Greek Islands
18. Trover Shop
19. Botanic Gardens
20. The Chancery
21. The Capitol

days (it's closed Sunday and Monday) and in December when it overflows with strawflowers and Christmas greens. But it's a treat any time and a good place to start any tour of Capitol Hill. Munching a breakfast doughnut, you can wander east on North Carolina Avenue four blocks to the giant elms and Mary Bethune statue in **Lincoln Park** (*2*), **North Carolina and Eleventh Street, N.E.,** then back west on East Capitol Street to about Sixth Street, north one block to A Street, N.E., then eastward. This gives you a sample of the next best feature of Capitol Hill: its houses.

Start with the mammoth old brick castles in the **600 block of East Capitol Street** (*3*), with their towers, balconies, and lightning rods. In the early part of this century, when Capitol Hill was a place of grand townhouses and alley stables, with much the air of a separate small town, these were the townhouses of the rich and mighty, with libraries and billiard rooms and back stairs to the servants' quarters. When the era of the auto lured the rich and mighty to the suburbs, the big houses became tourist homes (which some still are) and then apartments. Today the apartments are giving way, in some cases, to restoration-minded families in search of living room. Once you could buy one of those 20-room castles for around $100,000—complete with a Dante-esque furnace, oak paneling, and a tower room where your daughter can dream of knights and princesses. But those days are gone.

Not all of the Capitol Hill's houses, however, are monuments to Edwardian and Victorian megathink. Along A Street, N.E., which harbors some of the Hill's most intriguing houses, lies a selection of smaller homes inventively restored with as much attention to fun as to period. Notice the insistent red and yellow gingerbread of **617 A Street, N.E.** (*4*), and the whimsical windows and the waving arm of **407 A Street, N.E.** (*5*), just two blocks west. Tucked away on almost every street on the Hill are similar examples of its residents' search for personality and diversity in their houses—qualities that vastly enrich the neighborhood environment as a whole.

Most homeowners have chosen old houses for their vehicle, while others have accented their block with new houses in harmonious contemporary design. Good examples can be seen at **314 and 316 Ninth Street, S.E.** where the horizontal, almost Japanese lines of masonry and wood seem to widen the narrow lots and renew their vertical, more traditional surroundings. While you're on Ninth Street don't miss the happiest Victorian of them all—it's number 335—the yellow-brick turret which might have sprung straight from Oz.

The interaction between people and their houses on Capitol Hill enriches both, as well as the neighborhood around them. Three case studies come to mind:

Thomas V. Kelly is unofficial mayor of Capitol Hill, having been born there 50-odd years ago in his father's house at 404 Constitution Avenue, N.E., and now living at **420 Constitution Avenue, N.E.** (*6*). During a scrappy 1930s boyhood, he helped hold the Depression at bay with after-school gardening jobs at the house where he lives now, a rambling 19-room colossus, which stretches down Constitution and around the corner onto Fifth Street. Throughout a long, distinguished career as a reporter, feature writer and resident Puck of the old *Washington Daily News,* he dreamed of owning the house some day, as much for its history as for its size. It was built, he knew, around 1870 by Major Samuel Walker, a former Union Army officer who, in a brief tour as Washington's Chief of Police, raided a red light district at the foot of Capitol Hill. Walker also ordered the names of the congressmen seized in the raid to be published in the *Evening Star,* a move which contributed to the briefness of his tenure.

Five blocks east of the Kellys and seven blocks south at **534 Tenth Street, S.E.,** there is a small, two-story gray-brick house with a pillared porch. The seemingly unremarkable house is a monument to the vision and perseverance of Chris and Martha Wright, two people in their early thirties who took a chance on Capitol Hill when its fortunes were lowest.

They moved to Washington in 1968, just after the riots that followed the assassination of Dr. Martin Luther King, Jr., and promptly bought a house, or rather, a structure. The brick walls were standing, but that was about all. The windows had been broken out, the plumbing stolen, the yard piled high with debris. They bought it for about $13,000. Two years and $10,000 later they had made it a warm, comfortable little home, with a yard overflowing with flowers and a megalomaniac fig tree.

They learned carpentry and plumbing, pried their dining room floor from the parquet of the old Willard Hotel, where they also got plumbing at auction. Today they have a house they could sell for more than $100,000. If they were interested in selling, which they aren't.

Bigger visions loomed in the mind of Tim Temple when he

saw the hulking stucco at **228 Ninth Street, S.E.**—a haunted house, whose three or maybe four floors scattered rats and vermin on its neighbors. That was in 1969. Temple, a motorcycling stockbroker in his late thirties, persevered through a four-year title fight to buy the property, then rebuilt the carriage house for himself with such features as a balcony-hung bedroom and a spiral staircase. Now he's plowing his way into the main house with a pickup construction crew of retired bartenders and bearded geniuses, installing solar heating, sculptured fireplaces, and light shafts, making up the design for the house as he goes.

There are, of course, a thousand such stories on Capitol Hill. The faces of the houses themselves hint at some of them. But as you make your morning rounds and watch the pretty young women legging their way up A Street to jobs in the Dirksen Building, remember they may have been up all night plastering walls.

Capitol Hill is also a good place to go looking for roots. Blacks can find special meaning at the **Museum of African Art** (*7*), **316 A Street, N.E.** Feminists may find it meaningful to look in at the **National Woman's Party** (*8*), **144 Constitution Avenue, N.E.,** and meet a suffragette. Every American can sense the roots of government and rule of law at the **Supreme Court** (*9*), **First and East Capitol Streets, N.E.** Genealogists can tap the **Library of Congress** (*10*) **across East Capitol Street from the Supreme Court.** Shakespearean scholars can further their knowledge of the Bard at the **Folger Shakespeare Library** (*11*), **201 East Capitol Street, S.E.** General history buffs can look in at the **American Historical Association** (*12*), **400 A Street, S.E.** Political conservatives can take comfort in the **Liberty Lobby** (*13*), **Third and Independence, S.E.,** which has almost as many antennae on the roof as the Russian Embassy.

These places are all worth a look as you wander back toward Pennsylvania Avenue to explore the shops and restaurants of Capitol Hill. Look into **Mr. Henry's** (*14*), **601 Pennsylvania Avenue, S.E.,** the **Hawk and Dove** (*15*), **329 Pennsylvania Avenue, S.E.,** and **Jenkins Hill** (*16*), **223 Pennsylvania Avenue, S.E.**—these are all restaurant-bars, but they're more than that. They all function as neighborhood community centers. Georgetown has more and fancier bars, but they rarely perform the same function because they are flooded with non-Georgetowners.

On Capitol Hill, your bar is a place where you can meet a friend, receive a telephone call or just drop in from time to time to see what's going on. On Sunday mornings, Jenkins Hill holds a champagne brunch that—for less than $9 at this writing—entitles you to eggs Benedict and all the champagne you can drink. **Cool Breeze's at 501 Eleventh Street, S.E.,** has some of the best home-made pies on the Hill, and on weekends the Sicilian fair makes way for the most reasonable sumptuous omelettes in the area.

Take a look in the **Trover Shop** (18), **227 Pennsylvania Avenue, S.E.,** and get an idea of what the people who run your government are reading. And **Kramer Books and Records,** just down the avenue at **336 Pennsylvania,** is a good place to eavesdrop on legislative assistants discussing their bills as they browse.

Before the luncheon crowd rolls in, save yourself a seat at the **Taverna Greek Islands, 307 Pennsylvania Avenue, S.E.** (17), an island of shishkebab and feta cheese on flat bread. It's bound to inspire even the hamburger-loyal 12-year-old who wouldn't be caught dead out of McDonald's. Chase yours with a Harp ale from Ireland and for dessert try the galaktoboureko—a flaky pastry filled with custard.

There is much more to tell you about the neighborhood. The area east of Union Station has sprouted some exciting, new restaurants. Over on 8th Street, S.E., across from the Marine Barracks is the newly restored **Barracks Row,** a hubbub of antique and craft shops. John Philip Sousa was born in a house at 6th and G Streets, S.E., and buried at the Congressional Cemetery near the Kennedy Stadium along with hundreds of senators and representatives. And there are the marvelously foggy liberal politics of the Hill, which in 1972 inspired one Democratic mass meeting to concern itself, among other things, with equal political representation for interracial homosexual couples.

But you're getting the idea.

So spend your afternoon looking at the trees on the Hill (what a wealth of sycamores and elms!) and peep into the publicly subsidized jungle of the **Botanic Gardens** (*19*)—that greenhouse at one foot of the Capitol grounds.

The evening you can spend at another foot of Capitol Hill in **The Chancery, 704 New Jersey Avenue, N.W.,** (*20*), another neighborhood bar which caters to Georgetown Law School students. It features a mural with pictures of Bobby Kennedy, Ralph Nader, and Oliver Wendell Homes; a series of good bluegrass bands; and a bartender who serves the best Irish coffee in town.

But before then, take a moment at dusk and walk out on the

terrace of the **Capitol Building** (*21*). While you stand there with the Washington Monument in the distance and the nation's capital spread out before you in the twilight, you can watch the lights wink on, one by one, along the streets of the city. It's one of the minor delights of a summer night for anyone, and it's a part of life on Capitol Hill.

# *Georgetown and Alexandria*

## By Laura Longley Babb

### GEORGETOWN

Georgetown is a two-faced town. Saturdays along M Street and Wisconsin Avenue one face is presented, at its worst, or best. If you join the shoving, elbowing streams on those streets, you may find yourself living a scene from Nathanael West. There the bead and bauble dealers stake out sidewalk sales territory; a smart boutique titillates the throngs with real live moving mannequins in the window; a flower-vendor hawks daisies in front of the Little Tavern hamburger joint; suburban migrants, bejeaned-George-towners-for-a-day, move as a pack on the scent of a gourmet coffee shop; and an endless wave of overheating automobiles and drivers twists slowly, slowly, down Wisconsin Avenue.

But behind all this, in the milder pace of a weekday midmorning, you can discover the sleepy, shaded streets like N and R,

Laura Longley Babb is editor for books of *The Washington Post Magazine*.

Dumbarton and Thirty-first, the inscrutable federal and Victorian mansions of old wealth and new power, the high-walled gardens, the neat narrow houses of Washingtonians on the move, up. This is the neighborhood that achieved chic after Eleanor Roosevelt encouraged New Dealers to move in and begin renovating the larger places that, in an earlier day, had housed the port's river princes and land barons.

A port is, after all, what Georgetown was—and may yet become again. It was a rather small port, even in the scale of those two-centuries-ago days, and woodlands and tobacco fields were near. If, today, you wander down by the Potomac, you might imagine burly men hauling great hogsheads of tobacco onto a wooden ship—and those burly men would have been shouting and singing, most likely, in two accents: British and African.

Down in this neighborhood were streets that attested to the water ties: Bridge and Falls (now M Street), Water and High (Wisconsin Avenue), Wapping Causeway, Fishing Lane. But the town those streets cut up, laid out in 1751, was a Maryland town, for Georgetown wasn't part of the District of Columbia then, because there was no District (not to mention a U.S.A.). That came a little later—and happened here. Down at Suter's Tavern George Washington got together with a group of commissioners in March of 1791 and hammered out the historic agreement: the acquisition of the tobacco fields and foggy bottoms that would make up the federal city.

You can walk to the site of Suter's under the Whitehurst Freeway at K and Thirty-first Streets—but you might feel it's not worth the time or footwear. So let's start about a block north of that site, near the start of the C&O Canal, which flows gently, even sweetly (depending on the heat and stagnation of the stream), through Georgetown.

*Go to Thirty-first and the Canal, opposite the Canal Square shopping complex.*

### The Towpath and Thomas Jefferson Street

The Canal, one of George Washington's ideas and investments, was built to open up the region to commerce from the north and west. Later, that early Patowmack Canal, company and wa-

# Georgetown Walking Tour

1. Chesapeake & Ohio Towpath
2. Towpath Houses
3. Potomac Masonic Lodge #5
4. Old Stone House
5. Thomas Sim Lee Corner
6. Narrow House, 1239 N
7. Decatur House
8. Laird–Dunlop–Lincoln House
9. Jacqueline Kennedy House
10. Kissinger Residence
11. Gun-barrel Fence
12. Dumbarton House
13. Evermay
14. Mt. Zion Cemetery
15. Oak Hill Cemetery
16. Montrose Park
17. Dumbarton Oaks
18. Scott–Grant House
19. Tudor Place
20. Bowie House
21. Cooke's Row
22. "Emilio" House
23. Methodist Episcopal Church
24. St. John's Episcopal Church
25. Bodisco House
26. JFK House
27. Burnt Row
28. Cox Row
29. Halcyon House
30. "Quality Hill"
31. Prospect House
32. Georgetown University

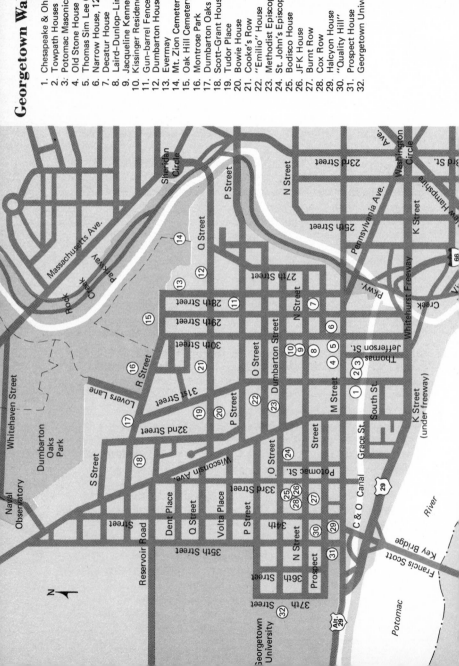

terway, were taken over and extended by the Chesapeake & Ohio. Until Hurricane Agnes whipped through and emptied the C&O, as it came to be called, this was a navigable waterway with barges, boatmen, and mules. People lived along the Canal, too, and still do. If you pick your way east on the cobbled Towpath, you can see the cozy pastel houses, about the size of large match-boxes and built around 1870. They're known as the Towpath Houses.

Upon reaching Thomas Jefferson Street, look to your immediate left for Number 1058. This was the Potomac Masonic Lodge, #5, built in 1810; members of this lodge officiated at the laying of the Capitol's cornerstone in 1793. At Number 1047 (a spot now occupied by a rambling brick-and-glass office complex), Thomas Jefferson lived while serving as Secretary of State under George Washington.

*Walk one block north on Thomas Jefferson Street to M Street. Directly across M is the Old Stone House. This is where we're heading, but please go either half a block west or east to a light—there is none here.*

**Saved!**

Built back in 1765, the honey-colored Old Stone House, 3051 M Street, is a neatly restored middle-class home outfitted with the modest furniture and utensils typical of the families who once lived here. Open daily 9:30 to 5, the stone walls make for a cool, dark retreat on those white-hot days when the solar death rays take their toll. There's also a casual garden that beckons strollers to sit among the fruit trees and flower beds.

A few steps down M Street is another good home rescued from the wrecker's ball: the Thomas Sim Lee House, 3001 M Street. Lee was an important figure, friend of George Washington and twice governor of Maryland, but it's his red-brick rowhouse that is really remarkable today. In 1951, bought by some George-town residents who restored the structure to "adaptive use" as a shop, the governor's house became one of the first concrete applications of the Old Georgetown Act. That Act has since saved other buildings of historic and architectural merit.

*From the Lee Corner, continue north on Thirtieth Street to N Street. Along the way, look for Number 1239—Georgetown's*

The quiet crowding of Georgetown is consistent, in scale, and pedestrian.

Watergate.

C&C Canal, Georgetown

*narrowest abode, measuring a meager 11 feet in width. (But that's a palace compared to ones you'll find in Alexandria!)*

### Decatur Detour
At N, you might turn east to 2812—a block and a half off our path—to see the discreet federal home Susan Wheeler Decatur moved into after her husband Commodore Stephen Decatur was slain in a duel. Supposedly she thought that in secluded Georgetown she would never encounter her husband's opponent. (As far as anyone can tell, she never did.)

### Other Retreats
Turning west on N from Thirtieth Street, you'll come upon the retreats of two other well-known individuals who suffered similar tragic experiences. Number 3014 N Street, a substantial brick home built by Scotsman John Laird in 1799 and later owned by Judge James Dunlop, it became the haven of Robert Todd Lincoln after the Civil War and his father's murder. And just across the street at 3017, high on an ivy-covered hillside, is the elegant eighteenth century dwelling which Jacqueline Kennedy purchased and retreated to after President Kennedy's assassination.

By cutting through the backyard of 3017, you'd almost be in Henry Kissinger's house. It would, however, be far wiser to round the corner from N to Thirtieth to Dumbarton Street. You can't miss 3018 Dumbarton, an attractive white brick home: if the security guards don't tip you off, the two "No Parking" signs and absence of garbage bags should.

### Fence to Arms

Check your bearings and our map and proceed to the northwest corner of Twenty-eighth and P Streets. Marching around 2803 P is a fence made from a hundred musket barrels. Seems that back in the mid-nineteenth century a clever locksmith named Reuben Daws picked up a load of antiquated guns from the Washington Navy Yard, simply stuck the stocks into the wall, attached spikes to the muzzles, and—*voilà!*—had himself a good, cheap fence.

### Dumbarton—House, Not Oaks

Ambling north along Twenty-eighth and a few steps east on Q you come to Dumbarton House (2715 Q Street, N.W.), not to be confused with Dumbarton Oaks up on R Street. One of George-town's oldest (1747) late-Georgian homes, the stately place was remodeled in 1805 by Benjamin Latrobe and was occupied by the first Register of the Treasury, Joseph Nourse. Back when it was known as Bellevue, it sat smack in the center of present-day Q Street. But in 1915, when Q was cut through, the house was hoisted to its hillside site. It's now owned by the Society of Colonial Dames, and—just as in 1934 when Eleanor Early breathlessly described it in *And This Is Washington!*—"everything in it is extremely elegant, and *correct.*" The Dames won't charge you admission to see the elegant and correct furnishings, but they do accept contributions. (Open Monday through Saturday 9 to noon; closed Sundays, holidays and the months of July and August.)

### Evermay

For a glimpse of what paradise might be, go back to Twenty-eighth, turn north, and keep climbing until, on your right, through the iron gates crowned with gold, past the glorious magnolias, you see a genteel Georgian manor house. This is Evermay.

The brick home, whose address is 1623 Twenty-eighth Street (although it hardly needs one at all), presides over land Samuel Davidson bought from the Beall family in 1794, after he sold the site of Lafayette Square and the White House to the federal government. Today Evermay remains in private and privileged hands—the Belin family's. They've owned it now for more than half a century, and one can understand why they might never let it go. As *The Post*'s Sarah Booth Conroy has written: "Standing before the south façade of the house, and looking down at the treetop view, topped here by the Washington Monument, there by the Capitol Dome, it is easy to see why Davidson sold the feds the marshland and kept his castle site. At night, the lights of Washington make a second Milky Way for Evermay's entertainment."

For your entertainment, the grounds—exquisite Italianate terraced gardens—have been open to the public on garden tours. Watch the papers in the spring: you might be lucky.

### At the Top of the Georgetown Heights

Beyond Evermay, at the top of Twenty-eighth Street, lies Oak Hill Cemetery and next to it on the east, Mt. Zion, one of Washington's oldest black cemeteries, where more than 8,000 freedmen and slaves are buried. Now under restoration, Mt. Zion once was two burial grounds, both with black-ownership histories dating back to mid-nineteenth century. One was an old Methodist burial ground, the other was organized in 1843 by the Female Union Band Society of freedmen.

Oak Hill, far differently, was given and endowed by one rich man—banker and art patron William Wilson Corcoran, who also made a gift of the ornate Gatehouse at Thirtieth and R in 1849. Not far from that exclusive entrance is a delightful Gothic Revival chapel, often likened to a perfect paperweight, which James Renwick designed and built in 1850.

(There are many notables buried here, their gravesites marked with either modest or ostentatious memorials. Maybe the most touching memorial of all in Georgetown, though, is far from any cemetery. Down near the Canal, at 1066 Wisconsin Avenue, low on the front façade of what's now a shop and once was the Vigilant Firehouse, is this inscription: "Bush, the old Fire Dog, Died of Poison, July 5th, 1869. R.I.P.")

### Dumbarton Oaks

To the west of Oak Hill is Montrose Park and beyond that a romantic walkway which, since 1900, has officially been called

Lovers Lane. The path for pairs marks the eastern extremity of the real estate known as Dumbarton Oaks, 3101 R Street, N.W. *(See* Chapter XIV, "Natural Life," for a full description of the Renaissance gardens, and Chapter VIII, "Art," on the pre-Columbian, Byzantine, and medieval collections.)

This sprawling preserve was once part of the patent of a Georgetown forefather named Ninian Beall. The house, the main part at least, was built around 1800 by Judge William Hammond Dorsey. Over the years it changed as it changed residents—some of them noted names like John C. Calhoun, who entertained the Marquis de Lafayette there in 1824. Finally, in 1920, the place passed to Robert Woods Bliss and his wife. They restored the building, brought the lush lawns and gardens back to life, and then turned everything, including their extensive art collections, over to Harvard University. (It was under Harvard's auspices that the Dumbarton Oaks Conference was held in 1944, leading to the formation of the United Nations.)

Today the collections and gardens are open to the public, but the hours aren't terribly convenient: closed July 1 through Labor Day; otherwise open 2-5 P.M. daily—except the art collections, which are closed Mondays.

### Civil War Sidetrip

During the Civil War, Lieutenant General Henry W. Halleck lived in Alabaman A. V. Scott's large home at 3238 R Street, and it's said that President Lincoln would consult with Halleck here. General Ulysses S. Grant also spent a summer here after the war.

### Architectural Attractions

South to Dumbarton Street from R on (or not far off) Thirty-first Street there are several outstanding and/or outlandish structures.

First and maybe finest is Tudor Place, at 1644 Thirty-first Street. And, happily, it's nowhere close to American-mock-English-Tudor. William Thornton's masterpiece of regency style, Tudor Place was built early in the nineteenth century by Thomas Peter, husband of Martha Parke Custis, the first First Lady's granddaughter. (For a good view, go to the northwest corner of Thirty-first and Q Streets.)

Facing Tudor House on Q Street is a generous late-Georgian home built by Washington Bowie, of the same family as the inventor of the Bowie knife and the hero of the Alamo. It's now an Episcopal Church Home.

Also on Q Street, numbers 3007–3027, are four fanciful Victorian villas put up by Henry Cooke. The row is called, of course, Cooke's Row.

A more contemporary flight of fancy can be found nearby at 3115 O Street. The wood-shingled house is done up in a dozen colors, plus a daisy, and is signed "Emilio."

### En Route to Wisconsin

Back on Thirty-first, continue south to Dumbarton and turn west, where you'll pass the Methodist Episcopal Church at number 3127. In this church, a dejected President Lincoln reportedly wept during services in March, 1863, and here poet Walt Whitman tended the wounded and dying when the church served as a Union hospital.

At Wisconsin Avenue, the pulsing artery of shops and restaurants, jog back up to O Street. (Suggestion: There are any number of neighborhood haunts for something to warm you up or cool you down before trekking on.)

*On the west end of Georgetown, the route—with a couple extra steps here and there—takes you along O Street to Thirty-third, to N, to Thirty-fourth, to Prospect, to Thirty-seventh, and up to the gates of Georgetown University at Thirty-seventh and O Streets.*

### The West End

Along the way, here are the highspots:

• The District's oldest (founded 1794) Episcopal Church—St. John's—on the corner of O and Potomac Streets.

• The gracious Bodisco House, 3322 O Street, which was the Russian Embassy for many years. It's dubbed Bodisco after the elderly Russian ambassador, Baron Alexander de Bodisco, who brought to this home his 16-year-old bride, American schoolgirl Harriet Williams.

• The Kennedy House, 3307 N Street. Senator John F. Kennedy bought this comfortable place in 1957 as a gift for his wife Jacqueline after their daughter Caroline's birth. From here, they moved to the White House.

- 3308-3320 N Street. Called Burnt Row for the devastating fire that swept through these houses in 1833.
- 3327-3339 N Street. Called Cox Row for Georgetown mayor Colonel John Cox, who in 1817 built these fashionable federal townhouses, all set serenely back from the bustling street.
- Halcyon House, southwest corner of Thirty-fourth and Prospect Streets, was erected in 1787 and was the residence of the country's first Secretary of the Navy, Benjamin Stoddert.
- "Quality Hill," 3425 Prospect, built in 1798, seems to have acquired its name from the character of the neighborhood.
- Prospect House, 3508 Prospect, a late eighteenth century mansion, was the home of Secretary of the Navy James E. Forrestal during World War II. After the war, when the White House was being renovated and the Trumans were living in Blair House, Prospect House was leased as the presidential "guest house."

### Ivory Tower

Walking through Georgetown, one happens upon Georgetown University, which spills over the grounds beyond the gate at Thirty-seventh and O Streets. But the university really should be seen first from the Virginia shore of the Potomac, from where the Gothic spires of Healy Hall create a castles-on-the-Rhine horizon.

Those of us without wheels can content ourselves with a pleasant walk through the campus. Stop in Old North, the original college building (1792), and Healy, begun in 1877. And don't miss the statue of Archbishop John Carroll, founder of Georgetown, which is the oldest (1789) Jesuit institution in the country.

From the university, you can return via O Street to the cramped sidewalks of Wisconsin, where you might choose to join the informal parade past the boutiques, bead vendors, and flower carts. But if you came equipped with car, pile in, find your way down to K Street (under the Whitehurst Freeway). There is a right turn on to the Rock Creek Parkway that takes you past the Kennedy Center. Take the Parkway along the river to Memorial Bridge. Cross it and head toward National Airport and Alexandria on the George Washington Memorial Parkway south to Alexandria, where you can continue your tour even farther back through American history.

## ALEXANDRIA, VIRGINIA

The tour buses clip through Alexandria, stop briefly at Christ Church, continue their appointed rounds to Mount Vernon, and on the return leg, cut the engines for fast forays into the souvenir shops.

Alexandria, the Old Town port section, should not be blitzed through. Get out of your car, or off your bus. Hang around awhile. Because within the space of a few blocks and about 60 minutes, just rambling around, you can walk down a cobbled street called Captain's Row, lift a mug at Gadsby's Tavern, step back into our nation's past anywhere along the way.

A lot of American history was played out in this seaport, where today the local landmarks represent important periods —Alexandria as a tobacco port built up by Scottish merchants; the colonial, commercial, and social capital; and, during the Civil War, a city of southern sympathy and northern occupation. Curiously, it was that trying time that kept Old Town out of the spray of cannon and intact today.

But then, Alexandria is hardly a backwater town untouched by time, nor is it a Williamsburg without the cellophane wrapping. It's actually a sprawling city, of which the Old Town port is only a part, though one that feels like a small neighborhood much the way Capitol Hill does, where faces become familiar enough to evoke friendly greetings, where run-down old houses are personally restored by their owners. (On many of the buildings, by the way, you'll see the official oval plaques of an Historic Buildings Survey.)

In history and architecture, Alexandria is similar to Georgetown. But don't visit here expecting a Georgetown "scene." So far, Alexandria lacks the discos and bracelet dealers, and that suits the locals just fine. They seem quite satisfied with their river views at almost every turn, with their congenial Snack Bar down by the water on King Street, with their Christmas Walks and Scottish Games.

In 1669, John Alexander purchased this land along the Potomac, and some 63 years later Scottish merchants put up a shipping warehouse. By 1748 the hamlet had mushroomed and it finally was incorporated as a town. Among its early "founding fathers," bearing surnames that recur in the town's history, were William Ramsay, John Carlyle, Thomas Lord Fairfax, and Lawrence Washington. And one strapping surveyor, George Washington, helped lay out Alexandria, so-named for the first patent holder.

Some years after that one Robert E. Lee grew up in Alexandria, mostly in the sober-faced red-brick house known as **Lee's Boyhood Home, 607 Oronoco.** He and his family lived there until he left for West Point. It's open to the public: Monday–Saturday 10-4, Sunday noon-4. (Small admission.) Next door—and the architectural twin of that house—was the **Hallowell School, 609 Oronoco.** Lee took his lessons here from a learned and well-liked Quaker. Lee's uncle, **Edmund Jennings Lee,** built the house at **428 North Washington** in 1799; and across the street is the **Lee-Fendall House, 429 North Washington,** graced by a towering magnolia. Built by Philip Richard Fendall, whose first and second wives were both Lees, it's now a delightful Lee museum, open daily 9-5 (small admission). An even earlier boyhood home of Lee's is nearby—**407 North Washington,** where the family lived in the rear wing of the house.

There's another historical footnote in the four attractive houses called **Brockett's Row, 301-307 North Washington.** According to historian Mary Powell, before Robert Brockett built this pleasing row—around 1840—there had been on the site "a row of shabby frame houses" where "drunken dances and 'wakes' kept a turmoil in the neighborhood."

Take a look, in passing, at the small, narrow houses at **523 Queen.** People were little in the early days. Take a look, too, at the flat-faced, half-house at **511 Queen**—you'll find this sort of house throughout Old Town Alexandria. They're called "flounders," and there's some delightful dispute over the origins of the name and structure. One argument has it that in order to secure their deeds, each owner—who had to build within two years—built a wing first. Supposedly each had planned to add a main building and never did. Another view is that the high English tariff on glass was responsible for the flat, windowless walls—which look like the flounder fish. And there you have it—maybe.

Just a few steps away is where Robert E. Lee's cousins

lived—**Lloyd House, 220 North Washington.** Here Lee learned he'd been selected as commander of the Army of Northern Virginia. A few steps more and you come to the house that is remembered as the home of Lee's father, the dashing Revolutionary War hero **"Light Horse Harry" Lee, 611 Cameron.**

An elegant Fairfax family home, originally designed and built in the late eighteenth century by William Yeaton, is down the block—the **Yeaton-Fairfax House, 607 Cameron Street.**

**Christ Church, Washington and Cameron Streets,** holds a silver plate on the communion rail, rubbed shiny by hands large and small; it marks the spot where the Confederate leader was confirmed. Another plate marks his simple pew, No. 46. George Washington worshipped here too, "weather and roads permitting." He kept pew No. 60 (price 36 pounds, 10 shillings). In continuous use since February 27, 1773, the Church is open weekdays 9-5, Sundays 2-5; try to attend a Sunday morning service—8 and 10:30. At the early service, the rays from the east pour through the splendid Palladian windows, lighting the elevated pulpit and parishioners' faces.

Washington had a small brick townhouse at **508 Cameron.** (It's been privately rebuilt to its original state, but is not open to the public. But don't miss, walking by, the curious mirrored gadget at the right front window. It's called a "busybody" and allows a nosy person inside to see who's at the door or on the street.) You'll find the good general at **Gadsby's Tavern,** too **(132 North Royal),** where he was toasted at "birth-night balls" and where he presided over a number of events, such as the one in 1775 that resulted in the adoption of the colonial rights assertions called the "Fairfax County Resolves," written by George Mason—the "Pen of the Revolution."

But turn away from history for a moment, back to the present—and listen. It's quite possible that from **Market Square, Fairfax and King Streets,** your ear will catch the strains of a string concert playing along with the fountain, or the skirl and rattle of the Alexandria Pipes and Drums, a crack corps costumed in full Highland regalia. **Carlyle House (1752), 121 North Fairfax,** also bears witness to the Scottish beginnings of Alexandria. Trustee John Carlyle, who hailed from Dumfries, Scotland, modeled his house after Craigiehall in West Lothian. It was a grand house then, and is now (open to the public) thanks to extensive restoration. Besides being architecturally impressive, the house is historically important, for it was here, in April, 1755, that British General Edward Braddock—with George Washington in tow—met with five royal governors to discuss his French and Indian War. They brought up, too, a not-so-bright idea for taxes to pay for that ill-fated campaign—later, the Stamp Act helped provoke the American Revolution.

About that time, William Ramsay, the town's first Postmaster and first and only Lord Mayor, moved into a yellow house. Today, **Ramsay House, King and Fairfax Streets,** considered Alexandria's oldest (*c.* 1742), wears the Ramsay tartan on the door and welcomes visitors as headquarters of the Alexandria Visitors Center. (*See* last page of this chapter.)

Turn away from history once more, and visit the **Torpedo Factory, King and Union Streets.** It's a vast workshop/showroom for artists and carftspeople, open daily 10-5. On the neighboring streets and alleys are most of the town's quaint gift and curio shops—many of them delightful.

There is some recent history to the Torpedo Factory: it was where torpedoes were once made and where, later, captured Nazi war records were stored. There's even history in **Captain's Row,** the **100 block of Prince Street,** where sea captains built their homes and where cobbles were laid by Hessian prisoners of war.

One of the town's outstanding examples of Greek revival plays a contemporary role today: the **Athenaeum Gallery, 201 Prince,** the former Bank of the Old Dominion. This creamy, cantaloupe-colored building, whose front-yard tree explodes in matching hue every fall, is open Tuesday–Saturday 10-4, and occasionally on Sundays for special exhibitions. In this affluent quarter, too, is the rambling **Fairfax House, 207 Prince,** built by Colonel William Fairfax in 1752. **Dr. Elisha Cullen Dick** occupied the fine residence at **209 Prince;** by the way, he had nothing whatsoever to do with David Copperfield. But as a physician he did attend Washington in the general's final hours, and, as was the custom, stopped the clock at the moment of death. **Dr. James Craik,** a friend of both Washington and Dr. Dick, and Surgeon General of the Continental Army, was also with Washington at his death. His unassuming home was at **210 Duke.**

There are two "flounders" along our path here—at **202 Duke,** and at **321 South Lee.**

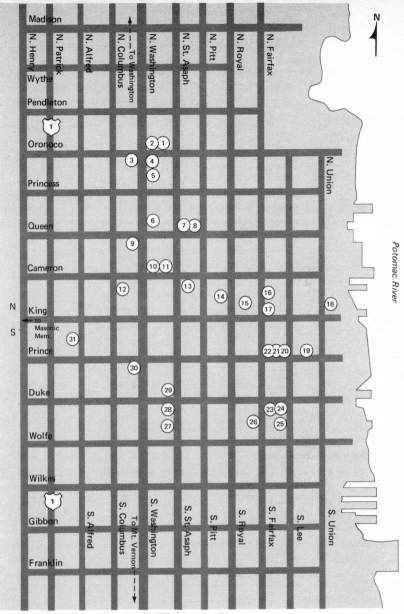

# Old Town Alexandria Walking Tour

**(Major points of interest, numbered to follow text.)**

1. Lee's Boyhood Home
2. Benjamin Hallowell School
3. Edmund Jennings Lee House
4. Lee-Fendall House
5. 407 No. Washington Street
6. Brockett's Row
7. Little House 523 Queen Street
8. 511 Queen Street flounder
9. Lloyd House
10. "Light Horse Harry" Lee House
11. Yeaton-Fairfax House
12. Christ Church

13. George Washington Townhouse
14. Gadsby's Tavern
15. Market Square
16. Carlyle House
17. Ramsay House— Alexandria Visitors Center
18. Torpedo Factory
19. Captain's Row
20. Athenaeum
21. Fairfax House
22. Dr. Elisha Cullen Dick House

23. Dr. James Craik House
24. 202 Duke Street flounder
25. 321 South Lee Street flounder
26. Old Presbyterian Meeting House
27. 317 S. St. Asaph flounder
28. Lafayette House
29. Taylor House
30. Lyceum—No. Va. Bicentennial Center
31. Friendship Fire Company

The austere **Old Presbyterian Meeting House** (1774) is at **321 South Fairfax** (open 9-4 weekdays, Saturdays until 1 P.M. Sunday services at 11 A.M.). Though it burned in 1835, the outer walls and the old clock withstood the blaze. Behind, in a corner of the manicured churchyard criss-crossed by neat brick walks, is the tomb of the Unknown Soldier of the American Revolution.

Glance at **317 South St. Asaph,** another of the "flounders."

When people speak of George Washington, as one does all through a tour of Alexandria, in the next breath there's almost always the general's doting admirer, the Marquis de Lafayette. He too was—and still seems to be—around Alexandria. In 1824, some years after the Frenchman's outstanding service in the American Revolution, he returned to our country as a national guest. During that visit he stayed in the gracious home known today as **Lafayette House, 301 South St. Asaph.** On that same visit, Lafayette tried to address the throngs from 301, but needing a higher podium he stepped up on **Robert Taylor's** front steps at **601 Duke.**

The **Lyceum Company** is a good next stop. It was not a business, but a lecture-and-debating society, and was restored as the George Washington Northern Virginia Bicentennial Center, **Prince and Washington Streets.** (See below.)

There seems little doubt of George Washington's fondness for this town. He kept active in local affairs—he was a founder of the **Friendship Fire Company, 107 South Alfred,** a volunteer outfit whose engine house with red-and-white cupolas still stands (open weekdays 10-4). He even bought the town its first fire engine for a hefty $400.

### Information on Events

For more visitor information and details on such special events as the garden tours, annual Christmas Walk and Scottish Games, contact:

The **Alexandria Visitors Center, Ramsay House, 221 King Street, 549-0205.** Open daily 10–5:00. At 10:30 and 1:30 daily there is also a 13-minute color film about Alexandria. And on Tuesday through Saturday a conducted walking tour follows it. The Center also offers visitors: free bus or car parking in metered or one and two hour zones; tour planning; foreign language guides by advance notice; assistance in making reservations for entertainment, dining and/or overnight accommodations.

**George Washington Northern Virginia Bicentennial Center,** at the **Lyceum, 201 South Washington Street, 750-6677.** Open daily 9–5. Gift shop open Monday through Saturday 10–4:30, Sunday 1–4:30. This Center is, obviously, oriented more to the region, with exhibits, brochures, and a very helpful staff. Certainly worth stopping in for additional information and trip planning.

The **Alexandria Community Y** (not affiliated with the YWCA), **602 Cameron Street, 549-0111.** Office open 8:30–4:30 Monday through Saturday. Walking and bus tours complete with docents, sometimes costumed.

**Doorways to Olde Virginia, Box 7053, Alexandria 22307; 548-0100.** This private organization conducts special group tours, behind the scenes and inside the homes, of Old Town Alexandria. Also bus trips to outlying plantations.

# XXI
# Getting HELP

*Help*

| | |
|---|---|
| Police | 911 |
| Ambulance | 911 |
| Fire | 911 |
| Police Department Information | 626-2007 |
| Doctors Referral (Medical Bureau) | 223-2200 |
| All-Night Drugstore | 628-0720 |
| Travelers Aid | 347-0101 |
| Emergency Counseling: | |
| Hot-Line | 527-4077 |
| Hot-Line | 949-6603 |
| Suicide Prevention | 629-5222 |
| Rape Crisis Center | 333-7273 |
| Poison Control Center | 835-4080 |
| Animal Bites | 626-2000 |

*Area Codes*

| | |
|---|---|
| District of Columbia | 202 |
| Maryland | 301 |
| Virginia (Northern) | 703 |

*Visitors Information*

| | |
|---|---|
| American Revolution Bicentennial Administration | 634-1776 |
| Public Citizen Visitors Center | 659-9053 |
| Washington Area Convention & Visitors Bureau | 857-5500 |
| Daily Tourist Information | 737-8866 |

*Transportation*

| | |
|---|---|
| Airport Limousine Service | |
| Baltimore | 347-7766 |
| National and Dulles | 471-9801 |
| Amtrak-Union Station | 800-523-5720 |
| Downtown Ticket Office (business hours only) | 484-7540 |

Taxis ................................... see the Yellow Pages
Greyhound Bus Station ........................... 289-5100
Trailways Bus Station ............................. 737-5800
City Metrobuses (routes & schedules) ............... 637-2437
Tourmobile .......................................... 554-7950
Washington Metropolitan Transit Commission ........ 331-1671

*Government*

Burea of Engraving and Printing .................... 566-2000
U.S. Capitol ........................................ 224-3121
Department of Defense (Pentagon) ................... 545-6700
Federal (Agency) Information Center ................ 755-8660
Library of Congress ............................... 426-5000
U.S. Supreme Court ............................... 393-1640
    Visitors Information ......................... 638-0220
National Archives .................................. 523-3000
White House ....................................... 456-1414

*Stage—Music—Dance*

Arena Stage ....................................... 638-6700
Ford's Theatre .................................... 347-6260
Kennedy Center for the Performing Arts
    Box Office Information ......................... 254-3600
    Dial Instant-Charge: ...........................
        Concert Hall ............................. 857-0900
        Opera House ............................. 857-0900
        Eisenhower Theatre ...................... 857-0900
    American Film Institute Theatre ................ 785-4600
National Theatre
    Box office ..................................... 628-3393
    Instant Charge ................................ 466-8500
Wolf Trap .......................................... 938-3800
Olney Theatre ...................................... 924-3400

*Museums*

Air and Space ...................................... 628-4422
Arts and Industries Building ........................ 628-4422
Corcoran Gallery of Art ............................ 638-3211
Freer Gallery of Art ............................... 628-4422
Hirshhorn Museum .................................. 628-4422
Museum Of African Art ............................. 547-7424
National Collection of Fine Arts .................... 628-4422
National Gallery of Art ............................. 737-4215

National Geographic Society ......................... 857-7000
National Museum of History & Technology ............ 628-4422
National Museum of Natural History .................. 628-4422
National Portrait Gallery ........................... 628-4422
Phillips Collection .................................. 387-0961
Renwick Gallery ..................................... 381-5811
Smithsonian ......................................... 628-4422
    Dial-A-Museum ................................. 737-8811

*Parks*

Coming Park Events ..................................426-6700
Dial-A-Park (Today's Events).........................426-6975
D.C. Department of Recreation .......................629-7226
Hains Point..........................................
    Tennis...........................................783-5360
    Golf.............................................638-7037
National Capital Parks ..............................426-6700
National Zoological Park .............................381-7228
Rock Creek Park......................................426-6835
Summer-in-the-Parks .................................426-6770
Theodore Roosevelt Island............................426-6922

## HELP FOR INTERNATIONAL VISITORS

*Help*

International Visitors Information Services .............872-8747

*Currency Exchange*

American Security & Trust, Fifteenth Street ............
    and Pennsylvania Avenue, N.W....................624-4024
National Bank of Washington, 1129 Twentieth ..........
    Street, N.W......................................624-3560
Riggs, 1503 Pennsylvania Avenue, N.W. ...............624-3984
    Night information ...............................624-3980
Deak & Company, 1800 K Street, N.W. ...............872-1233
Bank of Virginia, in the Continental Telephone Building (near Dulles
    Airport) ........................................750-7361
Duty-Free Shop, Dulles Airport terminal building.. ..(703) 661-8815
First and Merchants National.........................
    Bank, Dulles Airport terminal building..............471-7498
Teletrip, at National Airport.........................979-8383

# Index